D1312049

PSYCHOTHERAPY
IN MANAGED HEALTH CARE

THE OPTIMAL USE OF
TIME & RESOURCES

CAROL SHAW AUSTAD
WILLIAM H. BERMAN
EDITORS

American Psychological Association
Washington, DC

Copyright © 1991 by the American Psychological Association. All rights reserved. Except as permitted under the United States Copyright Act of 1976, no part of this publication may be reproduced or distributed in any form or by any means, or stored in a database or retrieval system, without the prior written permission of the publisher.

First printing July 1991
Second printing May 1994

Published by the
American Psychological Association
750 First Street, NE
Washington, DC 20002

Copies may be ordered from
APA Order Department
P.O. Box 2710
Hyattsville, MD 20784

In the United Kingdom and Europe, copies may be ordered from
American Psychological Association
3 Henrietta Street
Covent Garden, London
WC2E 8LU England

Cover designed by Donya Melanson Associates, Boston, MA
Typeset by Easton Publishing Services, Inc., Easton, MD
Printed by United Book Press, Inc., Baltimore, MD
Technical editing by Judy Nemes
Production coordinated by Nancy Niemann

Library of Congress Cataloging-in-Publication Data

Psychotherapy in managed health care: the optimal use of time and resources /edited by Carol Shaw Austad and William H. Berman.
  p.   cm.
  Includes index.
  ISBN 1-55798-108-6 (acid-free paper)
  1. Psychotherapy—Practice—United States. 2. Managed care plans (Health care)—United States. 3. Mental health services—United States—Management. I. Austad, Carol Shaw. II. Berman, William H., 1954–
  [DNLM: 1. Managed Care Programs—economics—United States.
  2. Managed Care Programs—organization & administration—United States.
  3. Psychotherapy—economics—United States. W 275 AA P985]
  RC 465.6.P79 1991
  616.89′14′0973—dc20
  DNLM/DLC
  for Library of Congress   91-21994
                                                                                 CIP

Printed in the United States of America

Contents

FEB 9 1995

Contributors

Jerry Adams,   Staff Psychologist, Kaiser Permanente, San Diego, California.

Carol Shaw Austad,   Assistant Professor of Psychology, Central Connecticut State University, Marcus White Hall, New Britain, CT, and Staff Psychologist, Community Health Care Plan, Wallingford, Connecticut.

Cynthia Belar,   Chief Psychologist, Kaiser Permanente Medical Care Center, Department of Psychiatry, Los Angeles, California.

William H. Berman,   Assistant Professor of Psychology, Fordham University, Bronx, NY and Adjunct Assistant Professor of Psychology in Psychiatry, Cornell University Medical College, White Plains, New York.

Nicholas A. Cummings,   Executive Director, American Biodyne Center, South San Francisco, California.

Patrick H. DeLeon,   Special Assistant, Office of Senator Daniel Inouye, Washington, DC.

Louis J. Destefano,   Assistant Professor of Psychology in Psychiatry, New York Hospital–Cornell Medical College, White Plains, New York.

Charles E. Folkers,   Director of Mental Health, Rhode Island Group Health Association, Providence, Rhode Island.

Donald M. Gragg,   Physician-in-Charge, Chemical Dependency Recovery Program, Kaiser Permanente Medical Care Center, Los Angeles, California.

Marsha Gunstad,   Program Manager of Adolescent Diagnostic and Consultation Team, Metropolitan Clinics of Counseling, Minneapolis, Minnesota.

Karen H. Henault,   Clinical Coordinator of IMPACT, River Valley Services, State of Connecticut Department of Mental Health, Middletown, Connecticut.

Michael F. Hoyt,   Chief Psychologist, Kaiser-Permanente Medical Care Center, Hayward, California.

Hyman L. Kempler,   Associate Director, Pain Management Program, and Psychologist, Kenmore Center, Harvard Community Health Plan, Boston, Massachusetts.

Jeremy Kisch,   Chief of Mental Health Services, Community Health Care Plan; Assistant Clinical Professor, Department of Psychiatry, Yale University School of Medicine.

Daniel Y. Patterson,   Vice President and Medical Director, American Psych-Management, Inc., Arlington, Virginia.

Patricia J. Robinson,   Staff Psychologist, Group Health Cooperative of Puget Sound, Seattle, Washington.

Herbert C. Schulberg, Professor of Psychiatry and Psychology, Western Psychiatric Institute and Clinic, Pittsburgh, Pennsylvania.

C. Paul Scott, Clinical Associate Professor of Psychiatry, University of Pittsburgh School of Medicine; Director of Psychiatric Education, St. Margaret Memorial Hospital Family Practice Residency, Pittsburgh, Pennsylvania.

Charles F. Sherman, Director of Operations, United Behavioral Systems, Inc., Minneapolis, Minnesota.

Robert Sovner, Chief Psychopharmacologist, Mental Health Department, Harvard Community Health Plan-Medford Center, Medford, Massachusetts.

Nina M. Steefel, Staff Psychologist, Community Health Care Plan, New Haven, Connecticut.

Kirk Strosahl, Staff Psychologist, Group Health Cooperative of Puget Sound, Central Mental Health Service, Seattle, Washington.

Gary R. VandenBos, Director of Communications, American Psychological Association, Washington, DC.

Preface

The history of this book begins long before our own personal involvement in managed mental health care. The past 25 years have seen major economic and social changes in health care. From a fiscal standpoint, the annual cost of health care in the United States increased from $75 billion in 1968 to $438 billion in 1988, accounting for more than 11% of the Gross National Product, and far outpacing general inflation rates. As a result, consumers and businesses became increasingly reluctant to pay for unlimited health care and expressed an expectation that medical care providers should be professionally and economically accountable for their decisions. From a societal viewpoint, health care has been increasingly viewed as a basic right for all Americans. Both of these trends have led to the massive growth of managed health care.

Our own history in managed care began in the latter part of 1983, when we accepted jobs at Community Health Care Plan in New Haven, Connecticut. We knew little about managed care except that health maintenance organizations (HMOs) provided comprehensive health care, including mental health care, to a subscriber population, and that no one could have more than 20 sessions of psychotherapy per calendar year. We were drawn, however, to the egalitarian distribution of mental health services and to the preventive, holistic philosophy of managed health care. We did not know that our own personal histories would become so intimately involved with managed health care.

Like many practicing mental health clinicians, both of us had had some experience in crisis intervention and brief treatment. Our predominant academic training and clinical experience, however, had been with long-term psychodynamic and humanistic psychotherapy. As a result, we were intellectually and emotionally unprepared for the managed care model of treatment in which six sessions was the norm. As we struggled with the limits of the benefits package, we began to realize that most people sought mental health care for relatively well defined "problems in living," rather than for chronic or severe problems. Many patients presented with marital dysfunction, family crises, or relationship or developmental problems that did not fit into discrete psychiatric categories. We also discovered that these patients usually wanted help in solving these problems quickly and efficiently in order to return to their prior lifestyle. Few of them sought major or extensive psychological intervention, although many wanted to talk about their lives. Some of our patients with major depressions, anxiety disorders, or psychotic disorders responded quickly and significantly to psychotropic medication, which then allowed them to talk in therapy about the social/interpersonal problems that contributed to their current dysfunction.

As we matured clinically in this setting, we became generalists, mental health family practitioners, collaborating with primary care physicians and specialty providers to provide a wide range of mental health services to a wide range of patients. We found that the "natural duration" of single episodes of psychotherapy was short-term, with more than one episode over time. We had an "Aha!" experience as we discovered that intermittent involvement with patients seemed to reflect a "natural" schedule of therapy.

More than once, a patient might call back a year or two after a single session of therapy to ask for another appointment. He or she would explain that the brief contact had been helpful, and a new problem had arisen that needed to be discussed. The managed care experience coalesced for us as we realized that therapy did not have to occur on a weekly basis or in 50-minute chunks to be helpful. Our definition of psychotherapy changed as our patients showed an ability to reengage in therapy after a brief contact and a long hiatus.

Although we read reports of "the threat of HMOs" and the dangers of these alternative care settings, we believed many of our patients benefited from our efforts. As we met with other managed care therapists, we realized that many of them had adopted psychotherapy practices that facilitated symptom relief, fostered personal growth, and provided a valuable interpersonal experience for the patient. Moreover, these practices centered around humanistic and democratic values. Many had developed a "sociological awareness" that concern for the individual and the collective group was needed if we were to fulfill our moral and social obligations.

Aside from a few papers by early contributors such as Nicholas Cummings, Michael Bennett, and Patrick Coleman, there was little published information on how managed care therapists actually practiced their trade. As a result, we decided to gather and record the clinical wisdom of these providers, so that others could begin to use these techniques and begin to test their efficacy both through research and clinical practice. We wanted to make a proactive contribution to the flow of information about managed care and mental health. We undertook this task in the belief that informed clinicians represent the first step toward revolutionizing the mental health care system.

This book was conceived as an initial effort to outline models for practice and to describe current approaches to the provision of mental health care within the economic and social realities of our society. Our goals were to:

- Delineate models of biopsychosocial intervention within prepaid health care systems;
- Describe interventions for particular patient populations developed in or applied to prepaid settings;
- Identify particular problems and issues of concern, and needed directions for the future.

We have not addressed the philosophical aspects of the current changes in health care. Neither have we solved the moral and ethical questions inherent in any treatment model in which an essential service is subject to profit motives and a free-market system; we assume that the mental health care delivery system is subject to greed and misuse. In addition, this book does not encompass the total range of therapies or the total range of disorders. Managed mental health care remains in its infancy.

The material presented here is the beginning of a model of mental health services that is appropriate for the majority of people seeking functionally necessary psychological services. The first section provides a broad overview of the social, economic, and historical factors contributing to the current state of managed mental health care. The relationship between mental health and general health care is examined, and the commonalities among short-term psychotherapies as practiced both in general settings and in managed health care are identified. The settings for managed health care are also described, and the economic and organizational limits on managed mental health practice are highlighted. There are several issues in this area that remain unresolved and will require the attention of both practitioners and administrators. Such issues include cost-shifting, exclusion criteria, and care of the chronically ill. Finally, the roles of different mental health practitioners are described, with a clear emphasis on a multidisciplinary approach to mental health delivery.

Part Two provides theories and models for the practice of mental health in the managed setting. The general philosophical orientation to psychotherapy in managed health care is that of intermittent psychotherapy throughout the life cycle. This approach takes into account the developmental stage, personal strengths, and current state of the patient in formulating brief, targeted inverventions. Individual therapy for psychological problems is not the only approach used in managed mental health. Group psychotherapy and behavioral medicine are also essential components of comprehensive mental health care. The theories underlying these approaches, and how they can be applied in a managed care practice are explored. The integration of medical and psychological services, the treatment of patients requiring more extended intervention, and the availability of programmatic interventions characterize both of these programs. Psychopharmacologic intervention is the fourth treatment approach that is essential to high-quality mental health care. An approach to psychopharmacology that emphasizes collaboration among specialists in primary medicine, mental health, and psychopharmacology is described and delineated. Part two ends with a description of the processes involved in learning psychotherapy in a managed health care setting, and the resistances people have toward brief therapy.

Section three is designed to provide specific guidelines for working with many of the commonly encountered patient populations in managed care. Inpatient and outpatient procedures for working with adolescents and their families are described in detail. Procedures for providing innovative and integrative treatment for depressed patients and psychotic patients in a managed care setting are also discussed. These chapters particularly emphasize the ways in which managed health care can provide more effective care for these patients. The single most common referral problem in managed health care is relationship difficulties. In this section, the treatment of such problems using cognitive and behavioral techniques is also addressed. The remaining chapters discuss the treatment of disorders that present special difficulties within the managed care setting, including personality disordered patients, chemical dependency patients, chronic pain patients, and somatizing patients.

The final section of the book summarizes the current status of managed health care and discusses future directions for practice, training, and research. The current legislative status of managed health care is examined, and its impact on the delivery of services is discussed. Areas of concern and caution, the potential for expanded practice, and the importance of training in managed care service delivery are highlighted. Finally, we summarize the current practice of managed mental health and describe a model of quality assurance that is relevant to the intermittent, developmental, outcome-based approach to mental health services that defines it.

This book is the product of many years' work and many peoples' contributions. Just as the practice of managed mental health is a collaborative endeavor, so this book was truly a collaborative endeavor; authorship was decided by alphabetical order, not by contribution. It is impossible to thank all those who have contributed to the growth and development of this volume. Jeremy Kisch, the medical staff, and the mental health staff and support personnel of Community Health Care Plan have all contributed their ideas, concern, and commitment to the patients we served. Nicholas Cummings and many of our other colleagues have provided not only chapters, but also enthusiasm, encouragement, and new ideas. Special thanks are due to William O. Sherman who has provided many hours of moral support and technical computer assistance. John Clarkin, Steven Hurt, and Kurt Geisinger have also provided ideas, technical facilities, and computer assistance. At the America Psychological Association, Gary VandenBos, Brenda Bryant, Julia Frank-McNeil, and our editor Mary Lynn Skutley have waded patiently through several drafts and helped us negotiate the process of book editing, a task we were as unprepared for in 1988 as we were to enter the managed health care field in 1983. Our spouses, Arnold Austad and Ellen Raynes Berman have given their time, support, and editorial advice in more ways than we can count. Finally, we owe an unpayable debt to our patients and our contributors, who have truly taught us all how to be more effective therapists in the managed health care setting.

Carol Shaw Austad
William H. Berman

Part I

Introduction

1

Carol Shaw Austad and William H. Berman

Managed Health Care and the Evolution of Psychotherapy

The evolution of psychotherapy and the American health care delivery system are inextricably linked. Psychotherapists can no longer practice as if psychotherapy were independent of its economic environment, and medicine can no longer be conducted as if the physical and psychological were independent of one another. The recognition of stark economic realities and the emerging discovery of the relationship of mind to body in health conditions have created new opportunities to integrate the practice of health and mental health care, thereby improving the efficacy of both (Feldman, 1986; Tulkin & Frank, 1985). Alternative health care, frequently called managed health care, is an important catalyst that can facilitate this process (Altman & Goldstein, 1987; de Lissovoy, Rice, Gabel, & Gelzer, 1987).

The past two decades have witnessed outstanding changes in the structure of the American health care delivery system. Three trends are shaping the use and delivery of mental health services. First, costs have increased so dramatically that employers, insurers, and individual consumers are no longer willing to pay unlimited amounts for health care without close scrutiny and accountability. Second, the mind–body dualism that has dominated American medicine is being tempered by increasing evidence that psychological factors and physical health reciprocally influence each other (Frank & McGuire, 1986). This has made the inclusion of mental health benefits essential to adequate health care (Durenberger, 1989). Third, the field of mental health has placed increasing emphasis on short-term, symptom-focused, active interventions that use both somatic and psychological methods (Goldman, 1988; Marmor, 1980). The effects of these overlapping trends, stemming from multiple philosophies, can be felt throughout the mental health delivery systems and nowhere more strongly than in managed health care systems.

This chapter will discuss each of these significant trends before defining and describing the elements of psychotherapeutic practice in managed health care.

Changes in American Health Care Delivery

The Economics of Health Care

While the majority of Americans believe health care should be available to all (Callan & Yeager, 1991; Durenberger, 1989), people are, in general, disconcerted about what they consider to be unnecessarily high medical costs. Government and employers are the primary payers of health-related services, financing 80% of all expenditures. (The remaining 20% represents unsystematized out-of-pocket payments; Goldsmith, 1984). These payers have made efforts to contain the dramatic increases in their costs (Dorwat & Chartock, 1988). One unexplored frontier for cost saving is mental health. As much as 25% of health costs are incurred by mental health care, the third largest single source of health-related expenses. Cost containment measures are spurring significant changes in health benefits and models of health and mental health care delivery systems (Bennett, 1988; Berman et al., 1988; Bittker, 1985; Fielding, 1984; Kisch & Austad, 1988).

The growing concern and frustration over escalating health care costs have inspired the formation and proliferation of alternative health care delivery systems. These systems are now referred to as "managed health care," and were created in hopes of containing costs and delivering high-quality care (Ellwood, 1988; Faltermeyer, 1988). The idea of managed care is not new and possesses historical roots that go back to the early 1900s. Current conceptions of managed health care emerged from the concept of "prepaid care": a comprehensive package of health services provided on a contractual basis with a predetermined provider or providers for a preestablished fee. Although a detailed history is beyond the scope of this chapter, and several excellent reviews are available (Nelson, 1987; Starr, 1982), a short synopsis of the major historical highlights of managed health care and mental health services will shed some light on their evolving relationship.

The History of the HMO and Mental Health Services

Health maintenance organizations (HMOs) began in the early 1900s as maverick forms of health care delivery. They were founded as democratic service delivery systems that provided affordable and accessible health care to specific populations (Nelson, 1987). Initially, HMOs were controversial and were vehemently opposed by a majority of the medical profession. They were used by poor and middle-class laborers and farmers who found that prepaid care eliminated the threat of a sudden, unexpected onslaught of medical bills. By the early 1970s, prepaid health care became widely accepted because of the support of labor, industry, government, and consumers.

The federal government showed its support for the development of HMOs by passing the HMO Act of 1973. This provided financing through low-cost loans and grants and decreased legal restrictions that had inhibited the growth of group and prepaid practice. Several basic models of managed care were developed. The Staff Model HMO generally offers the patient comprehensive medical services and hires providers as salaried employees or contractors who work in central locations. In the Group Model, a contractual agreement exists between the HMO and a group of practitioners to provide specified services in either a centralized location or in private offices. In the Independent Practice Model practitioners contract to provide specific services from their own private offices. Payment in these arrangements (except for the salaried staff model) can be reimbursed on a prearranged fee-for-service schedule or on a capitated basis (provider at risk to deliver all necessary services for the set fee).

A Preferred Provider Organization combines fee-for-service care with financial incentives for patients to use a selected provider panel, but the freedom to use non-preferred providers for nondirective. Providers are not at risk, but maintain an exclusive fee-for-service billing arrangement with a predetermined patient group. In mixed models, features of two or more models of managed care are combined (Fox, 1990; Hillman, 1989). Today, a number of models have evolved that combine the features of the original models and add other characteristics. The generic term "managed health care" is used to describe them and the HMO is now a subcategory of the larger class. The structure of HMO models continues to change. The American Managed Care Review Organization newsletter (1991) shows that as enrollment increases, HMOs tend to merge into "network" models. An example is a group model HMO that develops an IPA network to expand the service area. The merging of the HMO and IPA models qualifies this as a network model managed care organization.

Psychological intervention was not routinely included as part of the benefit structure in early prepaid health plans. Mental health benefits have been a recent addition. Thanks to the pioneering efforts of the United Auto Workers and the American Psychiatric Association in conjunction with Group Health Insurance of New York, pilot projects were conducted in which mental health services were included in general medical benefits (Bennett, 1988; Nelson, 1987). Mental health care became a required part of general prepaid health care when the federal HMO Act of 1973 mandated that in order to qualify for federal assistance, HMOs had to include short-term, outpatient mental health evaluation and treatment. The current federal statute directs that an HMO must offer short-term, outpatient mental health evaluation and crisis intervention services as well as 60 days of inpatient psychiatric care (DeLeon et al., 1985).

Nevertheless, the incorporation of mental health benefits into managed health care has been accompanied by controversy and reluctance on the part of many payers. Corporate sponsors and insurers are concerned about "moral hazard": if people are free to use mental health benefits, overutilization may result in prohibitively expensive costs (Goldman, 1988).

Mental Health in General Health Care

Despite the objections, many mental health practitioners contend that mental health services have the potential to increase the efficacy of medical care (Tulkin & Frank, 1985). One of the strongest arguments against the concern of overutilization has been the demonstration of the "medical offset effect": that is, the use of mental health services produces a reduction in the use of general medical health services. Extensive research has demonstrated that short-term outpatient psychotherapy reduces medical costs over a two-to-three-year period (Jones & Vischi, 1979; Mumford, Schlesinger, Glass, Patrick, & Cuerdon, 1984). In one example, a six-year study of medicaid enrollees showed that psychiatric treatment reduced the use of other physician services, especially X-ray and laboratory testing (Goldensohn & Fink, 1979). In another set of studies at the San Francisco Kaiser Permanente

Center, data were collected to test how mental health services affected subsequent medical utilization (Cummings & Follette, 1968, 1976; Cummings & VandenBos, 1978; Follette & Cummings, 1967). VandenBos and DeLeon (1989) summarize the findings from this literature, indicating that research consistently shows that individuals in emotional distress who seek psychological services tend to be higher users of all general medical services before they receive psychological intervention. During the first year patients receive psychotherapy there is no evidence of an offset effect, in part because the total cost of their health care does not change. Mental health services have been substituted for less appropriate and unnecessary general medical expenditures. A significant decline in medical utilization does occur in the year following psychological services, however. The use of psychological services in medical care appears to be cost-effective, in part by reducing the demand for unnecessary medical care (Jones & Vischi, 1979; Levitan & Kornfield, 1981; Mumford et al., 1984).

While the medical offset phenomenon illustrates that psychological factors and physical health influence each other (Frank & McGuire, 1986), a second trend has enhanced justification for including mental health benefits in health plans. Psychotherapists are developing circumscribed interventions to be used in treating the psychological elements of specific medical conditions. Such targeted interventions deal with specific aspects of medical care, including stress and pain management; smoking cessation; weight control; medication and diet compliance; and recovery and adaptation to surgery and chronic illness. Many medical and psychological practitioners no longer arbitrarily separate the medical and psychological worlds (VandenBos & DeLeon, 1988).

Psychotherapy in Mental Health Care

Psychotherapy is a form of treatment provided to people to repair or to prevent debilitating emotional, social, and behavioral dysfunction (Newman & Howard, 1986). It is no coincidence that brief psychotherapy is becoming popular at this time in our particular culture. Short-term treatment provides the opportunity to deliver quality care to diverse patients throughout this country.

Prior to World War II, the vast majority of mental health services were provided on an inpatient basis for the seriously and chronically mentally ill. Psychotherapy was used only by those who could afford to pay for such expensive services out of pocket. In the subsequent half-century, the number and types of available mental health interventions have dramatically increased. A focus upon the role of family and environmental influences upon psychological disorders has diminished the dominance of the medical model of "mental illness." The primary site of service delivery has changed from the state mental hospital to outpatient mental health centers. A concomitant increase in the amount of services and the number and types of mental health providers occurred between the 1950s to the 1990s. The recipients of mental health services have grown to include not just the severely and chronically disturbed, but any individual or family experiencing emotional distress. Today, psychotherapy is no longer reserved for the elite and is considered to be an effective form of health care intervention for a wide variety of people and problems (Garfield & Bergin, 1986).

The earliest forms of short-term therapy were devised for both clinical and practical reasons. Psychodynamic therapists felt that more patients might benefit more quickly if some of the psychodynamic techniques were modified. These therapists reminded their colleagues that Freud himself believed in and used short-term techniques (Davanloo, 1980; Mann, 1973; Sifneos, 1979). The primary goal of these models was the development of short-term techniques which are consistent with, and refine psychodynamic theory. A secondary goal was to meet the demands of clinical necessity associated with the pending limitations of private health insurance coverage and clinic waiting lists (Davanloo, 1980; Mann, 1973). Since the early 1980s, other dynamically oriented brief psychotherapies have used a range of object relations (Strupp & Binder, 1984), interpersonal and ego psychological models (Garfield & Bergen, 1986).

Cognitive and behavioral techniques such as Meichenbaum's self-instructional training, Lazarus' Multimodal Therapy, and Beck's Cognitive Therapy demonstrate that positive change can occur through the use of highly structured, problem-oriented, brief techniques in ways that require much less time than insight-oriented therapies (Masters, Burish, Hollon, & Rimm, 1987). Strategic, short-term therapies such as those of Haley (1976), Watzlawick (1963), the Ericksonians (Bugental, 1987) and the existentialists (Frankl, 1955; Glasser, 1969) are other popular forms of short-term techniques that are intended to produce effective, even dramatic, changes through brief forms of interventions (Lazarus, 1973; Marmor, 1980). Finally, crisis intervention models of treatment arose from practical necessity. With a goal of returning a disordered individual to his or her pre-emergency level of functioning, the advances in crisis intervention work have been technical, applied, and atheoretical (Bloom, 1984). The crisis intervention models are a result of practical, problem-solving necessity.

The above brief history of short-term therapy leads into the notion that today's trend in the evolution of psychotherapy is to develop specific, targeted treatment interventions for particular problems such as depression, anxiety, attention deficit disorders, and chemical dependency. Specific models of short-term therapy, programmatic interventions, semistructured group treatment, behavioral regimens, and psychoeducational programs have been created to address a range of other psychological problems (VandenBos & DeLeon, 1989). As interventions become more specific and targeted, these mental health practices fit well into health care systems that emphasize health maintenance and prevention rather than sickness (DeLeon, Uyeda, & Welch, 1985). Psychotherapists performing such psychotherapy constitute a mental health care delivery system (VandenBos & DeLeon, 1989).

In summary, shifts in the theory and practice of psychotherapy, recognition of the reciprocal relationship of physical and psychological disturbances, together with today's inflated health care costs have contributed to a revised view of mental health services in managed health care. Although these factors affect the practice of all mental health care to some degree, they are predominant factors in affecting the practice of psychotherapy. Such programs encourage the fair and equitable distribution of services to the greatest number of people (Kisch & Austad, 1988). The field of mental health needs methods of psychotherapeutic intervention that are philosophically and pragmatically compatible with good managed health care systems. Some interventions have been developed; others are in the process of being developed. All of the therapies practiced in managed health care have elements in common. The following section details these commonalities.

Psychotherapy in the HMO Setting

"HMO psychotherapy" is psychotherapy practiced within a managed health care setting, particularly in a staff model setting in which the parameters of treatment have been modified both consciously and unconsciously, to be compatible with the philosophy, theory, and economic and pragmatic conditions of a managed care system.

Most therapists who work in HMO settings find settings well suited for the provision of mental health services. Staff and group model facilities in particular provide comprehensive health care in a setting where medical and mental health professionals can interact, consult, and collaborate (Feldman, 1985). Practitioners find significant differences between many of the demand characteristics of the fee-for-service and the HMO settings. As a result, traditionally trained therapists are not always philosophically or pragmatically prepared to work at the HMO.

Interviews with a small sample of staff model managed care therapists showed that 55% knew nothing or very little about the nature of the HMO before they worked there, and that over 70% felt their graduate training had not adequately prepared them for this kind of work (Austad, Sherman, Morgan, & Holstein, 1991). Managed care membership have heterogenous problems, needs, and expectations often not encountered in private practice settings. Therapists sometimes reported feeling ill-equipped to deal with the intensity, complexity, and volume of work with which they were often faced. They found themselves needing to change their traditional practice patterns to make them fit into the organizational context of the prepaid health care setting (Austad, 1990). The extent of these adaptations vary. It appears that therapists who have embraced the philosophy of managed health care and have worked successfully in these settings seem to have adapted one of three major methods of accommodation.

First, HMO psychotherapists often favor models of psychotherapy which, by nature, fit within the HMO framework. Many of the cognitive–behavioral therapies and behavioral medicine techniques (Tulkin & Frank, 1985) need no modification in order to be compatible with the HMO setting. For example, in this volume, Robinson's chapter on treating couples illustrates how the cognitive–behavioral model can be implemented readily within the prepaid health care setting. Beck's cognitive group therapies for depression or anxiety, and Interpersonal Therapy as described in Schulberg and Scott's chapter further illustrate of how already existing models can be used with little or no modification. Belar's chapter *illustrates similarly* how behavioral medicine's multidimensional targeted interventions, which call for the integration of mental and physical health, also find a home in the managed health care sector.

Second, some therapy models are partially compatible with many managed care systems but require some modification which can, at times, yield innovative improvements in the treatment approach. For example, Kempler's chapter on pain management demonstrates how his HMO environment can integrate psychological and medical treatment and therefore facilitate the holistic treatment of the chronic pain patient. Folkers and Steefel point out how, at RIGHA Health Care Plan, group therapy techniques interact with the "closed managed care system" to enhance the treatment of a variety of patients ranging from the borderline personality to people embroiled in developmental transitions. Strosahl has adapted short-term cognitive behavioral methods for use in the treatment of personality disorders within managed care contexts. Donovan (1987, 1989) has modified psychodynamic methods to make it possible to treat patients in managed care settings who are usually thought to be poor candidates for traditional short-term psychodynamic therapy. The work of the therapist is to search for, reframe, and reverse the pathogenic belief that prevents the patient from being free to use more productive self constructions.

Third, some resourceful clinicians have designed new models of therapy, tailored when traditional theories did not provide solutions to the wide range of mental health problems at the HMO. For example, Cummings, who was chief psychologist at Kaiser Permanente in Northern California describes managed care therapy models in two chapters in this book concerning the "somatizing patient" and "intermittent psychotherapy throughout the life cycle." He describes specific targeted interventions that are useful in treating specific psychological problems. This seminal work has earned him the title of "Father of Managed Care Psychotherapy." Bennett and Wisneski (1979) at Harvard Health Care Plan describe a developmental, intermittent model in individual therapy similar to that of Cummings. Budman and Gurman (1988) have developed a system of therapy called the interpersonal-developmental-existential (I-D-E) model therapy. It provides a frame of reference that allows the therapist to reframe patient problems as core issues of loss, distorted beliefs, developmental dysynchronies, lack of meaning, desire for symptomatic relief, interpersonal problems, or personality disorders.

The Characteristics of HMO Psychotherapy

HMO therapies adhere to the basic principles common to all short-term therapy models (Bauer & Kobos, 1987), but they also incorporate some uniquely "HMO" characteristics. Both types of characteristics will be described and discussed.

Characteristics Common to All Short-Term Therapies

HMO models are based on the assumption underlying most short-term psychotherapy models (Bauer & Kobos, 1987) that is, that significant psychological change can occur, or be set in motion, in a short time. Time constraints are incorporated as a working ingredient of psychotherapy. Assessment is early and accurate. Intervention is prompt. By definition, therapy is goal-directed and focal. Rapport, or a good working alliance, between patient and therapist must blossom promptly.

Focused assessment. All short-term therapists, and especially the managed care therapist, need to achieve a rapid, accurate assessment of a patient's problem and to arrive at a clear, specific formulation of an effective treatment plan. The managed care therapist must be competent at formulating both a psychiatric diagnosis and a working formulation that will guide both pharmacological and psychosocial interventions as needed (Bittker & George, 1980). In many cases, assessment and intervention are intertwined with the test interventions used to clarify the assessment.

Rapid response to need/crisis intervention preparedness. Prompt handling of emergencies is absolutely essential to effective treatment. Early access to psychotherapy can avoid uncontrolled clinical problems and overintensive therapeutic involvement (Bonstedt & Baird, 1979). The managed care therapist, particularly the staff model therapist more than many short-term therapists, often has generous organizational support to help in handling crises. In staff and group model HMOs a referral can be as simple as a walk to a different location in the building. The availability of urgent visit programs, access to emergency appointment time, follow-through programs at hospital discharge, temporary holding environments, and extensive medical backup are essential for preventing or limiting unnecessary exacerbation of acute mental health situations (Bittker & George, 1980; Budman & Gurman, 1988; Cummings, 1988). Therapists are trained to think quickly, develop a working alliance and diagnosis, and intervene on short notice.

Clearly defined treatment goals and responsibility for therapy. In brief therapy, the patient and therapist must define specific, achievable goals that are consistent with both the patient's subjective experience and the therapist's objective understanding. The patient and therapist must clearly contract for the purpose, the schedule, and the duration of treatment. This clearly fosters an atmosphere in which the patient assumes much of the responsibility for therapeutic work. (Bittker & George, 1980). The patient is actively involved in bringing relevant material to the sessions, cooperating in extra session assignments, and implementing behavioral change outside of therapeutic contacts.

Active therapist. The role of the therapist is not authoritarian, but authoritative. He or she possesses a variety of clinical skills to lead the patient in a positive, productive direction. The therapist is responsible for structuring therapeutic contacts, recommending particular interventions, and involving others as indicated.

Characteristics Unique to "HMO Psychotherapy"

Psychotherapy conducted in HMO and other managed health care settings also has characteristics that distinguish it from other models of short-term therapy. The factors that make the practice of psychotherapy within managed health care unique include the following:

Primary care orientation. In the primary care model of medicine, the physician coordinates the general health care of the patient. The doctor–patient relationship is stable and consistent, but the frequency of contact is determined by the clinical need of the patient. The patient consults with the doctor when there is a reason to do so. Consequently, the physician follows a patient in brief episodes over an extended time span.

HMO psychotherapists apply this primary care perspective to mental health practice. The psychotherapist is like the "psychological family doctor" (Cummings, 1986) who treats the patient in "interrupted continuity" (Morrill, 1983). The patient is followed in brief episodes over longer periods of the lifespan (Anderson, 1981). This allows long-term observation with less intensive (but not necessarily less profound or effective) "intermittent" therapeutic input. It seems only appropriate that if the medical model is to be used metaphorically in the treatment of psychological dysfunction, the role of the therapist should be parallel to the role of the family doctor.

In the context of a primary care medical setting, there is a blending of the medical and psychotherapeutic involvement that encourages a balanced, holistic view of the patient (Meier, 1981; Patrick, Coleman, Eagle, & Nelson, 1979). Both physician and therapist attend to the relationship between mental and physical well-being, making possible new treatment formats such as resolving problems identified as themes or ongoing conflicts through a succession of interrupted crisis episodes (Morrill, 1983).

Developmental orientation. The application of the primary care orientation, that is, following the patient in brief episodes over long periods of time, is most compatible with a certain philosophy of life span development. This philosophy contends that the individual is both open and vulnerable to crises that can occur at developmental junctures or milestones (Levinson, 1978). However, it is seldom used in models of adult psychotherapy. Observation of patients over time in the HMO indicates there is a "natural flow" to the involvement in psychotherapy. This supports the notion that psychotherapy can be a continuous, intermittent interaction between therapist and patient that extends throughout the life cycle (Cummings, 1986). Staff model HMOs are particularly suited to this perspective because they generally provide accurate, long-term records of the patient's physical and mental health while he or she is a member.

Effective parsimony and flexible use of intervention, alternative treatment approaches, and programmatic intervention. Use of the "least extensive, least expensive, least intrusive interventions" is paramount (Bennett, 1986; Bennett & Wisneski, 1979; Bonstedt & Baird, 1978). The frequency, length, and timing of treatment varies according to patient needs. In addition, the managed care therapist is able to choose from among an array of lower-level interventions. Time can be used efficiently through the use of programmatic forms of intervention. For example, the therapist is acquainted with the role of group therapy, psychoeducation, and community resources as important components of mental health treatment (Boaz, 1988). A group psychotherapy program that provides a range of interventions offers an important alternative to individual therapy. Use of family intervention, self-help groups, and partial hospitalization are important tools of the HMO psychotherapist.

Pragmatic therapeutic alliance. Cummings, in his chapter on intermittent therapy throughout the life cycle, (this volume) has described the implicit contract between therapists and patients in managed care setting: "I will provide the best possible care, if you agree to make me obsolete as quickly as possible." The intermittent model of intervention assumes that as soon as the patient no longer needs the therapist, the therapist recedes into the background of the patient's life. When necessity or clinical need dictates, the therapist again is readily available to help the client deal with whatever problem arises. Commitment to the client is seen from a very different point of view from that of the long-term traditional therapist.

The HMO psychotherapist agrees that he or she (or the system) will maintain a long-term relationship with a patient and the patient's family if indicated. The patient can trust that the therapist will offer efficient, effective, parsimonious, and minimally intrusive therapeutic interventions. There is a strong reality base in the alliance. There is a recognition that the entire managed care membership is a group whose health needs must be met. The therapist encourages autonomy and independence rather than transference and dependence. Therapist and patient must incorporate the reality of limited time and resources as well as a compassion for others who have psychotherapeutic needs. Patients sense that they are responsible (Adler, 1963) for using the resources altruistically; thus, they accept the limitations and use the services in a cost-effective manner (Spoerel, 1974).

The alliance between the therapist and the HMO patient is nontraditional but pragmatic. It is a "twentieth century coalition" for mental health involving both consumerism and a sociological awareness of the needs of other HMO members. Patient satisfaction is considered an important criterion of success.

Medical/nonmedical collaboration. The mental health provider works within an open system involving primary care, specialty medicine, and mental health. Nonmedical and medical health practitioners work in close contact with physicians and psychiatrists, allowing for a ready integration of psychopharmacology and psychotherapy. Some primary care physicians are well educated about caring for patients with mental health problems and will supervise patients on psychotropic medications when they are able to consult with psychiatric specialists and mental health professionals (Kisch & Austad, 1988). Conversely, the mental health professional can view the patient through the eyes of the primary care physician who has a large data base about a patient and his or her family.

Willingness to be monitored: Utilization review. Because of an awareness of escalating medical costs and a social concern, the managed care therapist tries to deliver the least intrusive and the most cost-effective therapy possible. The therapist understands that review can foster this process and philosophically is committed to the notion that peer review is helpful.

Controversies In and About Managed Health Care

Mental health care in managed health care continues to be a target of controversy. Some object strenuously to the types of psychotherapy used by managed care therapists claiming that it represents a superficial, or "bandaid" approach to solving mental health problems. Others have noted that the managed care movement abandoned its social objectives in favor of economic gains, trading national health care for increased profits (Bennett, 1988).

No system can exist without systemic problems. Community mental health centers, government facilities such as the Veteran's Administration and state mental hospitals, and private clinics all have weaknesses in their service delivery. Both superior and inferior clinicians can be found in any setting. Just as there are superior managed care systems, there are also inferior ones. They are not unique in presenting problems to the consumer and the provider. The following are the most common problems:

Potential role conflicts. A managed health care provider can be torn between quality and productivity. The managed care therapist is expected to treat, and treat well, greater numbers of patients than is typical in many other settings. The most difficult part of the job can be dealing with the numbers of people and the intensity of the work (Austad & Holstein, 1989). Maintaining high productivity levels while delivering optimal care can be arduous, and both the managed care system and the therapist must guard against burn-out. HMO therapists must learn to balance their interests with those of the organization. Chapter 7 addresses some of these issues.

Barriers to utilization of mental health services. In an organization that possesses financial incentives to minimize care there may be a temptation to undertreat, especially in "for profit" managed care systems. However, checks and balances are contained in the professional integrity of the staff. The majority of providers feel obliged to object to and report the incidence of unethical behavior. Furthermore, the temptation to overtreat in the fee-for-service sector is just as real as the temptation to undertreat in managed health care. Equal consideration should be given to both potential abuses. Although there are numerous heated debates about the ills of undertreatment, few words are spoken about the abuses of overtreatment. Whether a fee-for-service or prepaid practice, one assumes that the professional will treat the patient within the bounds of standard practice. The professional is obliged to candidly and truthfully inform patients of the benefits and limitations of treatment. Problems can arise when marketing personnel misrepresent services and barriers to treatment arise such as waiting lists and nonreferrals. Concerns regarding quality of care issues are addressed in the final chapter of this book.

Limited benefits. Mental health benefits offered by managed care organizations vary considerably (Lange, Chandler-Guy, Forti, Foster-Moore, & Rohman, 1988). Claims have been made that the benefits of managed health care are restrictive and deny patients needed access to care. Extensive research on utilization of mental health care suggests that more than 90% of the population using mental health services can be treated within the average benefit limits (Taube, 1988; Wells, Manning, & Benjamin, 1989; Phillips, 1985). In a national survey, Levine, Glasser, and Jaffee (1988), found that the organizational characteristics of managed health care systems varied considerably, but of the 94% of plans that provide mental health care benefits approached a median of 30 days of mental health inpatient coverage per member per year (PMPY) (with 82% of the plans having no copay) and 20 ambulatory mental health visits (or 40 group visits) PMPY (with a mean copay of $4 per visit after the first 10 visits). The national average for psychotherapy sessions is four to six (Phillips, 1985). Thus, the clinician works in the confines of the benefit package, but these "limitations" are in line with "what is!" A stressor unique to managed health care can result from the need to correct unrealistic member expectation regarding entitlement and what therapy can realistically achieve (Boaz, 1988). In addition, serving the chronic, underprivileged populations within the managed care setting is a problem that has not been solved (Califano, 1986). The final chapter addresses these issues in more detail.

Undervaluing of psychotherapy. Some medical staff may express antipathy toward psychotherapy, whereas others have come to recognize that psychotherapeutic intervention can make a significant contribution to the well-being of their patients (Feldman, 1986). It is the responsibility of psychologists to continue to educate the medical profession as to the usefulness of psychotherapy. The managed health care setting is ideal for this because of the frequent contact and proximity of the departments of physical and mental health.

Unfamiliarity of professionals with managed care work. Whenever there is change, there is resistance to change, and HMO therapists face resistance from the traditional establishment as well as peer objections. The managed care therapist may not be understood, accepted, or held in high regard by colleagues who are opposed to and do not understand what they are doing. Managed health care settings are foreign to many private practitioners and to many traditional therapists. A lack of formal and on-the-job educational training of staff members can be an obstacle to dispensing adequate mental health care.

Opportunity or Challenge?

Although some see managed care as a danger, others see it as an opportunity to enhance mental health practice (LaCourt, 1988). Many who work in managed health care regard it as an exciting setting that brings with it the challenge to help troubled people in the most efficient, effective way possible. Managed care providers consistently rate the HMO as a fairly positive place to work and one that gives fairly comprehensive services (Lange et al., 1988). In another survey of more than 300 HMO practitioners (Austad, et al., 1991), many described the HMO as an innovative and inspiring environment in which to deliver psychotherapy.

The following quotes are from interviews with HMO therapists and represent the kind of thinking that evolves among health practitioners who work in managed health care (Austad et al., 1991). When asked how working in the HMO had affected their development as persons, one staff model HMO psychotherapist, a veteran of 10 years, stated:

> . . . in terms of getting in touch with the kinds of things that trouble your neighbor next door or the person across the street or the person living in the lower income sections of your town or employees at the telephone company versus employees of the post office and so forth, we've seen people from all these different settings . . . it's given me the opportunity to share a little more the human experience . . . and get in touch with who we are living with, who the people on the street are . . . I think I've become a more tolerant accepting person . . . nothing much surprises me. I suppose that happens to most clinicians, but if you were in private practice and you only saw well-heeled populations with certain kinds of problems, it wouldn't be the same. I think I've become a more understanding person as a result of being in an HMO . . .

Another therapist who had been working in an HMO for five years stated:

> I think I'm a wiser individual . . . when I count the number of patients that I've seen and the number of problems and life experience that I've heard about . . . I'm wiser and more mature . . . and I'm confident about my skills as a therapist in being able to work with a variety of different kinds of problems. I've heard so many stories from so many people that I really understand life a lot better by having had these relationships . . .

This book is a testimony to our changing health care systems and their effect upon the practice of psychotherapy. The chapters contain information from dedicated and innovative clinicians who want to deliver quality care effectively and efficiently. They have adapted the parameters of familiar therapy systems to fit the HMO delivery system. In doing so, they have created resourceful ways to help others and are advancing the evolution of psychotherapy. Their chapters represent not only technical contributions, but also messages of compassion, altruism, and cost effectiveness. This book is thus about the evolution of psychotherapy.

References

Adler, A. (1963). *The practice and theory of individual psychology*. Patterson, NJ: Littlefield, Adams.

Altman, L. A., & Goldstein, J. M. (1988). *Impact of HMO type on mental health service delivery: Variation in treatment and approaches*. Paper presented at Group Health Association of America, Seattle, WA.

American Managed Care and Review Association Newsletter. (1991), *22*(6), 8.

Anderson, R. O. (1981). Shifting from external provision of mental health services in a health maintenance organization. *Hospital and Community Psychiatry, 32*(1), 31–

Austad, C. S., & Holstein, L. (1989, August). *The HMO psychotherapist and the private practitioner: A comparison*. Paper presented at the 97th Annual Convention of American Psychological Association, New Orleans, LA.

Austad, C. S., Kisch, J., & DeStefano, L. (1986). The health maintenance organization: II. Implications for psychotherapy. *Psychotherapy, 25*(3), 449–454.

Austad, C. S., Sherman, W. O., Morgan, T., & Holstein, L. (1991). *The HMO psychotherapist*. Unpublished manuscript.

Bauer, G. P., & Kobos, J. C. (1987). *Brief therapy: Short-term psychodynamic intervention*. Northvale, NJ: Jason Aronson.

Bennett, M. (1986). Maximizing the yield of brief psychotherapy: Part II. *HMO Mental Health Newsletter*, *1*, 1–4.

Bennett, M., & Wisneski, M. J. (1979). Continuous therapy within an HMO. *American Journal of Psychiatry, 136*, 1283–1287.

Bennett, M. J. (1988). The greening of the HMO: Implications for prepaid psychiatry. *American Journal of Psychiatry, 145*(12), 1544–1548.

Berman, W. H., Kisch, J., DeLeon, P. H., Cummings, N. C., Binder, J. L., & Hefele, T. J. (1988). The future of psychotherapy in the age of diminishing resources. *Psychotherapy in Private Practice, 5*(4), 105–118.

Bittker, T. E., & George, J. (1980). Psychiatric service options within a health maintenance organization. *Journal of Clinical Psychiatry, 41*, 192–195.

Bloom, B. L. (1984). *Community mental health.* Belmont, CA: Brooks/Cole.

Boaz, John T. (1988). *Delivering mental healthcare: a guide for HMOs.* Chicago: Pluribus Press.

Bonstedt, T., & Baird, S. H. (1979). Providing cost effective psychotherapy in a health maintenance organization. *Hospital and Community Psychiatry, 30*, 129–135.

Budman, S. H., & Gurman, A. S. (1988). *The theory and practice of brief psychotherapy.* New York: Guilford Press.

Bugental, J. F. T. (1987). *The art of the psychotherapist: Subtle skills of the life-changing enterprise.* New York: Norton.

Califano, J. (1986). *America's Health Care Revolution: Who lives? Who dies? Who pays?* New York: Random House.

Callan, M. F., & Yeager, D. C. (1991). *Containing the health care cost spiral.* New York: McGraw Hill.

Cummings, N. A. (1986). The dismantling of our health systems: Strategies for the survival of psychological practice, *41*, 426–431.

Cummings, N. A. (1988). The emergence of the mental health complex: Adaptive and maladaptive responses. *Professional Psychology: Research and Practice, 19*(3), 323–335.

Cummings, N., & Follette, W. (1968). Psychiatric services and medical utilization in a pre-paid health plan setting: Part II. *Medical Care, 6*, 31–41.

Cummings, N., & VandenBos, G. (**1978**). The general practice of psychology. *Professional Psychology, 10*, 430–440.

Davanloo, H. (1980). *Short-term dynamic psychotherapy.* New York: Jason Aronson.

DeLeon, P., Uyeda, M. K., & Welch, B. (1985). Psychology and HMOs: New partnership or new adversary? *American Psychologist*, 1122–1124.

de Lissovoy, G., Rice, T., Gabel, J., & Gelzer, H. (1987). Preferred provider organizations one year later. *Inquiry, 24*, 127–135.

Donovan, J. (1987). Brief dynamic psychotherapy: Toward a more comprehensive model. *Psychiatry, 50*, 167–183.

Donovan, J. (1989). Brief dynamic psychotherapy: Characterological intervention and the physical position of the patient. *Psychiatry, 52*, 446–461.

Dorwat, R. A., & Chartock, L. R. (1988). Psychiatry and the resource-based relative value scale. *American Journal of Psychiatry, 145*, 1237–1242.

Durenburger, D. (1989). Providing mental health care services to Americans. *American Psychologist, 44*, 1293–1297.

Ellwood, P. (1988). The Shattuck Lecture—Outcomes management: A technology of patient experience. *New England Journal of Medicine, 318*(23), 1549–1556.

Faltermayer, E. (1988, October 10). Medical care's next revolution. *Fortune*, pp. 126–130.

Feldman, S. (1985). *Psychology and HMOs*, (Chairman's message.) Available from the Special Interest Group Organization, Division 38, American Psychological Association, 1200 17th St., N.W., Washington, D.C.

Feldman, S. (1986, Spring). Mental health in health maintenance organizations: A report. *Administration in Mental Health, 13*(3), 1–3.

Fielding, S. L. (1984). Organizational impact on medicine: The HMO concept. *Social Science and Medicine, 18*(8), 615–620.

Flinn, D. E., McMahon, T. C., & Collins, M. F. (1987). Health maintenance organizations and their implications for psychiatry. *Hospital and Community Psychiatry, 38*(3), 255–263.

Folette, W., & Cummings, N. (1967). Psychiatric services and medical utilization in a pre-paid health plan setting: Part I. *Medical Care, 5*, 25–35.

Fox, P. D. (1990). Foreward: Overview of managed care trends. *The insider's guide to managed care* (pp. 1–12). Washington, D.C., The National health lawyer's association.

Frank, R. G., & McGuire, T. G. (1986). A review of studies of the impact of insurance on the demand and utilization of specialty mental health services. *Health Services Research, 21*(2), 241–265.

Frankl, V. E. (**1955**). *The doctor and the soul: An Introduction to logotherapy.* New York: Knopf.

Garfield, S., & Bergin, A. (1986). Introduction and historical overview. In Garfield & Bergin, A. (Eds.) *Handbook of psychotherapy and behavior change* (pp. 3–22). New York: Wiley.

Glasser, W. (1965). *Reality therapy: A new approach to psychiatry.* New York: Harper & Row.

Goldensohn, S., & Fink, R. (1979). Mental health services for medicaid enrollees in a prepaid group practice plan. *American Journal of Psychiatry, 136*(2), 160–164.

Goldman, H. H. (1988). Mental health and substance abuse services in HMOs. Paper presented at Providing Mental Health Care Today: Key Decision Points for HMOs, Group Health Institute, Seattle, WA.

Goldsmith, J. C. (1984, Fall). Death of a paradigm. *Health Affairs, 5*–19.

Haley, J. (1976). *Problem solving therapy: new strategies for effective family therapy.* San Francisco: Josey Bass.

Hillman, A. L. (1988). Financial incentives for physicians in HMOs. *The New England Journal of Medicine, 31*, 1743–1748.

Hsiao, M. C. (1987). The resource-based relative value scale: Toward the development of an alternative physician payment system. *Journal of the American Medical Association, 258*(6), 799–802.

Inglehart, J. K. (1988, Spring). Competition and the pursuit of quality: A conversation with Walter McClure. *Health Affairs,* 79–90.

Jones, K. R., & Vischi, T. R. (1979). Impact of alcohol, drug abuse, and mental health treatment on medical care utilization: A review of research literature. *Medical Care, 17,*(Suppl.), 1–90.

Kisch, J., & Austad, C. S. (1988). The health maintenance organization: I. Historical perspective and current status. *Psychotherapy, 25*(3), 441–448.

LaCourt, M. (1988). The HMO crisis: Danger or opportunity? *Family Systems Medicine, 6*(1), 80–93.

Lange, M. A., Chandler-Guy, C., Forti, R., Foster-Moore, P., & Rohman, M. (1988). Providers' view of HMO mental health services. *Psychotherapy, 25*(3), 455–462.

Lazarus, A. (1973). Multimodal therapy: Treating the basic id. *Journal of Nervous and Mental Disorders, 156*, 404–411.

Levin, B. L., Glasser, J. H., & Jaffee, C. L. (1988). National trends coverage and utilization of mental health, alcohol, and substance abuse services within managed care settings. *American Journal of Public Health, 78*, 1222–1223.

Levinson, D. (1978). *Season's of a Man's Life.* New York: Ballantine Books.

Levitan, S. J., & Kornfield, D. S. (1981). Clinical and cost benefits of liaison psychiatry. *American Journal of Pyschiatry, 138*, 790–793.

Mann, J. (1973). *Time limited psychotherapy.* Cambridge, MA: Harvard University Press.

Marmor, J. (1980). Historical roots. In Davanloo, H., *Short-term dynamic psychotherapy* (pp. 3–13). New York: Jason Aronson.

Masters, J. C., Burish, T. G., Hollon, S. D., & Rimm, D. C. (1987). *Behavior Therapy,* New York: Harcourt Brace Jovanovich.

Meier, G. (1981). HMO experiences with mental health services to the long-term emotionally disabled. *Inquiry, 18*, 125.

Morrill, R. G. (1978). The future for mental health in primary health care programs. *American Journal of Psychiatry, 135*, 1351–1355.

Mumford, E., Schlesinger, H. J., Glass, G. V., Patrick, C., & Cuerdon, T. (1984). A new look at evidence about the reduced cost of medical utilization following mental health treatment. *American Journal of Psychiatry, 141*, 1145–1158.

Nelson, J. (1987). The history and spirit of the HMO movement. *HMO Practice, 1*(2), 75–85.

Newman, F. L., & Howard, K. L. (1986). Therapeutic effort, treatment outcome, and national health policy. *American Psychologist, 41*(2), 181–187.

Patrick, C., Coleman, J., Eagle, & Nelson, J. (1978). Chronic emotional patients and their families in an HMO. *Inquiry, 15*, 166–173.

Phillips, E. L. (1985). *A guide for therapists and patients to short-term therapy.* Springfield, IL: Charles Thomas Publishers.

Riche, M. (1987, November). Behind the boom in mental health care. *American Demographics*, pp. 33–37.

Schwartz, W. (1987). The inevitable failure of current cost-containment strategies: Why they can provide only temporary relief. *Journal of the American Medical Association, 257*, 220–224.

Sifneos, P. (1979). *Short-term dynamic psychotherapy*. New York: Plenum Press.

Spoerl, O. H. (1974). Treatment patterns in prepaid psychiatric care. *American Journal of Psychiatry, 131*, 56–59.

Starr, P. (1982). *The social transformation of American medicine*. New York: Basic Books.

Strupp, H. H., & Binder, J. L. (1984). *Psychotherapy in a new key: A guide to time-limited dynamic psychotherapy*. New York: Basic Books.

Sullivan, R. (1985, December 2). Hospitals moving to prepaid care. *New York Times*, pp. 1, B4.

Tulkin, S., & Frank, G. W. (1985). The changing role of psychologists in health maintenance organizations. *American Psychologist, 40*, 1125–1129.

VandenBos, G., & DeLeon H. H. (1988). The use of psychotherapy to improve physical health. *Psychotherapy, 25*, 335–343.

Watzlawick, P., Beavin, J. H., & Jackson, D. D. (1967). *The pragmatics of human communication*. New York: Norton.

2

Daniel Y. Patterson and William H. Berman

Organizational and Service Delivery Issues in Managed Mental Health Services

The Setting

American PsychManagement, Inc. (APM) is a private mental health benefits firm in Washington, D.C. APM specializes in the design, delivery, and management of mental health benefits to self-insured companies, insurance carriers, labor unions, and health maintenance organizations. Its services include benefit redesign, catastrophic case management, preadmission certification, concurrent care review, and retrospective utilization review. In addition, it provides preferred provider organizations and capitated mental health benefit plans for health maintenance organizations. Prior to joining American PsychManagement, Dr. Patterson was Director of Psychiatry, Kaiser Permanente of Mid-Atlantic States.

Thanks in part to the efforts of the Committee on the Costs of Health Care (Roemer, 1985) and the growing labor movement (Kisch & Austad, 1988), health insurance has now become an absolute given in employment settings (Tolchin, 1989). Benefit packages enable employers to lure employees without having to increase salaries and other direct costs. Conversely, labor unions have made health benefits a significant bargaining chip in contract negotiations (Freitag, 1989). More recently, large employers have become self-insurers in an attempt to provide benefits while controlling costs.

Business–health coalitions have made the control of mental health and substance abuse costs one of their top agenda items for the coming decade (Kessler, 1986). Mental health and substance abuse (MH/SA) care in some companies accounts for 25% of the employers health care costs (Sullivan, Flynn, & Lewin, 1987), with inpatient treatment accounting for 23% of all hospital days (Keisler & Sibulkin, 1987). Moreover, costs of the mental health component of health care are rising at a dramatic 27% per year (Winslow, 1989). Increasingly, the business community expects that health insurance benefits will be required for all employed persons, even for those receiving minimum wage (Tolchin, 1989). Recent changes in Medicare legislation have significantly increased access to a minimum acceptable amount of mental health care for the elderly (Durenburger, 1989). Employers feel an urgent need to minimize the spiraling health costs that affect corporate profits, and they want to clearly define the limits of their financial responsibility for employee health care.

At the same time, employers have witnessed a significant breakdown of traditional health insurance programs due to competition from managed care programs and the phenomenon of spiraling adverse selection. This "meltdown scenario" can be described as follows. High utilizers of mental health services (and medical/surgical benefits) are reluctant to change long-established relationships with providers, and continue to use their benefits to the maximum. This maximum utilization drives up indemnity insurance premiums by affecting the actuarial tables used in determining premium rates. The high indemnity rates lead to the exit of healthy low utilizers at their company's next benefit conversion point (open season) as they turn to managed care programs that meet their medical needs at more reasonable rates. These low-utilizing subscribers are essential to the indemnity plans to balance the overall costs of insurance for the total group. The exodus of the low utilizers in turn leaves a higher concentration of high utilizers in the indemnity insurance plan, further driving up the indemnity insurance premiums. The spiral of adverse selection and increasing costs can continue uncontrolled until the indemnity premiums are beyond the reach of all but the most ill, or the most wealthy. All of these factors have produced a growing aversion to fee-for-service care and indemnity reimbursement plans among business and insurers and an increasing affinity for managed care delivery systems. Managed care managers, corporate benefits managers, and the practitioners who provide the services need to understand the types of managed health care delivery systems, the benefits and limitations offered to subscribers, and the organizational and professional problems in managed care. To achieve these goals, this chapter will address the following:

1. The advantages and disadvantages of various types of managed mental health delivery systems;
2. The most likely benefits, limitations, and exclusions of managed mental health care, and the relationship between private and public mental health care;
3. The professional roles and conflicts in managed mental health service delivery.

Types of Managed Care Systems

Although there is an extensive array of systems for service delivery, there are two general models of MH/SA managed care delivery: (a) the staff or group model health maintenance organization, referred to in this paper as an HMO; and (b) the private office practice, fiscal control-based Preferred Provider Organization/Independent Practice Association (PPO/IPA) model. Each form has its advantages and disadvantages, emphasizing some services and benefits while minimizing other components of service delivery.

The staff model HMO was one of the first forms of widely accepted alternate delivery system and has been in existence for more than 50 years (Kisch & Austad, 1988). Staff model HMOs and their siblings, the group model, employ full-time and part-time practitioners to provide MH/SA services. Enrollees pay a set fee for all services, have minimal paperwork, and have deductibles and copayments that are generally significantly lower than those found in indemnity insurance. Offices are situated either as an integral part of primary care, or (particularly in HMOs with larger enrollments) in a separate wing or building dedicated to mental health services. In the staff model, the providers are employees of the HMO. In the group model, the providers are a separate corporate entity that usually contracts with the HMO at a capitated rate.

The staff model HMO at its best can be the most organized and cost-effective delivery system. Care is provided in a centralized facility with a uniform charting procedure and consistent and coherent staff training. Many of the early HMOs fostered group cohesiveness and a sense of purpose in providing health care (Bennett, 1988). Comprehensive, integrated treatment can be offered most easily in such HMOs, and the utilization of services and quality of care can be measured and monitored. The closed system of a staff model HMO facilitates cost containment. A clinician is always available, and emergencies are easily handled within the HMO.

Staff model HMOs have disadvantages as well. First, they inherently limit the choice of provider to physicians and therapists who are on their staff. In addition, they run the risk of recruiting poor quality providers with less skill or limited training who have been unable to function in private practice. Increased routinization, decreased flexibility, and decreased autonomy all contribute to this different form of "adverse selection" (Fielding, 1984). Furthermore, providers on salary sometimes behave less flexibly and are perceived as being less concerned with their patients (Luft, 1981; Mechanic & Aiken, 1989). Staff model HMOs have at times been found to "control" utilization with long waits for routine appointments or onerous referral procedures (Glassner, Duggan, & Hoffman, 1975; Mechanic & Aiken, 1989). At their worst, staff model HMOs in financial straits have incentive to pressure their MH/SA clinicians to practice in a less than optimal manner.

The IPA and its cousin (from the delivery perspective) the PPO provide services to a given population at a discounted fee-for-service rate. IPAs are health plans, in which enrollees can pay a set fee for all covered health services, and providers can be paid a discounted fee-for-service rate out of the capitation-based risk pool. Such HMOs often provide financial incentives for lower utilization. In the PPO, the providers are reimbursed on a fee-for-service basis, but at a discounted rate. The provider benefits from decreased paperwork and improved claims turnaround, and the patient is afforded reduced or absent deductibles and copayments. IPA/PPO providers maintain private practice offices, and managed care activities constitute only a portion of their practice.

These models have the advantage of offering the enrollee a much greater choice of clinicians than staff model HMOs. IPA/PPO systems offer less risk of pressuring their clinicians into providing substandard care, since individual monitoring is infrequent, and providers have the option of resigning from the panel. In addition, there is sufficient competition that poor and substandard services will be forced out of the market fairly quickly. Cost control procedures are often more difficult in these systems, since organizational contact with providers is less direct, and providers are less committed to the organization.

On the negative side, IPAs and PPOs often depend on deeply discounted fees and withholds that are never returned to the provider. Utilization review procedures are quite cumbersome and are often adversarial. Moreover, IPA/PPO sysstems guarantee no direct provider accountability and no organized system to handle emergencies. This can result in inconsistent care or frequent uncontrolled costs. For example, providers are at liberty to refuse patients if their practice "is full," in an attempt to select so-called "good patients with nice problems." Conversely, they can potentially pad their practice by recommending continued treatment after the insurance benefits are depleted. The reliance on primary provider/gatekeepers with capitation agreements increases the potential for underreferral for necessary services due to profit motives. Finally, PPO/IPAs are less likely to develop briefer treatment approaches. This results in longer, unplanned psychotherapy, or inappropriate psychopharmacology that substitutes anxiolytics and hypnotics for antidepressant and antimanic treatments (Burns, Smith, Goldman, Barth, & Coulam, 1989).

From the above descriptions one can see that both the staff model HMO and the IPA/PPO delivery systems offer benefits and risks to the individual subscriber. Staff and group model HMOs offer the most organized, comprehensive, and efficient care, and encourage an egalitarian treatment philosophy rather than a simple cost-containment perspective. PPO/IPAs offer greater freedom of choice of practitioners, increased flexibility in service utilization, and ease of reimbursement for providers. Abuses are possible in both. In the staff model, excessive work loads threaten to elicit substandard care; in the PPO/IPA, costs may be higher, utilization review is limited, and "cream-skimming" by individual providers is possible. The downside risks of indemnity plans are self-evident: the costs of current insurance coverage are prohibitive. The challenge for current health planners is to create delivery systems that maximize the advantages of managed mental health care, while limiting and controlling the potential for abuse.

Benefits, Limitations, and Exclusions in Mental Health Services

The major aims of managed mental health are control of overutilization and the delivery of cost-effective services. These aims are addressed by indemnity insurance, such as Medicare, in two ways. Inpatient mental health benefits in all nonpsychiatric and some psychiatric hospitals are limited by the Diagnostic Related Grouping (DRG) prepayment strategy. DRGs have resulted in significant decreases in costs (Taube, Lave, Rupp, Goldman, & Frank, 1988), but they do not handle outliers well.[1] The control for outpatient mental health cost is through yearly and lifetime dollar caps and through use of deductibles and copayments (e.g., Manning, Wells, Duan, Newhouse, & Ware, 1986). These approaches run the risk of establishing an elitist system and blocking early access, which may increase overall costs in the long run (Durenberger, 1988, 1989).

---

[1] Outliers are defined by utilization review companies and insurers as cases that lie outside defined statistical standards, such as two standard deviations beyond the mean for a given diagnosis or DRG.

Federal HMO legislation set the required mental health benefit package (for those seeking federal qualification) at 20 individual psychotherapy sessions per member per year. In practice, HMO MH/SA benefits usually include additional inpatient benefits, even though not all are federally qualified (Levin, Glasser, & Jaffee, 1988). Programs vary, however, in the requirement for and amount of co-payment (Levin & Glasser, 1979), which may serve as a deterrent to utilization.

Empirical research and the experience of the senior author have shown that 4–6% of HMO members are referred for mental health services (Diehr, Williams, Martin, & Price, 1984; Wells, Manning, & Benjamin, 1986), and that 90% of those patients can be treated within the 30-day inpatient and 20-visit outpatient limit (Cummings, 1990; Taube, Goldman, Burns, & Kessler, 1988; Wells et al., 1986).

High Users of Mental Health Services

Based on these data, only 0.5% of an HMO membership cannot be treated within the standard benefit package and have a greater need for services. These high users absorb almost 50% of the total dollars for mental health care. At least one-third of these high utilizers suffer from significant disability (Taube et al., 1988; Kisch & Austad, 1988). For patients who need ongoing, intensive mental health interventions in order to function, these services must be provided either by the managed care facilities or by the public sector.[2]

It is likely that business coalitions on health will draw state and local officials into substantive discussions as to the appropriate role of the public and the private sectors in the delivery of mental health and substance abuse treatment, with particular reference to the catastrophic or high utilizer group. The goal of these discussions will be to develop (a) clear operational definitions of what is ordinary versus catastrophic; (b) adequate and appropriate funding for each sector's designated task; and (c) a meshing of delivery systems that will create a seamless interface between the private and public delivery systems.

Severe versus chronically ill. The provision of catastrophic and long-term mental health treatment clearly differs from medical/surgical treatment, both in the way services are used and in the source of care. Catastrophic medical/surgical illnesses are virtually always treated in the private sector, even when treatment is supported by public dollars through programs such as medicare; there are no state hospital facilities that undertake renal transplants. In contrast, chronic *mental* illnesses have traditionally been treated in state psychiatric facilities, and more recently in community mental health centers.

In practice, many HMOs provide services for a broad range of patients, including

---

[2] Some portion of those patients who use more than 20 sessions per year are using them for educational, professional, or personal growth purposes, simply because the benefit is available. This practice is known in the insurance industry as "moral hazard," referring to the tendency of some people to use nonessential services simply because those services are free. While discretionary uses of psychotherapy are perfectly appropriate for the individual, health care insurers including managed health care systems are under no obligation to provide this type of psychotherapy. There is no data on the prevalence of such discretionary care, but some have suggested it to be as high as two-thirds of the high utilizers.

those with psychotic disorders. It is likely that the private sector will continue to provide MH/SA services to the large majority of patients, and the public sector will provide services for the chronically and catastrophically mentally ill.

The rationale for separating what Taube et al. (1988) referred to as the "high-impaired high-utilizers" (the chronically ill) from the rest of mental health utilizers is not simply a cost issue (although cost factors do enter in, to be sure). There is increasing evidence that it is extremely difficult to provide adequate services to the severely ill in capitated programs. Mainstreaming seriously mentally ill people into HMOs presents significant organizational and service delivery problems (Christianson, Lurie, Finch, & Moscovice, 1989). For example, a very large population is needed in order to effectively provide the necessary services. The base rate of persons with severe psychiatric disorders who are dependent on an employed family member is about 6:10,000 (Shadish, 1989), so that a managed care panel of fewer than 100,000 will not have sufficient numbers of chronic psychiatric patients to make a comprehensive chronic care program economically feasible. Moreover, the cost of a comprehensive chronic care program is too great for an individual HMO unless it has a very large nonchronic population to offset it.

The alternative, integrated mental health systems for the chronically ill (IMHs), differ in significant ways from HMO capitation programs (Mechanic & Aiken, 1989). Since virtually all patients in IMHs are at high risk and have a high need for intensive services, capitation payments are based on the estimated need for care for a full year for a single patient. The private sector is developing IMHs as an alternative to the public mental health programs in providing effective services for these high-risk patients (Babigian & Reed, 1989).

Defining chronic mental illness. There is a developing consensus among managed mental health specialists that specific operational criteria should be used to define chronicity, and *not* diagnosis per se. Diagnosis alone does not accurately predict chronicity (Harding, Zubin, & Strauss, 1987), and many psychoses and personality disorders can be effectively treated in HMOs.

The four most common operational criteria for transferring patients from standard managed mental health/substance abuse benefits into public treatment settings happen when the following are:

1. A definitive recommendation of long-term residential or hospital treatment has been made;
2. The patient is on medical or psychiatric disability retirement or is an adult financial dependent by virtue of a psychiatric illness;
3. A patient has been hospitalized more than four times for a psychiatric illness, indicating an illness that is refractory to standard psychiatric interventions, and;
4. A patient has been hospitalized psychiatrically but refuses to comply with appropriate outpatient treatment.

In all of these cases, the need is apparent for more intensive treatment than is typically available in private sector care. Day hospital, residential treatment, or intensive psychological intervention are difficult to provide without a sufficiently large population from which to draw.

Operational exclusionary criteria in the outpatient arena are less clear, and harder to establish. A frequent HMO inclusion criterion has been that a condition must be "amenable to crisis intervention or short-term evaluation and treatment." However, there is reason to believe that this criterion will be eliminated in the near future as vague and impossible to realize. As more and more brief treatments are developed, and the emphasis on intermittent treatment over time increases (see Cummings, *in this volume*), such a criterion becomes irrelevant. HMO clinicians have often been persistent and ingenious in treating heretofore "untreatable" patients within the context of the HMO benefits. This is especially true in the staff model HMO which encourages a "work smart" approach (see DeStefano & Henault, and Strosahl, in this volume). Many so-called chronic schizophrenic, borderline, and conduct-disordered patients have been treated within 20 individual or 40 group therapy visits per year.

An alternative criterion may be a relatively clear definition of biopsychological necessity, involving a combination of functional impairment and symptomatic presentation. This cannot be limited to patients with DSM-III R diagnoses, however, since more than half of patients seen in HMOs would qualify for only the so-called V-codes (difficulties in marriage, social, or personal life) that do not meet specific diagnostic criteria, but do cause significant distress.

The Problem of Cost-Shifting

It is important that the private and public mental health systems agree on the operational criteria for exclusion from any private insurance, in order to prevent charges of cost-shifting. Although not foreign to the medical/surgical care, cost-shifting is a special problem in the MH/SA area. Allegations of cost-shifting abound in the managed care areas, although the evidence of it is scanty. In contrast, cost-shifting in the private practice arena is common. Mental health clinicians in the private insurance/fee-for-service system and private psychiatric inpatient facilities frequently shift patients from their care to state-funded facilities (hospitals, clinics) for a variety of reasons, including management difficulties and inability to pay full fee.

In the private practice sector, difficult patients are often returned to the private practice pool with the patient retaining insurance coverage. Alternative arrangements for the patient's care do not have to be made directly. The clinician has only to notify the patient by certified mail and continue to provide care during a decent interval. Those private patients who are turned over to the public mental health sector can also be shifted with little impact. There are no regulatory guidelines affecting this kind of action by private clinicians, and the number of cases per clinician is so small as to make effective regulation impossible. Patients who are released have little recourse, except lengthy and difficult court actions or professional ethics complaints.

In contrast, managed mental health clinicians, especially those in staff model HMOs, are restrained from cost-shifting by policy and peer pressure. Case-shifting to public mental health facilities can be more easily scrutinized by regulatory agencies. If the patient is not a candidate for public care, the patient cannot get care from clinicians outside the HMO unless he or she is willing to pay for the full cost of such care. The HMO clinician's peers and supervisors are unlikely to accept transfers of difficult patients with equanimity.

Professional Issues in Managed Mental Health

The types of managed care systems and the benefits provided by those systems provide the external structure within which mental health services can be delivered. However, the issues of access to services, and who provides those services also need to be clarified. Referral procedures, staffing, and the roles of different mental health disciplines are common sources of debate and conflict (see Austad, Berman, Cummings, Hoyt, Koran, & Wright, 1989). The remainder of this chapter will discuss these issues, offering possible alternatives to the sometimes heated debates over turf and role. We are aware that there is a wide range of systems in existence, and that the present options are not the only choice. Future models may use different structures and guidelines for operation. However, at the present time, choices based on a staff model delivery system are the most efficient (Kessler, 1986; Patterson, 1986). We are assuming a delivery system that provides the minimum mandated benefits including 30 inpatient days and 20 individual or 40 group outpatient sessions per member per year.

Referral Procedures

Several procedures for referral have been used in HMOs. In some, particularly IPAs, the primary provider serves as a gatekeeper, and at times functions as a barrier to access to all specialty providers. Although there appear to be some short-term economic gains from this process, we are of the opinion that, for both economic and ethical reasons, this is not an appropriate procedure. The only rationale for establishing a barrier to treatment is when there is concern that neither the patient nor the specialty provider will accurately evaluate the need for specialty services. Clearly this should not be the case for mental health. First, primary providers are likely to underestimate, rather than overestimate, the need for mental health care (Wells, Manning, Duan, Newhouse, & Ware, 1987). Second, a well trained mental health staff can be expected to distinguish those who need mental health care from those who can be treated in primary care, and make the appropriate referrals.

With these assumptions, referrals for mental health can come from three sources. First, patients are referred by a primary provider (physician, physician assistant, or nurse) based on either a request or the assessment by the provider that mental rather than physical health services are needed. Second, patients can be self-referred. These are patients who either have sought mental health care in the past and know when additional treatment is needed, or who can clearly recognize an emotional or interpersonal problem for which contact with a medical provider only delays the appropriate intervention. Even in cases where little mental health care is needed, within a staff model, the cost of seeing a mental health provider is no greater than the cost of seeing a primary provider. Third, referrals can come from other specialty providers. Referrals from obstetrics/gynecology are particularly common, as women may be more open and honest with their gynecologist. However, referrals from neurology, pediatrics, and oncology are also common.

Staffing Patterns

The relative contributions of the various mental health disciplines has been a topic of much discussion in the literature (and some litigation). Such "turf" issues raise concerns about livelihood and autonomy as well as real issues of competence and expertise (Berman, 1989). Both theory and practice indicate that a range of providers is essential for quality mental health service (Cheifitz & Salloway, 1985; Patterson, 1986), and that few roles are not interchangeable; the majority of research on disciplinary differences shows no significant effect for discipline. However, research and practice are often at variance with abstract beliefs. For example, the American Psychiatric Association has recommended that the chief of mental health in staff model HMOs should be a psychiatrist (American Psychiatric Association, 1989). In fact only 55% of HMOs have a chief of mental health at all, and only 42% of those are headed by a psychiatrist; the rest are headed by psychologists (28%), social workers (17%), or nurse clinicians (13%) (Shadle & Christianson, 1988).

The pragmatics of staffing for psychiatrists, psychologists, masters-level mental health professionals (including nurse clinicians and social workers), and chemical dependency counselors may be determined best by the types of services provided in HMOs. In practice, each discipline has several appropriate functional roles that maximize the practitioner's training and experience. Regardless of educational degree, however, all full-time practitioners should be expected to see an average of seven to eight patients per day, including individual and group contacts.

Inpatient Services

Inpatient treatment is the most restrictive and invasive component of mental health care. Research has consistently documented that outpatient treatment is less costly and promotes less disruption in family and work life than inpatient care. Inpatient care is also the most expensive component of a managed mental health system. For the benefit of both the HMO and patients and their families, inpatient hospitalization and the inpatient-outpatient interface must be managed efficiently if the mental health program is to be cost-effective.

The underlying rule is that the more control the HMO has over the pace of treatment and length of stay, the less costly will be the hospitalization. Ideally the HMO provides its own inpatient treatment. However, case flow and start-up costs make this impossible except in the largest plans. (A minimum of 150,000 enrollees is needed to provide case flow for a 12-bed unit.)

Providers in managed mental health should be in control of admission to and discharge from the hospital. It has been our experience that the next most efficient procedure is to have staff psychiatrists with attending privilege at a local hospital.[3]

---

[3] Since only a handful of states provide hospital admitting and attending privilege for nonphysicians, we have no data on their possible role in this regard.

When this option is available, the psychiatrist not only controls admission and discharge, but also provides a liaison function between inpatient and outpatient care. He or she is completely informed as to the availability of outpatient care, the patient's family background and past history, and medication issues. As a result, both the number and duration of hospitalization can be kept to a minimum.

Outpatient Services

The foundation of a cost-effective outpatient managed care program is the family mental health practitioner (FMHP). Just as the medical family practitioner synthesizes the roles of internist, pediatrician, obstetrician and general surgeon, but chooses the family as his unifying focus, the family mental health practitioner has the same broad approach and unifying focus. Ideally, the FMHP develops an ongoing relationship with the patient's family, as well as a database of information relevant to the case. FMHPs assess nonemergency patients and families, identify the appropriate family unit for treatment, and undertake brief psychotherapy (usually no more than 10 sessions), leaving the door open for additional strategic treatment opportunities in the future. The FMHP should be comfortable working with any family unit—individual, couples, or families—and should be eclectic in approach (behavioral, cognitive, psychodynamic, etc.), but short-term in orientation. The FMHP can implement many of the programmatic treatments described in this book and provide most of the treatment for the interpersonal and intrapersonal problems that commonly present for therapy.

The most common, and least costly practitioner to fill this role is the masters-level clinician. In practice, master's-level clinicians consistently have formed the largest provider category in staff and group model HMOs. In 1982, psychiatrists and doctoral psychologists accounted for 24% and 19% of full-time-equivalent mental health providers, respectively (Levin & Glasser, 1984). Like the FMHP, they can function largely independently, yet work in conjunction with medical, psychiatric, and psychological staff.

Retraining of master's-level clinicians for the FMHP role will require significant effort and time, since social workers and psychiatric nurses have often been trained only in long-term psychotherapy approaches. Psychologists and psychiatrists may choose to work as FMHPs also, allowing patients the freedom to choose their own clinicians. Salaries may be lower for FMHPs compared to specialists, since the competition for FMHP positions is greater. Doctoral-level practitioners who choose to function as FMHPs may also need retraining, but may have had some significant exposure to brief treatments already. In general, doctoral-level providers will be encouraged to contribute to more specialized treatments in which advanced experience and training are more relevant.[4]

There are specific problems that require more intensive and structured outpatient programs in order to prevent inpatient care and to reduce unnecessary utilization of medical services. Substance abuse, chronic pain, medical treatment

---

[4] It is possible that the benefit package could be tailored for a dollar-equivalency limit rather than a session limit. In such a system, the number of contacts with a doctoral-level clinician would be less, reflecting the increased cost of service for these providers. However, such a system has never been used and would have many logistical and organizational problems.

compliance, eating disorders, and major mental illness (schizophrenia, bipolar disorder, major depression, and panic disorder) all have been shown to benefit from outpatient psychosocial interventions. Psychologists can make a significant contribution in developing and directing such programs with the assistance of psychiatrists, FMHPs, and substance abuse counselors.

The role of psychologists needs to extend beyond direct clinical service (Cheifitz & Salloway, 1984, 1985). Psychologists are most often placed in charge of directing all outpatient psychotherapy programs and are responsible for both training and supervising masters-level staff. In addition, psychologists often have significant expertise in child and adolescent psychotherapy and can provide significant specialty care in pediatric mental health when the problems exceed the expertise of the FMHP. Finally, psychologists can have a central role in health-related issues (Cheifitz & Salloway, 1984):

> "The development of pertinent and practical health education . . . techniques, the application and supervision of these techniques, and the measurement of their effects, all seem to be challenges calling for response by health psychologists. (p. 162)

Of course, others have argued that psychologists can provide the bulk of services (Berkman, Bassos, & Post, 1988; Cummings, 1988) although the cost of such programs may be greater than that of more multidisciplinary programs.

The treatment of psychoses and severe mood disorders requires the use of psychopharmacologic agents, medical monitoring, and differential diagnosis of medical disorders. Other psychiatric disorders also involve varying degrees of medical management. The role of psychiatrists in managed mental health should be designed to provide services to these patients. Psychiatrists can provide supervision and direct medical and pharmacologic services to drug-responsive disorders (see Sovner, in this volume, for a discussion of a psychopharmacology service).

Since psychiatrists are centrally involved in inpatient treatment, they can also provide direct service and consultation in tracking care from emergency triage to crisis intervention and/or inpatient care to follow-through care. Although they need not be the exclusive providers in this domain, the comprehensive treatment of severely disturbed patients benefits from the involvement of medical personnel. In practice, psychiatrists do tend to see more severely disturbed patients than do psychologists (Knesper, Belcher, & Cross, 1989). Psychiatrists can function as generalists who provide the same services as other mental health providers, including pharmacotherapy (Bennett, 1988; Flinn, McMahon, & Collins, 1987). Like other doctoral-level providers, however, they are significantly more costly.

Caring for seriously ill patients requires teamwork and often involves more than one discipline. FMHPs can often provide services such as long-term maintenance and aftercare supervision. Psychologists often direct and supervise intensive structured outpatient programs such as day hospitals and partial hospitals, outpatient drug and alcohol rehabilitation, and long-term group maintenance programs. Psychiatrists can provide medical coverage and facilitate the transition among inpatient, partial hospitalization, and outpatient services.

Long-term outpatient services. In general, mental health services will be provided within the benefit package and provided by clinicians in the panel. Continued treatment, or the recommendation for long-term outpatient treatment will be carefully monitored. As noted before, there is a small population of patients who require long-term psychotherapy. Long-term treatment is essential to any comprehensive mental health delivery system (see Cummings, this volume, for a supporting view). Psychotherapists with specialized skills in various approaches to a long-term intensive treatment can include psychiatrists, psychologists, and masters-level clinicians.

Decisions as to who needs (as opposed to wants) long-term psychotherapy should be made, initially, by FMHPs. For example, one screening criterion is repeated exacerbation of symptoms or significantly increased medical utilization when mental health care is stopped. Once a referral for long-term intervention is made, a clinician administrator or utilization review committee can evaluate the recommendation of the FMHP. The committee can provide an effective gatekeeper function to prevent unnecessary utilization of long-term psychotherapy, yet allow the FMHP to maintain a good relationship with the patient. On the other hand, patients who appropriately need long-term psychotherapy will be identified by the managed care program directors through standard utilization review procedures. Such reviews identify patients who are excessive utilizers of the mental health and medical care services. The continuing appropriateness of such long-term psychotherapy should be monitored in ongoing utilization reviews to ensure that appropriate treatment is being provided.

To avoid a conflict of interest, FMHPs and specialty providers will work only within the primary provider/short-term psychotherapy system and will not treat enrollees with intensive long-term psychotherapy. These clinicians will refer appropriate patients to long-term psychotherapy based on severity of psychopathology and upon the specialty skills of the long-term psychotherapist. A separate panel of long-term psychotherapists will be used for this small patient population.

Conclusion

Managed mental health care has multiple organizational structures, ranging from the staff model HMO to various forms of PPOs and group practice organizations. Each approach balances the economic and service delivery benefits in different ways; while IPAs offer the most flexibility of services, for example, they tend to be more costly because the flexibility precludes some cost controls. Choices must be made based on individual and community needs, which must include the cost of medical care for the community.

Managed mental health is not the panacea of mental health delivery. There are some patients who will not benefit from managed mental health. For example, chronic psychiatric patients probably will be underserved in traditional managed care. The solution to the treatment of chronic patients is far from clear. We have suggested criteria that might be used to identify these patients and recommended discussions between the private and public sector as to how best to provide services to them.

All mental health disciplines can play important roles in managed care delivery. Regardless of discipline, managed mental health care providers will require a major practical and theoretical reorientation. Long-term psychotherapy will be available, but to a much lesser extent and with much more attention to biopsychological necessity and maintenance of quality treatment. In this system, all providers will have to choose among the roles of family mental health provider, specialty provider either in the inpatient or outpatient domain, or the alternative role of a long-term intensive outpatient psychotherapist. Academic training facilities will be needed to provide curricula to accommodate the increasing emphasis on short-term intervention.

This chapter has outlined the structure within which managed mental health care is practiced. We have discussed the way services are provided, what services can be provided, and the limitations of managed mental health care. It is clear that managed mental health, in the long run, will not belong to any one mental health provider group. The remainder of this book defines the nature of managed mental health given the structures we have described.

References

American Psychiatric Association. (1989). *Guidelines for psychiatric practice in staff model health maintenance organizations.* Washington, DC: American Psychiatric Association.

Austad, C. S., Berman, W. H., Cummings, N. J., Hoyt, M., Karon, B., & Wright, R. (1989, August). *The pros and cons of managed mental health care.* Symposium conducted at the 97th Annual Convention of American Psychological Association, New Orleans, LA.

Babigian, H., & Reed, S. (1989). An experimental model capitation payment system for the chronic mentally ill. *Psychiatric Annals, 17,* 604–609.

Bennett, M. J. (1988). The greening of the HMO: Implications for prepaid psychiatry. *American Journal of Psychiatry, 145,* 1544–1549.

Berkman, A. S., Bassos, C. A., & Post, L. (1988). Managed mental health care and independent practice: A challenge to psychology. *Psychotherapy, 25,* 434–440.

Berman, W. H. (1989, August) Central issues in the HMO psychotherapy debate. Discussant for the symposium, *Managed Health Care Effects on the Practice and Evolution of Psychotherapy,* at the 97th Annual American Psychological Association Convention, New Orleans, LA.

Burns, B. J., Smith, J., Goldman, H. H., Barth, L. E., & Coulam, R. F. (1989). The CHAMPUS tidewater demonstration project. *New Directions in Mental Health Services, 43,* 77–86.

Cheifitz, D. I., & Salloway, J. C. (1984). Mental health services in health maintenance organizations: Implications for psychology. *Professional Psychology: Research and Practice, 15,* 152–164.

Cheifitz, D. I., & Salloway, J. C. (1985). Patterns of mental health services provided by HMOs. *American Psychologist, 39,* 495–502.

Christianson, J. B., Lurie, N., Finch, M., & Moscovice, I. (1989). Mainstreaming the mentally ill in HMOs. *New Directions in Mental Health Services, 43,* 19–28.

Cummings, N. A. (1988). The emergence of the mental health complex: Adaptive and maladaptive responses. *Professional Psychology: Research and Practice, 19*(3), 323–335.

Cummings, N. A. (1990, August). Managing mental health care: An alternative to having it manage us. Paper presented at the 98th Annual Convention of the American Psychological Association, Boston, MA.

Diehr, P., Williams, S. J., Martin, D. P., & Price, K. (1984). Ambulatory mental health services utilization in three provider plans. *Medical Care, 22,* 1–13.

Durenberger, D. (1988). Rectifying an archaic payment policy. *American Journal of Psychiatry, 145,* 81–82.

Durenberger, D. (1989). Providing mental health care services to Americans. *American Psychologist, 44,* 1293–1297.

Fielding, S. L. (1984). Organizational impact on medicine: The HMO concept. *Social Science and Medicine*, *18*(8), 615–620.

Flinn, D. E., McMahon, T. C., & Collins, M. F. (1987). Health maintenance organizations and their implications for psychiatry. *Hospital and Community Psychiatry*, *38*, 255–263.

Freitag, M. (1989, August 17). The battle over medical costs. *The New York Times*. New York Times, pp. D1, D4.

Glasser, M. A., Duggan, T. J., & Hoffman, W. S. (1975). Obstacles to utilization of prepaid mental health care. *American Journal of Psychiatry*, *132*, 710–715.

Harding, C. M., Zubin, J., & Strauss, J. S. (1987). Chronicity in schizophrenia: Fact, partial fact, or artifact? *Hospital and Community Psychiatry*, *38*(5), 477–486.

Keisler, C. I., & Sibulkin, A. (1987). *Mental hospitalization: Myths and facts about a national crisis.* Newbury Park, CA: Sage.

Kessler, K. A. (1986). Benefit design, utilization review, case management, PPOs contain costs. *Benefits Today*, *3*(10), 1–2.

Kessler, K. A. (1986, September 9). Cost containment: Prospects for controlling mental health benefits costs improving. *Business Insurance*, *20*, 47, 50.

Kisch, J., & Austad, C. S. (1988). The health maintenance organization: I. Historical perspective and current status. *Psychotherapy*, *25*(3), 441–448.

Knesper, D. J., Belcher, B. E., & Cross, J. G. (1989). A market analysis comparing the practices of psychiatrists and psychologists. *Archives of General Psychiatry*, *46*, 305–314.

Levin, B. L., & Glasser, J. H. (1979). A survey of mental health service coverage within health maintenance organizations. *American Journal of Public Health*, *69*, 1120–1125.

Levin, B. L., Glasser, J. H., & Jaffee, C. L. Jr. (1988). National trends in coverage and utilization of mental health, alcohol, and substance abuse services within managed health care systems. *American Journal of Public Health*, *78*, 1222–1223.

Luft, H. (1981). *Health Maintenance Organizations: Dimensions of Performance.* New York: Wiley-Interscience.

Manning, W. G., Wells, K. B., Duan, N., Newhouse, J. P., & Ware, J. E. (1986). How cost sharing affects the use of ambulatory mental health services. *Journal of the American Medical Association*, *256*, 1930–1934.

Mechanic, D., & Aiken, L. H. (1989). Capitation in mental health: Potentials and cautions. *New Directions in Mental Health Services*, *43*, 5–18.

Patterson, D. Y. (1986). Provider productivity and other issues in HMO mental health. *HMO Mental Health Newsletter*, *1*(11), 1–5.

Roemer, M. I. (1985). I. S. Falk, the committee on the costs of health care and the drive for national health insurance. *American Journal of Public Health*, *75*, 841–848.

Shadish, W. R. (1989). Private sector care for chronically mentally ill individuals. *American Psychologist*, *44*, 1142–1148.

Shadle, M., & Christianson, J. B. (1988). *The organization of mental health care delivery in HMOs.* Excelsior, MI: Interstudy.

Sullivan, S., Flynn, T. J., & Lewin, M. E. (1987). The quest to manage mental health costs. *Business and Health*, *4*, 24–28.

Taube, C. A., Goldman, H. H., Burns, B. J., & Kessler, L. G. (1988). High users of outpatient mental health services: I. Definition and characteristics. *American Journal of Psychiatry*, *145*(1), 19–24.

Taube, C. A., Lave, J. R., Rupp, A., Goldman, H. H., & Frank, R. G. (1988). Psychiatry under prospective payment: Experience in the first year. *American Journal of Psychiatry*, *145*, 210–213.

Tolchin, M. (1989, September 24). Sudden support for national health care. *The New York Times*, pp. E4.

Wells, K. B., Manning, W. G., & Benjamin, B. (1986). Use of outpatient mental health services in HMO and fee-for-service plans: Results from a randomized controlled trial. *Health Services Research*, *21*, 453–474.

Wells, K. B., Manning, W. G., Duan, N., Newhouse, J. P., & Ware, J. E. (1987). Cost-sharing and the use of general medical physicians for outpatient mental health care. *Health Services Research*, *22*, 1–17.

Winslow, R. (1989, December 13). Spending to cut mental health costs. *The Wall Street Journal*, A1.

Part II

Theoretical and Conceptual Perspectives in Managed Mental Health Care

3 ─────────────────────────────────────

Nicholas A. Cummings

Brief Intermittent Therapy Throughout the Life Cycle

The Setting

American Biodyne is a mental health maintenance organization that was founded in 1985. It is a privately held Delaware corporation that provides unlimited mental health/chemical dependency outpatient and hospitalization services to enrollees of Blue Cross/Blue Shield, Humana, Lincoln National, and several other health plans in 10 states. It currently serves contracts representing 2.5 million covered lives.

Traditional Models of Psychotherapy

The Biodyne model of psychotherapy is derived from data on thousands of patients and more than 30 years of the author's personal experience. It evolved in response to the need for a form of brief psychotherapeutic intervention that was not only meaningful, effective, and efficient in helping people to deal with problems in living, but that also could be financed as a free benefit to health insurance enrollees. This response began in the 1950s when psychotherapy was an exclusion in all health plans (Cummings, 1986, 1988; Cummings & Fernandez, 1985) and resulted in the development of the nation's first comprehensive prepaid mental health plan. Years later this model became the treatment methodology at American Biodyne, and has come to be known as the Biodyne model.

As a clinician at Kaiser Permanente dealing with multiple patients and presenting problems, it was apparent to the author that traditional models of psychotherapy were not comprehensive enough to care for all patients' clinical needs all of the time. Specific assumptions of the orthodox models of psychotherapy produced obstacles to change rather than change itself. It is important to identify and understand these troublesome suppositions in order to appreciate the underlying rationale for the Biodyne model. These premises of traditional therapy are as follows:

There is a "right" or "best" model of psychotherapy. Theory, techniques, and methods from different models have not been integrated and synthesized because schools of thought have tended to compete with one another rather than consolidate their knowledge. Proponents of each orientation have been more concerned with proving which therapy is "right" or "best" than with integration of the best.

The "ideal therapist" exists, that is, someone who can do all things for all people (Cummings & VandenBos, 1979). Experience has shown that when it comes to difficult patients (schizophrenics, addicts, borderline personalities, etc.), an individual therapist may do very well with some types, adequately with others, and poorly with still others.

Patients and their problems should conform to a model of therapy. The therapy should not conform to the needs of the patient. Many traditional therapies dispense one method of treatment regardless of the nature of the patient's difficulties. Specific psychotherapy models characteristically treat every patient with the type of therapy the psychotherapist has to offer. Thus, if the therapist is a Freudian analyst, the patient is likely to "get the couch," regardless of whether the presenting problem is alcoholism, marital discord, or job difficulties. If the therapist is a Jungian analyst, the patient is going to "paint pictures." If the therapist is a behaviorist, the patient is going to be "desensitized."

Psychotherapy "cures" mental health problems. Therapy uses a concept of cure that is based on a medical as opposed to a psychological model. This concept has held back psychotherapy more than any other (Cummings & VandenBos, 1979). Because both patient and therapist "only get one chance," therapists keep patients in treatment until they are sure that every recess of the unconscious has been analyzed as to its conflicts. Traditional models of psychotherapy often assume that if the patient has another problem three years after the patient and therapist terminate, the therapist has not done the job correctly. For decades George Albee (1968) has chided the psychological community for practicing in the house of medicine. Psychologists are finally extracting themselves from that house, but they still continue to use medicine's concept of cure.

Termination is a difficult and painful process. One of the major problems for the therapist doing brief therapy based on traditional models is that the therapist constantly experiences separation anxiety and thus is continually under the stress of encountering loss. Haley (1978) suggests that many psychotherapists gravitate to long-term therapy because the constant separation anxiety imposed upon them by brief therapy is too painful, especially if there has been early bereavement or rejection in the therapist's own history.

The Biodyne Model of Psychotherapy: Principles of Brief Intermittent Psychotherapy

The Biodyne model of psychotherapy challenges the above-mentioned assumptions of traditional therapy, replacing them with assumptions that appear to be more relevant to modern-day mental health problems. First, a therapist's role should be similar to that of the family doctor. Second, a developmental view of man that gives up the concept of cure and termination and reflects the intermittent nature of psychological problems is a productive and fruitful model for psychotherapeutic interventions. Third, therapeutic interventions that are "targeted," or specific and parsimonious, are the most beneficial for dealing with these psychotherapeutic problems.

The Therapist: Psychological Family Doctor

The Biodyne model of psychotherapy can best be described as "brief intermittent therapy throughout the life cycle" (Cummings, 1983). Psychotherapy consists of brief, intermittent episodes that meet recurring crises throughout the patients' life cycle. In an era when health care is fractionated among many specialists who seldom confer with each other, the psychotherapist can be the unifying practitioner who remembers and cares. This means that when a patient presents with a problem, the therapist takes the problem seriously but not necessarily at face value, and he or she treats that problem. The psychological practitioner behaves like the old-fashioned family doctor who remains in touch with all the patient's needs and confers with the other specialists treating the patient for various conditions. Just as the patient visits his or her family doctor when he or she catches influenza or breaks a leg, so the therapist also treats the patient intermittently, as and when the need arises. "Necessary and sufficient treatment" is the keynote of the Biodyne model.

The Developmental View

Since the therapist sees the patient at important junctures over the life span, he or she becomes a unifying and caring agent in the patient's life. Patients continue to grow beyond the actual course of therapy, which serves as a "yeast" for years to come.

This form of intermittent therapy is based on a developmental view of the life cycle coupled with a notion similar to that of Freud's repetition compulsion. The first response to the first trauma in life becomes the prototype of every subsequent response to later life traumas. A person's attempt to solve the crisis is predictable from one trauma to another because it is a recapitulation of the initial adaptation to the stresses of life.

Life contains a number of typical and predictable developmental crises. These situations arise out of normal developmental tasks such as entering school, the advent of adulthood, becoming a parent, getting a divorce and/or separation, midlife changes, and adapting to old age and, ultimately, death. This author believes that, during these crisis points, the individual will repeat the original response to the first trauma or stress in childhood. The response may be depression, phobia, hysteria, or some other defensive adaptations. It may be somatization as illustrated in the child who, under the stress of separation anxiety, exclaims "Mommy, my tummy hurts too much to go to school and take my spelling test." Once established, a prototype becomes the typical way of adapting to life's crises and any other anxiety-provoking stimuli. The prototypical way of responding will be repeated during the life cycle in response to new threats.

Therapeutic intervention during these crises helps the individual to learn new and more effective methods of dealing with perceived threats. After a new prototype is adapted in therapy, the individual ventures out into the world to help himself or herself to cope with problems. The patient returns to the therapist when he or she needs to accommodate the new response styles to life situations. However, a significant difference between the Biodyne model of therapy and traditional models is that each new crisis after the initial therapy requires relatively few additional sessions, regardless of its severity. Our patients learn "life change" skills, or a new process of dealing with problems, and are quickly restored to health.

Targeted Interventions and the Blending of Techniques

The most efficient psychotherapy model is one that incorporates the best that each of the schools of psychology and psychotherapy have to offer, yet specifically fits the most appropriate intervention to the patient's problems. The Biodyne model uses over 60 targeted therapies (Cummings, 1983). Specific techniques are used for specific problems. In order to see the value of this strategy, one might well ask, would you go to a physician that treated everyone who came in the door with penicillin, whether one person had a broken leg from skiing or another had pneumonia? Of course you wouldn't. Fifty years ago all physicians practiced in that manner, since they had five different medications. If one did not work they gave the next one. If that didn't work, they gave the third and so on until they exhausted their repertoire of five favorite medications. At that time the list of the pharmacopeia of the United States was contained in one volume. Not so any more. Physicians have literally thousands of specific treatments for specific conditions, but psychotherapists have not followed the lead of medicine in this area. In reality, the combined schools of psychotherapy have already developed far more specific treatment approaches than most practicing clinicians ever dream of. But, psychotherapists are stuck in the rut of doing what they were initially trained to do regardless of the patient's condition. The Biodyne model makes use of effective treatment techniques that have evolved from all therapy models and combines them into effective therapy. The treatment plan is tailored to the specific needs of each individual patient and the therapist does not have to make the patient fit the model. It frees the therapist from the concepts of the ideal therapist (where the therapist has to be all things to all people), cure, and termination.

Giving up the concepts of "cure" and "termination." The Biodyne model abandons the notion of cure as the accepted primary goal of treatment (Cummings & VandenBos, 1979). That view, perhaps, has held psychotherapy back more than any other concept. Keeping a patient in treatment to guarantee that anxiety will never again plague the patient is absurd, as anxiety is a normal accompaniment of living.

Under the Biodyne model, therapy is not terminated. It is interrupted. Of the patients who come, 85% opt for brief therapy. They enter this model, use it, and come back when they have the need. Therapists often track them for 10, 20, or even 25 years, and find that patients spend less time in psychotherapy overall than they would in traditional, extended therapy. This practice of intermittent therapy over the years can sometimes span generations within one family; the author has treated both children and grandchildren of patients.

Parameters of Biodyne's Brief Intermittent Psychotherapy

Since the parameters of brief, targeted therapy are totally different from those of long-term therapy, many traditional therapists need to be retrained in order to learn it. Brief therapy means more efficient rather than less therapy. It is a model that has generated a number of effective, targeted interventions. Space permits a brief discussion of only a few of them.

Hit the Ground Running

Budman and Gurman (1988) used this term to indicate that the first session must be therapeutic. The belief that effective therapy must be preceded by history-taking (a duty often performed by a social worker) has never been substantiated empirically. It is important for a therapist to know some of a patient's history, but it is impossible to know all of the histories of every patient seen. In the Biodyne model of intermittent therapy, a therapist might not learn all of a patient's history until he or she comes back five or six years later. It is important for the clinician to know the *salient* history, and particularly, the first, and consequently the recurrent manner in which the patient has met psychological trauma. To ensure that the first session is therapeutic, the therapist must attempt to do the following:

Perform an Operational Diagnosis

An "operational diagnosis" is different from a vague psychiatric diagnosis that uses the *Diagnostic and Statistical Manual of Mental Disorders* (DSM III-R), (American Psychiatric Association, 1980) to label a person. Instead, operational diagnosis focuses on one issue: "What brings the patient here today rather than last week or last year?" The answer to this question holds the key to the real reason *why* the patient is in therapy. The operational diagnosis is essential in order to arrive at an appropriate treatment plan. It is best to reach an operational diagnosis in the first session or as soon as possible thereafter.

Examples of operational diagnoses abound: A diagnosis of "alcoholism" could not be considered operational because there is no immediacy involved—the patient may have been alcoholic for some time. If, on the other hand, the therapist learns that the patient's boss has cautioned the patient that he must get help or be fired the next time he misses work on a Monday, the basis for an operational diagnosis has been reached. Similarly, a further example might be that of a woman who has been sexually unresponsive throughout her marriage but who comes to seek therapy now because she discovers that her husband is having an affair and her marriage is seriously threatened.

Frequently patients present themselves because their attitudes and behaviors have created situations that are intolerable. They may want the situation rectified without the therapist tampering with the problem that created the situation in the first place. Addicts are an excellent example of the above. Their unspoken, implicit contract is most often, "Help me alibi through the legal difficulties resulting from my drinking, but allow me to continue to drink." Proper assessment of the operational diagnosis and discerning the patient's implicit contract are critical to formulating a successful treatment plan.

Replace the Implicit Contract with a Therapeutic Contract

Every patient makes an implicit contract with the therapist in the first session. In many cases the therapist misses the implicit contract and erroneously concludes that both patient and therapist are working toward change in the patient. Fritz Perls (personal communication, September, 1972) has cautioned that patients often do not come to therapy for treatment or to change themselves. They come to have the therapist "make it all better," presumably without much effort on their part.

As Paul Watzlawick (personal communication, May, 1972) has pointed out, if the patient gives the therapeutic contract and the therapist disregards it, the patient, anxious to please will usually comply with the therapist's definition of the contract. Patient and therapist then unwittingly become involved in a wrestling match that the therapist erroneously labels "resistance." Although there is such a thing as resistance, 80% of what most therapists term resistance may be the therapist's failure to recognize the patient's goals in treatment. For example, if a patient comes into the office of a therapist and says, "Doctor, I'm glad you have this comfortable chair because I'm going to be here a while," and the therapist does not respond to that statement, the therapist has, by default, made a contract for long-term, nontherapeutic therapy. In short, he has agreed to be nontherapeutic. If the patient says, "I want to come in here and save my marriage, but whatever I do, I'm going to end up getting divorced," the therapist has just made a contract for that patient to divorce. And if the therapist spends the next two years trying to save that marriage the therapist is going to wonder, "Why? What's happening?" The therapist does not realize that the patient's initial contract was that he or she wanted to be able to say after the divorce, "I did everything to save my marriage, I even entered psychotherapy." Space does not permit the hundreds of examples of clinical errors that occur because the therapist did not listen for the therapeutic contract.

After detecting the patient's implicit therapeutic contract, therapist and patient need to discuss it. It is appropriate for the therapist to refuse treatment if the patient insists on his or her own therapeutic contract, but most patients, once their implicit contract is verbalized and discussed extensively, will opt for a legitimate therapeutic goal. The therapist nevertheless must use all of his or her therapeutic acumen to ascertain that the patient is not merely reiterating what he or she thinks the therapist wants to hear.

Once the contract is clear and mutually agreed upon, the therapist makes clear a second part of the contract for short-term, intermittent psychotherapy. The therapist needs to say, "Now that our goals are clarified, I would like to add the following to that contract: I will never abandon you as long as you need me. In return for that, I want you to join me in a partnership to make me obsolete as soon as possible." Perfunctory agreement should not suffice. This aspect of the contract should be discussed thoroughly so that the patient agrees to the amendment and realizes that this is an important part of the working therapeutic agreement. Thus, the stage is set for the patient to take responsibility for his or her own treatment and life change.

Do Something Novel in the First Session

It is important to find something novel and unpredictable to do in the first session. This cuts through the expectations of the "trained patient" and creates a mental set that problems will immediately be addressed. Although for some patients the mere experience of someone truly listening is novel, psychotherapists tend to over-rely on this intervention. Doing something novel most often means doing the unpredictable. The result is to catapult the patient into treatment in spite of their resistance. This technique is particularly effective with jaded and covertly cynical patients, such as those with character disorders and borderline personalities.

Give Homework Assignments

Giving homework in the first session and thereafter will make the patient realize that he or she is expected to be responsible for his or her own therapy. Tasks must be meaningful in light of the patient's goals and the therapeutic contract.

Ignore "Drop Out"

If a therapist takes the above steps, therapeutic "drop out" will be avoided. Patients know when to discontinue treatment better than therapists do. When the time comes, the therapist can discuss the issue with the patient and invite him or her to resume treatment whenever problems that require help arise again.

Cases Illustrating Brief Intermittent Psychotherapy

Case Illustration No. 1: "Amazing Grace"

The case of the patient the entire staff of our center called "Amazing Grace" illustrates the principles presented above: hit the ground running, perform an operational diagnosis, elicit the implicit contract, help the patient assume the first step in self-responsibility, and do something novel. Patients come with their own agenda and expectations. Grace was no exception. She was referred by a colleague who, after seeing her for three years felt such hostility toward her that he disqualified himself from treating her. He warned me that Grace, a "schizoholic," would generally alternate between three behaviors: she would appear drunk at one session, urinate in the chair in the next session, and finally, do some semblance of therapeutic work in the third. One never knew which of the sessions would be the urination session. To protect himself from the consequences, he put the kind of rubber sheet used in a baby's crib over the therapy chair. All attempts to stop this erratic behavior resulted in Grace's falling to the floor, stopping breathing, turning blue and becoming cyanotic, at which point the therapist called the paramedics to resuscitate her, literally saving her life. With this in mind, I decided to assume certain educated risks, and became an authority on cyanosis during the next couple of weeks. At the first therapy session, I warned Grace that urinating in the chair would end our therapeutic relationship. I did this on the grounds that it would be deleterious to continue treating a patient who was behaving in a most regressed, antitherapeutic fashion and to impotently expect change in the face of extreme opposition. Grace's reaction to my warning was to clear her throat and spit on the carpet. When I asked her to clean it up, she countered that I had not told her she could not spit on the carpet.

I explained that there were many unacceptable kinds of behavior, as she was quite aware, and that I had no intention of warning her about every one of them. Any recurrences of such incidents would result in our terminating therapy.

Grace stared at me without saying a word for several minutes before falling to the floor. She stopped breathing, and began to turn blue, which is a symptom of cyanosis. Instead of calling the paramedics, I did what I had prepared and planned to do and went to my desk to retrieve my camera. I discovered, much to my dismay, that the camera was empty. While I searched frantically for the film I talked excitedly to Grace, encouraging her to keep up the performance so it could be recorded for medical history. Every once in a while, Grace would open one eye and stare at me in total disbelief.

Finally, when I got the camera loaded and began to take pictures, my flash did not work. Before I could get the flash attachment functional with a new battery, Grace was back in her chair apparently ready to begin a more constructive relationship. I saw Grace four times before going to the next step in her therapy.

Grace's behavior frequently brought her to San Francisco's various hospital emergency rooms, and her cyanotic attacks had often been repeated there. After my fourth session with Grace, I obtained her permission to have my telephone number at the emergency rooms, with instructions that I should be called if her behavior became troublesome. As expected, Grace did subsequently become cyanotic during an emergency room intervention, and I was summoned to deal with her. This first time, the fact of my physical presence was enough to cause her to stop the behavior. Subsequently, a brief exchange by telephone sufficed. Within three weeks Grace had stopped the behavior completely.

The case of Grace illustrates how the "primary patient" can sometimes be the therapist. The primary patient was very obviously the psychiatrist who referred Grace, and secondarily, the emergency room staff who dealt with her "cyanosis." After a further 18 sessions, Grace and I terminated. During this time, she had changed her appearance from that of a bag lady to that of a self-respecting human being, had begun to groom herself, and stopped drinking. Although she was still schizophrenic, she was no longer a schizoholic who felt compelled to go through life getting attention by exhibiting antisocial behaviors.

Case Illustration No. 2: Kevin

At this point, I shall review the concept of intermittent brief therapy and provide a history of some of its techniques by illustrating them with a case that spans two decades. In 1967 I was confronted with a young man of 28 whom we shall call Kevin. He arrived in my waiting room with no appointment, as a "drop in." Kevin was in a state of severe drug withdrawal and looked very disheveled. When I first saw him, I wondered how schizophrenic he might be. I had no history or prior knowledge of him. In the first session, I learned that Kevin had graduated from Purdue University with a degree in elementary school teaching. On Wednesday of his first week of teaching on his first job, he had been unable to cope and had run out of the classroom. Without stopping at his parents' home, where he lived, he had hitchhiked to San Francisco from Indianapolis. He arrived with just what he had on his back and in his pockets. He was introduced to drugs and within three weeks had become what I would term a "cafeteria addict,": that is one who will ingest anything put before him or her, be "high" all the time, yet still claim not to be addicted to anything. Detoxification is a problem with such addicts. While the withdrawal syndrome is predictable in users of heroin, barbiturates, alcohol, or anxiolytics, it is extremely risky in a cafeteria addict, and it is difficult to plan appropriate intervention.

At Purdue, Kevin appeared to have been a very isolated young man. He had never had a date. His social life consisted mainly of returning to his parents' house on weekends, and going to skid row with a couple of bottles of cheap wine where he could get the alcoholics intoxicated and then perform fellatio on them. To all intents and purposes, Kevin at this time could have been considered either schizophrenic or certainly borderline ambulatory schizophrenic.

It was apparent that Kevin did not want to overcome his addiction, but simply wanted to be made to feel better. He was startled when I refused him a second appointment and became desperate when I explained that he would have to commit to staying clear of drugs for six months in order for therapy to be effective.

After some pleading on Kevin's part, I promised him a second appointment if he could refrain from drug-taking for 72 hours, a goal I considered to be well within the realm of possibility. On the 70th hour Kevin called and requested an appointment. I denied it, suspecting that he might not be able to hold out for the last two hours. Kevin reacted angrily, accusing me of being "crazy," but did, in fact, keep his promise and called again when the agreed upon time period had expired.

At that second appointment I began to prepare him to enter a 20-session group addiction program. He required six individual sessions before he entered group.

While brief therapy ranges from one to twenty sessions, sessions can be spaced at intermittent intervals. Kevin was seen three days after the first session and as the need arose thereafter, until he was ready to enter our drug therapy program in 1967. Like those of most other patients in our brief therapy program, Kevin's sessions were spaced according to his clinical needs.

After Kevin graduated from the group addiction program, he stayed free of drugs and went back to work. His first job was relief work at the Post Office, his second was driving a cab, and his third, which he started when he finished the drug treatment program, was as an eligibility intake worker in the County Hospital.

In 1968 Kevin came back to see me. Over the intervening year, he had married, and his wife, Carol, was pregnant. Kevin told me that even though therapy had helped him a great deal, he felt that his self-image was too low to allow him to think of himself as a father to his forthcoming child. In therapy, Kevin established that his self-esteem had risen enough that he was able to get married and maintain a happy married relationship. After four sessions, he felt comfortable about the impending birth.

Kevin was not seen in 1969. By 1970, he was not only the proud father of a son now a little over two years old, but Carol was pregnant again. They were in the process of buying their first house and Kevin needed to borrow money from his father-in-law, whom he hated, as a down-payment for the house. In three sessions, I helped Kevin to raise his self-esteem to the point where he bought the house. He also settled his antagonism toward his father-in-law, and they became very good friends over the next two or three years.

In 1971 Kevin returned for one session concerning a marital problem. He was harboring much anger toward Carol, which was being expressed through premature ejaculation. The symptom cleared. A few months later in 1971, Kevin called to say that as a result of the one session regarding his premature ejaculation, he wanted to go into couples' therapy. I referred him to one of my colleagues at American Biodyne, who saw Kevin and Carol for six marital sessions. During this time, Kevin resolved his overidentification with his first son. He had been convinced that his first son was going to turn out to be a "creep" like himself.

In 1972 Kevin returned once more, this time very anxious about the fact that he was about to take a civil service examination to become a probation officer. He had been hired under temporary aegis as a probation officer for the county, had completed six months' probation work, and would lose his job if he did not pass the examination. Kevin and I decided in that session that he would enter biofeedback training. After 12 sessions of biofeedback training Kevin passed the civil service examination in the top eight and became a permanent probation officer for the county. In 1973 Kevin was not seen at all, although his wife Carol was seen by another therapist for four sessions.

In 1974 Kevin and Carol bought their first duplex. Kevin returned to therapy because he felt very nervous about buying their first real property and was not sure if he was "good enough" to be a landlord. It took five sessions to resolve this issue. Kevin and Carol did buy the duplex, the first of four that they now own.

In 1975 Kevin came to see me in a homosexual panic. He came to the office unannounced and waited, shaking, for about three and a half hours until I was able to see him upon completion of my scheduled appointments. He told the following story. One of his apartments was rented to a tall, handsome man toward whom Kevin had become very sexually attracted. One day Kevin was there to collect the rent, and some abortive fondling occurred under the pretext that Kevin was to have a sexual experience with this man and waive the rent. But Kevin was overcome by panic, and before he did anything else, he jumped into his car, drove to my office, and ensconced himself in the waiting room. In five sessions, Kevin resolved his homosexual panic.

I did not see Kevin again until 1977. When I asked what the problem was that brought him in, he replied that he had just come in for a check up. We talked for a session and I told him to call when he felt the need. In 1978 Kevin returned to boast that after two sons he was proud to be the father of a baby girl.

In 1979 I saw Kevin's older son, who was having a school problem. I also saw the younger son twice and Kevin three times. I did not see Kevin at all in 1980. In 1981, he visited me three times in regards to his potential promotion to supervisor in the probation office. He had become, in the estimation of his employers, the number one probation officer in the county. By that point, he was being assigned all of the interesting cases. Kevin was worried about becoming a "paper pusher" who sat at a desk; he wanted to do real field work. At the end of three sessions Kevin felt able to make his decision, and decided to become a supervisor.

In 1983 Kevin had two sessions. He had been offered a top Federal Department of Justice job and did not know if he wanted to accept it. Again, after some discussion he took responsibility for making his own decision and appears to be thoroughly enjoying the assignment that he eventually accepted.

In both 1987 and 1988, Kevin came in for single sessions. Both of his sons have since graduated from high school and have gone on to college.

Conclusion

Kevin and his family were seen over 20 years, during which there were individual sessions with Kevin, his wife, and his two sons. There were a number of forms of intervention—drug therapy, couples' therapy, biofeedback, and emergency sessions. Over this period, a total of 93 sessions occurred. If Kevin had been seen in continuous long-term therapy for five years, would the outcome have been better? It certainly would have involved more than 93 sessions. But would it have produced the contented and happy marital, occupational, and life adjustment that Kevin made with the help of this brief intermittent psychotherapy throughout his life cycle? Doubtless, I shall see Kevin again, as I shall Carol. If the family is like other families I have worked with over the past 25 or 30 years, the chances are that one day I will see not only Kevin's children, but perhaps even his grandchildren. The cases of "Amazing Grace" and Kevin illustrate the model that has been described in this chapter and which I call brief, discontinuous psychotherapy throughout the life cycle. The approach could also be described as one that promotes the general practice of psychology, or, if you will, the notion of the psychologist or therapist as the psychological family practitioner.

References

Albee, G. (1968, June). The short unhappy life of clinical psychology: R.I.P. *Psychology Today*, pp. 29–31.

American Psychiatric Association (1980). *Diagnostic and statistical manual of mental disorders* (3rd ed.). Washington, DC.

Budman, S. H., & Gurman, A. S. (1988). *The theory and practice of brief therapy*. New York: Guilford Press.

Cummings, N. A. (1983). *Biodyne training manual of brief intermittent therapy throughout the life cycle*. San Francisco: Biodyne Institute.

Cummings, N. A. (1986). The dismantling of our health system: Strategies for the survival of psychological practice. *American Psychologist, 41*(4), 426–431.

Cummings, N. A. (1988). The emergence of the mental health complex: Adaptive and maladaptive responses. *Professional Psychology: Research and Practice. 19*(3), 323–335.

Cummings, N. A., & Fernandez, L. E. (1985, March). Exciting future possibilities for psychologists in the market place. *Independent Practitioner*, pp. 38–42.

Cummings, N. A., & VandenBos, G. R. (1979). The general practice of psychology. *Professional Psychology, 10*, 430–440.

Haley, J. (1978). *Problem-solving therapy*. New York: Harper & Row.

4 _____

Charles E. Folkers and Nina M. Steefel

Group Psychotherapy

The Setting

Rhode Island Group Health Association (RIGHA) was founded in 1971 as a staff model health maintenance organization (HMO) and was the first HMO to be federally qualified. Membership is currently over 94,000, with five health centers and two affiliated medical groups in Rhode Island and southeastern Massachusetts. Two of the centers operate on a family practice model, and the other three are multispecialty centers. Each center has a Mental Health Services department staffed with clinicians specializing in child/family, substance abuse, and adult mental health practices. A seven-day-per-week substance abuse day treatment program was begun in 1988 as an alternative to inpatient detoxification and rehabilitation treatment. Department chiefs are psychologists or psychiatrists. The clinical staff consists of approximately 45 full-time equivalents. In 1990, RIGHA became a division of Harvard Community Health Plan.

One approach for developing high quality, innovative and cost-effective mental health interventions in the managed care setting is to cultivate methods of group psychotherapy. This clinical tool has much unexplored potential to fulfill one of the mandates of managed care—to distribute services in a fair and equitable fashion by serving as many as possible. Traditional group psychotherapy, which evolved from the explorations of therapists trained in traditional individual therapy techniques, is now being further shaped within the managed care setting. Where previously therapists worked to find effective methods of short-term individual therapy, practitioners of group psychotherapy are following a parallel development toward short-term group methods.

Traditional Group Psychotherapy

Definition

Yalom (1970) states that "the essence of the therapy group is interaction; each member must continually communicate and interact with the other members" (p.

180). According to Schein (1965), "A psychological group is any number of people who (1) interact with one another, (2) are psychologically aware of one another, and (3) perceive themselves to be a group. The size of the group is thus limited by the possibilities of mutual interaction and mutual awareness" (p. 67). Orlinsky and Howard (1986) describe group psychotherapy as one to two therapists working with between two and twelve unacquainted and unrelated patients. In a therapeutic setting group members can see themselves, their behaviors, and the behaviors of others within the group context and can receive support from others in their efforts toward change.

History

"The earliest writings on group psychotherapy tended to deal almost exclusively with individual behavior or with the therapeutic process. Consideration of the dynamic aspects of the group-as-a-whole . . . were largely neglected" (Scheidlinger, 1982, p. 29). By the late 1930s, Kurt Lewin, an experimental and applied social psychologist working in Germany, had developed the "field theory" approach to human psychology. Viewing behavior within the context of its current psychological field led to clinical practice that focused on the "here and now" and to the idea that a social group provided the "ground" for each individual within it (Yalom, 1970).

Work at the Tavistock Clinic in London during the 1940s expanded the knowledge of group phenomena. Wilfred Bion (1959) was especially interested in understanding group dynamics, and much of his work contributed to research on organizational psychology.

Solomon Asch (1955) wrote "For psychologists, group pressure upon the minds of individuals raises a host of questions they would like to investigate in detail" (p. 318). This research resulted in his now classic study of "high conformer" and "low conformer" behavior in groups. The study added to the understanding of the implicit and explicit norms or rules that operate in groups.

Henry Ezriel (1957), a psychoanalyst who worked at the Tavistock Clinic, stated that the leader of a psychoanalytic group is "nothing but a passive projection screen except for his one active step of interpretation." The therapist takes the role of the "good" parent to deal with group transference while still attending to all of the individual transference relationships with group members.

Behavioral groups provide peer pressure as a source of reinforcement for members, and the behaviorally oriented group leader teaches the members to give or withhold reinforcers effectively. The group setting also provides opportunity for the members to observe others as possible models for their own behavior.

Humanistic groups are relatively unstructured at the start, and the leader works to build norms that provide psychological safety and opportunity for growth. Respect and acceptance for whatever level of participation group members are presently able to contribute is basic to group work (Rogers, 1971).

In the 1970s, small group work began to be supplanted by large group awareness training programs (LGATs). These groups, made available to the public by profit-making businesses, "examine philosophical, psychological, and ethical issues concerning personal effectiveness, decision-making, personal responsibility and commitment" (Fisher, Silver, Chinsky, Goff, & Klar, 1990). Participants are assumed to benefit from insights gained through the group experience and to be able to apply group lessons to their everyday lives. Examples of such groups are EST, Lifespring, Actualizations, Insight, Relationships, and Forum which evolved from EST.

Group Versus Individual Therapy

The effects of traditional group treatment have not been as fully researched and developed as those of individual therapy. However, there are some who believe it may be an important clinical tool that is underused; indications of this usefulness are grounded in research. Orlinsky and Howard (1986) report that in the majority of the 12 studies they reviewed, there were no significant differences in therapeutic outcome between individual and group treatment. They conclude that it may make little difference to clinical success whether therapy is delivered in an individual or group format.

Because there is presently no conclusive evidence that individual therapy is more clinically effective than group treatment, practitioners have no reason to heed the unsupported misgivings about brief group therapy; in fact, reported research indicates that short-term group therapy is at least as effective as individual therapy for a number of patients (Dick & Wooff, 1986; Shapiro, Sank, Shaffer, & Donovan, 1982).

Group treatment can have an advantage over individual modalities in dealing with transference issues because statements made by peers may be more understandable to a group member than are statements made by a therapist; "help-rejecting complainers" are often confronted by fellow group members more effectively than they could be by a therapist. According to Sperry (1989), "time-limited groups tend to decrease transference and decrease the incidence of regression, while increasing coping and interpersonal skills and reality testing." (p. 57)

Short-Term Group Therapy as Practiced in HMO s

Definition

To help clarify what time-limited group therapy is, Sperry (1989) lists the technical characteristics shared by most time-limited groups. These are "(a) therapeutic management of temporal limitations; (b) limitation of therapeutic goals; (c) centering the therapeutic content in the present; (d) direct management of the sessions by the therapists; (e) rapid early assessment; (f) promptness of intervention; (g) flexibility on the part of the therapist; (h) ventilation or catharsis as an important element in the process; (i) a quickly established interpersonal relationship from which to obtain therapeutic leverage; and (j) appropriate selection of patients, since not all patients can profit from a brief therapeutic contract." (p. 53)

Among the goals for time-limited group therapy drawn by Sperry from his literature review are "(a) amelioration of distress or symptom reduction; (b) prompt establishment of the patient's previous emotional equilibrium; [and] (c) promoting efficient use of the patient's resources (i.e., increasing sense of mastery or self-control, emphasizing adaptation, aiding behavioral change, providing cognitive re-structuring, and social effectiveness)." (p. 53)

Sperry (1989) states that "until recently, effective group therapy meant long-term, ongoing treatment lasting from 2 to 5 years" (p. 51). There is even a question as to whether the model of long-term therapy is carried out in practice. Studies by Stone and Rutan (1984) in a private setting and by Klein and Carroll (1986) in a community mental health setting indicate that a majority of group members drop out early: 40% before the end of the first year, and 75% before the end of the second year in a private setting and 52% by the end of the twelfth session in the community mental health setting.

Sperry points out that at present there is no exact definition of what would be considered time-limited group treatment. "The mean number of sessions for individual time-limited treatment is about 25. . . . For time-limited group therapy, there is a trend toward fewer sessions with a mean of 12 to 15 sessions." (p. 52) According to Sperry, time-limited group sessions usually last one to one and one half hours, scheduled on a weekly basis." (p. 52) The effectiveness of time-limited therapy, group or individual, as compared to long-term therapy, is supported increasingly by research (Bernard & Klein, 1977, 1979; Budman & Gurman, 1988; Imber, Lewis, & Loiselle, 1979; Klein, 1983).

History

Support for the use of group therapy as an effective tool in the HMO setting can be found in a brief history that illustrates the evolving discovery of the therapeutic strengths inherent in groups and their processes (Sabin, 1981). Kurt Lewin, a social psychologist, founded the Research Center for Group Dynamics in 1945 to further explore and test out his "field theory." While providing a training workshop for community leaders, Lewin agreed to a request by three participants that they sit in on a staff discussion of the day's group sessions. Hearing their own behavior discussed in an objective fashion proved to be a powerful experience for them. This serendipitous discovery developed into what is the now familiar process of "feedback."

Lewin's organizational workshop format, including the new idea of feedback, was the basis for work done at Bethel, Maine, training group members in group process. It was a summer spent at Bethel that shifted Carl N. Zimet (1979), a past president of the Division of Psychotherapy of the American Psychological Association, from his previous strict psychoanalytic framework to a belief in the effectiveness of group work. He also gained an understanding of the benefit of combining intellectual and affective aspects of therapy through group experience. The Bethel, Maine, Basic Skills Training (BST) Group was soon influenced by clinicians added to the training staff and grew into the training or "T-group." The T-group, a laboratory method of training or reeducation, was widely used in human relations training because it produced powerful learning experiences (Schein & Bennis, 1965). Participants were able to gain personal insight into their own and others' attitudes and feelings about the group events they observed and shared.

In the early 1950s, skill training based on the BST group model was carried out at the University of California, Los Angeles. The T-group, also called the sensitivity training group, the encounter group, or the personal growth group, was considered by the faculty to be the "therapy group for normals." The social climate of California and the 1960s stretched the concept of sensitivity and awareness toward the creation of more radical groups for individuals searching to expand their personal growth.

The proliferation of these groups with their myriad claims of beneficial results prompted Lieberman, Yalom, and Miles (1973) at Stanford University to research the phenomena. The results of their study of 18 encounter groups representing 10 different methods, all using formats that included only 30 hours of treatment time, showed that specific leader activities correlated with outcome. These activities include a high level of warmth and positive support, a rich cognitive framework that can help participants make sense of their experience, and a constant attention to group process in order to prevent scapegoating and to enhance wide participation.

In 1979, Carl N. Zimet, building on insights gained during a summer at Bethel, Maine, was one of the first to describe and discuss the "developmental task and crisis group." He called this group therapeutic intervention a new concept, though not a method, which he believed would help practitioners deal with the drastic changes he predicted were soon to come in the provision of psychological services within the American health care system. Zimet was also one of the first to publish the idea that the cost-effectiveness of treatment and the clinical effectiveness of treatment would be intimately related in the future. He suggested that the high costs of hospitalization for both mental and physical illness encouraged a greater emphasis on prevention, and proposed group therapy as a cost-effective way to provide remedial as well as preventive mental health care. He pointed to the high cost of one-to-one psychotherapy, which has not been proven more effective than group care, and to the apparent savings possible when preventive psychotherapy permits a lowered expenditure for medical care.

Basic Models of Therapy

Some basic models for group therapy are particularly suited to time-limited work and are consistent with the goals described above. The experiential model, the psychoeducational model, the crisis intervention model, and the developmental stage model are discussed below from a theoretical aspect. First, we will discuss the traditional model for each type of group; then, we will discuss a specific model from health maintenance organization (HMO) experience.

The Experiential Model of Group Psychotherapy

An experiential group helps people become more aware of themselves, their own social behavior, and the social interactions of others.

Traditional models. In the business world experiential groups are called T-groups or training groups; in school or community settings experiential groups are often labeled sensitivity or personal growth groups. Experiential groups are also used in hospital settings to encourage patients' interaction and social responsibility and to help patients be more aware of how they affect others.

People who are basically able to cope with their lives and have at least minimal social skills and awareness are appropriate members. These group experiences can enrich members' lives and help them perform better in work and social settings (Schein, 1965; Yalom, 1975).

Experiential groups typically have certain identifiable stages (Brammer, Shostrom, & Abrego, 1989). First is the inclusion stage during which group members are primarily concerned about themselves and how they relate to the total group. Building group cohesion and setting goals, both personal and group, are important tasks to accomplish at this time. According to Yalom (1975) "Cohesiveness in group therapy is the analogue of relationship in individual therapy."

Once group stage one is established, issues of power and control arise. This is the conflict stage, group stage two. The leader's task is to create an open climate for the working through of conflict and confrontation. Group members' tasks are to learn how to manage conflict constructively and to share responsibly in the determination of the group direction.

Resolution of the conflict stage leads to the affection stage, group stage three. Both positive and negative feelings can be expressed and some members begin to take emotional risks. The emerging sense of trust allows the group to begin to "work" toward their goals.

The fourth stage is termination. This is an important and difficult period for group members. In ongoing groups, termination issues are dealt with whenever a member leaves; in time-limited groups, termination is experienced by all members at the same time. It is a time for recognizing what has been gained and for learning how to separate and say goodbye. One leadership task for this stage is to help members conceptualize what the group has meant to them and what plans they have to carry this into life after group. A followup session several months after termination can lead to further evaluation from a different perspective.

The HMO model. The HMO supports the idea of outpatient treatment that allows patients to work on important personal issues without breaking from their normal living situation, or having to utilize treatments that are more disruptive to a patient's life and more costly to the health care provider. This allows resources to be reserved for those who need more intensive individual treatment and supervision. For many patients, the temporary social structure and support of an experiential group provides a safe and effective setting within which they can gain new awareness and appropriate coping behaviors. Thus it is neither a luxury for life enrichment nor a treatment mode for severely disabled patients; rather it is a safety zone that allows a member to personally regroup.

For the HMO, the experiential group provides such a setting in a cost-effective manner; inpatient treatment, which is more disruptive to a patient's life and more costly to the health care provider, can be reserved for those who need the continuous provision of treatment and supervision.

Examples of experiential groups that could be used in the HMO setting are: groups for couples with relationship problems, for patients who have recently left inpatient settings, and for socially awkward men.

The Psychoeducational Model of Group Psychotherapy

A psychoeducational group is used for teaching skills pertaining to a specified topic within a therapeutic setting. These groups are structured around a planned agenda in order to reach preestablished goals in a limited period of time.

Traditional models. Cognitive–behavioral methods are the techniques predominantly used in psychoeducational groups (Beck, 1976; Ellis, 1962). Group building can occur quickly because goals are preset, sessions are focused and group members are usually ready to share within the topic area. Since the group is time-limited and structured, termination is a natural result of completing the training.

Both training and education benefit from the energy and focus that a group provides; the format gives an opportunity to use didactic exercises and group discussions. For the therapist, the group forum also can provide an efficient way to teach, for example, relaxation techniques, cognitive strategies to combat depression, stress reduction, and behavior changes helpful for dealing with medical conditions. Through use of a psychoeducational group, therapists can avoid the tedium of repetitive work with a seemingly unending string of individuals.

The HMO model. The HMO is an organization committed to maintaining health and therefore supports preventive and health-enhancing programs; this is a departure from the traditional "medical model" for providing treatment. Whether an educational program is planned by the mental health department or is provided by a separate health education segment of the organization, the format of the psychoeducational group is "a natural." Compared to individual sessions, psychoeducational groups are cost-effective to the HMO both in terms of economics and efficiency, and thus can be profitably made available to patients.

Examples of psychoeducational groups that could be used in the HMO setting are: groups for parents of preschool children, for driving phobics, and for relaxation training.

The Crisis Intervention Model of Group Psychotherapy

A crisis intervention group is a way to provide care quickly for patients whose condition might rapidly deteriorate should they have to wait for conventional treatment arrangements (Allgeyer, 1973). The goal is to intervene quickly, while someone is disorganized psychologically, in order to support the patient's regathering of coping skills.

Crisis intervention groups grew from the work of Eric Lindemann (1944) on grief and mourning and from the work of Gerald Caplan (1964) relating poor management of crises by adult psychiatric patients to worsened ability to function after the crisis had passed. Both Lindemann and Caplan pointed the way toward preventive services and the training of members of the community to provide these services.

Traditional models. Traditionally, crisis work has been done with individuals who need immediate help. Crisis hot lines and prevention teams have trained nonprofessionals or paraprofessionals ready to talk on the phone or to provide onsite intervention. Community mental health facilities offer 24-hour emergency services as a result of the provision for crisis intervention that was a part of the Community Mental Health Centers Act of 1963.

Some examples of crisis groups developed in the 1960s are short-term, heterogeneous groups (Allgeyer, 1970 & 1973; Strickler & Allgeyer, 1967) used with well selected "disadvantaged" patients. These groups were described as useful for treating problematic or culturally deprived patients who were difficult to keep in treatment. The groups met for six to eight sessions.

Crisis groups can be a part of a triage process that sets priorities for provision of treatment, a stage in an intake system, or the chosen treatment method for prevention of post-traumatic stress disorder. For some patients, the group may provide sufficient treatment to allow them to get beyond their crisis situation; for others the group may be a stepping stone to other treatment.

The HMO model. For the HMO, the use of crisis groups makes it possible to manage a variable flow of patients seeking treatment in a timely and appropriate way. The quick response inherent in a crisis group setting supports the HMO goal of case containment while allowing efficient triage and effective mobilization of treatment resources. For those patients for whom waiting could lead to deterioration from their current levels of functioning, the crisis group provides a "safety net" while case-specific planning is done.

Examples of crisis groups that could be used in the HMO setting are: groups for recent victims of crime, groups for survivors of natural catastrophies, and groups for patients who feel they are in crisis.

The Developmental Stage Model of Group Psychotherapy

The developmental stage group brings together patients who are relatively close in age but who have a variety of presenting problems. Erikson's (1963) psychosocial developmental stages provide the rationale for the formation of this sort of group. Members are moving through the same transition even though the particular issues to be worked through may vary.

Traditional models. The developmental group has existed serendipitously in the past, for example, when youth counselors worked with adolescents in a neighborhood center or therapists worked with the elderly in a retirement community. As a planned treatment modality, developmental groups grew up in a short-term therapy context (Budman, Bennett, & Wisneski, 1981).

The HMO model. One goal of the HMO is to provide appropriate treatment for a large and varied membership; the developmental group allows common treatment of patients with heterogeneous presenting problems by establishing a unifying focus on age-relevant developmental tasks. By working through shared life issues and by keeping the focus on age-related themes, a process of change begins that will continue beyond the end of the group. For example, young adults will struggle with issues of intimacy, while middle-aged adults will be concerned with assessing their life's work and with mortality.

Since group members are close in age and have similar issues and concerns, they quickly "join" and are able to begin the working-through process. In order to have such a cohesive focused group, members are carefully selected. Normal aspects of development are stressed; psychopathology is deemphasized, and members build an age-appropriate context from which to view their current lives.

These groups are suitable to the HMO because they foster the notion of "intermittent therapy throughout the life cycle," the idea that people benefit from moving in and out of treatment in accordance with the particular path of each individual's life.

Examples of developmental groups that could be used in the HMO setting are: groups for recently retired men, groups for new parents, and groups for single young adults.

Interaction of Short-Term Therapy and the Staff Model HMO

Short-term group therapy in an HMO setting makes good sense from a theoretical point of view, and several models for group work have been presented. Although clear models derived from theory provide a framework for clinical work, the knowledge gained from experience provides the guidelines for practical application. The first author of this chapter has built a background of experience from building the group therapy program at Rhode Island Group Health Association (RIGHA), a staff model HMO. The following discussion is a distillation of his clinical observations and experience.

Although the practice of group psychotherapy in HMO settings has the same theoretical roots as group practice in social service agencies, mental health centers, clinics, hospitals, and private practices, there are several aspects of its context that are different. These differences are present whether the specific HMO is a group or staff model organization with its own facilities and mental health clinicians or is an Independent Practice Association (IPA), Preferred Provider Organization (PPO), or other "dispersed" model.

Practice Issues Influenced by the HMO System

Closed versus open system. An HMO is a "closed system." Unlike traditional indemnity insurance plans, it controls costs by retaining some of the freedom to choose where and by whom care will be given to members. HMOs provide treatment for covered conditions by using nonspecialists whenever possible; in order to see specialists, referral of members by their primary care providers or by a gatekeeper clinician is frequently required.

The mental health department of an HMO represents a specialty area, but within the department efficient staffing suggests that therapists be generalists rather than subspecialists. Patients seeking treatment frequently assume that care from a specialist is superior care. In a medical context, for many conditions, the procedure or the medication prescribed by an internist or family physician, for example, will be identical to that prescribed by a dermatologist or ophthalmologist. In a mental health context, "generic psychotherapy" is likely to be prescribed for a whole range of problems.

In an open system, patients may seek out specialists in grief, incest, depression, panic, and so on. In a closed system, a patient is more likely to get a specific treatment targeted to his or her specific needs by a generalist. A group therapy program can significantly expand the ability of the staff to offer specialty treatments; the result can be that specialty care will be both the most clinically effective and the most cost-effective.

It is the authors' belief that closed systems with group programs have the potential to secure for patients the most appropriate care, where open systems would not. Three sorts of cases that the first author has dealt with clinically might illustrate this point. Closed systems with good internal communication can plan to consistently route the following types of patient to proper treatment.

First, there are the borderline, narcissistic, or manic patients who often are difficult to provide for. They easily pass through a series of incomplete treatments with multiple clinicians because they tend to leave treatment impulsively and they possess a sense of entitlement that is never satiated in individual treatment.

Second, there are the somatizing patients whose core anxiety or depression problem goes untreated while multiple physical work ups are pursued in the search for a physical diagnosis.

Third, there are the patients whose emotional and behavioral life style (e.g. tobacco and other substance abuse, marital conflict, worrying) is producing physical health problems that recur despite appropriate medical treatment.

In all the above cases, a coordinated system that includes specialized group treatment can keep these patients from "falling through the cracks."

Diversity of clientele. A second characteristic of the HMO is the diversity of its clientele. Since its membership is most often a benefit of employment, there is wide variability in the socioeconomic and cultural characteristics of its members. Therapy groups most often contain heterogeneous populations with homogeneous clinical conditions. Any group is likely to contain members who differ in gender, ethnicity, employment, and so forth. While authors such as Yalom (1985) point out that heterogeneity of group membership is an important factor to be considered within the group treatment context, our experience (at the HMO) has been that this issue tends to be less of a problem than anticipated.

First, such issues of differentness and belonging constitute "grist for the mill" of the group process and are at the heart of the content of group work. Second, forces at work in the group therapy milieu seem to move participants to appreciate other's common humanity rather than their dissimilarity. Third, the HMO ideal can guide the mission of HMO mental health care so that preventive and health enhancing services have a place alongside the treatment of psychiatric disorders. This departure from the medical model may be welcomed by some as a liberation from inappropriate constraints. These services can also be provided by special health and education programs, and liaison work with other departments may be necessary. Psychoeducational groups are effective formats for teaching "wellness."

Applications in group psychotherapy programs. Keeping the above characteristic in mind, RIGHA developed a group psychotherapy program that played a central role in the delivery of mental health services in its prepaid health care system. This program was intended to increase cost effectiveness, to make specialty treatments practical, to solve logistical problems in the operation of the department, and to offer preventive and health enhancing interventions to the healthier members of the plan. Doing so required the assessment of clinical and organizational needs, designing groups in a creative and flexible manner, and the provision of necessary support and encouragement to the group therapy program.

Administrative guidelines. The following guidelines for administrators establishing group therapy in HMO practice have been developed from the RIGHA experience.

1. *Establish a group therapy program.* This requires systematic planning that begins with the "big picture" of the department's clinical program. Without this sort of guidance, group formation can become merely a matter of who is willing to start another group, what room is available, and which patients to exclude. If the group therapy program comprises a core of group therapists involved in planning, peer supervision, and review, the energy generated can be self-sustaining and will result in high-quality treatment by clinicians who believe in their work and enjoy it.

2. *Develop groups that make sense.* Assessing the need for therapy groups involves two considerations: cost-effectiveness and clinical need. The first consideration has a rather straightforward role in group program development. The second includes taking inventory of the cases that are either presenting for treatment, on the waiting list, or in clinicians' case loads. What clusters are discernible? If evening appointments are being monopolized by marital therapy cases, a couples group or a communication skills workshop might make sense. If panic disorders or chronic depressions or grief reactions are numerous, consider groups organized around those diagnoses. If a number of patients with those diagnoses happen also to be young adult women with conflicts over intimacy, consider a women's group. If routine medication recheck appointments are unsatisfying to both patients and their psychiatrists and nurses, consider a medication group.

Not every group that is efficient is also practical, but the value of starting with an overinclusive "brainstorming" approach permits the limits of conventional wisdom about group therapy to be expanded, sometimes in surprising ways.

3. *Capitalize on staff strengths.* Clinical staff members will inevitably have different personal styles, clinical interests, and areas of expertise. Unless staff are hired for very specific purposes, a perfect match of clinicians and clinical needs will seldom occur. When the matching and modifying process of program development is a participatory one, with staff members designing their own groups in consultation with colleagues and in response to department needs, two valuable benefits accrue: creativity and a sense of motivation through ownership. The depression management group described below is an example of a group developed in a participatory manner.

4. *Support the program.* Administrative support of the group therapy program can make the difference between good morale and bad. If therapists believe their

efforts and initiative are unappreciated, interest will lag and quality of care will almost inevitably suffer. Recognition should be given both directly and indirectly. Positive feedback from clinical supervisors and administrators is worth giving explicitly. An effort to provide material support and clerical support for groups also conveys that the program is valued. Provision of release time for group development, record keeping, and supervision also offers recognition that group treatment is not just an afterthought to the mental health program.

5. *Integrate groups into treatment planning.* When group therapy referrals are solicited only when a new group is forming, the group program is, in fact, functioning as an afterthought. To avoid this, the structure of intake and the disposition of "patient flow" in the department need to accommodate group therapy referrals, and conversely, the structure of the group program must permit smooth and timely referrals.

Clinical development guidelines. The following guidelines for the clinical development of groups include some universal considerations that apply to any short-term group therapy program.

1. *Grooming for the group.* A common difficulty in practicing brief group therapy is the amount of time required by some individuals to become oriented to the culture of group psychotherapy. For example, they need to focus on introspection, emotions, self-disclosure, and so on. Particularly in process-oriented groups, the individuals who profit and contribute the most seem to be those with some prior therapy experience. They not only know "what to do," but they also have a notion of what they want to address in the group. When patients present for intake who appear to be good candidates for group treatment but whose grasp of the process is weak, the evaluating therapist may offer a two-stage treatment plan: a brief course of individual therapy to bring relevant skills into focus, followed by group therapy to begin working through those issues. The grooming stage can make the wait for the start of a short-term group productive, rather than an inconvenient interruption.

2. *Making the referral.* Many patients for whom group treatment would be appropriate—even ideal—hold the prejudice that group therapy is second-best and that individual treatment is the "good stuff." In order to overcome this false assumption, and to make referral to group therapy an agreeable process with the expectation of success, several factors are important. First, in order to seem credible to his or her patients, the referring clinician must believe in the effectiveness of group therapy. Second, a brief rationale for using group treatment, a description of how it operates, and confrontation of the patient's ambivalences are essential to the allaying of doubt and to producing expectancies for success. Third, the grooming strategy discussed above has the additional advantages of offering the apprehensive candidate some individual attention at the outset of treatment in such a way that the subsequent group therapy is regarded as good treatment or the treatment of choice.

3. *Intermittent or serial treatment.* Since utilization of mental health services in many prepaid settings is controlled chiefly by benefit limits and copayments, continuous long-term therapy is a rarity. Intermittent attention over the years is quite common, however, and group treatments can be highly useful and effective in this approach. In some cases, the patient will not be prepared for a group ex-

perience until other issues are addressed. In others, incidents and insights from an earlier group experience will serve as working examples and reference points in later work. A patient with multiple problems will be able to address them over time in a series of groups. Not only can this approach help the patient to focus on one problem at a time rather than to flounder among too many issues, but entrance into a series of specialized groups can have the effect of fostering a positive independence rather than a regressive passivity.

4. *Relating to the organization at large.* Functioning as part of a medical system at large, the mental health department of a prepaid health care system is well placed to promote the ideal of holistic health. The conventional wisdom is that many (or most) medical office visits are for problems that are either primarily psychological or strongly influenced by emotional or behavioral factors. To a mental health department, this may be perceived as an opportunity to offer health-promoting and preventive interventions, or as a threat of overwhelming utilization by an expanded clientele. A well planned program of group offerings, such as lectures, workshops, discussions, self-help, or, of more formal courses sponsored by health educators, medical staff, or outside consultants can contain utilization in a way which benefits both patient and health plan.

5. *Special considerations for non-staff-model HMOs.* A programmatic approach to group psychotherapy like the one advanced here is most suited to the centralized varieties of HMOs, such as staff model, group practice, or hospital-based systems. Dispersed organizations such as IPAs have more difficulty developing a coordinated program of group treatment. The existence of a discrete mental health department in a centralized system favors the sort of grass roots program development process described here; open panel systems will necessitate an administrative (top down) process, by which specific group treatments would be contracted out to providers or agencies. The idea of adding to a system yet another administrative role of coordinator of group therapy, of course, can run afoul of both efficiency-minded administrators and independent-minded private practitioners. The job should not require a great amount of time, however, and, with a little creativity, the development of therapy groups by participating clinicians who consult with a coordinator should be a positive collaborative experience. The importance of effective communication and coordination in these systems is more difficult and even more crucial than in a group or staff model organization.

6. *Coordinating the program.* To accomplish program development, peer supervision, training, problem solving, and housekeeping functions like scheduling, it is necessary to find time for group therapy staff meetings. The time taken may be regarded as "lost" treatment hours, but used judiciously, these hours will lead to effective and efficient group treatment. Memos and newsletters can also enhance the program. Using the clerical staff for mailings, scheduling, typing, copying, and procuring supplies can help support a large and active program.

Staff model HMOs have been a natural setting for providing the type of group therapy Zimet envisioned. Both remedial and preventive short-term therapy groups are being used in current programs. For example, the George Washington University Health Plan in Washington, D.C. has combined several techniques into a Coping Skills Program, which is a time-limited group for anxious or depressed patients. Another program at Harvard Community Health Plan (HCHP) provides a variety of short-term groups. The patients whom HCHP therapists treat in short-term groups have characterological, neurotic, and situational problems, have major areas of dysfunction, and are often severely hampered by symptoms. Examples from the HCHP program include a crisis group, a women's group, and a developmental group that is described later in the chapter.

Examples of Groups Developed for HMO Practice

Three examples of short-term therapy groups developed specifically for HMO practice follow. The first two are from RIGHA; the third is from HCHP. These groups are practical applications related to the four theoretical models presented earlier. The Depression Management Group combines the experiential and the psychoeducational models; the Crisis Group follows the crisis intervention model; and the Adult Developmental Group follows the developmental stage model.

Depression Management Group

This hybrid of psychoeducational, cognitive, behavioral, group process, and experiential elements had two ancestors in the program at RIGHA: a five-session anxiety management group with a psychoeducational approach; and a behavioral group for depression that emphasized rating scales, charting, inventories, and graphing (Lewinsohn, 1978). The latter had been led by a consultant on a somewhat irregular basis and required more motivation than could be mustered by many patients.

The Depression Management Group was designed for patients with chronic depression. Considerable creative energy was brought to bear on the issues of motivation and engagement because depressed people tend to be amotivated and withdrawn. Some ideas, such as establishing a "buddy system" within the group for support and monitoring, or asking each member to select a relative or friend as a "sponsor" who would attend several group meetings, were ultimately dropped. Other ideas, such as a fifteen-minute free discussion period at the end of the session with the therapist(s) absent, were incorporated in successive cycles of the group. Trial and error and patient feedback guided these changes.

Even the developers of this pilot group were surprised by how well the educational and the group process approaches enhanced each other. Each of 12 sessions had a topic relating to an aspect of depression and included discussion time during which personal sharing and interaction were encouraged. The thematic presentations seemed to dissipate social anxiety and promote group identification in a particularly helpful way for depressive individuals. Conversely, having a group culture of trust and acceptance seemed to make it possible for unlikely topics (such as secondary gain, suicide, and anger) to be discussed with appreciation and little defensiveness.

A variety of handouts, homework assignments, poems, and the like, were gleaned from many sources and were sometimes modified. Each time the group was offered, the "curriculum" changed somewhat in response to the needs and requests of the particular mix of individuals. The effectiveness of the group was reflected in pre-

and posttest self-report scores and in the clinical impressions of therapists who resumed individual treatment with patients they had referred to the group.

The following details are offered as a snapshot of the group at one point in time. The group began with an orientation meeting. Our staff decided to accept all referrals without holding screening interviews and to use this initial orientation meeting to screen members informally. The meeting would also give them a "sample experience" so that they might decide whether the group would meet their needs.

The orientation meeting began with a brief presentation during which the therapist explained the structure and rationale of the group. After this explanation, the total group was divided into subgroups and the members were assigned a small group exercise. After completing the exercise, they returned to the larger group for discussion.

Subsequent meetings followed a relatively stable format. A bridging period at the start of the meeting gave members a chance to update the group on their progress and to become more comfortable interacting with others. The therapist(s) might answer questions during this period and encourage the group to reach out to its quieter members. The therapists also kept the anxiety level moderate. They then gave information to the patients in a brief lecture format.

A sample list of session topics follows:

1. Introduction to depression
2. Thinking and feeling
3. Helplessness and control
4. The sick role
5. Understanding
6. Anger
7. Assertion
8. Relaxation
9. Behavior change
10. Pleasant events
11. Review and conclusions
12. Endings and losses

After each session's presentation, a discussion or an exercise might follow, designed to demonstrate the point of the presentation as well as to promote interaction among group members. Homework assignments were given each week. The therapist reminded the group of the number of sessions remaining and reactions to the "countdown" were solicited. In the final sessions, members were asked what they found to be helpful and not helpful. Their responses not only permitted the format of the group to be further refined, but they also gave a sense of the value of the group experience to each participant.

Crisis Group

The principal incentive for the development of this group at RIGHA was to solve the following dilemma: Patients presenting in acute distress could be seen on a same-day basis for evaluation, but follow-up often meant either crowding the already full schedule of the evaluating clinician or putting the patient at the top of the list for case assignment. In either event, the result was to lengthen the wait for those seeking nonurgent treatment; ·and, if these patients also went into crisis while waiting, a vicious cycle would ensue. A further complication was that many patients in crisis would require evening appointments that were scarce and already in demand.

The evening Crisis Group was planned to give clinicians a disposition alternative that could accommodate patients within a week and follow them through a six-week period, a time typical for such crises to diminish, as suggested by other clinicians (Donovan, Bennett, & McElroy, 1981). The size of the group was limited to a maximum of six members with no more than two referrals each week because new members need time to tell their stories. One coleader of the group was a psychiatrist who could see to the medication needs of group members. The only explicit referral criterion (apart from common sense ones) was that patients referred to the group were experiencing a decrement in functioning as the result of a relatively discrete event to which they were reacting. They might also have chronically poor functioning at baseline, but the goal of the group was to return them to their previous baseline level of functioning.

The group met for 90 minutes one evening per week. The cotherapists were active, maintaining relatively tight control over the group process. They employed quasi-rituals to structure the experience and to impart a sense of group culture. A poster-size sheet of paper was used to record information about each of the members when they first told their story of crisis. A time line, a genogram of all involved significant others, and a list of feelings, worries, or symptoms might be included. The sheets were taped to the wall of the group room each week, providing members with a reference point for each others' situations as well as for their own. Returning members gave brief summaries and updates. The therapists tried to enforce brevity to make sure that all members would have a turn. The therapists also pointed out the common elements in members' situations to promote empathy, interaction, and understanding. Not surprisingly, the feedback members offered was usually in the form of concrete advice. After six, not necessarily consecutive sessions, a member was terminated from the group as initially agreed upon. Patients could, but often did not, continue to seek additional forms of therapy.

This group was a challenging clinical forum. The level of members' distress and the need to guide the group process very actively made it an extremely demanding group to lead.

Adult Developmental Group

Probably the best known paradigm for HMO group therapy was developed at HCHP (Budman & Gurman, 1988). To accommodate large numbers of members presenting for treatment of neurotic, character, and adjustment problems, a program of fixed-length therapy groups was established that began with the assumption that the life difficulties encountered by individuals would tend to center around developmental themes. The importance and usefulness of developmental groups in the context of current social conditions was predicted by Zimet at his presidential address to the Division of Psychotherapy of the American Psychological Association in August 1977 (1979).

The Midlife Group was a fifteen session group for patients aged 35 to 50. Those selected for the group were distressed enough to need treatment, were willing to enter a short-term group for treatment, and met other specified criteria (Budman, Bennett, & Wisneski, 1981). Candidates for the group were interviewed and educated about the developmental focus and goals for the group.

The group of six to ten men and women was run as a 12-session closed group. The midlife patient, who is at a time of reassessment, often feels stuck with limited possibilities, needs to make new choices, and feels pressured by the passing of time. The leaders of the group made use of these issues for focusing therapy, and the patients worked through these stages within the group setting as they moved toward termination.

In order for these groups to operate well, it is essential that the emphasis be practical and that appropriate referring, screening, and orientation be accomplished efficiently and effectively. Developing group cohesion, maintaining a clear focus, and keeping an awareness of the time-limited nature of the group are important therapeutic tasks.

Potential Problems in an HMO Group Psychotherapy Program

When a group program is not designed but merely develops in response to budget limitations, two major abuses may ensue. First, group formation can be haphazard and inappropriate. When administrative and clinical planning are not systematic, groups may be established arbitrarily. Second, when a group program grows unplanned, the treatment that is provided will be poor. Good treatment results from a programmatic approach to assessing clinical and organizational needs and from a creative and flexible approach to designing groups. The provision of strong support encourages high quality treatment by clinicians who believe in their work and enjoy it.

Conclusion

Effective psychological groups provide a therapeutic setting within which members can see themselves, their own behaviors, and the behaviors of others. Experiential groups provide a microcosm of social and intrapsychic relationships within which members can feel some sense of safety while taking chances that seem too frightening in a large social scene. Psychoeducational groups are structured around a planned agenda and specific areas of skill and knowledge. Crisis groups provide quick response, active support, structure, and a focus on individual self-reports. Developmental groups allow the sharing of age-appropriate life issues among members who might otherwise feel isolated in their struggles toward healthy maturity.

Short-term group therapy has developed naturally from traditional group therapy. By focusing clearly on goals and facing the realities of time limitations, the curative aspects of the group process can work effectively and efficiently. It therefore can play a central role in the delivery of mental health services in a prepaid health care system.

The HMO has characteristics that encourage the use of group therapy. First, it is a closed system and has the potential both to set up good internal communication and to route patients in a consistent way to group treatment. The practical application of group theory can lead to the development of specialized groups as a way to meet defined and identified needs. Second, because of its connection to company benefit programs, the HMO has a diverse membership. This diversity is well accommodated by the group process, which creates a therapeutic milieu for building an appreciation of differences. Third, the underlying premise of the HMO to maintain health means that education is a necessary part of HMO services. Presentations for groups of members are a key part of wellness programs.

Short-term group therapy makes good use of HMO resources. Therapists are available to more than one member at a time, and group members themselves become resources for each other. The time-limited dimension of short-term group therapy discourages any tendency to overtreat or keep patients in groups longer than they need to be there. On the other hand, regular availability of short-term groups allows members to move easily back into treatment at a later time. Use of a group therapy program can increase cost-effectiveness, make specialty treatments practical, solve logistical problems in the operation of a department, and permit preventive and health-enhancing interventions to be offered to a large and varied membership.

References

Allgeyer, J. M. (1970). The crisis group: Its unique usefulness to the disadvantaged. *International Journal of Group Psychotherapy, 20*, 235–239.

Allgeyer, J. M. (1973). Using groups in a crisis-oriented setting. *International Journal of Group Psychotherapy, 20*, 235–239.

Asch, S. E. (1955). Opinions and social pressure. In A. P. Hare, E. F. Borgatta, & R. F. Bales (Eds.), *Small groups: Studies in social interaction* (pp. 318–324). New York: Alfred A. Knopf.

Beck, A. T. (1976). *Cognitive therapy and the emotional disorders*. New York: New American Library.

Bernard, H., & Klein, R. (1977). Some perspectives on time-limited group psychotherapy. *Comprehensive Psychiatry, 18*, 579–584.

Bernard, H., & Klein, R. (1979). Time-limited group psychotherapy: A case report. *Group Psychotherapy, Psychodrama, and Sociometry, 32*, 31–37.

Bion, W. R. (1959). *Experiences in groups and other papers*. New York: Basic Books.

Brammer, L. M., Shostrom, E. L., & Abrego, P. J. (1989). *Therapeutic psychology*. Englewood Cliffs, NJ: Prentice Hall.

Budman, S. H., Bennett, M. J., & Wisneski, M. J. (1981). An adult developmental model of short-term group psychotherapy. In S. H. Budman (Ed.), *Forms of brief therapy* (pp. 305–342). New York: Guilford Press.

Budman, S. H., & Gurman, A. S. (1988). *Theory and practice of brief therapy*. New York: Guilford Press.

Caplan, G. (1964). *Principles of preventive psychiatry*. New York: Basic Books.

Dick, B. M., & Wooff, K. (1986). An evaluation of a time-limited programme of dynamic group psychotherapy. *British Journal of Psychiatry, 148*, 159–164.

Donovan, J. M., Bennett, M. J., & McElroy, C. M. (1981). The crisis group: Its rationale, format, and outcome. In S. H. Budman (Ed.), *Forms of brief therapy* (pp. 283–303). New York: Guilford Press.

Ellis, A. (1962). *Reason and emotion in psychotherapy*. New York: Lyle Stuart.

Erikson, E. H. (1963). *Childhood and society*. New York: W. W. Norton.

Ezriel, H. (1957). The role of transference in psychoanalytic and other approaches to group treatment. In *ACTA Psychotherapeutica, 1, (Suppl.)*.

Fisher, J. D., Silver, R. C., Chinsky, J. M., Goff, B., & Klar, Y. (1990). *Evaluating a large group awareness training: A longitudinal study of psychosocial effects*. New York: Springer-Verlag.

Imber, S., Lewis, P., & Loiselle, R. (1979). Uses and abuses of the brief intervention group. *International Journal of Group Psychotherapy, 29*, 39–49.

Kazdin, & Bellack, A. S. (Eds.). *The clinical psychology handbook*. New York: Pergamon Press.

Klein, R. (1983). Group treatment approaches. In A. E. Hensen, P. M. Lewinsohn, R. F. Munoz, M. A. Youngren, & A. M. Leiss (Eds.), *Control your depression*. Englewood Cliffs, NJ: Prentice-Hall.

Klein, R., & Carroll, R. (1986). Patient characteristics and attendance patterns in outpatient group psychotherapy. *International Journal of Group Psychotherapy, 36*, 115–132.

Lieberman, M. A., Yalom, I. D., & Miles, M. D. (1973). *Encounter groups: First facts*. New York: Basic Books.

Lindemann, E. (1944). Symptomology and management of acute grief. *American Journal of Psychiatry, 101*, 141–148.

Orlinsky, D. E., & Howard, K. I. (1986). Process and outcome in psychotherapy. In S. L. Garfield, & A. E. Bergin (Eds.), *Handbook of psychotherapy and behavior change* (pp. 331–381). New York: Wiley.

Rogers, C. R. (1971). *Carl Rogers on encounter groups*. New York: Harper & Row.

Sabin, J. E. (1981). Short-term group psychotherapy: Historical antecedents. In S. H. Budman (Ed.), *Forms of brief therapy* (pp. 271–282). New York: Guilford Press.

Scheidlinger, S. (1982). *Focus on group psychotherapy*. New York: International Universities Press.

Schein, E. H., & Bennis, W. G. (1965). *Organizational psychology*. Englewood Cliffs, NJ: Prentice-Hall.

Schein, E. H., & Bennis, W. G. (1965). *Personal and organizational change through group methods*. New York: Wiley.

Shapiro, J., Sank, L. I., Shaffer, C. S., & Donovan, D. C. (1982). Cost effectiveness of individual versus group cognitive behavior therapy for problems of depression and anxiety in an HMO population. *Journal of Clinical Psychology, 38*, 674–677.

Sperry, L. (1989). Training in time-limited group therapy. *The Journal of Training & Practice in Professional Psychology, 3*(2), 47–62.

Strickler, M., & Allgeyer, J. M. (1967). The crisis group: A new application of crisis theory. *Social Work, 12*, 28–32.

Stone, W. N., & Rutan, J. S. (1984). Duration of treatment in group psychotherapy. *International Journal of Group Psychotherapy, 34*, 93–109.

Yalom, I. D. (1975). *The theory and practice of group psychotherapy*. New York: Basic Books.

Zimet, C. N. (1979). Developmental task and crisis groups: The application of group psychotherapy to maturational processes. *Psychotherapy: Theory, Research and Practice, 16*, 2–8.

5 _____

Cynthia Belar

Behavioral Medicine

The Setting

Prior moving to the University of Florida, Gainesville in 1990, Dr. Belar was Chief Psychologist at Kaiser Permanente, Los Angeles. The Kaiser Permanente Medical Care Program was established in 1933 and is currently the largest prepaid health maintenance organization in the country. Membership is over six million throughout its twelve geographic regions; the Southern California region has two million enrollees and ten medical centers. The Los Angeles Medical Center serves a population of approximately 360,000 members. It consists of both outpatient clinics and a 752-bed medical/surgical hospital, plus a number of specialized programs (e.g., cardiac surgery, neurosurgery, radiation therapy) that serve the membership of the entire region.

The Los Angeles Medical Center Department of Psychiatry was established in 1960 and is responsible for providing services related to the mental health benefit, which covers all "psychological counseling" and "psychological testing." Currently the staff includes 17 psychiatrists, 13 clinical psychologists, 30 psychiatric social workers, 3 marriage and family counselors, and 3 clinical nurse specialists. Staff are organized into six general multidisciplinary clinical teams and the Behavioral Medicine Service. Members are entitled to services based on their particular health plan benefit. A simplified overview of plans is (a) no charge for consultations to inpatients on medical/surgical units and in the emergency room; and (b) outpatient sessions at varying rates (e.g., 20 sessions at no charge and $5 per session thereafter; $10 per session for the first 20 sessions followed by private sector rate; or, $20 per session for the first 20 sessions followed by private-sector rates).

Behavioral medicine is "the interdisciplinary field concerned with the development and integration of behavioral and biomedical science, knowledge and technique relevant to health and illness and the application of this knowledge and these techniques to prevention, diagnosis, treatment and rehabilitation" (Schwartz & Weiss, 1978, p. 250). As a field, behavioral medicine is not the province of any one discipline, nor does it embrace any particular theoretical orientation. Individuals within the field who are trained to provide psychological intervention services, the focus of this book, come from the disciplines of psychology, nursing, social work, and psychiatry. Within psychology, the term clinical health psychology is often used

65

to describe this area of professional practice (Belar, Deardorff, & Kelly, 1987; Million, 1982).

If one adopts an integrated biopsychosocial perspective of health, the major conceptual model within behavioral medicine, then all *mental* health is really a subset *within* the domain of health. Nevertheless the term behavioral medicine is often used to describe clinical services that are *different* from traditional mental health services. Whereas the population focus of the latter is often described as psychiatric, and the targets of psychological interventions are often viewed as mental and not necessarily physical health, behavioral medicine services often target medical/surgical populations and their related health outcomes. Unfortunately, such language may perpetuate the already pervasive mind–body dualism in health care (see also the chapter on depression by Schulberg and Scott, in this volume). However, it has served to establish the identity of areas of research and clinical practice that have literally mushroomed over the past decade, and it is on these areas of practice that this chapter will focus.

The Growth of Behavioral Medicine

The roots of behavioral medicine date back to the fifth century B.C. and the Hippocratic school of medicine. Psychosomatic medicine as a field, however, emerged between 1920 and 1950. At that time, two major frameworks dominated: psychodynamic and psychophysiologic. For example, Franz Alexander (1950) developed his specificity theory of illness based upon psychoanalytic theory, and Harold G. Wolff (1953) developed a psychophysiological stress model of disease. In Alexander's model, specific unresolved unconscious conflicts produced specific somatic disorders (e.g., frustrated oral dependency needs resulted in duodenal ulcer). Wolff systematically studied the effects of psychological stimuli on physiological processes (e.g., the effects of stress on blood pressure in hypertensives versus normals). During these decades, mind–body processes passed from the province of philosophy and religion to become respectable subjects of scientific inquiry.

The subsequent years produced significant developments in both theoretical and applied aspects of behavioral medicine, as noted by Belar, Deardorff and Kelly (1987):

> The past three decades have been marked by a decrease in the influence of psychodynamic theories, an increased focus on psychophysiological processes, the addition of social and ecological dimensions, and the development of psychological interventions to prevent or ameliorate disease and improve the health care system. (p. 3)

As a field, behavioral medicine has grown rapidly from the mid-1970s to the present. The Academy of Behavioral Medicine was established in April 1978, with Neal E. Miller as its first president. In November 1978 this author attended the organizational meeting of the Society of Behavioral Medicine in Chicago, and in that same year the *Journal of Behavioral Medicine* was begun under the editorship of W. Doyle Gentry.

Gentry (1984) summarized some of the reasons for the rapid growth of behavioral medicine. These factors included:

1. The failure of biomedical models to adequately explain health and illness, with a subsequent search for more adequate explanatory models;
2. The increased, nationwide concern about issues such as quality of life and prevention of illness;
3. The shift in focus from infectious disease to chronic disease as the major challenge in medicine, with the concomitant recognition of the influence of life-style factors in chronic disease[1];
4. The increased maturity and sophistication of research in the behavioral sciences, including the application of learning theories to disease etiology and illness behavior; and
5. The increased cost of health care and the search for alternatives to the traditional health care system.

Behavioral Medicine in Prepaid Health Care

One alternative to the traditional health care system has been the health maintenance organization (HMO). As indicated in previous chapters, the numbers of HMOs and other models of health care service delivery have increased dramatically in the past decade. For example, a recent InterStudy report (1987) indicated that there were 626 operational HMOs in the United States in 1986, triple the number found in 1981. The developmental roots of the HMO are in political, social, and economic reform movements in American society (Kisch & Austad, 1988). Quality health care that is accessible and affordable to all is the underlying philosophy of the HMO. However, spiraling health costs and efforts at cost containment have played a significant role in this model's current growth (see Austad and Berman, in this volume).

Behavioral medicine services find a natural home in prepaid health care for a number of reasons. First, the organizational structure of many prepaid plans lends itself to a biopsychosocial model of health care. Health plans that incorporate services provided by physicians, physician assistants, nurses, physical therapists, dietitians, psychologists, and medical and psychiatric social workers can foster the kind of multidisciplinary teamwork that is essential to effective biobehavioral interventions. Moreover, since prepaid health care is a "closed system," pressures on one part of the system affect other parts of the system. In this context, the integration of psychosocial and physical health care becomes essential not only for humanistic and "community standard of care" values, but also for efficient operation of the HMO itself and for cost-effective treatment of health plan members.

Many of the major biomedical problems addressed in health care involve some aspect of psychosocial functioning. Lifestyle problems such as diet, exercise, and

---

[1] A significant shift in national health policy was reflected in the 1979 release of *Healthy people: The Surgeon General's report on health promotion and disease prevention* (Department of Health, Education, and Welfare, 1979). As the role of behavior in health became more prominent, there was more impetus for the development of behavioral interventions to facilitate health.

addiction (e.g., to smoking or alcohol) affect coronary artery disease, pulmonary disease, and stroke. The management of psychosocial stress and interpersonal difficulties has significant impact on heart disease, depression, and diabetes. Although many of these disorders require somatic treatment to reduce the immediate seriousness of the illness, they also benefit from modifications in the psychosocial sphere. Other chronic problems, such as low back pain, can be treated somatically, but primarily for amelioration of symptoms rather than cure. Behavioral methods have been developed as alternatives to somatic interventions when those interventions are ineffective, are excessive given the severity of the problem, or produce serious side effects (e.g., drug dependence). Attention to these preventive and behavioral aspects of health can benefit significantly the individual in terms of improved health, and society in terms of decreased costs, decreased sick days, and increased productivity.

It is an important concept in modern health care that a treatment model involving behavioral medicine services can be quite cost-effective as well as efficacious. Cost-effectiveness is related to both the *treatment* of disease and the *prevention* of future health problems (behavioral health). For example, the prepaid health care system obtains financial benefits from *maintaining the health* of its members. In contrast, fee-for-service practitioners benefit economically from the *treatment of disease*. Thus effective behavioral health programs that facilitate prevention of disease have the potential for long-term financial rewards for HMOs with stable memberships.

In the treatment of disease, there have been a number of studies highlighting the importance of biobehavioral interventions in the reduction of medical costs (DeLeon & VandenBos, 1988). While a review of these data is beyond the scope of this chapter, a few examples are provided. Schlesinger, Mumford, Glass, Patrick, and Sharfstein (1983) studied claims submitted from 1974 to 1978 by federal employees to Blue Cross/Blue Shield. Two study groups were formed: (a) patients diagnosed as having either diabetes, asthma, hypertension, or ischemic heart disease who had received psychological treatment; and (b) patients with similar diagnoses who had not received psychological treatment. Medical costs three years later for patients seen only within the "physical health care system" were $950. The average cost for patients who in addition had received psychological services averaged $579. Even when adding in the cost of providing psychological services, a five percent reduction in total cost was obtained for patients suffering from these disorders.

A meta-analytic study by Mumford, Schlesinger, and Glass (1982) found that "psychological interventions" consistently promoted recovery from surgery and heart attack. The greatest benefits were on speed of recovery (two days fewer hospitalization) and fewer complications after discharge. These authors also found evidence that psychotherapeutic interventions were more effective than educational approaches, but that combined approaches were perhaps the most effective.

More recently, Schneider (1987) has reviewed studies assessing the cost-effectiveness of biofeedback and behavioral medicine treatments for patients with problems involving headache, hypertension, chronic pain, heart disease, or surgery. Although long-term follow-up is generally not available in the field, quite promising results were found with respect to evidence for reduced physician visits, medication usage, medical care costs to patients, hospitalization, and mortality rates as well as increased quality of life (e.g., fewer side effects from medications). The most common interventions employed were packages including some form of psychophysiological self-regulation and stress management, usually cognitive behavioral in nature.

In conclusion, behavioral medicine is clearly in the best interests of the patient, as it provides a comprehensive treatment program for medical disorders that maximizes physical, social, and personal gain, while minimizing costs, side effects, and invasive procedures. In addition, research has demonstrated that behavioral medicine interventions are cost-effective with respect to both short-term and long-term savings in health care delivery.

Components of Behavioral Medicine Services

As indicated above, behavioral medicine services involve a biopsychosocial approach to the assessment and treatment of health and disease. Services are not limited to specific methods or based upon a particular psychological theory. Rather the approach is multidimensional, involving physiological, affective, cognitive, and behavioral features of the individual and his or her environment.

Assessment in Behavioral Medicine

Some critics of prepaid health care view "programs" of treatment as lacking the ability to take individual differences into account. Such is not the case. Prior to designing a particular behavioral medicine intervention, a careful assessment of the individual problem is essential. In the biopsychosocial model for assessment that is used in effective behavioral medicine service, the clinician assesses the interactions among the person, the disease, and the person's environment (Engel, 1977; Leigh & Reiser, 1980). Belar et al. (1987) have articulated specific targets for assessment (patient, family, health care system, and sociocultural context) and the kinds of information to be obtained for each target (biological/physical, affective, cognitive, behavioral). See Table 1 for a summary of this model.

In each domain of assessment, the clinician strives to understand the patient's current status, changes since onset of the illness, and past history. Focus is not only on identification of problems, but also on delineation of assets, resources, and strengths of the patient and his or her environment. Assessment methods may include interviews with the patient, attending physician, nursing staff, or significant others, as well as the use of diaries, questionnaires, psychometrics, behavioral observation, psychophysiological monitoring, and archival searches. Thus the assessment process is an integrative one that compiles information from a wide variety of sources.

It is important to note that in the assessment process, information obtained in one target area may influence the interpretation of findings in another target area. In the biological sphere, the type and location of symptoms (e.g., genitalia, heart) can affect the meaning the patient attributes to the illness; medication (e.g., Valium) may affect physiological recordings obtained; and endocrine dysfunctions clearly affect mood states (e.g., hypothyroidism). In the social sphere, legislative policies

Table 1.   Targets of assessment

Nature of information	Patient	Environment Health care system	Family	Sociocultural context
Biological or Physical	Age, sex, race Physical appearance Symptoms, health status Physical exam Vital signs, lab data Medications, drugs Psychophysiological data Constitutional factors Genetics History of injury, disease, and surgery	Characteristics of the treatment setting Characteristics of medical procedures and treatment regimens Availability of prosthetic aids	Characteristics of the home setting Economic resources Size of family Familial patterning (history of headache) Other illness in family members	Social services Financial resources Social networks Occupational setting Physical job requirements Health hazards
Affective	Mood Affect Feelings about illness, treatment, health care, providers, self, family, job, and social network History of affective disturbance	Providers' feelings about patient, illness, and treatment	Members' feelings about patient, illness, and treatment	Sentiment of culture regarding patient, illness, and treatment
Cognitive	Cognitive style Thought content Intelligence Education Knowledge about disease Health beliefs Attitudes and expectations regarding illness, treatment, health care, and providers Perceived meaning of illness Philosophy of life	Providers' knowledge Providers' attitudes toward patient, illness, and treatment	Knowledge about illness and treatment Attitudes and expectations about patient, illness, and treatment Intellectual resources	Current state of knowledge Cultural attitudes toward patient and illness
Behavioral	Activity level Interactions with family, friends, providers, and coworkers Health habits Health care utilization (previous medications and psychological treatment) Compliance Ability to control physical symptoms	Providers' skills in educating and training patients Reinforcement contingencies for health and illness	Participation in patient care Reinforcement contingencies for health and illness	Employment policies Laws regulating health care practice, disability, provision of care, health habits Handicapped access Customs in symptom reporting and help seeking

From C. Belar et al., *The Practice of Clinical Health Psychology*. Copyright 1987 Pergamon Press, Inc. Reprinted by permission of Pergamon Press, Inc.

affect "the sick role" behavior of a patient (e.g., criteria for disability awards), and prosthetic characteristics of the environment affect the patient's activity level (e.g., environmental barriers for the wheelchair-bound). Finally, in the psychological sphere, cognitive capacities and health belief models affect ability to comply with treatment regimens (e.g., preparing for home dialysis); family overprotectiveness affects patient self-care (e.g., decreased strength in the chronic back pain patient); and providers' beliefs about disease affect patients' emotional responses (e.g., staff values concerning homosexuality and AIDS).

In addition, the clinician needs to have an understanding of how the setting in which the assessment occurs may affect data obtained. For example, in the presence of her oncologist for whom she wanted to be a "good patient," one woman denied depression, only to break down after the physician left the room. Competent interpretation of assessment data depends upon a firm grounding in the theoretical and empirical health psychology literature. In developing the case conceptualization, information is weighted based on known mediating relationships and prior clinical experience.

HMO assessment practices differ from those in traditional settings by their *integration* into the treatment process. Elaborate "standard battery" work ups followed by staff consultation followed by treatment, delay service delivery and have little practical value for the patient. While individual screenings for each patient are usually conducted prior to referral to specific treatment programs, detailed assessment is generally an ongoing part of the treatment process. Assessment in the HMO is especially facilitated by the presence of a medical record for each health plan member that contains a wealth of information from a variety of health care professionals regarding the individual's health status and past relationship with the health care system.

Intervention in Behavioral Medicine

Interventions in behavioral medicine are also multidimensional and can be aimed at targets related to the patient's physiology, affect, cognitions, or overt behavior. As noted by Belar et al. (1987) interventions can be applied at the level of the patient, his or her health care providers, the patient's family, or the sociocultural context itself. Examples of behavioral medicine interventions at the patient level include: (a) relaxation training for prevention of anticipatory nausea related to chemotherapy; (b) development of a self-monitoring and cuing protocol to increase compliance with a medication regimen; (c) utilization of biofeedback to decrease incontinence; (d) play therapy using coping models to decrease hospitalization anxiety in children; (e) antidepressant medication for chronic pain patients; (f) anger management for Type A behavior patterns; (g) provision of sensory and procedural information about stressful medical procedures; and (h) behavioral skills training in insulin self-injection.

Interventions at the level of the environment include: (a) redesign of living space (e.g., for the blind patient, ordered placement of food in the refrigerator); (b) supportive therapy for the patient's family to decrease an anxiety-laden home atmosphere; (c) training of the patient's family to reinforce well behavior versus sick-role behavior; (d) provision of burnout prevention workshops to nursing staff; (e) redesign of intensive care units to promote patient orientation; (f) education of physicians regarding psychosocial factors in disease; (g) negotiations with employers to facilitate gradual return to work; (h) advocacy for behavioral health legislation (e.g., controls on smoking in the work place); (i) allocation of resources to improve access to behavioral specialists within the health care plan; and (j) education of the health plan membership regarding breast self-examination. One could also conceptualize clinical research activities as interventions, because contributions to the body of knowledge concerning effective diagnostic and treatment strategies will affect the future quality of patient care within the plan.

In choosing an intervention, the behavioral medicine specialist must be aware of the possible positive and negative effects that changes in one target of intervention might have on other areas of functioning or ongoing treatments. For example, relaxation training can produce shifts in insulin needs. Thus if relaxation training is used in patients with diabetes, careful medical monitoring is required so as to avoid producing an unstable diabetes. Another example is the effort to produce a greater sense of mastery and independence via training in self-care activities. While the patient might benefit, family members might become more anxious because a "professional" is not performing the particular technique (e.g., self-catheterization); concern may be so great that family members actually discourage the implementation of the procedure.

The specific intervention strategies used in behavioral medicine include maximizing placebo effects, supportive counseling, verbal insight psychotherapies, education and information, crisis intervention, relaxation training, imagery procedures, hypnosis, biofeedback, systematic desensitization, modeling, skills training, behavioral rehearsal, contingency management, self-monitoring, cuing, cognitive strategies, and pharmacotherapy. Intervention strategies are often used in combination and are sometimes targeted at staff or family members. Collaboration between behavioral and medical professionals is almost always required.

Overview of Behavioral Medicine Services

To further elucidate the role of behavioral medicine in prepaid health care, a number of behavioral medicine intervention programs will be described, and issues in the provision of these services will be discussed. More detailed descriptions of treatments for specific patient populations can be found in other chapters of this handbook (see Kempler's chapter on pain treatment, in this volume). The programs described below are those currently provided by the Behavioral Medicine Service of the Department of Psychiatry at the Kaiser Permanente Medical Care Program, Los Angeles Medical Center. They are not meant to be an exhaustive account of either the current or potential role of behavioral medicine services in prepaid health care.

The Behavioral Medicine Service of the Los Angeles Medical Center Department of Psychiatry is headed by a psychiatrist (Medical Director) and a clinical psychologist (Clinical Director). It has three subcomponents, the Consultation and Liaison Team, the Behavioral Medicine Outpatient Team, and the Behavioral Health Service.

The Consultation and Liaison Team is a multidisciplinary group of psychiatrists, clinical nurse specialists, and psychologists that interacts with both inpatient medical/surgical units and the hospital's emergency area. In the emergency room, members of the team provide management of acute psychiatric emergencies. In the inpatient areas they offer assistance in differential diagnosis (e.g., dementia versus depression), management of psychosocial issues, and evaluation of patients for suitability for participation in specialized medical treatment programs (e.g., cardiac transplant, liver transplant, bone marrow transplant, home respirator). In addition they provide interventions for patient or staff problems as appropriate (e.g., groups for AIDS patients, stress management groups for nursing personnel).

The Behavioral Medicine Outpatient Team is the ambulatory equivalent of the Consultation and Liaison Team. Its members provide a variety of psychological consultations and treatment services to the outpatient medical/surgical clinics. Problem foci have included coping with illness, noncompliance with medical regimens, neuropsychological assessment and diagnosis, presurgical screening (e.g., penile prosthesis surgery), and psychophysiological management of disorders such as spastic colitis, Raynaud's Disease, and hypertension. Ongoing specialized programs are offered for headache, coping with chronic pain, cardiac rehabilitation, and caretakers of Alzheimer's patients. This team is also multidisciplinary, consisting of a psychiatrist and clinical psychologists, including clinical neuropsychologists.

The Behavioral Health Service is the outreach arm of the department providing health promotion groups designed to modify health behaviors that may be risk factors for later health problems. Programs include Stop Smoking, Weight Management, Assertiveness Training, Dealing with Anger, Interpersonal Communications, and Stress Management. These programs are usually eight-week structured groups with very specific targets of intervention. A clinician with a master's degree in psychology coordinates and staffs this component.

Sample Behavioral Medicine Programs

Alzheimer's Caretakers Group (Klein, 1988)

This is a five-week group conducted to facilitate the functioning of caretakers of health plan members with irreversible dementia. The goals of this program are: (a) to provide information about the disease and the problem-solving skills needed to care for the patient with progressive dementia; (b) to provide emotional support to caretakers; and (c) to teach skills in responding to the patient's cognitive and behavioral impairments and learning how to modify the patient's environment so that it is conducive to adaptive functioning consistent with residual abilities. The 1.5 hour sessions are led by a clinical neuropsychologist. Each session is divided between formal presentation of information and group discussion. Specific topics include:

Session 1: Medical and psychological aspects of dementia, including current research efforts and experimental treatments;

Session 2: Resources for the patient and family, including available medical, psychological, social, community, and nursing home services;

Session 3: Legal and financial considerations involved in having a family member with dementia;

Session 4: Videotapes provided by the Alzheimer's Disease and Related Disorders Association, with discussion of the various manifestations of the disease process and related family problems;

Session 5: Skills in conservation of emotional and physical resources of caretakers.

Group discussions emphasize learning new methods to deal with family and daily life problems. Group members have the opportunity to share feelings and concerns as well as suggestions for problem resolution.

Headache Program

The Headache Program has two components. The Headache Clinic (Belar, 1987a) is a half-day per week clinic run by the Behavioral Medicine Outpatient Team in collaboration with the Department of Neurology. Patients suffering from chronic headache who have not responded to a number of previous treatments (usually medication) and who have had a neurological work up within the past year are referred by primary care providers throughout the medical center as well as by other neurologists. In the Headache Clinic, patients are evaluated by a neurologist and a clinical psychologist; after a team conference, a treatment plan is recommended. Treatment recommendations may include individual psychotherapy, medication (e.g., prophylactic, abortive, psychotropic, analgesic), psychophysiological self-regulation training, and/or the Headache Management Group (described below). A psychiatric consultant and a family practitioner with expertise in the assessment and treatment of myofacial pain syndromes are also available for consultation and treatment.

The second component of the Headache Program is the Headache Management Group (Frautschi & Belar, 1986) provided by the Behavioral Medicine Outpatient Team. This group meets for ten weekly 1.5 hour sessions and is led by a clinical psychologist. A new group begins each month. Patients suffering from migraine, muscle contraction, and combined headache are referred from both primary care providers and specialists (e.g., neurologists, neurosurgeons) throughout the medical center. Patients may or may not have been seen in the Headache Clinic depending upon whether another neurologic opinion is indicated. The group is focused and directive, and includes self-monitoring, relaxation, biofeedback, cognitive restructuring, and bibliotherapy. The goals of the Headache Management Group are: (a) to educate the patient about the causes, exacerbating factors, and treatment of headache; (b) to individualize the patient's understanding of the headache problem through functional analyses and diary methods; (c) to teach skills in relaxation, physiological self-control methods, and imagery to reduce headache activity and to increase tolerance for pain; (d) to teach skills in cognitive–behavior therapy that decrease maladapative thinking; and (e) to increase skills in coping with stress. Depending upon the individual problem, the patient may be receiving no other concurrent services, may be followed by a physician (psychiatrist or neurologist) for medication, or may be in marital, individual, or family therapy.

Each group session combines didactic presentation and group discussion, skills training in self-regulation, and homework assignments. In the first session, the structure of the group is explained, and the importance of homework assignments, such as headache diaries and educational readings, is stressed. Headache diaries are reviewed in each session to facilitate identification of triggers and consequences of headache, and to increase skills in self-monitoring.

Relaxation training is started at the second session. Patients are taught the usefulness of progressive muscle relaxation and breathing, and actually practice this form of relaxation in the group. In-group practice of this or other relaxation methods (autogenics, cue-controlled relaxation, imagery) is repeated each session. Finger temperature and electromyograph frontal area monitoring are also provided. The importance of daily home practice of relaxation with finger temperature monitoring is stressed throughout the program.

Beginning in the third session, cognitive and affective components of the program are introduced. Patients are taught to attend to automatic thoughts and to begin to keep thought records. They learn to consider alternative thoughts and to work through examples in everyday life. Group support and discussion are particularly important in cognitive restructuring, as patients often identify others' distorted cognitions and provide each other with alternative thoughts. Throughout the program there is an emphasis on generalization and maintenance of gains as well as techniques for coping with pain.

After graduation, patients can attend a monthly "alumni group" that is designed to facilitate relapse prevention. Return for occasional "booster" sessions and continued problem solving is encouraged by the group therapist.

Stop Smoking Program (Hook, 1985)

Smoking is also approached from the biopsychosocial model. The Stop Smoking Program consists of eight one-hour sessions held weekly. Program goals include: (a) education concerning the physical and psychological effects of smoking on health; (b) education concerning the physiological and psychological aspects of smoking cessation; (c) skills training in strategies of smoking cessation and maintenance; and (d) education about other resources to support nonsmoking behavior. The group leader uses didactic presentations, audiovisual aids, bibliotherapy, and group discussion as a means to encourage member involvement in goal setting, implementing behavior change protocols, peer support, homework assignments, and group experiential exercises.

Specific topics addressed include education about the physiological, psychological, and social aspects of smoking. In addition patients are taught to use substitute behaviors, environmental management, and cognitive restructuring techniques. They are also taught methods of coping with emotional and behavioral side effects of smoking cessation, as well as problem-solving strategies and assertion training to deal with internal and external urges to smoke.

Cardiac Rehabilitation Program (Frautschi, 1987)

The goal of behavioral medicine participation in the Los Angeles Medical Center's Cardiac Rehabilitation Program is to assess patient psychological factors known to be related to increased risk for coronary disease and poor rehabilitation from myocardial infarction. The psychologist involved provides consultation and intervention services to both patients and staff regarding these issues. The Heart Health Questionnaire was developed to provide information about traditional physical and behavioral risk factors; in addition the intake packet includes psychometric instruments to assess stressful life events, trait anxiety, depression, trait anger, anger expression, and Type A behavior patterns.

The specific interventions provided will depend upon the problem areas identified in the intake evaluation, or at a later point by staff. Interventions may include relaxation training, cognitive restructuring, anger/anxiety/depression management, and/or psychotropic medication. Treatment is currently individual in format. Self-paced "Coping with Coronary Heart Disease" training modules that include workbooks and videotapes are currently being developed in an effort to maximize efficiency in providing some parts of these interventions.

Coping with Pain Group (Belar, 1987b)

The goals of the Coping with Pain group are: (a) to educate the patient concerning the emotional, cognitive, psychophysiological, and behavioral components of the pain experience; (b) to decrease pain and suffering as much as possible through the development of skills in pain management and coping with pain; and (c) to increase healthy behavior through maximizing function in recreational, social, vocational, and interpersonal activities. Chronic pain problems addressed have included post herpetic neuralgia, phantom limb pain, back and neck pain, interstitial cystitis pain, and postmastectomy incisional pain.

The Coping with Pain group is led by a clinical psychologist. There are eight, weekly 1.5 hour sessions, with follow-up provided by an alumni group. Topics covered include: understanding the chronic pain syndrome; sensory, affective, cognitive, and behavioral components of pain; self-monitoring; goal setting; pacing; relaxation; pain control strategies; interpersonal interactions around pain; dealing with the health care system; coping with stress; generalization; and maintenance. The first hour of the session is divided between didactic presentations and group discussions; the last half-hour is spent in skill training in various pain management strategies. Homework assignments include relaxation, self-monitoring, and working toward specific individual goals in the areas of family, recreational, and vocational functioning. Patients may be concurrently receiving services in the physical therapy department; many are followed by the consultant psychiatrist for either low-dose antidepressants (used for their analgesic effects) or for pharmacologic treatment of a significant clinical depression.

Issues for Behavioral Medicine in the HMO

Unlike the fee-for-service world in which a practitioner tends to feel responsible only to patients currently in treatment, the HMO clinician is responsible for health care services to the *membership*. Thus the practitioner is challenged not only to provide quality care at the level of direct service, but to consider issues such as accessibility of care to health plan members and how to most efficiently manage professional time and treatment resources. For many professionals this context stimulates activities in the area of program development.

An example is the problem of headache. At the Los Angeles Medical Center services were originally designed to meet the needs of known headache sufferers in an efficient manner. The treatments themselves do not differ from those reported in the literature and provided in private practice and academic medical center settings. However, there was also concern by staff about the problem of headache in the *membership*, the base rate of which is, of course, much higher than those referred for treatment. In order to address this issue, behavioral medicine staff present to other disciplines' in-service education meetings at regular intervals in an effort to update knowledge in the field. They also make themselves available to consult in the development of educational materials to be sent to the entire membership. Finally, staff are currently considering a "minimal therapist contact" package in which information about the nature and methods of treatment of headache can be easily exported to the outpatient medical/surgical clinics to promote patient self-management of headache by members. Obviously this is a fertile field for health services research, as the risks and benefits of such approaches are not well documented.

Another issue in the delivery of behavioral medicine and mental health care relates to the accessibility of services. The Department of Psychiatry, which houses the Behavioral Medicine Service, has a policy of "no waiting list." This is based in part on crisis theory and the need to maximize opportunities for intervention, and also on a strong belief in prevention. In the Behavioral Medicine Service, many patients are referred from other health care providers but, as with all of the Department of Psychiatry, patients may self-refer at any time. Only about one-half of the department's patients are physician-referred. Thus a patient may present with a problem (e.g., headache) that has not yet been adequately evaluated from a biomedical perspective. Behavioral medicine clinicians often need to refer to other medical/surgical specialties in order to clarify the biologic component within the biopsychosocial model. These specialties are easily accessible in an integrated HMO system such as Kaiser Permanente. Collaboration is fostered not only by the HMO system itself, but by the need for mental health practitioners to practice ethically and responsibly within the limits of their competence.

A professional practice issue in behavioral medicine has always been the occasional need to serve as a patient advocate. Consultants often find themselves mediating between the health care system and the patient. A previous psychiatric diagnosis can sometimes affect physicians' willingness to pursue medical evaluations, and the physician–patient relationship has been known to be less than adequate on occasion. It has also been said that in the HMO, there is an increased need for *all* health care professionals to take on patient advocacy roles, because the patient has less autonomy and control than in fee-for-service health care. The patient is dependent upon the employer's benefit offerings, health plan enrollment periods, and the HMO's policy about changing physicians. The behavioral medicine clinician has special obligations in patient advocacy and should act as an internal critic, if necessary, of unfair policies or colleagues' practices.

Finally, a special problem for behavioral medicine services within the HMO is related to the pervasiveness of mind–body dualism throughout American health care policy. Separate insurance benefit packages are usually developed for *mental health* and *physical health* problems, with psychological consultations and therapies covered under the mental health benefit. Mental health benefits in fee-for-service insurance plans often require large copayments that effectively limit utilization; in HMOs mental health benefits are often more restricted than medical/surgical benefits. If the patient (or employer) has not purchased a type of health plan insurance with good coverage for psychological interventions, covered physical health problems might not be adequately addressed.

A few examples might clarify this issue:

1. Even if the treatment of choice for a headache problem is psychophysiological, these treatments are psychological and thus provided under a mental health benefit.

2. The expenses of a penile prosthesis surgery might be fully covered. However, the cost of a presurgical psychological evaluation to determine whether this surgery is appropriate, or whether sex therapy is indicated, might involve a significant copayment that could either provide a barrier to service or affect the patient's attitude toward the examination itself and potentially bias results.

3. The biofeedback treatment of fecal incontinence with its behavioral training of anal sphincter control is decidedly psychological. Is it mental health treatment?

If the HMO's organizational structure is that of unbundled health plan benefits (i.e., coverage for specific services that is contracted out to several professional groups rather than integrated within one professional group), behavioral medicine practice may be more severely restricted as the mind–body split becomes even more reified. Implementation of the biopsychosocial model requires integrated health care.

The very growth of behavioral medicine services and research demonstrating significant positive health outcomes may help to challenge the mind–body dualism now prevalent in national health care policy. Clarification of whether it is the procedure or the problem that defines coverage, and who are the appropriate providers of treatment will be necessary. The outcome has significant implications for enrollees of prepaid health plans, whose physical health can be markedly improved by psychosocial interventions as well as for HMO clinicians who use *psychological interventions* to address *physical health* problem.

References

Alexander, F. (1950). *Psychosomatic Medicine*. New York: Norton.

Belar, C. D. (1987a). *Headache Clinic*. Kaiser Permanente Program Guide, Los Angeles.

Belar, C. D. (1987b). *Coping with Pain Group*. Kaiser Permanente Program Guide, Los Angeles.

Belar, C. D., Deardorff, W. W., & Kelly, K. E. (1987). *The practice of clinical health psychology*. New York: Pergamon.

Department of Health, Education, and Welfare. (1979). *Healthy people: The surgeon general's report on health promotion and disease prevention*. Washington, DC: U.S. Government Printing Office.

Engel, G. L. (1977). The need for a new medical model: A challenge for biomedicine. *Science, 196,* 129–136.

Frautschi, N. (1987). *Psychosocial Components of the Cardiac Rehabilitation Program*. Kaiser Permanente Program Guide, Los Angeles.

Frautschi, N., & Belar, C. D. (1986). *Headache Management Group*. Kaiser Permanente Program Guide, Los Angeles.

Gentry, W. D. (Ed.). (1984). *Handbook of behavioral medicine.* New York: Guilford.

Hook, S. (1985). *Stop Smoking Program.* Kaiser Permanente Program Guide, Los Angeles.

InterStudy. (1987). *The InterStudy Edge.* Excelsior, MN: InterStudy.

Kisch, J., & Austad, C. S. (1988). The health maintenance organization: I. Historical perspective and current status. *Psychotherapy, 25*(3), 441–448.

Klein, R. (1987). *Alzheimer's Caretakers' Group.* Kaiser Permanente Program Guide, Los Angeles.

Leigh, H., & Reiser, M. F. (1980). *Biological, psychological, and social dimensions of medical practice.* New York: Plenum.

Millon, T. (1982) On the nature of clinical health psychology. In T. Millon, C. J. Green, & R. B. Meagher (Eds.), *Handbook of clinical health psychology.* New York: Plenum.

Mumford, E., Schlesinger, H. J., & Glass, G. V. (1982). The effects of psychological intervention on recovery from surgery and heart attacks: An analysis of the literature. *American Journal of Public Health, 72,* 141–151.

Schlesinger, H. J., Mumford, E., Glass, G. V., Patrick, C., & Sharfstein, S. (1983). Mental health treatment and medical care utilization in a fee-for-service system: Outpatient mental health treatment following the onset of a chronic disease. *American Journal of Public Health, 73,* 422–429.

Schneider, C. J. (1987). Cost effectiveness of biofeedback and behavioral medicine treatments: A review of the literature. *Biofeedback and Self-Regulation, 12,* 71–92.

Schwartz, G. E., & Weiss, S. M. (1978). Behavioral medicine revisited: An amended definition. *Journal of Behavioral Medicine, 1,* 249–251.

VandenBos, G. R., & DeLeon, P. H. (1988). The use of psychotherapy to improve physical health. *Psychotherapy, 25,* 335–343.

Wolff, H. G. (1953). *Stress and Disease.* Springfield, IL: Charles C. Thomas.

6

Psychopharmacology

Editors' Note.   Psychopharmacology has a central role in all mental health care. While medications often have significant side effects, and can be problematic if improperly used, psychoses, severe depressions, and some panic disorders respond well to psychoactive medications. However, the practice of psychopharmacology is not as well defined as its efficacy. In everyday practice, a great deal of psycho-pharmacology is provided by internists and by nonmedical providers in conjunction with psychiatric specialists. This is rarely discussed openly but has significant implications for the training, practice, and cost of mental health care that includes pharmacotherapies. The two parts of this chapter address conceptual and practical issues as they are relevant to managed mental health care. In the first part, Kisch discusses the importance of collaboration among the different types of providers in managed mental health and highlights some of the major issues. In the second part, Sovner discusses the practice of psychopharmacology using one approach to collaborative psychopharmacology. The parts are separate, and neither author necessarily endorses statements written by the other author.

Jeremy Kisch

The Need for Psychopharmacological Collaboration in Managed Mental Health Care

The Setting

Community Health Care Plan (CHCP) is a staff model health maintenance orga-
nization (HMO) located in the greater New Haven area. Founded in 1972 by Dr.
Isadore Falk through the American Federation of Labor and Congress of Industrial
Organizations (AFL-CIO), there are currently approximately 68,000 members over
a number of satellite centers. Mental health services are delivered by a multidisci-
plinary staff headed by the Chief of Mental Health Services, a psychologist. The
mental health benefit includes up to 25 fully covered outpatient therapy sessions with
no copayment (with a $2,000 limit) and up to 60 inpatient psychiatric hospitalization
days and 45 substance abuse treatment days.

Rapid and far-reaching changes in the field of mental health are necessitating
collaborative relationships between physicians and other healthcare professionals.
Three forces in particular are fostering the need to develop a model of "collaborative
psychopharmacology"—advances in the use and effectiveness of psychoactive medications, the proliferation and differentiation of mental health care professionals,
and the rise of alternative forms of health care delivery.

The Growth of Pharmacological Intervention

Although less than 40 years old, psychopharmacology has altered the nature of
mental health practice and has important implications for the treatment of mental
health problems (Bassuk, Schoonover, & Gelenberg, 1983).

First, long-term, severe, and slowly remitting disorders can often be contained,
ameliorated, and controlled through the use of psychotropic medications. Psychotherapy, a method of empathic and/or persuasive discussion within a professional
relationship, is often not a sufficient treatment for individuals suffering from serious
mental conditions with protracted courses. High quality, effective treatment of pa-

tients who are mentally and emotionally compromised often requires the integration of both psychopharmacological and psychological interventions.

Second, medication can also influence psychotherapeutic practice style. Since psychotropics decrease symptom severity, psychotherapy can be briefer and more focused. A therapist can attend to a patient's presenting problem rather than to the reorganization of an individual's life (Elkin, Pilkomnis, Docherty, & Sotsky, 1988; Kisch & Austad, 1988; Kisch & Machover, 1989).

Third, major inflation in the costs of health and mental health care is forcing a revision of the priorities and practices of hospital-based care (Wallace, 1987). Psychotropic medications are tools that can help prevent psychiatric hospitalizations as well as decrease the frequency and length of an inpatient stay. Seeing unnecessary hospitalization as a nonproductive interruption within an individual's life is part of the newly emerging philosophy of health care (Caton & Gralnick, 1987).

The above factors mean that the use of psychoactive medications is becoming an essential part of routine mental health treatment.

The Proliferation of Professional Differentiation

The number of practitioners who provide some form of outpatient mental health treatment has grown from 50,000 to 250,000 in the past two decades (Spencer, 1986). The number and type of professionals contributing to the care of patients who require psychotropic medications have also increased significantly. Psychiatrists, psychologists, primary care physicians, nurses, social workers, and family practitioners are members of this growing body. This proliferation has occurred within the context of a shortage of psychiatrists as well as an uneven distribution of practitioners between rural and urban areas.

Primary physicians (i.e., internists, pediatricians, and family medicine practitioners) are significant providers of mental health services. Some estimate that about 60% of American mental health care is provided by general physicians (Thompson & Thomas, 1987). The use of psychoactive agents to treat insomnia, anxiety, depression, pain, hyperactivity, psychosomatic conditions, substance abuse, and so forth has further augmented the role of primary medicine in the behavioral arena. Modern-day nurses are increasingly responsible for treatment (Grossman, 1987).

In more than 20 states, trained nurse practitioners already have limited prescription privileges and provide effective treatment, particularly for the underserved populations (Barclay, 1990). A model program that illustrates the potential effectiveness of interdisciplinary collaboration among psychopharmacologists, nurses, and primary care physicians is described in the second part of this chapter. Through the Department of Defense, psychologists are also participating in pilot programs in which they are training to prescribe a limited number of psychotropic medications (Ray, 1990).

A multidisciplinary approach to treatment may be new to mental health but not to medical practice in general. Complementing the development of medical specialization has been the growth of allied health professions and nonphysician providers capable of delivering medical care, often, but not exclusively, in conjunction with and under physician supervision (Garfield, 1976).

The Growth of Managed Care and the Collaborative Process

Health maintenance organizations (HMOs) have already played a leading role in developing integrated models of health care delivery by allowing maximal participation of physicians' assistants, midwives, nurse practitioners, optometrists, psychologists, and others. In addition, HMOs have encouraged helpful clinical interactions among primary care physicians, psychiatrists, and nonphysician mental health providers. Although collaboration can enhance the quality of care, the actual process is complex. Turf issues arise in an interaction where there is so much variation in the educational, training, social, professional, and legal backgrounds of the participants. Facilitating cooperation requires work and willingness on the part of all health care providers who treat individuals with diagnosable mental disorders.

Collaborative Psychopharmacology in Managed Care

Collaborative prescribing has received little direct attention. Because the implications for treatment are so great, it is important to study the process formally.

In mental health practice generally, and in HMO mental health specifically, the psychotherapeutic aspect of treatment, if it exists, will often be provided by a psychologist or another nonphysician mental health professional. The initial diagnostic assessment that a patient might benefit from medication may be made by an individual who is not licensed to prescribe. This professional may initiate a referral to a physician, who may not necessarily be a psychiatrist. In these situations, prescription may be thought of "generically" as a recommendation as to what interventions will be helpful in treating the patient.

The right to prescribe medication defines the dividing line between physicians and the allied professions involved in health care. Unfortunately, competition and control issues between practitioner groups stimulate arguments over lines of responsibility and authority. In actual clinical practice, primary care physicians often informally collaborate with nonphysician mental health professionals. Nevertheless, most psychotropic prescriptions are actually written by primary care physicians (Kisch & Austad, 1988). The relationship between primary medicine and psychiatry also varies between providers and settings. Psychiatrists and their physician colleagues have still not resolved the issue of where the appropriate boundaries of practice lie, and the areas of overlap are extensive. However, the prevailing psychiatric viewpoint is as follows. Psychiatrists only should prescribe psychotropic medication. Primary care physicians tend to underdiagnose mental conditions, and when symptoms of mental disorder are recognized, they are too often medicated inadequately and inappropriately. Nonphysicians often compound these errors as well as misdiagnose the symptoms of organic disease masked in behavioral symptomatology. Furthermore, nonphysicians have difficulty in competently monitoring and treating potential physical side effects that might arise from psychotropic medications.

These arguments are countered by those who believe that formal training could provide the nonphysicians with the necessary knowledge to prescribe. In many health care settings, nonphysicians already assist competently in the initiation and monitoring of psychotropic medication. Limited prescription privileges for physician assistants and nurses practicing within health care settings already exist in some states. It is argued that psychologists who received advanced training in psychopharmacology would increase access to and availability of needed treatment particularly in underserved areas.

Psychologists are licensed by almost all states to diagnose and treat mental disorders. The right to diagnose presupposes the ability to differentiate conditions for which medication may be appropriate. But psychologists are licensed to treat solely by psychological methods. When medication is indicated, referral must be made to a physician. Unfortunately, this division of effort has sharpened a false bifurcation in that psychotherapy and psychopharmacology are seen as treatment alternatives rather than as complementary interventions.

Physicians, including psychiatrists, cannot provide the totality of services that now make up mental health care. Of necessity there must be an integrated network of clinical practitioners. This network facilitates continuity of care between psychotherapeutic and psychopharmacological providers of care. Conversely, nonphysician psychotherapists cannot proceed as if their techniques are an alternative to medical approaches and still provide realistic care. Group practice, particularly the staff model HMO, presents a fertile arena for innovative development in the relationships between these disciplines and allows for pharmacological intervention in mental health care, a form of *collaborative psychopharmacology*. The variations of collaborative models that have arisen in HMOs, often on an informal basis, incorporate common elements including direct case consultation, coordination of care between medical and mental health, and participation of mental health in non-mental-health encounters (Feldman, 1986).

It is crucial that all providers of health and mental health care spell out clearly their interrelationship in key areas of practice. Since the HMO centralizes a variety of practitioners in a coordinated practice, it has played a pioneering role in fostering systematized interaction among physicians, psychiatrists, and nonphysician psychotherapists. The setting encourages a wide latitude of practice for physicians by supporting the continuing role of the physician in the total needs of the patient. As the entrance point for specialty services, the primary care physician has the opportunity to provide an initial intervention or critical support after referral for psychotherapy. Psychiatry is able to provide consultation and liaison to a primary care physician or to a nonphysician psychotherapist when needed. Psychiatric time can be reserved for consultation and supervision or extended to the most difficult patient management situations. Psychiatrists can also provide for the education and updating of physicians and nonphysician psychotherapists.

There are many possible permutations and combinations of the collaborative model of managed health care can take. The second part of this chapter illustrates one specific model of pharmacological collaboration in a staff model managed care system. If there is to be a significant outreach to all individuals who could profit from some form of mental health service, a collaborative model integrating the presence of the primary care physician, the expertise of the psychiatrist, and the energy and dedication of the nonphysician psychotherapist is vital. The HMO has demonstrated that it is possible for precisely such a mix to occur to the advantage of practitioners and patients alike.

References

Barclay, A. (1990, August). Psychopharmacology: A plan for specialty training for clinical psychologists. In *Issues in psychopharmacology training for clinical, counseling, and developmental psychologists*. Symposium conducted at the 97th Annual Convention of the American Psychological Association, Boston.

Bassuk, E., Schoonover, S., & Gelenberg, A. (1983). *The practitioner's guide to psychoactive drugs*. New York: Plenum Press Medical.

Caton, C., & Gralnick, A. (1987). A review of issues surrounding psychiatric hospitalization. *Hospital and Community Psychiatry, 38*, 858–863.

Elkin, I., Pilkonis, P., Docherty, J. P., & Sotsky, S. (1988). Conceptual and methodological issues in comparative studies of psychotherapy and pharmacotherapy: I. Active ingredients and mechanisms of change. *American Journal of Psychiatry, 145*, 909–917.

Feldman, S. (1986). Mental health in health maintenance organizations: A report. *Administration in Mental Health, 13*, 165–179.

Fink, P. (1985). Psychiatry and primary care: Can a working relationship develop? *General Hospital Psychiatry, 7*, 205–209.

Garfield, S. (1976). Evolving a new model for health care delivery. *Orthopaedic Review, 5*(3), 19–21.

Grossman, J. (1987). The psychiatric alcohol and drug algorithm: A decision for the nurse reviewer. *Quality Review Bulletin, 13*, 302–308.

Kisch, J., & Austad, C. (1988). The health maintenance organization—I. Historical perspective and current status. *Psychotherapy, 25*, 441–448.

Kisch, J., & Machover, R. (1989). Psychotherapy in the HMO. *HMO Practice, 4*, 98–101.

Ray, O. (1990, August). A model curriculum in psychopharmacology. In *Issues in psychopharmacology training for clinical, counseling, and developmental psychologists*. Symposium conducted at the 97th Annual Convention of the American Psychological Association, Boston.

Spencer, C. (1986). Psychology systems compares costs, utilization, between psychiatric PPO and fee-for-service providers. *Spencer's Research Reports, 335*, 12–86.

Thompson, T., & Thomas, M. (1985). Teaching psychiatry to primary care internists. *General Hospital Psychiatry, 7*, 210–213.

Wallace, C. (1987, July 3). Employers turning to managed care to control their psychiatric care costs. *Modern Healthcare*, pp. 82–83.

Robert Sovner

A Psychopharmacology Service Model

The Setting

The Harvard Community Health Plan (HCHP), Health Centers Division, is a staff model managed health care setting in the greater Boston area serving a population of approximately 210,000 members. The Medford Center has a capacity membership of 38,000. Its mental health department provides comprehensive psychiatric services (including various forms of psychotherapy) and handles approximately 200 requests for mental health services per month. HCHP members are offered up to 20 hours of outpatient mental health care per calendar year. At the time that the Psychopharmacology Service was created, the Medford Mental Health Department was staffed by 16 clinicians (3 of whom were staff psychiatrists).

A health maintenance organization (HMO) is an ideal setting in which to practice modern clinical psychopharmacology. The potential for providing high-quality, cost-effective drug therapies to treat psychiatric disorders is greater than in any primary or specialty care setting. Managed care, particularly in a staff model offers the context of a comprehensive medical and mental health system that can decrease hospital stays and increase coordination of care (Schlesinger, 1986).

HMOs can support pharmacotherapy through (a) coordination of treatment and follow-through among all primary and specialty services; (b) decreased potential for drug abuse by close monitoring of utilization and compliance; (c) increased potential for psychotherapeutic and psychopharmacologic specialization within mental health; (d) close collaboration around novel and nonstandard treatment protocols; and (e) availability of well-trained staff for backup, nonessential contacts (e.g., medication refills), and side-effect triage.

Brief psychotherapy in prepaid health care has a burgeoning literature (see Bennett, 1988; Bittker, 1985; Bonstedt & Baird, 1979; Cummings, 1988 and, for example, this volume). In contrast, surprisingly little attention has been paid to the implementation or cost-effectiveness of psychotropic drug therapy services in HMO settings (Shader, 1988). Discussions of the "medical management of psychopharmacologic agents" are generally limited to opinion papers (Sharfstein & Goldman, 1989) or studies of organic mental disorders (Goldman, Cohen, & Davis, 1985). I know of only two empirical studies on managed care psychopharmacology. A study of lithium carbonate use found that ongoing training in the medical management of bipolar disorder significantly increased the quality of care provided in a prepaid health plan (Feldman, Wilner, & Winikoff, 1982). Another study found that a portion of those patients who seek psychiatric treatment and/or receive medication prescriptions for depression have a persistent or relapsing depression at the 12-month follow-up (Hankin & Locke, 1982).

In this chapter, I describe the delivery of psychopharmacologic services within an HMO. First, I will discuss the psychopharmacologist as consultant to primary medicine.[1] Second, I will describe a specialized psychopharmacology service that I developed at HCHP, in which both an MD–psychopharmacologist and nurse clinicians play a central role in managing the treatment of a large number of patients receiving psychotropic drug therapy. I will also present case studies in the form of psychotropic drug protocols that have been used in the HMO mental health department.

Psychopharmacology Services to Primary Medicine

A large proportion of mental health services are provided by the primary care provider (e.g., internists, family practitioners). For example, the frequency of mental health service use increases by more than 100% when mental health contacts by primary providers are included in the total estimate of mental health contacts (Horgan, 1985; Manning, Wells, & Benjamin, 1987; Regier, Goldberg, Burns, Hank, Harper, & Nyez, 1982; Schurman, Kramer, & Mitchell, 1985). In addition, as many as 20% of patients in primary care have a treatable depression (see Schulberg & Scott, this volume). The use of psychotropic drugs in primary care without a formal psychiatric diagnosis raises this estimate to an even higher level (Patrick, Eagle, & Coleman, 1978; Wells, Manning, Duan, Newhouse, & Ware, 1987). All too often, these prescriptions provide subclinical doses, are discontinued prematurely, or are continued for longer than necessary (Katon, 1987; Schulberg, Block, & Coulehan, 1989).

Psychiatrists and psychopharmacologists can provide a useful consultative function to primary medicine without significantly increasing the cost-shifting to mental health. A consultation function for psychopharmacology independent of mental health is similar to the model of treatment used by a variety of medical specialties, including cardiology. For these subspecialties, a patient receiving treatment from internal medicine is referred to cardiology to verify diagnosis and treatment. Usually the patient is seen once, recommendations are made or current treatment is approved, and the patient is returned to internal medicine for follow-up.[2]

There are several situations in which a single psychopharmacology consultation could be more effective and useful than a mental health referral. First, patients

---

[1] A psychopharmacologist is a psychiatric subspecialist with a high degree of expertise (either by fellowship training or experience) in the diagnosis and treatment of drug-responsive psychiatric disorders.

[2] Coleman's group at Community Health Care Plan in New Haven examined a consultation-based mental health system in the 1970s (Coleman & Patrick, 1978; Patrick, Eagle, & Coleman, 1978). They described a program in which 75% of the mental health care was provided by primary care providers (internists, physician assistants, and nurses) while consulting with members of the mental health staff. However, this model of intervention has disappeared in the ensuing 15 years, in favor of specialty mental health departments that provide the bulk of mental health care.

who have previously refused referral to the mental health department but who require psychotropic medication could be evaluated by a psychopharmacologist with no overt mental health involvement. Second, patients who enroll in the plan and are already receiving maintenance doses of lithium carbonate or neuroleptics may need little more than a single psychopharmacology consultation. Third, patients with complex medical problems might benefit from psychotropic medication. This consultation model would clearly be inappropriate for schizophrenic or severe personality disorder patients, or patients who have a history of inpatient hospitalization. These patients require psychosocial as well as somatic treatment.

Psychopharmacology Specialty Services Within HMO Mental Health Care Departments

As a way to provide cost-effective, high-quality drug therapy services, the Medford Center of HCHP established a Psychopharmacology Service (PS) to maximize the clinical impact of a part-time consultant psychopharmacologist who had been hired to assess and treat patients with psychotropic drug-responsive disorders (Sovner, Bailey, & Weisblatt, 1990). The PS was established to offset increasing demands for pharmacologic intervention as part of the mental health service, in part, because there was a shortage of psychiatrists in the mental health department. All PS visits were counted toward the patient's mental health benefit (20 hours per year) and were not treated differently from other types of clinical visits.

A two-tier system was developed that maximized cost-effective patient care. The primary strategy used two Master's-level psychiatric nurse clinical-specialists to provide initial evaluation, follow-up, and maintenance services regarding psychotropic medication to patients. This was done in accordance with preestablished drug protocols. The psychopharmacologist provided initial evaluations, supervised cases, signed prescriptions, and evaluated cases that were beyond the expertise of the nurse clinical-specialists. Using nurses in an expanded role is a cornerstone of the mental health delivery system at HCHP (Mian, Tracy, & Tulchin, 1981). The PS, therefore, was able to build on this already accepted practice of interdisciplinary collaboration.

The role of the nurse clinical-specialists was quite broad, and encouraged practice to the extent of their expertise. After conferring with the psychopharmacologist or another staff psychiatrist, these psychiatric nurses recommended and initiated drug therapy for patients they assessed as part of their general mental health duties. The nurse clinical-specialists required an average of 45 to 60 minutes to screen patients, depending on the extent of prior evaluation by internal medicine or mental health. They also provided follow-up evaluations for patients enrolled in the PS.

The psychopharmacologist carried out initial assessments, began treatment, provided ongoing care, and referred patients for follow-up care to the nurse clinical-specialists. The psychopharmacologist usually was able to complete an initial evaluation in 30 to 45 minutes depending on the complexity of the case. All patients who received nurse-initiated drug therapy were referred for a consultation with the psychopharmacologist and were seen within a three-week period. Thus the psychopharmacologist provided ongoing evaluation and backup for the nurse clinicians.

Initial Referral and Assessment

The referring clinician contacted the PS support staff and an appointment with either the nurse clinical-specialists or the psychopharmacologist was scheduled. Patients who were considered to be diagnostic puzzles or who had complex histories of treatment were generally evaluated by the psychopharmacologist. Clinical and medical data were forwarded in the patient's chart and reviewed prior to assessment for psychotropic medication.

There were three principal referral sources to the PS. First, primary mental health clinicians referred patients whose clinical history, presenting symptoms, and mental status warranted a medication consultation. In these cases, the consultation verified the diagnosis and determined the proper medication and initial pharmacologic treatment plan. Second, patients who exhibited masked depression or panic disorders, or who were resistant to a mental health referral, were referred directly from internal medicine or neurology for pharmacologic evaluation. The third group was self-referred, consisting predominantly of patients who were already receiving a maintenance dose of either a neuroleptic, antimanic, or antidepressant medication.

Consultations were behavioral and data-based. Initial pharmacology assessments were facilitated, in many cases, by patients having already been medically screened by an internist. Observable and quantifiable target symptoms were identified and used to evaluate treatment response at follow-up appointments. Drug treatment was guided by a set of protocols for starting and titrating the daily dose of preferred psychotropic agents. There were no a priori limitations on patients the nurses could follow or medications they could monitor; in practice, however, medically complicated patients were treated only by a psychiatrist.

Follow-up Visits

If medication was prescribed at an initial evaluation visit, the patient was told that he or she would be followed in the PS. It was explained that all subsequent follow-up visits would be for medication-response assessments only and that other clinicians within the department would be available for psychotherapy, stress management, and other forms of psychosocial intervention. Those patients who were being followed by a primary mental health coordinator were referred back, and coordination of treatment was maintained between the primary provider and the nurse clinical-specialists.

Follow-up assessments were used exclusively to monitor the patient's clinical response to medication. The target symptoms highlighted in the treatment protocol and identified during the evaluation were compared to the patient's condition at initial evaluation and (if available) at presymptomatic baseline. When indicated, medication blood levels were drawn prior to the follow-up visit, so that they were available as part of the assessment. In addition, side effects that commonly follow from the particular medication were evaluated. Periodic evaluations of tardive dyskinesia were conducted for patients taking neuroleptics. The nurse clinical-specialists titrated their patients' daily drug doses against clinical response, blood levels, and side effects.

The two nurse clinical-specialists monitored treatment in 30-minute follow-up appointments scheduled every two to four weeks. The psychopharmacologist scheduled routine follow-up visits for 15 minutes every two to four weeks. The psychopharmacologist found the shorter time period sufficient to assess treatment response and adverse effects for most patients, probably due to greater experience. When a patient was stable on medication, follow-up visits could be reduced to once every two to six months. This was sufficient for those patients needing indefinite maintenance medication.

Prescriptions

The nurses usually wrote their own prescriptions and had them signed by the psychopharmacologist or a staff psychiatrist. The psychopharmacologist's use of 15-minute follow-up visits insured that he or she would be free several times per hour to sign prescriptions. They also left him or her free on a frequent basis for "hallway" consultations and for crises which might require more than the scheduled time.

PS emergencies such as consultation for hospital admissions, and acute drug side effects would sometimes occur when the psychopharmacologist or nurse clinical-specialists were not on site. Three mechanisms were available to address these problems. First, the MD–pharmacologist was often available by telephone for indirect consultation. When this was not the case, or when direct contact was needed, these crises were handled by mental health clinicians who provided on-call services on a rotating basis during normal office hours. Finally, a psychiatrist was always on site during normal office hours to deal with emergency medication issues. During evenings and weekends, the normal health on-call procedures were followed.

Drug Protocols

The purpose of using psychiatric nurse clinical-specialists was to combine knowledge about medical aspects of psychotropic drug response with knowledge of psychiatric syndromes and diagnosis. The operation of the PS was in accordance with HCHP policies, American Nursing Association guidelines, and Massachusetts state regulations. According to the regulations of the Massachusetts Board of Registration in Nursing, nurses who function in an expanded clinical role can evaluate and treat patients provided that drug therapy is prescribed in accordance with established treatment protocols. Also, the prescribing physician must assess the patient, although not necessarily prior to the initiation of treatment (Board of Registration in Nursing, January 22, 1988).

A number of drug protocols were established at the Medford Center for the use of antidepressant, antipanic, and antimanic medications. These protocols were not unique or unusual. The models on which they were based were drawn from treatment recommendations that have appeared in various publications (e.g., Hyman & Arana, 1987). The use of objective inclusion criteria, pretreatment medical evaluation and treatment/dosage protocols were easily integrated into clinical practice. Tables 1 and 2 provide examples of protocols used for nortriptyline (a tricyclic antidepressant) and lithium carbonate, respectively. Both protocols include basic diagnostic criteria and exclusion criteria as the first step. Then medical evaluation

Table 1.   Nortriptyline Treatment Protocol

Initiate drug treatment for any patient who meets the following criteria:
   Patient suffers from a major depression (DSM III-R 296.2 or 296.3) with any three of the following symptoms:
      Sleep disturbance
      Appetite disturbance
      Fatigue
      Diminished interest
   Patient does not have history of or presently has panic attacks
   Patient has not had an unequivocal response to another tricyclic antidepressant
   Patient does not have a history of manic or hypomanic episodes

Pretreatment medical monitoring:
   Less than 40 years old: laboratory assessment not indicated if patient is in good health (if health problems, refer to MD).
   40+ years old: EKG

Treatment initiation protocol[a]
   Days 1–2: 10 mg at bedtime[b]
   Days 3–4: 20 mg at bedtime
   Days 5–8: 30 mg at bedtime
   Days 9–13: 40 mg at bedtime
   Day 14: 50 mg at bedtime
   Day 28: Obtain blood level
   Titrate dosage based on clinical response and blood level (target = 50–150 ng/ml

Medical monitoring of treatment
   Less than 40 years old: none needed.
   40+ years old: EKG after six months.

Note. EKG = electrocardiogram
  [a] Patient should take entire daily dose in a.m. if amphetamine-like reaction develops (e.g., racing thoughts, jitteriness)
  [b] Patient should not increase daily dose if a positive response occurs or significant adverse reactions develop. Contact clinician.

is specified, and dosage titration guidelines are given. Finally, ongoing laboratory work as appropriate is recommended. These protocols are simple to follow and implement, and, in conjunction with ongoing supervision, provide quality treatment for patients.

Evaluation of the Psychopharmacology Service

Patient Contact

Patient contact data is collected as part of the Mental Health Department's review of staff productivity. A three-week sample of the productivity of the PS was analyzed after the service had been in operation for one year to determine the number and type of patients seen by the three clinicians. The productivity of the clinicians is displayed in Table 3.

The nurse clinical-specialists, who worked for four and eight hours per week, respectively to the PS, treated 25 and 39 patients. The psychopharmacologist was able to evaluate up to five new patients per week and carry a caseload of 120 patients during 14 hours per week of on-site time. Approximately one seventh of the psy-

Table 2. Lithium Carbonate Treatment Protocol

Initiate lithium therapy for any patient who has one of the following:
  Patient suffers from a depressive disorder with any three of the following symptoms:
    Hypersomnia
    Hyperphagia
    Fatigue
    Diminished interest
    History of manic or hypomanic episodes
  Patient is manic
  Patient is hypomanic with the following symptoms:
    decreased need for sleep
    mild euphoria
    mild overactivity
    pressured speech
    history of depressive episodes
  Patient is depressed and has a history of bipolar disorder and/or response to lithium therapy.

Pretreatment medical assessment
  Less than 40 years old:
    Chemistry profile (BUN, Creatinine)
    Serum electrolytes
    Thyroid function (T-3 Uptake, T-4, TSH)
    Urinalysis
  40^+ years old:
    Chemistry profile (BUN, Creatinine)
    Serum electrolytes
    EKG

Treatment initiation protocol (use 300 mg capsules)
  Days 1–3: 300 mg twice/day
  Day 4: Draw blood for lithium blood level
  If lithium level < .4 mEq/L, increase to 300 mg in a.m. and 600 mg at night until follow-up appointment (two weeks).
  Target blood level: 0.7–1.2 mEq/L)

Medical monitoring of treatment
  Less than 40 years old:
    Thyroid function every 6 months
    BUN and Creatinine every 6 months
  40^+ years old:
    Thyroid function every 6 months
    BUN and Creatinine every 6 months
    EKG every 12 months

Note. EKG = electrocardiogram

chopharmacologist's time was spent in supervision, administrative meetings, and unscheduled contacts. Referrals to the nurse clinical specialists prevented backlogging of patients followed by the psychopharmacologist and facilitated rapid evaluation and treatment of new patients who required consultation with the psychopharmacologist.

Table 4 lists the types of mental illnesses treated by the PS. The mood and anxiety disorders predominated. It is interesting to note that there were no schizophrenic patients in the PS caseload. These data are consistent with the total mental health department caseload and are an accurate reflection of the types of patients who are referred for psychopharmacology treatment at the Medford Center. That is, the vast majority are ambulatory, nonpsychotic depressed or anxious patients.

Table 3. Psychopharmacology Service Patient Contacts During a Three-Week Survey Period

Clinician	Total Hours During Study Period	Initial Evaluations	Total Follow-up Visits	Non-Visit Prescriptions	Caseload
Psychopharmacologist	42	16[a]	42[b]	68[c]	120
Nurse A	12	——	18[d]	——	25
Nurse B	24	——	40[d]	——	39
Total	78	16	100	68	184

Notes. [a] Visits were for 45 minutes. Six of 16 were referred to nurse clinicians for follow-up during survey period.

[b] Visits were for 15 minutes.

[c] Includes all prescriptions other than those written during patient visits, e.g., telephone request. Thirty-four prescriptions (50%) were written for patients being followed by nurse clinicians.

[d] Visits were for 30 minutes.

Table 4. Diagnostic Categories of (Psychopharmacology Service) Patients During a Three-Week Survey Period ($N = 120$)

Affective disorders:	81%
Unipolar depression: (all types)	65%
Bipolar illness:	16%
Anxiety/Panic disorders	12%
Psychoses[a]	4%
Organic mental disorders	3%

Note. [a] Includes schizoaffective disorder and atypical psychoses. There were no cases of schizophrenia.

Patient Satisfaction

No specific mechanism for monitoring patient satisfaction was used by the PS. However, in staff-model HMOs there are a number of feedback mechanisms that provide unobtrusive measures of performance. First, a patient advocate is always available to patients for feedback, complaints, and member input. In these cases, clinicians are invariably informed of the complaint. Second, internal medicine will get feedback from patients directly during office visits, and indirectly by observing the degree of treatment compliance. These data sources indicated that patients were quite satisfied. During the first year of operation, no one refused to be followed by a nurse clinician for medication. Issues related to not being seen by "the expert" were rare and were handled by a "second opinion" consultation with the psychopharmacologist. When dissatisfaction was voiced, it tended to be related to problematic provider–patient matches rather than treatment problems.

Staff feedback was positive because consultations were being provided more quickly than before the program was instituted, and treatment response was monitored closely by trained staff. In general, mental health staff supported the development of the PS. First, the PS improved access time to drug therapy services for patients referred by other mental health clinicians. Second, the PS decreased the number of medication patients handled by the other psychiatrists, freeing them to also engage in psychotherapy and other nonsomatic interventions.

Because the PS can provide somatic treatments in a timely manner with sufficient coordination of treatment, it may be more efficient to provide the biological treatments through a subspecialty service. Psychopharmacology can be provided in a cost-effective way by combining the services of psychiatric nurse clinical-specialists and psychiatrists or psychopharmacologists.

Quality Assurance

Although both staff and patient satisfaction appear to be high, it is important to develop specific mechanisms for maintaining assurances of quality care in this form of service delivery system. Two approaches were used to maintain quality of care. First, the psychopharmacologist evaluated all patients, either prior to treatment or within three weeks of treatment-initiation if drug therapy was started by a nurse. Second, each nurse clinician received 30 minutes of supervision from the psychopharmacologist for every four hours of psychopharmacology care provided. Each week during the supervision time, the status of all the patients in the clinician's caseload was at least briefly reviewed. Having the psychopharmacologist see all the patients at least once and sign prescriptions for them on a regular basis facilitated the process. In addition, there were informal "hallway" consultations that went on throughout the day regarding such issues as the management of emergent side effects and the choice of a specific treatment for a particular patient. In complicated or treatment-resistant cases, the psychopharmacologist would carry out a second consultation either at the nurse's or patient's request.

The Psychopharmacology Service as a Model for Future Use

The purpose of the PS was to maximize the provision of psychotropic drug treatment in an HMO mental health department by enhancing the use of a psychiatric subspecialist with nonphysician clinicians. The PS demonstrated that psychiatric nurses can fulfill an important function of patient care in a subspecialty setting. This model for delivering drug therapy services is being implemented at a second HCHP site. Future research in our setting will be able to provide a cost/benefit evaluation based on the number of patients served, duration of treatment, duration of contacts, and response rate compared to mental health services without a PS.

The success of the service was attributable to four factors. First, the introduction of nurse clinical-specialists to clinical care positions at HCHP did not begin with the PS. Nurse clinicians have provided direct service to enrollees for many years, particularly in internal medicine, pediatrics, and obstetrics–gynecology. This practice is also consistent with the expanded use of nurses in other outpatient mental health settings (Shelley & Fieve, 1974).

Second, the PS was not a separate service, but rather a subspecialty component of a larger mental health department. All patients who were seen in the PS had already been evaluated by a primary mental health coordinator who was responsible for the overall management of the case. Drug therapy therefore was part of an integrated treatment plan coordinated by the mental health department. Because the PS was highly focused on biochemical interventions, "turf" issues related to sharing clinical responsibility were infrequent. Mental health clinicians did not feel that the psychopharmacology staff interfered in their patients' psychosocial treatment.

Third, outpatients treated by the PS of the Medford Center were generally stable, and not suffering from psychotic disorders. The applicability of this kind of program to populations with a higher percentage of psychotic and/or crisis patients remains an open question. However, there is no a priori reason to assume that it would not function as well.

Fourth, the time flexibility of the PS greatly increased the efficiency of the service. The 15-minute allocations for follow-up visits by the psychopharmacologist may be the most controversial part of the PS. The role of time in HMO therapy has been addressed elsewhere in this volume (see Cummings on intermittent brief therapy, and Hoyt, both in this volume). Mental health care is one of the few health services in which visits are rigidly defined by the time period allowed and not by the service rendered. Health services schedule visits according to a rough time estimation that varies depending on the procedure (e.g., 15 minutes for a routine follow-up visit; one hour for an endoscopic examination). In contrast, mental health services usually make no distinctions between psychotherapeutic and psychopharmacologic visits. Mental health clinics usually adhere to the traditional 45- to 50-minute hour and 25-minute half-hour appointments even for drug therapy follow-ups. The PS experience indicates that 15-minute follow-up visits are sufficient for medication assessments in a stable outpatient population. As the nurse clinical-specialists develop greater expertise and experience, they too may be able to schedule 15-minute contacts, further increasing the efficiency of the PS.

Nurse clinical-specialists are the ideal clinical specialists for a psychopharmacology subspecialty. The prescription and monitoring of psychotropic drug therapy requires a basic knowledge of medicine and pharmacology that is part of a nursing education. Given the salary differential between psychiatrists (who seem to be increasingly difficult to attract to HMO settings) and nurses, it seems appropriate to use nurses for the bulk of psychopharmacologic care and reserve the psychiatrists for the more complicated or medically difficult cases.

Obviously the PS requires a more differentiated approach to mental health and mental illness. If all patients are essentially treated the same, then having a psychopharmacology subspecialty may not be the most appropriate model. However, there is growing evidence that we can begin to target specific interventions for patient populations based on diagnosis, family, social, and psychological factors (Frances, Clarkin, & Perry, 1984). When more focal, specific interventions are appropriate, then a separate PS is very likely to be successful.

The possibility of splitting psychopharmacology from mental health care is particularly feasible in HMOs where it is less likely to be used simply as a means of eliminating psychotherapy altogether (because of statutory requirements for psychotherapy services), or as a means of placing psychotherapists under the supervision of medical staff. Obviously caution would be needed in implementing such a separation in order to avoid the establishment of barriers to psychosocial treatments. However, separating psychopharmacology and psychotherapy services could facilitate provision of more comprehensive treatments for disorders such as panic disorder with agoraphobia, obsessive–compulsive disorder, and schizophrenia by increasing the available number of sessions for behavior or family therapy and eliminating the battle over who is ultimately qualified to provide treatment. It would also eliminate charging a patient on the basis of the service provider rather than the service itself. If an internist, for example, prescribes an antidepressant, no charge is made toward a mental health benefit.

In summary, a psychopharmacology service is a cost-effective way to provide drug therapy services for patients with mental disorders that have a clear-cut biological component. In many respects, staff model HMOs are an ideal environment for such programs. The on-site availability of medical backup, emergency care, and other mental health services provides a level of support and treatment coordination unavailable in many other settings. An HMO-based psychopharmacology service, therefore, can provide very high-quality mental health care in a cost-effective way.

References

Bennett, M. J. (1988). The greening of the HMO: Implications for prepaid psychiatry. *American Journal of Psychiatry, 145*, 1544–1549.

Bittker, T. E. (1985). The industrialization of American psychiatry. *American Journal of Psychiatry, 142*, 149–154.

Board of Registration in Nursing. (1988, January 22). Massachusetts regulations governing the practice of nursing in the expanded role. *Massachusetts General Laws* c. 112, s. 80B [244 CMR 4.00].

Bonstedt, T., & Baird, S. H. (1979). Providing cost effective psychotherapy in a health maintenance organization. *Hospital and Community Psychiatry, 30*, 129–135.

Coleman, J. V., & Patrick, D. L. (1978). Psychiatry and general health care. *American Journal of Public Health, 68*, 451–457.

Cummings, N. A. (1988). The emergence of the mental health complex: Adaptive and maladaptive responses. *Professional Psychology: Research and Practice, 19*, 323–335.

Feldman, J., Wilner, S., & Winickoff, R. (1982). A study of lithium carbonate use in a health maintenance organization. *Quarterly Review Bulletin, 8*, 8–14.

Frances, A., Clarkin, J., & Perry, S. (1984). *Differential therapeutics in psychiatry: The art and science of treatment selection.* New York: Brunner/Mazel.

Goldman, H. H., Cohen, G. D., & Davis, M. (1985). Expanded medicare outpatient coverage for Alzheimer's disease and related disorders. *Hospital and Community Psychiatry, 36*, 939–942.

Hankin, J. R., & Locke, B. Z. (1982). The persistence of depressive symptomatology among prepaid group practice enrollees: An exploratory study. *American Journal of Public Health, 72*, 1000–1007.

Horgan, C. M. (1985). Specialty and general ambulatory mental health services: Comparisons of utilization and expenditures. *Archives of General Psychiatry, 42*, 565–572.

Hyman, S. E., & Arana, G. W. (1987). *Handbook of psychiatric drug therapy.* Boston: Little, Brown.

Katon, W. (1987). The epidemiology of depression in medical care. *International Journal of Psychiatry in Medicine, 17*, 93–112.

Manning, W. G., Wells, K. B., & Benjamin, B. (1987). Use of outpatient mental health services over time in a health maintenance organization and fee-for-service plans. *American Journal of Psychiatry, 144*(3), 283–287.

Mian, P., Tracy, K., & Tulchin, S. (1981). Expanded roles for mental health nurses within an HMO. *Hospital and Community Psychiatry,* 727–729.

Patrick, D. L., Eagle, J., & Coleman, J. V. (1978). Primary care treatment of emotional problems in an HMO. *Medical Care, 16*, 47–60.

Regier, D. A., Goldberg, I. D., Burns, B. J., Hank, J., Hoeper, E. W., & Nyez, G. R. (1982). Specialist/generalist division of responsibility for patients with mental disorders. *Archives of General Psychiatry, 39*, 219–224.

Schlesinger, M. (1986). On the limits of expanding health care reform: Chronic care in prepaid settings. *The Milbank Quarterly, 64*(2), 189–215.

Schulberg, H., Block, M., & Coulehan, J. (1989). Treating depression in primary care practice: An application of decision analysis. *General Hospital Psychiatry, 11*, 208–215.

Schurman, R. A., Kramer, P. D., & Mitchell, J. B. (1985). The hidden mental health network: Treatment of mental illness by nonpsychiatric physicians. *Archives of General Psychiatry, 42,* 89–94.

Shader, R. I. (1988). Book review. *Journal of Clinical Psychopharmacology, 8,* 451–452.

Sharfstein, S. S., & Goldman, H. H. (1989). Financing the medical management of mental disorders. *American Journal of Psychiatry, 146,* 345–349.

Shelley, E. M., & Fieve, R. R. (1974). The use of nonphysicians in a health maintenance program for affective disorders. *Hospital and Community Psychiatry, 25,* 303–305.

Sovner, R., Bailey, K., & Weisblatt, R. (1990). An HMO psychopharmacology service: A cost-effective delivery system for psychiatric services in a managed health care system. *HMO Practice, 4,* 162–166.

Wells, K. B., Manning, W. G., Duan, N., Newhouse, J. P., & Ware, J. E. (1987). Cost-sharing and the use of general medical physicians for outpatient mental health care. *Health Service Research, 22,* 1–17.

7

Michael F. Hoyt

Teaching and Learning Short-Term Psychotherapy Within an HMO

The Setting

The psychiatry department at the Kaiser-Hayward Medical Center has 33 full-time clinicians (19 PhDs, 6 MSWs, 6 MDs, and 2 RNs) serving 153,000 members. The staff to patient ratio is 1:4,200, with outpatient, emergency room, and hospital consultation-liaison services being divided into adult, child and family, and behavioral medicine/chemical dependency functional teams. The Kaiser-Hayward facility is part of the Kaiser Permanente Northern California region, which serves more than 2,400,000 members.

Background: Psychotherapy in the HMO

The expansion of health maintenance organizations (HMOs) and the current controversies regarding how mental health services can best be provided (Austad, DeStefano, & Kisch, 1988; Cheifetz & Salloway, 1984; Cummings, 1986, 1988; DeLeon, Uyeda, & Welch, 1985; Goldensohn, 1977; Kiesler & Morton, 1988; Kisch & Austad, 1988; Shulman, 1988; Tulkin & Frank, 1985) have created a powerful context for the teaching and learning of psychotherapy skills. The adaptation of psychotherapeutic practice to the exigencies of the HMO benefit structure is resulting in the emergence of a universal treatment philosophy that cuts across heterogeneous systems and various specific treatment techniques. "HMO therapy," as Austad et al. (1988; Hoyt & Austad, in press) call this unique practice, has a number of distinguishing characteristics that include rapid setting of clearly defined goals, crisis intervention preparedness, interventions designed to minimize (not extend) the therapist–patient relationship, flexible and creative use of time limits, and continuous and comprehensive treatment for chronic patients. Also included are cooperative collaboration between medical and nonmedical staff, coordinated psychopharmacology and psychotherapy, and a view of termination that allows for a brief and intermittent "family doctor" style of practice. Efficiency is the watchword of HMO therapy and effective short-term treatment is the key to its success.

To learn, to practice, and to enjoy the complex technical skills of an effective brief therapist (in an HMO setting and elsewhere), one must have enthusiasm for short-term work (Malan, 1976; Sifneos, 1987) and remain open-minded about the often self-fulfilling theoretical assumptions that underlie long-term therapy (Hoyt, 1985, 1987, 1990; Winokur & Dasburg, 1983). Some of the therapist values that facilitate good short-term work include: a preference for pragmatism and parsimony; the appreciation and promotion of strengths rather than pathology and of solutions rather than problems; and the perspective that being in the world is more important than being in therapy (Budman & Gurman, 1983; 1988; Frances, Clarkin, & Perry, 1984; Rosenbaum, Hoyt, & Talmon, 1990). Drawing on their experience at Harvard Community Health Plan, Budman, Feldman, & Bennett (1979, p. 392) describe a good HMO therapist as someone who possesses sound psychodynamic training, interest and experience in a high-pressure medical setting, interest in group practice, and commitment to problem-oriented short-term psychotherapy. While one might disagree with the specification of psychodynamic training the thrust of their description is clear: skill, motivation, and orientation toward focused short-term therapy are prerequisites. Regardless of specific technical orientation (psychodynamic, cognitive–behavioral, family systems, etc.) the effective brief therapist will operate from a set of guiding assumptions or beliefs that are compatible with a short-term model.

Contrasting belief systems underlie long- and short-term therapy orientations. Therapists accustomed to operating within a long-term context will be unable to use short-term methods successfully without modifying some of their underlying assumptions. To support their view that treatment must be lengthy to be effective, the proponents of long-term therapy make the following theoretical assumptions:

1. Pathogenic early experiences must be slowly and fully uncovered.
2. Therapist–patient rapport and alliance must form gradually.
3. Patients must be allowed to regress.
4. Transference takes a long time to develop and should not be interpreted too early.
5. Consolidation of gains requires a lengthy period of working through.

These assumptions, which are not necessarily true, can become self-fulfilling prophecies and may be held as quasi-intellectual resistances to short-term therapy (Hoyt, 1985; 1987; 1990).

An alternative set of working assumptions are proposed by the proponents of short-term therapy:

1. Focused interventions can set into motion a whole system of changes.
2. Selected patients can rapidly form a good therapeutic alliance and early transference interpretations can strengthen the working relationship.
3. Generalized regression should be avoided and restricted as much as possible to the focal area.
4. Time limits increase and intensify the work accomplished so that gains are consolidated throughout treatment.
5. Reactions to termination can be interpreted and dealt with productively throughout short-term therapy because patients are considered able to tolerate separation anxieties.

These differences underscore the technical methods that typify short-term work: an explicit understanding that treatment is not "timeless;" a very active therapist; early transference interpretations; selective attention to a central focus; a strong adult-to-adult therapeutic alliance and avoidance of generalized regression; and early attention to termination as part of the working-through process. Therapists accustomed to operating within a long-term treatment context will need to adjust or suspend their underlying assumptions and beliefs before they will be able to adopt these short-term methods effectively and comfortably.

The strong HMO emphasis on brief treatment with "return to function" as a primary goal will engender, for some therapists and in some circumstances, a strong set of counterproductive responses. In addition to the usual countertransference difficulties engendered by the demands of certain patients (Hoyt, 1989; Hoyt & Farrell, 1984; Hoyt & Goulding, 1989), therapists' reactions may also derive from both sociocultural and personal sources. Conflicts may center on being a salaried employee, problems with authority, discomfort with frequent exposure of one's work to peers and quality control, and various impingements upon therapists' self-image (Goldensohn & Haar, 1974; Lange, Chandler-Guy, Forti, Foster-Moore, & Rohman, 1988). For a variety of reasons, focused treatment may be frustrating and restrictive for some therapists. As Bennett and Wisneski (1979) have cogently argued, however, one should not perpetuate the myth that brief therapy is pragmatic at the expense of loftier goals of personality change and self-realization. A more accurate and comprehensive view is that brief therapy may result in significant change and enduring growth as well as symptom relief, an observation Goldensohn and Haar (1974, p. 256) made in their discussion of transference and countertransference in an HMO: "Although our primary goal is return to function, our experience has shown that significant personality changes may result from short-term therapy with limited goals."

This is not to say that all long-term or open-ended therapy is necessarily inefficient or misguided, as some brief therapy enthusiasts have implied (Hoyt, 1985, 1988). Some patients and some problems do require extended treatment, and the promotion of brief therapy approaches with as many patients as possible may help to make resources available for those few who do require prolonged therapy. How decisions are to be made about who "needs" long-term therapy and whether it is to be included or excluded (at what and whose expense) in HMO mental-health coverage go beyond the scope of the present discussion. What is important here is to recognize that many apparently long-term problems can benefit greatly from innovative short-term treatment, and that therapists should have the theoretical ability, practice skills, and interest to consolidate a protracted storyline into a treatable central issue.

The HMO therapist needs to be something of a generalist, able to conceptualize problems and implement treatments parsimoniously. One is best equipped if one can use multiple perspectives (Gustafson, 1986; Rosenbaum, Hoyt, & Talmon, 1990). HMO practice involves seeing cases that require "differential therapeutics" (Frances, et al., 1984). No one therapist can be expert at everything, of course, so a good staff collectively should have practitioners who are able to offer and teach a panoply of skills (Hoyt & Austad, in press). When a patient's present needs don't match one's therapeutic inclinations, being able to make a good referral can be a blessing for all concerned. Sometimes it's *who* you know, not *what* you know, that gets the job done!

Good brief therapists know that a great deal more can be accomplished and often more quickly than may at first seem possible. All work does not have to be accomplished at once. The therapist also recognizes that, with some assistance, people do a lot on their own. There are also different ways to do and get psychotherapy, for example, many people benefit enormously from psychoeducational approaches such as classes, structured workshops, and recommended readings.

Still, there are situations where we have to face the limits of brief (or any) psychotherapy. Then we professional caregivers may experience a strong potential for guilt: What are we going to do for the people who need more? Should we feel guilty that we cannot be everything to everyone? Just as patients can form an institutional transference (Reider, 1953), clinicians can engage in *institutional countertransference* by overassuming responsibility in response to patients' neediness and dependency on the institution. If HMO therapists and trainees begin to feel as if "Mother HMO should take endless care of her children," it will be important to recall that our professional activity is based upon a contractual relationship, and that patients have bought a form of health coverage that specifies the limits of what will be provided. We certainly can be concerned about the plight of some patients and make efforts to help them find appropriate help, but it is grandiose to think that we can take care of all problems. As a nation, we are facing a crisis in the cost of health care services and there are no easy answers. We need to face the fact with concern rather than guilt that "There is a burgeoning need for clinicians to be willing and able to apply effective short-term therapy methods if the needs of more than a handful of patients are to be served" (Hoyt, 1985, p. 83).

Advantages and Disadvantages to Psychotherapy Training in an HMO

Learning to practice short-term psychotherapy in an HMO involves the development of both a positive attitude toward brief treatment and the acquisition of specific clinical skills. Psychotherapy training within a HMO mental health service helps trainees acquire these professional skills by providing them with the following learning experiences:

1. The relatively rapid turnover of patients ensures that a greater number will be seen than if only a few were accepted and followed for a long period of time. The shifting caseload results in valuable exposure to more persons, problems, diagnoses, and treatment options;

2. Trainees are exposed to the multiplicity of perspective that a good HMO staff comprises. Cotherapy, peer review, hallway consultations, and case study seminars are easily available and provide highly valuable learning situations. Trainees also benefit from both the extended intensive experience of a cotherapy partnership as well as from the variety of viewpoints that can be brought to bear as a case is discussed during a staff meeting.

Supervision may be held on a one-to-one basis or (if there are enough trainees) within a group so that several trainees can learn from each case.

3. Institutional support such as videotape equipment, one-way mirrored observation rooms, and hired consultants are frequently a resource in some HMOs. It is important that HMO therapists, both trainees and experienced staff, not let the immediate needs of direct service provision so preoccupy them that they neglect their own needs for support, consultation, and professional development.

4. Training and working within a HMO structure promotes the inculcation of HMO therapy values and beliefs. Observing successful outcomes in individual cases as well as seeing the system successfully serve the needs of a large and diverse catchment population helps trainees and staff to appreciate the necessity and utility of brief therapy.

There are also potential disadvantages to learning psychotherapy in a HMO, suggesting that developing clinicians should have experience with diverse approaches and/or settings to round out their HMO therapy training:

1. The rapid turnover of cases tends to overemphasize quick assessment and rapid intervention and to minimize opportunities for more prolonged working through and attention to termination. The pressures of patient selection and the initial phases of treatment (including crisis services) allow comparatively little time for detailed case study. A trainee who is not yet comfortable working parsimoniously with a diversity of patients may feel overwhelmed or put upon by the pressure of his or her caseload.

2. Even if one prefers brief or short-term therapy, some supervised exposure to good long-term treatment will help a therapist to appreciate both the power and the limitations of short-term work.

Resistances and the Structure of Brief Therapy

Teachers of short-term therapy have come to recognize a series of "resistances" or counterproductive beliefs and barriers that will need to be confronted and overcome before the learning and practice of short-term therapy can proceed comfortably:

1. The belief that "more is better," often held despite the lack of evidence justifying the greater expense of long-term or open-ended treatment.

2. The myth of the "pure gold" of analysis—the overvaluation of insight and misassumption that change and growth require "deep" examination of an individual's unconscious and psychohistory.

3. The confusion of the patient's interests with the therapist's interests—the tendency of therapists to seek and perfectionistically treat putative complexes rather than attend directly to the patient's complaints and stated treatment goals.

4. The demand for hard work—the need for the brief therapist to be active, intensely alert, selectively focused, intuitive, and risk-taking.

5. Financial pressures—the temptation to hold on to that which is profitable and dependable.
6. Countertransference and termination problems—the need to be needed and the difficulties of saying goodbye (Hoyt, 1985, 1987, 1990).

Any of these resistances may be manifested at any point in the course of learning and practicing brief treatment, although different ones most often occur during the early, middle, and late part of the course of treatment, related to specific issues and strains associated with the different phases.

Brief psychotherapy (as well as other, more prolonged treatments) has five sequenced phases: selection, beginning, middle, end, and follow-through (Hoyt, 1986, 1990). In actual practice, of course, the phases blend into one another rather than being so discretely organized. The structure tends to be epigenetic or pyramidal, each phase building on the prior so that successful work in one is a precondition for the next. Also, there is often an interesting parallel between the microcosm and the macrocosm: the structure of each individual session resembles the overall course of treatment (Gustafson, 1986; Hoyt, 1979, 1990).

The *selection phase* involves choosing patients for therapy who are likely to be successful (Malan, 1976; Sifneos, 1987) and who do not have major contraindications or impediments. This can create an interesting dilemma, since those patients who are most suitable for short-term treatment (possessing high motivation for personal change, psychological mindedness, responsiveness to trial interventions, etc.) are also those who make the most desirable long-term patients. On the one hand, working with more responsive, relatively less difficult patients is important for both trainees who are developing their short-term skills and confidence, and for more experienced staff who need to have a satisfying mixture of cases. On the other hand, however, a manifestation of therapist resistance in this phase of brief therapy is the temptation to keep patients in therapy longer than is necessary. Unjustified treatment extension is both poor management of limited resources and unethical so therapists and supervisors must guard against the temptation to extend treatment for the attractive at the expense of the less fortunate.

The *beginning phase* of brief therapy involves making contact, forming a working alliance, orienting the patient regarding how to use treatment, establishing parameters, finding a psychological focus, and making a treatment contract. The therapist conveys the essential belief and expectation that change can occur *in the moment* and that the patient has within himself or herself the power to be different or to remain the same (Goulding & Goulding, 1978; 1979; Hoyt, 1990). The skillful brief therapist helps the patient to recognize his or her responsibility and thus facilitates the shift toward the patient's greater sense of autonomy and self-determination. Rapidly circumscribing an area of treatment, promoting problem solving more than analyzing unconscious material, maintaining an adult-to-adult alliance, and early confrontation of transference regression and the patient's avoidance of personal responsibility will be essential brief therapy activities that some clinicians will resist.

The *middle phase* of brief treatment involves refining the focus and "working through." This is a broadly used term that means both making the unconscious conscious, and, more generally, applying the lessons of therapy and making changes outside the treatment situation. "Insight" or "understanding" may be a desirable means (or epiphenomenon) toward change, but it is seldom a sufficient therapeutic goal in itself. In the middle phase of treatment, brief therapists may find themselves resisting the focusing activity that is often demanded. They may be tempted to confuse their own interests or agenda with those of their patients (Hoyt & Goulding, 1989).

The *end phase* may be relatively intense, especially if issues of loss and mourning are paramount in the therapeutic work (Hoyt, 1979; Hoyt & Farrell, 1984; Mann, 1973), or the ending phase may be relatively matter-of-fact. Regardless, therapists (and supervisors) must deal with their own feelings about termination. A number of complex issues may be involved, such as the disappointment and suspensefulness of incomplete work, the sorrow of ending intimacy, unresolved personal problems of loss, the "need to be needed," countertransference pulls to avoid ending, rescuing the patient, cramming extra work into the last few sessions, and the problem of relinquishing something lucrative.

The *follow-through phase* involves the continuation of psychological work and change beyond the formal ending date of therapist–patient contact. In short-term therapy much more than in typical long-term treatment, change processes may be initiated but not worked through before treatment ends. There is also the possibility of serial short-term therapy, where the patient returns for treatment in the future, often for problems related to life–developmental issues (Bennett, 1983, 1984; Budman & Gurman, 1988; Cummings, 1977; Hoyt, 1985, 1990). If the short-term therapist is to feel comfortable working in a brief framework, the patient's continued work after treatment and the possible return to therapy should usually be viewed as opportunities for future change and growth, rather than as "unresolved pathology" or "premature termination."

Parallel Processes Between Therapy and Supervision: Phase-Specific Resistances

Aspects of the patient–therapist relationship may be repeated in the therapist–supervisor relationship (Alonso & Rutan, 1988; Dasberg & Winokaur, 1984; Ekstein & Wallerstein, 1972; Hess, 1980; Zalcman & Cornell, 1983). This may enhance a trainee's empathy for his or her patient while allowing the supervisor to demonstrate effective treatment techniques in the method of supervision (Frances & Clarkin, 1981; Hoyt & Goulding, 1989), a desirable situation in which partial development of the trainee depends upon modeling and identification with the supervisor. This is a potentially powerful learning situation, but one that is also subtle and subject to distortions and abuse. Analogous to the interactions between patients and therapists, trainees and supervisors may enter into games and transactions that have more to do with gratifying desires for superiority or dependency than with promoting learning and change (Hawthorne, 1975; Kadushin, 1968). Even if trainee and supervisor have good intentions, there may be a tendency in the supervision situation to enact in parallel process certain resistances that are related to the strains of the specific phase of patient–therapist treatment in progress.

The *beginning phase* of supervision parallels the initial processes of therapist and patient evolving a working relationship, forming a treatment focus, and establishing the patient's recognition of his or her responsibility for making changes. At this time, the supervisor must be especially careful to foster the trainee's budding sense of competency. The supervisor must support nascent efforts toward selective focusing, confrontation, and rapport building. Supervisors need to avoid being overly critical or dazzling trainees with their knowledge and technical skill lest they demoralize them, or promote excessive dependency rather than inspire hope and effort. The supervisor teaches the trainee how to use supervision, and depending on the trainee's level of skill and experience, the supervisor and trainee will have to select one or two major foci to emphasize in supervision. The old saying, "If you're too well rounded, you're not pointed in any direction!" cautions against a possible pitfall in both therapy and supervision. As in the treatment contract, it may be helpful to have the trainee set specific goals for each session and for his or her overall supervision (Barnes, 1977; Berne, 1972; Goulding & Goulding, 1978; 1979).

The *middle phase* of supervision parallels the patient–therapist work of enhancing the patient's sense of autonomy, refining the focus, and working through both within the transference and in relationships outside of therapy. At this stage, the trainee's presentation may become unfocused and may lack specificity and purpose. The supervisor may be tempted to take over, to change the focus radically (without sufficient reason), and/or to pursue topics closer to his or her interests than those of the trainee. The urge to diffuse the treatment may parallel the therapist–patient situation. The emergence of resistance or negative feelings toward the supervisor, who inevitably can not give the trainee all that is desired (just as the trainee can not satisfy the patient), needs to be handled tactfully. Calling attention to the parallel process may be instructive, although the supervisor has to be especially careful not to be critical or blaming comments (e.g., "You're just like your patient!"). Constructive handling of the trainee–supervisor relationship during the beginning phase will lay the groundwork for the successful confrontation of tensions during the middle phase.

In the *end phase* of supervision, termination is the issue. Just as the therapist may be experiencing feelings of incompleteness, or guilt, or both, and the urge to extend therapy and somehow "rescue" the patient, the supervisor may experience similar sentiments. He or she may desire to continue supervision beyond the cut-off date, may feel unrealistically that he or she has not done an adequate job, or may try to cram unassimilable amounts of clinical lore and wisdom into the last supervision meetings. The trainee, not feeling "totally educated" and competent, may invite and welcome these eleventh-hour desperations. However, it is better for therapist and supervisor to learn about countertransference through the experience rather than through enactment.

Conclusion

Interest in short-term therapy has increased tremendously in recent years and the basic belief of the effective brief therapist that significant and enduring changes can be facilitated quickly through skilled intervention has been increasingly borne out by both systematic research and individual experience (Koss and Butcher, 1986; Malan, 1976; Strupp & Binder, 1984). Clinicians need to be willing and able to practice effective brief therapy if the needs of more than a handful of patients are to be served. This reality, which is the backbone of HMO therapy, provides the mandate (Cummings, 1986; Hoyt, 1985; Kovacs, 1982) for the expanded teaching and learning of brief therapy (Clarkin, Frances, Taintor, & Warburg, 1980). A wide variety of specific theoretical and technical approaches have been developed, and much can be learned by reading, attending conferences and workshops, observation, and autodidacticism. The pressures and problems inherent in doing psychotherapy are quite pervasive, however, and we all are subject, from time to time, to developing counterproductive patterns or blind spots. Therapists who find themselves recently stuck or at a loss may benefit from consultation with a trusted peer or with a professionally skilled supervisor. Good supervision, like good therapy, pays for itself many times over.

References

Alonso, A., & Rutan, J. S. (1988). Shame and guilt in psychotherapy supervision. *Psychotherapy, 25,* 576–581.

Austad, C. S., DeStefano, L., & Kisch, J. (1988). The health maintenance organization: II. Implications for psychotherapy. *Psychotherapy, 25,* 449–454.

Barnes, G. (1977). Techniques of contractual supervision. In M. James (Ed.), *Techniques in transactional analysis for psychotherapists and counselors* (pp. 166–175). Reading, MA: Addison-Wesley.

Bennett, M. J. (1983). Focal psychotherapy: Terminable and interminable. *American Journal of Psychotherapy, 37,* 365–375.

Bennett, M. J. (1984). Brief psychotherapy and adult development. *Psychotherapy, 21,* 171–177.

Bennett, M. J., & Wisneski, M. J. (1979). Continuous psychotherapy within an HMO. *American Journal of Psychiatry, 136,* 1283–1287.

Berne, E. (1972). *What do you say after you say hello?* New York: Grove Press.

Budman, S. H., Feldman, J., & Bennett, M. J. (1979). Adult mental health services in a health maintenance organization. *American Journal of Psychiatry, 136,* 392–395.

Budman, S. H., & Gurman, A. S. (1983). The practice of brief therapy. *Professional Psychology, 14,* 277–292.

Budman, S. H., & Gurman, A. S. (1988). *Theory and practice of brief therapy.* New York: Guilford.

Cheifetz, D. I., & Salloway, J. C. (1984). Mental health services in health maintenance organizations: Implications for psychotherapy. *Professional Psychology: Research and Practice, 15,* 152–164.

Clarkin, J. F., Frances, A., Taintor, Z., & Warburg, M. (1980). Training in brief therapy: A survey of psychiatric residency programs. *American Journal of Psychiatry, 136,* 392–395.

Cummings, N. A. (1977). Prolonged (ideal) versus short-term (realistic) psychotherapy. *Professional Psychology, 4,* 491–501.

Cummings, N. A. (1986). The dismantling of our health system: Strategies for the survival of psychological practice. *American Psychologist, 41,* 426–431.

Cummings, N. A. (1988). Emergence of the mental health complex: Adaptive and maladaptive responses. *Professional Psychology: Research and Practice , 19,* 308–315.

Dasberg, H., & Winokaur, M. (1984). Teaching and learning short-term dynamic psychotherapy: Parallel processes. *Psychotherapy, 21,* 184–188.

DeLeon, P. H., Uyeda, M. K., & Welch, B. L. (1985). Psychology and HMOs: New partnership or new adversary? *American Psychologist, 40,* 1122–1124.

Ekstein, R., & Wallerstein, R. S. (1972). *The teaching and learning of psychotherapy* (2nd ed.). New York: International Universities Press.

Frances, A., & Clarkin, J. (1981). Parallel techniques in supervision and treatment. *Psychiatric Quarterly, 53,* 242–248.

Frances, A., Clarkin, J., & Perry, S. (1984). *Differential therapeutics in psychiatry: The art and science of treatment selection.* New York: Brunner/Mazel.

Goldensohn, S. S. (1977). Cost, utilization, and utilization review of mental health services in a prepaid group practice plan. *American Journal of Psychiatry, 131*, 256–260.

Goldensohn, S. S., & Haar, E. (1974). Transference and countertransference in a third-party payment system (HMO). *American Journal of Psychiatry, 131*, 256–260.

Goulding, R., & Goulding, M. (1978). *The power is in the patient.* San Francisco: Transactional Analysis Press.

Goulding, M., & Goulding, R. (1979). *Changing lives through redecision therapy.* New York: Brunner/Mazel.

Gustafson, J. P. (1986). *The complex secret of brief psychotherapy.* New York: Norton.

Hawthorne, L. (1975). Games supervisors play. *Social Work, 20*, 179–183.

Hess, A. K. (1980) (Ed.). *Psychotherapy supervision: Theory, research, and practice*, New York: Wiley.

Hoyt, M. F. (1979). Aspects of termination in a time-limited brief psychotherapy. *Psychiatry, 42*, 208–219.

Hoyt, M. F. (1985). Therapist resistances to short-term dynamic psychotherapy. *Journal of the American Academy of Psychoanalysis, 13*, 93–112.

Hoyt, M. F. (1986). Mental-imagery methods in short-term dynamic psychotherapy. In M. Wolpin, J. Shorr, & L. Krueger (Eds.), *Imagery 4.* New York: Plenum.

Hoyt, M. F. (1987). Resistances to brief therapy. *American Psychologist, 42*, 408–409.

Hoyt, M. F. (1988). Letter to the editor. *The Milton Erickson Foundation Newsletter, 9*(1), 5.

Hoyt, M. F. (1989). Psychodiagnosis of personality disorders: A guide for the perplexed. *Transactional Analysis Journal, 19*, 101–113.

Hoyt, M. F. (1990). On time in brief therapy. In R. Wells & V. Gianetti (Eds.). *Handbook of the brief psychotherapies,* New York: Plenum.

Hoyt, M. F., & Austad, C. (in press). Psychotherapy in a staff-model health maintenance organization: Providing and assuring quality care in the future. *Psychotherapy.*

Hoyt, M. F., & Farrell, D. (1984). Countertransference difficulties in a time-limited psychotherapy. *International Journal of Psychoanalytic Psychotherapy, 10*, 191–203.

Hoyt, M. F., & Goulding, M. (in press). Rapid resolution of a transference-countertransference impasse using Gestalt techniques in supervision. *Transactional Analysis Journal* (?).

Kadushin, A. (1968). Games people play in supervision. *Social Work, 13*(3), 23–32.

Kiesler, C. A., & Morton, T. L. (1988). Psychology and public policy in the "health care revolution." *American Psychologist, 43*, 993–1003.

Kisch, J., & Austad, C. S. (1988). The health maintenance organization: Historical perspectives and current status. *Psychotherapy, 25*, 441–448.

Koss, M. P., & Butcher, J. N. (1986). Research on brief psychotherapy. In S. W. Garfield & A. E. Bergin (Eds.), *Handbook of psychotherapy and behavior change: An empirical analysis* (3rd ed.), pp. 627–670. New York: Wiley.

Kovacs, A. L. (1982). Survival in the '80s: On the theory and practice of brief psychotherapy. *Psychotherapy: Theory, Research, and Practice, 19*, 142–159.

Lange, M. A., Chandler-Guy, Forti, R., Foster-Moore, P., & Rohman, M. (1988). Providers' views of HMO mental health services. *Psychotherapy, 25*, 455–462.

Malan, D. H. (1976). *The frontier of brief psychotherapy.* New York: Plenum.

Mann, J. (1973). *Time-limited psychotherapy.* Cambridge, MA: Harvard University Press.

Reider, N. (1953). A type of transference to institution. *Journal of Hillside Hospital, 2*, 23–29.

Rosenbaum, R., Hoyt, M. F., & Talmon, M. (1990). The challenge of single-session therapies: Creating pivotal moments. In R. Wells & V. Giannetti (Eds.), *Handbook of the brief psychotherapies.* New York: Plenum.

Shulman, M. E. (1988). Cost containment in clinical psychology: Critique of Biodyne and HMOs. *Professional Psychology: Research and Practice, 19*, 298–307.

Sifneos, P. E. (1987). *Short-term dynamic psychotherapy: Evaluation and technique* (rev. ed.). New York: Plenum.

Strupp, H. H., & Binder, J. L. (1984). *Psychotherapy in a new key: A guide book to time-limited psychotherapy.* New York: Basic Books.

Tulkin, S. R., & Frank, G. W. (1985). The changing role of psychologists in health maintenance organizations. *American Psychologist, 40*, 1125–1130.

Winokaur, M., & Dasberg, H. (1983). Teaching and learning short-term dynamic psychotherapy. *Bulletin of the Meninger Clinic, 47*, 36–52.

Zalcman, M. J., & Cornell, W. F. (1983). A bilateral model for clinical supervision. *Transactional Analysis Journal, 13*, 112–123.

Part III

Interventions with Specific Populations

8

Jerry Adams

Family Crisis Intervention and Psychosocial Care for Children and Adolescents

The Setting

The San Diego Kaiser Permanente Medical Care Program is part of the nation's largest health maintenance organization, serving over 380,000 members in San Diego County, most of whom enroll through their employers. All members have mental health benefits, which include up to 20 outpatient visits per calendar year. Specific contracts vary across subscriber groups, and some require substantial copayments for services provided.

Mental health services were available in six widely dispersed locations, through five divisions: (a) the Chemical Dependency Recovery Program; (b) the Adult Direct Services Division, an adult mental health service; (c) the Acute Psychiatry Service, including a "Crisis Team" located in the hospital Emergency Medicine Department (described in Wojdowski & Hartnett, 1985); (d) the Clinic Psychosocial Services Division, which provided "secondary mental health services" within primary care settings, for both adults and children (described in Adams & Kagnoff, 1983); and (e) the Child and Adolescent Direct Services Division (CADS).

The CADS staff included psychiatrists, psychologists, psychiatric social workers, and specially trained clerical staff. CADS offered or participated in a wide range of special services for children, adolescents, and their families including: a variety of psychotherapy groups; parenting classes, including classes on behavior management techniques, step-parenting, managing children with attention deficit disorder, teen issues, and separation and divorce; integrated medical/psychosocial chronic illness clinics, including pediatric hematology–oncology, diabetes, and neuropsychiatry; a child protection program, designed to provide preventive, early intervention, identification, and treatment services; and an enuresis and encopresis clinic (Carstens, 1988).

Preparation of this chapter was supported by the Kaiser Permanente Medical Care Program.

The author gratefully acknowledges the members of the Family Crisis Intervention Team who developed and nurtured this service; the support of innovation by Department Chief Dan Funkenstein, MD; and the guidance of Child and Adolescent Direct Services Coordinator Marcia Kagnoff, EdD, both for her role in development and maintenance of the FCIT and for her cogent comments on a draft of this paper.

Americans are fond of asserting that "our children are our most precious resource." Paradoxically, children and adolescents are often left to their own resources or are exposed to substantial risk in many situations:

- Many thousands of "latchkey" children raise themselves several hours a day, while realistic day care resources remain the subject of political debate (Fosarelli, 1984).
- Hundreds of thousands of youth run away from or are ejected from their homes (Hersch, 1988).
- Drug abuse impairs the functioning of millions of adolescents, many of whose parents contribute to the problem by either condoning the behavior or ignoring its existence (Kandel, 1982).
- Hundreds of thousands of adolescents are having children who, in turn, are at substantial risk for physical and emotional difficulties (Marecek, 1987).
- Thousands of children are abused or molested, while adults debate ways to accommodate how children communicate their experiences so their tormentors can be held accountable and the children can be protected (Dougherty, 1988).

This list of risks to our youth could be expanded substantially (Anderson, Williams, McGee, & Silva, 1987), and the number of children and adolescents affected multiplies daily, even as resources are curtailed (Klerman, 1988). Concurrently, the dramatic increase in the cost of health care and the move to make such care universally available (Enthoven & Kronick, 1989), have produced significant changes in its financing (see Austad and Berman, in this volume). Indeed, financial constraints have become a major determinant of health care practices in the United States. Advocates of mental health services for children are especially concerned about reduced funding, because children are so vulnerable and their needs often are overlooked.[1] Some express fear that profits will take precedence over the quality of care in prepaid mental health services. Bennett and Gavalya (1982) have described a comprehensive array of mental health services for children at Harvard Community Health Plan; however, little empirical research is available to clarify the fit between the needs and the available resources.

The economies of scale inherent in the large San Diego Kaiser Permanente health maintenance organization (HMO) made possible the development and implementation of a carefully planned, integrated array of services for youth and their families (Adams & Kagnoff, 1983). However, in that program from 1981 to 1989 there were annual increases in the rate of demand for psychosocial services for youth that ranged from about 10–30%. The combination of growing demands for services with stagnant or declining funding dictated an increased focus on efficiency and, in turn, heightened concern about the quality of services for children.

Another factor added to the challenge of meeting growing needs with shrinking resources: as many as a third of all requests for services for youth in the San Diego

---

[1] See Robin, 1982, for a moving review of the evolution of Western society's notions about the welfare of children.

Kaiser Permanente program involved a distinct crisis component, consistent with reports from other settings (Cooper & Wanerman, 1984). While available services were responsive to many needs, care for urgent cases was haphazard, relying on the individual clinician to fit cases into already heavy schedules. Only the most emergent cases were seen quickly, and many distressed patients had to wait for mental health services. This had a negative impact on patients, allowing them to consolidate maladaptive patterns of functioning. In addition, when routine care was disrupted by urgent cases, staff stress and patient complaints increased.

These considerations defined a significant challenge to our service delivery system: How could our mental health professionals respond rapidly and efficiently to increasing demands for urgent care for children, adolescents, and their families, without reducing more routine but equally important services? In response, the staff at Kaiser Permanente in San Diego identified the need for a family crisis intervention program as a pivotal component of our child and adolescent services. This program was designed to meet the need for crisis care while preserving the capacity to provide a broad spectrum of noncrisis psychosocial services. This led to exploration of the most efficacious way to develop such a service.

Development of the Family Crisis Intervention Team

"Crisis intervention" is a contractual benefit of most HMOs (Chiefetz and Salloway, 1985), but virtually none provide a clear definition of the services to be provided, and, ironically, little has been written to guide the application of crisis theory or practice in an HMO. Some authors on crisis intervention focus on any situation in which an individual expresses upset, regardless of its acuteness (e.g., Polk, 1982), while others concentrate on problem-solving techniques and community resources that could be brought to bear on the patients' problems (e.g., Fraser, 1986). In contrast, the Los Angeles Benjamin Rush Center for Problems in Living has long provided a very specific crisis intervention model (Jacobson, Wilner, Morley, Schneider, Strickler, & Sommer, 1965).

Gerald Caplan, the founder of community psychiatry, provided the now classic definition of a crisis (1961) as follows:

. . . a crisis is provoked when a person faces an obstacle to important life goals that is, for a time, insurmountable through the utilization of customary methods of problem solving. A period of disorganization ensues, a period of upset, during which many different abortive attempts at solutions are made. Eventually some kind of adaptation is achieved, which may or may not be in the best interests of that person or his fellows. (p. 18)

The Rush Center group found that while in crisis, people are unusually receptive to guidance and are especially open to restructuring their psychological processes, providing a window of opportunity for substantial positive change with appropriate intervention. As can be seen in the discussion below, crisis intervention differs from other forms of psychological treatment in a number of important ways; perhaps most central is its focus upon using the intense affect associated with the crisis state in order to enhance the prospects for constructive change. Success in this effort depends upon effectively addressing crucial current issues and their affective connections to suddenly reactivated past events while that affect is still readily available, a matter of days at most.

The Rush Center model originally had an individual treatment focus based in psychoanalytic theory (Jacobson, 1967), but also incorporated Caplan's (1961) community/prevention emphasis (Jacobson, Strickler, & Morley, 1968). Jacobson and his colleagues continued to refine their work over the next two decades. The concepts of that group appeared to be increasingly influenced by learning theory and more recently by cognitive psychology (see Jacobson, 1980, 1983; Hobbs, 1984).

Bonnefil and Jacobson (1979) described an adaptation of the Rush Center approach for families that is particularly relevant to this discussion. They emphasized the impact of a crisis upon all participating family members and provided guidelines for treatment. D. Jacobson (1980) described the application of the model to families experiencing a crisis in response to blending into step-families.

The San Diego Kaiser Permanente staff decided to adapt the Rush Center model (Jacobson, et al., 1965) to development of a new service to provide prompt and organized services to children, adolescents, and families in our system, who presented in a state of crisis. This program was called the Family Crisis Intervention Team (FCIT), the specific goals of which were (a) to provide patients in crisis rapid access to planned services; (b) to return patients to precrisis or improved functioning; and (c) to make each session a complete intervention, so that even patients who do not return gain some significant understanding of how to help themselves.

Interventions were structured in keeping with the Rush Center model (see Bonnefil & Jacobson, 1979; Bonnefil, 1980). The person requesting an appointment was asked to come in, along with the identified youth and anyone else in the family relevant to the presenting problem. Both parents were asked to participate, when they lived in the same household. In practice, the number of people attending the first session ranged from two to eight or so, but most commonly from two to four. The inclusion of young children was usually encouraged. Bonnefil (1980) noted that generally families presented when parents were in crisis, but that children may benefit by witnessing their parents' efforts, and sometimes by active participation. Experience demonstrated that even very young children can contribute greatly to the process in a direct way:

> A three-year-old boy, brought to a third session with his mother and 15-year-old half-sister because of baby sitter problems, sat passively on his mother's lap as the others heatedly described his father's difficult style of parenting. Suddenly the boy demanded loudly, "Stop talking!" With encouragement he revealed his distress at family arguments and the burden he had assumed of attempting to stop them. As his mother came to recognize this, she acknowledged fears that her husband had returned to using drugs, a major and previously unrevealed dynamic of this family.[2]

Family members were told that they had "up to six visits" to work on their concerns. In general, first meetings lasted from 90 minutes to two hours, with subsequent meetings lasting 45 to 60 minutes. Visits were usually scheduled weekly, but could be as frequent as several times a week if the family's needs so dictated.

---

[2] All clinical vignettes used in this paper were derived from actual case material, but facts were materially altered to ensure no patients can be identified.

An important premise of the FCIT was that people are capable of managing their own lives and making decisions regarding what is best for them. Consistent with this perspective, the timing of termination was decided primarily by the families themselves, with the guidance of the consultant. In some cases the consultant might urge continued treatment to protect a family member, such as a suicidal adolescent or an abused child.

Components of Evaluation and Treatment

The Rush Center model required an active, disciplined, and intensive approach to evaluation and treatment. The following tasks were accomplished in the first, particularly demanding session, and followed up in each subsequent meeting. The component tasks of family crisis intervention are presented here in a logical sequence, but the families were allowed to proceed in their own way, as long as all the components were covered with each family member present:

1. Determine Who is in Crisis

The initial call for an appointment provides important information. It is essential to know who is requesting the appointment and who suggested it. The latter may be someone outside the family, such as a school counselor, and the specified "problem" may not precipitate a crisis for the family. In a crisis situation, some members of the family may be in crisis while others may not. Care is taken to determine the level of upset and disruption experienced by each family member. Occasionally, even careful examination finds no one present to be in crisis, either because delay allowed some level of resolution or because a crisis had not actually occurred. In such a situation, a circumscribed problem of concern to the family is selected and addressed, still within six visits.

2. Determine the Symptoms of Each Person in Crisis

In any crisis situation, an important component of the evaluation is assessment of the specific dysfunctions and symptomatology in each individual, particularly in the identified patient. It is essential to assess risk to self or others and any acute psychotic symptoms and to evaluate the need to respond to these. Second, detailing the nature and severity of symptoms provides information regarding functioning of members and of the family system, which guides later steps of the intervention.

3. Identify the Hazard Leading to the Crisis, for Each Person in Crisis

The concept of hazard is central to the Rush Center model and refers to the specific life event that prevents fulfillment of an important need, and which for some people will result in a crisis. In general, the hazard involves a loss, which in some way represents a threat to the sense of self (Caplan, 1961). For example, divorce or the death of a loved one represents a potential block to many important needs; for some it produces a crisis in their lives beyond the normal grieving process. The hazard often is not evident, and the clinician must pursue its identification tenaciously. Some patients find the necessary persistence to be frustrating or irritating, but it is essential. Determining "why now" and "what's new" in the family situation will clarify the basis of the current crisis, and help to shape the interventions.

> An eight-year-old boy, upon returning from visiting his father in another state, was noncompliant and challenging with his mother and stepfather. A few weeks later, when criticized for this behavior, he said, in tears, that he did not want to live anymore. The hazard for the parents was obvious; they feared the loss of their son. However, the hazard for the boy was elusive. He had been disappointed by his father's inattentiveness during his stay with him and his lack of contact since, but this did not explain his sudden wish not to live. Only with persistent probing was it discovered that the night before he had telephoned his paternal grandmother, who had told him that the father had not called her for some weeks and therefore must not love her "either." This probably casual comment seemed to confirm the boy's fears that his father no longer loved him, and criticism by his other parents heightened the fear of abandonment, which represented the hazard from which his crisis developed.

4. Determine the Meaning of the Hazard (Loss), for Each Person

The meaning of the hazard determines the impact of the event upon an individual or family. Understanding it provides the focus for the rest of the intervention. As with any significant life event, the meaning is determined by a combination of both present and past aspects of the patients' lives as they experience the crisis.

The hazard within each life event for each family member may be different, and questioning each person is critical. For example, the death of a grandmother may be a hazard to the mother, while the hazard for the child may be the loss of his mother's attention while she is focused on her own mourning.

5. Determine Affective Connections to the Family's Past Experiences

During crises, usual coping strategies prove inadequate in part because the situation seems entirely unfamiliar, leading to a sense of helplessness. One of the factors that makes the Rush Center model so powerful is the focus upon understanding the emotional connections between the crisis feeling state and related past experiences.

The consultant helps family members to discover salient past affects by summarizing their current dissonant feelings and then asking, "When in your life have you felt *most* like you have been feeling during this crisis?", to elicit related prior experiences. Although many patients initially deny any such experiences, with gentle persistence most are helped to identify old emotions that have remained salient and contribute directly to the present crisis. Often recall of past feelings is accompanied by intense emotion. Many patients recall more than one germane experience, and together these may more fully reveal the reasons for the breakdown in current coping.

A 13-year-old boy whose mother had died of cancer four years earlier was stopped by his peers from intentionally walking in front of a speeding truck. He had had an argument with a special girlfriend, and he felt that without his mother he could not learn how to deal with girls. He acknowledged feeling depressed and hopeless, as he had when his mother died. He had been alone with her the day before she died, when she cried in apparent pain and tried to talk to him but could not; he did not know what to do and finally left. Since then he had been burdened with the sense that he "should have done something to help her," and cried profusely as he talked of this. Thus, the affect engendered by his current insecurity with girls and his longing for his mother's guidance related directly to his unresolved feelings about the loss of his mother and his sense of inadequacy in meeting her needs. By the third session he was able to remind himself how young he had been when she died, and that "nine-year-olds don't know much about how to help adults."

6. Determine the Relevant Past Coping Resources, for Each Person

In crisis intervention, it is necessary, but not sufficient, to identify the current hazard and its connection to past crises and losses. How the individuals and the family coped with the salient past hazard is equally important. Most people can recall a number of attempts to cope with a prior crisis, and recalling their previous coping strategies can help to identify an appropriate approach to the current situation:

A 14-year-old girl overdosed on pills after witnessing conflict among her best friends. She related her sad and frightened feelings to earlier years, when her parents had argued heatedly prior to their divorce. She recalled leaving the house on those occasions to avoid the distress she felt, but she had not considered leaving her friends during the conflicts because she felt responsible for stopping them. When she realized she had a workable alternative, she was able to leave when her friends fought, and felt much less overwhelmed by the conflicts.

7. Determine Components of the Crisis That Render Past Coping Resources Ineffective, for Each Person

People in crisis typically feel helpless and hopeless, so problems feel insurmountable. Identifying commonalities with past hazards and with prior coping strategies provides a focus for current efforts. Specifying the aspects of the current hazard that are new and require different tactics narrows the focus and reduces the sense of helplessness. As patients work through this process, they can experience their past mastery of similar difficulties and concentrate on developing coping strategies to deal with the novel aspects of the current crisis, rather than attempting to cope with what had seemed like a completely new situation:

A 13-year-old girl had lived with her divorced mother for six years but became depressed and suicidal when she learned that her father was going to marry the woman with whom he had lived for three years. She felt overwhelmed, until helped to realize that she had coped with her parents' divorce for years and now had only to learn to deal with the loss of her private fantasy that they would someday reconcile.

8. Formulate the Dynamic Relationships Among the Present and Past Interpersonal and Emotional Aspects of the Crisis for the Family

The dynamic formulation of the crisis and its complex of elements requires an understanding of how the various aspects interrelate. Past experiences identified as "most like" the current one must be related to the impasse producing the crisis and to the reactions of various family members. This formulation requires an understanding both of individual and family dynamics and of normal developmental and social processes. It is both highly challenging and a critical component of the intervention process.

9. Provide Family Members With a Cognitive Grasp of What Has Happened

When sufficiently clear, the formulation is communicated to the family as simply as possible so all members can understand it. Traditional psychodynamic therapies recommend great care in the amount and timing of any "interpretations" offered patients, based upon concern about readiness to accept them. In contrast, patients in crisis typically are found to be open to and able to benefit from a detailed account of relevant individual and family dynamics.

10. Support Affective Integration of What Has Happened

In addition to a cognitive understanding of the crisis, affective appreciation of the interrelationships between events and experiences is critical. While patients may readily comprehend the cognitive aspects, many defend themselves against the painful affects that make them meaningful; treatment is complete only when each person in crisis fully appreciates the still salient and painful emotions evoked by past experiences, as well as those related to the current situation. Because of the nature of crises, special attention must be given to feelings of guilt, anger, fear, and sadness. For example, loss through death may produce overt feelings of sadness and guilt, while anger is denied, but loss due to divorce may lead to denial of sadness but acknowledgement of anger and perhaps some guilt. Patients may need help experiencing the dissonant affects and often are freed by doing so to then address conflicts remaining from past experiences.

> A 33-year-old woman quit her job and moved to San Diego to be with a man she had met a few weeks earlier. She brought to the clinic her seven-year-old son who was "out of control" at home and school. After assessment the consultant explained that the boy was acting out his insecurity. This threatened the mother's fantasy of a wonderful new life because of her fear that her fiance would abandon them as the boy's father had, in response to her son's behavior. Her fears fed his, he acted out more, and his behavior increased her insecurity. The mother understood the cognitive explanation, but initially resisted the affective experience,

blandly asserting, "Maybe you're right." With guidance she was able to reexperience her feelings of abandonment by the boy's father, and the anger and guilt she had suppressed. As she reflected on the loss, she sobbed about the panic she had felt and how she had trusted the man; she could then acknowledge how difficult it was to trust the constancy of the new man in her life.

11. Mobilize Family Members' Coping Resources

It is important for people to appreciate both cognitively and affectively what has happened to them. However, the family also must deal directly with the current practical situation more effectively, and not return to the previous sense of helplessness. This may require direct support of the family's efforts to resolve the situation, guided by their new insight into prior effective efforts at coping with crises, and an understanding of the aspects of the new situation that contributed to the impasse. Even families that appear quite dysfunctional may have histories of surviving the most challenging difficulties. The consultant's respect for this strength can foster remarkable capacities to cope, even with situations that seem overwhelming to the consultant.

A primary resource for crisis resolution lies in social supports; ironically, it is often especially difficult for families in crisis to seek such support. Families may isolate themselves during a crisis or may have been isolated for a long time. In either case, enlarging their interpersonal support system may foster recovery. Patients with limited interpersonal skills require more active guidance, such as assistance in locating suitable self-help groups or other social contacts. With others, simple encouragement may be sufficient to reactivate friendships or extended family ties.

The final task is to aid family members in consolidating their gains, so that as new hazards arise, they can apply what they have learned in order to cope. The consultant guides review of what was learned and of ways it might be applied to future difficulties. The consultant typically is fairly inactive here, but may summarize when members cannot do so.

Some families demonstrate additional issues that could be addressed with a few more treatment sessions. However, for the crisis intervention consultant to pursue that effort would directly undermine the full impact of the model and compromise the discipline of the consultant. A central feature of the process is the enhancement of coping by family members, and fostering dependency is counterproductive. Similarly, for the consultant, commitment to supporting the family's mastery is paramount. As a result, the agreement of "up to" six visits was strictly enforced by all FCIT staff members. It is worthy of note that even the most seasoned of the consultants at the Rush Center maintain this strict standard, and it is one that experience strongly supports.

Disposition of a crisis case upon closing depends upon the interests of the family, the nature of any remaining problems, the consultant's judgment about the treatability of the family, and such factors as the nature of the mental health benefits available. Most cases served by the FCIT were considered completed at termination by both the consultant and the family, and required no additional services. Even those who expressed interest in additional treatment were encouraged to take a recess, so as to consolidate their gains from the crisis work; in part this meant learning to trust their own resources for coping, a component of the model that focuses on prevention of future crises. However, a few family members were referred directly to therapy groups or psychoeducational classes. Less than 10% of cases required and were thought likely to benefit from continuing family or individual services; most of these were transferred by prior arrangement to a therapist on another CADS team.

Special Challenges in Family Crisis Intervention

The challenge of applying the Rush Center model to children and families is substantial. Information abounds in each session, often expressed in bits and pieces by various family members; in addition, much of what children express may be conveyed through modeling clay, drawings, or restless behavior. Parents may resist exploration of family dynamics by focusing only on their children's symptoms. It is also common for families to defend a member who appears bothered by persistent questioning, diverting time and energy from the task at hand. Key individuals may not attend, such as a father who tells the mother to "do something" about a child's behavior, but then refuses to participate.

Successful crisis intervention depends upon avoidance of side issues that can foster incoherence and disarray. This is especially important in family work because of the overabundance of material and the number of people with separate notions about what is important.

The consultant sensitively supports and reinforces efforts to change. Praise that is too effusive or poorly related to patient behaviors can ring hollow and reinforce the patients' own sense of fragility and incompetence. On the other hand, failure to acknowledge constructive efforts may undermine the patients' confidence. Clarifying and acknowledging progress can provide an accurate perspective on the family's capacity to function independently.

Considerations in Retaining Staff to Do Crisis Intervention

Few therapists are trained in the sort of crisis intervention described here, yet nearly all clinicians practice what they consider to be "crisis intervention." Many assume there is nothing new to learn, or express resistance in a variety of other ways (see Hoyt, in this volume). However, therapists who are invested in mastering this approach emphasize the need to be highly disciplined and focused, and for specific training and ongoing support.

To support relearning, the CADS staff established a weekly seminar to study the available literature on crisis intervention. In addition, a workshop was arranged with a psychologist who helped develop and actively practiced in the Rush Center model. The new Family Crisis Intervention Team was formed and began seeing patients. Members presented new cases for team discussion on a regular basis. Members of the FCIT were uniformly positive about their work. All staff valued intervening soon after services were requested, while the affect associated with the crisis remained accessible. Morale on the team remained excellent, and burnout was not a significant problem.

The team also adapted a set of forms from the Rush Center designed to facilitate structured crisis evaluation and intervention planning. These were modified to allow the recording of data from all family members present. Completing these forms required detailing all of the elements of the crisis and the planned intervention, a key to disciplined work. The FCIT used these forms as an essential guide to maintaining the standards of the model. Prior to the first session, parents were given a questionnaire to complete that requested information about the family, the current problem, recent stresses, and various other relevant background issues. Adolescents were given a separate questionnaire, to elicit their views on similar matters. The referral form and the questionnaires were considered a central part of the clinical data base, along with the crisis evaluation and intervention planning form completed by the consultant.

Integration into the Larger CADS Program

Development and integration of the FCIT into the overall CADS child and adolescent care system required substantial organizational and professional planning.

A set of performance standards that embodied the priorities of the staff and clarified the interfaces and the responsibilities of providers both on and off the new team had to be developed. Criteria were established for redistributing staff to meet fluctuating demands: (a) families with emergencies were to be seen the same day, and all other crisis cases were seen within five calendar days of the request, preferably considerably sooner; (b) a full-time FCIT clinician was assigned four new urgent appointments and scheduled one "On Duty" slot per week; and (c) if additional cases were referred, they were assigned according to contingencies that included temporarily increasing caseloads and involving other staff. The primary goal was to ensure that crisis cases were seen rapidly.

Screening and assignment of cases were based on a rational decision-making process. Specially trained receptionists gathered substantial data from patients, guided by a set of "red flags" designed to highlight various risk factors. The receptionists also were encouraged to use their own interpersonal sensitivity to provide their "feel" for the urgency of the presentation. A clinician then reviewed all requests for services soon after they were received, deciding on scheduling priorities using any available data; this might include calling the person who requested the appointment. Patients were scheduled in accordance with the level of urgency. It was assumed that anyone in a genuine crisis would accept the first available appointment even if it were somewhat inconvenient, and this generally proved to be the case.

Plans for return appointments were made between the consultant and the family, based upon their shared view of what was needed. Typically appointments were scheduled at weekly intervals, but in especially intense situations they were more frequent. Termination, an integral part of the treatment process, was managed to further the family's sense of its own competence in handling difficult situations. As sessions progressed, the consultant played a less active role and supported the efforts of the family members to resolve problems.

Service Utilization

In 1987 CADS received about 2,500 requests for services. About 85% of these were scheduled for appointments; the remainder were handled by telephone, referred to more appropriate services, and so on. Of the over 2,100 families scheduled, about 35% or some 750 were assigned to FCIT consultants, whose collective work on the team represented about three to three and one-half "full time equivalents." Each full-time equivalent was scheduled to see about one new family in crisis per eight-hour day.

Presenting problems varied widely, but the most common involved attempts to escape intolerable situations: intense school avoidance, some type of suicidal behavior, runaway behavior, and/or substance abuse. Many young people presented as acutely depressed, and many others as agitated and very upset. A number of patients showed other anxiety disorders or were psychotic. Parents often complained of out-of-control behavior at home and school. Aggressive and even criminal behaviors were also common complaints, as were child molestation and abuse.

Family Member Acceptance and Satisfaction

Patient satisfaction with CADS services improved, with fewer complaints and more expressions of appreciation for the prompt service. In addition, most families readily comprehended and accepted the specific focus of the model, including attention to how each member was affected by the crisis. Very few patients had a fixed expectation for length of treatment, and nearly all those in crisis understood the reasons for the six-session limitation; only a few people with past therapy experience focused on "getting therapy," while the rest emphasized the need for problem resolution. Most FCIT cases terminated after fewer than six sessions, indicating that the time limitation did not impede the treatment process.

Observable Changes

One of the most tangible results of using this model was a substantial reduction in requests by frightened and angry parents for hospitalization of their children or adolescents. The rate of hospitalization for children and adolescents was low, even in the face of increasing demands. In 1987, from a membership of approximately 95,000 aged less than 18 years, 53 patients were hospitalized, or approximately 5.6 per 10,000, for an average of 24.3 days each. While no exactly comparable national figures for acute hospitalizations are available, the national admission rate appeared to be about 12.8 per 10,000, and the median length of stay to be between about 27 and 35 days (Manderscheid & Barrett, 1987).

In a small study of patient flow, family crisis intervention cases were seen for a mean of about 4.5 hours, which included a two-hour initial appointment and a mean of 2.5 additional appointments. Fewer than 20% of families were referred for additional care of any kind. FCIT families reapplied for subsequent help about as frequently as those seen in the more traditional service; this was true even though a fair number of FCIT families are "crisis prone" and often do not follow through well on interventions.

Limitations to the Approach

The effectiveness of crisis intervention depends largely upon addressing readily available affect generated by a recent breakdown in coping. Individuals who experience delay in getting help typically adopt some strategy intended to reduce their distress, and when this occurs, the model is much less effective. Our experience suggested that the interpersonal interplay within the family accelerated this process. If circumstances delayed contact for more than four or five days, the affect might again be sealed over; in some instances this occurred within 48 hours. When this happened, it still was possible to focus on a specific time-limited goal, but the dynamic potency of crisis intervention was unlikely to be achieved. Beyond this constraint, the approach proved to be applicable to most people presenting in crisis to our HMO's outpatient mental health service.

We must stress that family crisis intervention was not a panacea that effectively addressed all difficulties. Generally, long-standing problems of any sort were not likely to show significant change as a result of crisis intervention, although crisis elements superimposed on those problems may have been relieved and family members may have gained some perspective on how to cope with future crises. Most patients presenting with chronic problems were not triaged to the FCIT; the exceptions were referred on after crisis intervention, for any of a variety of services, some internal to our program and some in the community. As examples, adolescents with alcohol or drug problems were referred to our Chemical Dependency Recovery Program, while victims of molestation or abuse were typically referred to Parents, Daughters, and Sons United or other programs for ongoing care after crisis resolution. Also among the 10% of patients referred on for continuing care were psychotic and other poorly controlled patients who were followed by therapists on our routine treatment teams, as long as that could be managed within the constraints of the health plan contract; those who could not be were referred to outside agencies.

Crisis intervention may fail to meet the expectations of some parents and outside agencies. For parents who wish to leave their youngsters for "treatment," participation in a family approach may be unacceptable; they also may be dissatisfied with a short-term effort. Similarly, some agencies recommend long-term treatment as the only viable choice, sometimes based on a bias in that direction and sometimes for solid reasons (for example, in cases of extended molestation). In general, HMO contracts define relatively short-term benefits (Brady & Krizay, 1985) that are not designed to address such long-term needs.

Finally, some traditionally trained mental health providers find the Rush Center model unacceptable, for reasons varying from a sense that it must be too superficial, to discomfort with the level of discipline required and the demanding nature of the cases served.

Conclusion

Budman (1985) reviewed the literature concerning mental health services in HMOs and concluded:

> Given poor circumstances, the HMO mental health service gives health care providers the opportunity to do "more of the same" for less money and with fewer resources; under optimal circumstances it offers an enormous challenge, stimulating creativity and an expansion of new techniques, new areas, and new structures for providing mental health care. (p. 807)

The overall effect of the new modality represented by the FCIT was to improve patients' access to both crisis and routine care, to increase the effectiveness and acceptability of these services, and to challenge the staff to provide a demanding but rewarding core service for children and adolescents and their families.

References

Adams, J., & Kagnoff, M. (1983). Development of pediatric secondary psychosocial care in a health maintenance organization. *Children's Health Care, 12,* 4–10.

Anderson, J. C., Williams, S., McGee, R., & Silva, P. A. (1987). DSM-III disorders in preadolescent children. *Archives of General Psychiatry, 44,* 69–76.

Bennett, M. J., & Gavalya, A. S. (1982). Prepaid comprehensive mental health services for children. *Journal of the American Academy of Child Psychiatry, 21,* 486–491.

Bonnefil, M. C. (1980). Crisis intervention with children and families. *New Directions for Mental Health Services, 6,* 23–34.

Bonnefil, M. C., & Jacobson, G. F. (1979). Family crisis intervention. *Clinical Social Work Journal, 7,* 200–312.

Brady, J., & Krizay, J. (1985). Utilization and coverage of mental health services in health maintenance organizations. *American Journal of Psychiatry, 142,* 744–746.

Budman, S. H. (1985). Psychotherapeutic services in the HMO: Zen and the art of mental health maintenance. *Professional Psychology: Research and Practice, 16,* 798–809.

Caplan, G. (1961). *An approach to community mental health.* New York: Grune & Stratton.

Carstens, C. (1988). *The Enuresis Clinic parent's manual.* San Diego, CA: Keys to Learning.

Chiefetz, D. I., & Salloway, J. C. (1985). Crisis intervention: Interpretation and practice by HMOs. *Medical Care, 23,* 89–93.

Cooper, S., & Wanerman, L. (1984). *A casebook of child psychotherapy: Strategies and technique.* New York: Brunner/Mazel.

Dougherty, D. (1988). Children's mental health problems and services. *American Psychologist, 43,* 808–812.

Enthoven, A., & Kronick, R. (1989). A consumer-choice health plan for the 1990s. *The New England Journal of Medicine, 320,* 94–101.

Fosarelli, P. D. (1984). Latchkey children. *Developmental and Behavioral Pediatrics, 5,* 173–177.

Fraser, J. S. (1986). The crisis interview: Strategic rapid intervention. *Journal of Strategic and Systemic Therapies, 5,* 71–87.

Hersch, P. (1988, January). Coming of age on city streets. *Psychology Today,* pp. 28–37.

Hobbs, M. (1984). Crisis intervention in theory and practice: A selective review. *British Journal of Medical Psychology, 57,* 23–34.

Jacobson, D. S. (1980). Crisis intervention with stepfamilies. *New Directions for Mental Health Services, 6,* 35–43.

Jacobson, G. F. (1967). Some psychoanalytic considerations regarding crisis therapy. *The Psychoanalytic Review, 54,* 649–654.

Jacobson, G. F. (1980). Crisis theory. In G. F. Jacobson (Ed.), *New directions for mental health services: Crisis interventions in the 1980s.* San Francisco: Jossey Bass.

Jacobson, G. F. (1983). *The multiple crises of marital separation and divorce.* New York: Grune & Stratton.

Jacobson, G. F., Strickler, M., & Morley, W. E. (1968). Generic and individual approaches to crisis intervention. *American Journal of Public Health, 58,* 338–343.

Jacobson, G. F., Wilner, D. M., Morley, W. E., Schneider, S., Strickler, M., & Sommer, G. J. (1965). The scope and practice of an early-access brief treatment psychiatric center. *American Journal of Psychiatry, 121,* 1176–1182.

Kandel, D. (1982). Epidemiological and psychosocial perspectives on adolescent drug use. *Journal of the Academy of Child Psychiatry, 21,* 328–347.

Klerman, G. L. (1988). The current age of youthful melancholia. *British Journal of Psychiatry, 152,* 4–14.

Manderscheid, R. W., & Barrett, S. A. (1987) (Eds.). *Mental Health, United States, 1987* (pp. 81–84). Rockville, MD: National Institute of Mental Health.

Marecek, J. (1987). Counseling adolescents with problem pregnancies. *American Psychologist, 42,* 89–93.

Polk, G. C. (1982). Crisis theory: Application and utilization with hemodialysis patients and families. *Nephrology Nurse, 4,* 8–10.

Robin, M. (1982). Historical introduction to sheltering arms: The roots of child protection. In E. H. Newberger (Ed.), *Child abuse* (pp. 1–21). Boston: Little, Brown.

Wojdowski, P., & Hartnett, K. (1985). The HMO question. *Journal of Psychosocial Nursing, 23,* 23–25.

9

Marsha Gunstad and Charles F. Sherman

A Model of Adolescent Inpatient Short-term Treatment

The Setting

The Metropolitan Clinic of Counseling (MCC) in Minnesota was a privately owned, multidisciplinary mental health/chemical dependency service provider to health maintenance organizations and self-insured corporations in several states.

The management of child/adolescent inpatient services described in this chapter was developed and supervised by both authors while employed at the MCC-Minnesota (MCC-MN) operation. Credit is also given to Ida Swearingen, MSW, and the many other clinical and administrative personnel of MCC-MN who participated in the development of this operation.

Background and History: 1975–1985

While most literature on short-term inpatient programs (Abend, Kocholsky, & Greenberg, 1968; Evans, Chagoya, & Rokoff, 1971; Mirkin, Ricci, & Cohen, 1985) has considered a 30- to 90-day length of stay (LOS) to be reasonably short, the program we have developed and describe in this chapter has an LOS of only five to seven days. Before describing this program, we would like to describe its background and history.

During its first six years of operation, Metropolitan Clinic of Counseling (MCC) in Minnesota managed its inpatient child/adolescent services through a number of contracted inpatient psychiatrists and hospital psychiatric units. There was no required preadmission certification. Staff psychiatrists performed utilization review. Mental health inpatient utilization rates for the general population ranged between 20 and 40 days per 1,000 enrollees. These rates were reviewed by staff psychiatrists. The average LOS for adolescents between 1975 and 1981 was between 20 and 30 days. A multidisciplinary staff of psychologists (both PhDs and MSs) and social workers (MSWs) provided outpatient services. Referrals were also made to a panel of providers outside of MCC.

Appreciation is expressed to Riverside Medical Center for its cooperation in the development of this chapter. Great appreciation and respect is also expressed to William Routt, MD, for his support and courage in the development of this model.

A director of child/adolescent services was named in 1981 and assumed all responsibility for child/adolescent utilization reviews. From 1981 to 1985 the LOS for inpatient child/adolescent services remained relatively stable at 18 to 23 days. This reduction was achieved by limiting the inpatient psychiatric providers to three psychiatrists at two hospitals.

The Adolescent Diagnostic and Consultation Team: 1985–1988

While marketplace factors prevented MCC from hiring its own child psychiatrists, they also clearly defined the necessity of increasing control over the management of these cases. Intense and frequent use of outpatient services had enabled MCC to decrease its LOS for all populations. However, adolescent inpatient cases still had the longest LOS. Concern over continuing declines in capitation rates and higher operating costs, led MCC to develop an alternative model to traditional inpatient treatment.

A team of specialists skilled in structural and strategic family therapy were recruited in 1985. They began developing protocols to manage adolescent high-risk cases. The mandate to the Adolescent Diagnostic and Consultation Team (ADCT) was to do the following:

1. Provide intensive outpatient services to adolescents and their families as an alternative to inpatient treatment.
2. Follow adolescent cases upon discharge from a psychiatric hospital in order to reduce relapse.
3. Provide consultation to the MCC child/adolescent professional staff on high-risk adolescent cases.

Soon after its inception, ADCT demonstrated a reduction in admissions and LOS that more than compensated for its operating costs. In 1987 ADCT began to expand its therapeutic focus, with therapists following adolescents during their hospital stay and providing family therapy on the psychiatric unit as an alternative to the hospital staff.

The LOS for adolescents who were followed in the hospital by ADCT was reduced from between 12 and 15 days per case to between five and seven days. All child and adolescent inpatient services were performed in one hospital under the direction of two psychiatrists. ADCT staff are responsible for all family therapy services during hospitalization and immediately after discharge.

The Theoretical Model

Adolescents and their families who present in a hospital are in a state of crisis. When working with these families, our therapists view crisis as an agent of change and an opportunity to mobilize family resources.

Our theoretical approach, both on an inpatient and outpatient basis, is short-term and problem-focused. We have found the application of structural and strategic family therapy to be most effective in working with such families.

It is a basic tenet of this model that in order for a child's problematic behavior to change, parents must regain control of their child. The involvement of the family during a child's psychiatric hospitalization has been a treatment modality for over 10 years (Abrams, Fullner, & Whitaker, 1971; Harbin, 1979).

Traditional adolescent psychiatric hospitalization frequently serves to support a dysfunctional family hierarchy, that is, staff tend to replace parents rather than empower them (Anderson & Erstling, 1983). In order to deal with such incongruities in the family hierarchy, more adaptive interactional patterns must be implemented and maintained. In many cases, the child's family has been an important force in maintaining the problematic behavior. Its members can, therefore, play a significant role in ameliorating the problem. Families need to experience success in doing this, however, and it is our belief that a crisis unit in a hospital can be instrumental in providing such an opportunity.

It was essential to the realization of our treatment model within the hospital that we find an inpatient psychiatric facility that had a family systems therapy orientation. We contracted with Riverside Medical Center Adolescent Crisis Unit to provide our inpatient services. This unit is a 16-bed adolescent crisis unit located in Minneapolis. The Adolescent Crisis Program at Riverside Medical Center is an inpatient mental health program that provides assessment and treatment to adolescents, aged 12 through 17, who are in crisis situations that cannot be managed on an outpatient basis. These crises are often precipitated by such issues as suicidal thoughts or behavior, depression, or psychosis.

In the program's initial stages, MCC and hospital staff met to negotiate and to clearly outline what our mutual roles would be in working together. We emphasized our belief that a child's hospital stay needs to be short-term and intensive, with family involvement as a critical variable. Our basic assumption is that *treatment happens in the family*, although the hospital is useful for short-term stabilization of a crisis situation.

The unit was designed for adolescents who stayed in the program for up to 21 days, but we emphasized that we expected a shorter LOS than that expected by other referral sources using the adolescent crisis unit. It was also understood that MCC, in conjunction with our attending psychiatrist, would be responsible for monitoring LOS. Most importantly, MCC and ADCT needed to be viewed as the primary treatment team, even though the child was on the hospital's inpatient unit. In addition, we explained that discharge planning needed to begin as soon as the adolescent entered the hospital.

We built a team approach with the hospital staff. Each person involved with the adolescent during his or her hospitalization needed to communicate a unified message to the family. Although not all staff at the hospital agreed with our approach (that of short-term hospitalization), they worked diligently with us to present a united front to the parents. We had daily phone and in-person contact with the hospital staff to facilitate the communication necessary to achieve this.

As has been documented in previous literature dealing with short-term hospitalizations, administrative support is essential to the success of a short-term program (Hanrahan, 1986). "If administration officers do not support the clinical philosophy and treatment program, then chronic difficulties will occur" (Mirken et al., 1985). Riverside's administration was most supportive of MCC and ADCT's efforts to educate their staff about our treatment model. Toward this end, the hospital allowed therapists on their unit to attend weekly live supervision in our outpatient office.

Prior to implementing our family therapy treatment approach at Riverside Medical Center, MCC sought to add to the staff an attending child psychiatrist. When hiring a candidate for this position, we looked for the following qualities:

1. A commitment to brief therapy.
2. An ability to supervise brief therapy.
3. A commitment to the use of families in the treatment of adolescents.
4. A significant commitment not only to MCC's treatment philosophy, but also to the goals of quality service and cost containment.

To facilitate a unified treatment philosophy, we communicated frequently with the attending psychiatrist—both by phone and at the hospital. Formal treatment planning meetings were held weekly with the psychiatrist, ADCT Team, and members of the hospital team treating our clients. ADCT family therapists conducted daily informal consultations with the psychiatrist.

Admission Criteria

The criteria used to determine the need for adolescent hospitalization differ from those used by other community providers. Except for after hours, all admissions are reviewed by ADCT after discussion with the parents. The team used terms such as "stabilization," "family crisis," and "mobilizing the family" to begin to shape parental perceptions about the role of hospitalization in their child's treatment. Parents are educated about the appropriate and inappropriate use of the hospitalization. They were made aware that: (a) hospitals are not used for custodial care for adolescents pending out-of-home placement by the county social service agencies; (b) hospitals are not used to incarcerate adolescents who have run from homes or have been truant from school; and (c) psychiatric evaluations are not routinely done in an inpatient setting unless the adolescent is medically unstable, highly suicidal, or psychotic. In fact, without appropriate psychiatric indicators, hospitalization is seen as detrimental to an adolescent's development and may have many negative effects.

So what are the criteria for inpatient treatment of adolescents? In brief, they are:

1. High suicide risk (suicidal thoughts or plans, means to carry out plans, etc.).
2. Homicidal or severely assaultive behavior.
3. A psychiatric condition that requires confinement while medication is started or changed.

4. Drug toxicity.
5. Medical stabilization needed due to eating disorders.

Admitting Procedures

During Daytime Hours

All requests for admissions were directed to ADCT for provision of an evaluation of the adolescent and family if possible. When presented in an emergency room, the adolescent and parent(s) are evaluated first by the emergency room physician. This physician then notifies ADCT and a decision is made. Under all evaluative situations, a child psychiatrist is available to provide consultation, evaluation, and/or prescriptions for medication. However, the child psychiatrist has a secondary role and is used primarily for consultation.

When a decision is made to admit the adolescent, the preferred procedure is to have the family go to the hospital. If that is not possible, at least one parent accompanies the child. The hospital and attending physician are notified to expect the adolescent and family, and the attending psychiatrist calls the unit for orders. In almost all cases these include: watch status, history and physical examination, psychological testing (completed and interpreted within 48 to 72 hours), neurological assessment if needed, laboratory work (UR, CBC, SMA 12, T3, T4, TSH, serum creatinine), occupational therapy, and therapeutic recreation.

In addition, the parents and family members are requested to return within two days to begin discharge planning through family therapy sessions held two to three times per week. This participation is required of the family if admission to the unit is to be covered by their health maintenance organization (HMO) policy.

After Hours

Emergency or crisis after-hours calls are the responsibility of the general MCC professional staff. If an admission occurs, the adolescent and parents go to the hospital admitting department. Once again, the attending psychiatrist is contacted to provide orders for the unit after obtaining clinical information from the on-call staff. On the morning after an emergency admission, an ADCT staff member evaluates the patient on the unit, again, preferably with the parents and family members present.

Assessment

The goal of the crisis unit, as stated in its formal program description (Riverside Medical Center, 1988) is to assist the patient and family in problem identification and the development of strategies for resolving the crisis situation. Assessment/intervention groups within a multi-disciplinary milieu are utilized to meet this goal. The primary components of the Crisis Program are: individual and family assessment, occupational therapy, therapeutic recreation, group therapy, and social assessment. The program considers each of the fundamental needs of the patient: physical, psychological, spiritual, social, educational, developmental, familial, environmental, and recreational (Riverside Medical Center, 1988).

On admission, hospital staff begin an initial treatment plan. This is expanded and updated during the assessment component of the program. Assessment components of this unit include:

- Physical assessment.
- Speech and language evaluation (when indicated).
- Psychiatric assessment.
- Chemical dependency assessment (when indicated).
- Family assessment.

Diagnostic assessment, in terms of ADCT involvement, begins the moment there is a request for hospitalization. If the adolescent and his or her family has been seen by a family therapist on our staff, we provide pertinent information to the admitting psychiatrist. If the family has been involved with ADCT, much of the diagnostic assessment has preceded the request for hospitalization. In these cases, there is no need to duplicate psychological testing. In most ongoing cases, the treatment plan is formulated and discussed with the psychiatrist. The focus of treatment in the hospital is to identify (a) obstacles preventing the achievement of previously identified goals within the family, and (b) necessary modifications to the existing treatment plan.

Intervention

After the assessment is completed, hospital and ADCT staff develop an individual treatment plan that focuses on issues precipitating the child's admission. Patients and their families are assisted in developing their own care plan. This includes problem identification, goal setting, and actions they can take to resolve the crisis situation. The following case illustrates this approach:

> A 16-year-old female was admitted to the unit due to threats of suicide, several episodes of running away with friends, and alcohol abuse. She was agreeable to the idea of admission to the hospital as a means of sorting out her options and making some plans for the future. She had a one-hour interview with the psychiatrist, who determined that she was not psychotic or at high risk for suicide. Her alcohol abuse was determined to be episodic and reactionary to stress. No vegetative signs of depression were present. The running away with friends was in response to limit-setting attempts by her parents (viewed as punishment by her).
>
> A separate two-hour interview was held with the parents by a member of the ADCT staff who found the parents to be quite scared by their daughter's suspected sexual activity and threats of suicide. There was also a severe marital relationship problem and alcohol abuse by the father.
>
> Treatment goals were established that included:

1. Finding an interim placement for the daughter with a goal of returning home while continuing in family therapy.
2. Establishing curfew times acceptable to all.
3. Marital therapy for the parents.
4. Alcohol assessment for the father.
5. A no suicide/no run contract prior to discharge.

The Riverside program also provides peer interaction through daily activities and therapeutic groups. Structured patient education groups that address developmental needs use learning objectives to measure progress. There is no formal school component to this program. State law requires that programs in excess of 21 days provide for an educational component. Since the maximum length of stay is 21 days, the Minneapolis schools are not mandated by law to provide on-site education. The hospital social worker contacts the child's school in an attempt to delineate any school-related problems and facilitate a resolution before discharge.

Adolescents are observed on a daily basis as they participate in occupational therapy, verbal groups, and therapeutic recreation. According to the hospital (Riverside Medical Center, 1988), this structured environment allows for the incorporation of evaluation and intervention goals into a daily treatment program. Normative social/peer expectations and the achievements of the adolescent on a variety of developmental tasks provide the rationale for the structure of intervention. This environment allows the adolescent to act on new behaviors with therapeutic support from peers and professionals. Feedback regarding an adolescent's adjustment to the milieu is given to both the psychiatrist and ADCT staff to facilitate discharge planning.

In most cases where ADCT has been involved with the families prior to hospitalization the LOSs are shorter than in situations where ADCT has had no prior involvement. Hospital staff are immediately briefed about any prior therapeutic work. Everyone involved with the present hospitalization works in close coordination in order to resolve the crisis expeditiously.

In situations where the client is new to the ADCT staff, the hospital notifies us of any admission immediately, and our psychiatrist begins to coordinate a preliminary treatment plan. On the day of admission families are asked to contact ADCT to set up a family session. During our first phone contact with the family, we begin to emphasize the importance of the family's role in treatment. At the time of the crisis hospitalization, parents are generally feeling desperate. They may view the hospitalization as a way to put some distance between themselves and the problematic adolescent. They may also have a tendency to pathologize their child. Frequently a parent gives us a directive to "find out what is wrong with my child," and "fix it." In order to address these issues, we assure parents that we will provide a thorough and comprehensive diagnostic assessment for their child; at the same time we stress the importance of continued family involvement. To facilitate this, we set up the first family session within 24 to 72 hours. We ask that all family members living in the home be present when we first meet with the family in the hospital.

If the family is new to us, we will conduct the first session differently than we would with ongoing clients. It is most important in meeting with new families to form a connection that will facilitate a desire to continue in outpatient therapy. We explain in some detail why the ADCT staff is involved during their child's hospitalization. We emphasize the benefits of continuity of care, and our desire to work with the family both during the immediate crisis and after discharge. Throughout this initial family session, we emphasize our belief that family resources, once reorganized, provide the most effective means of immediate intervention and long-term, follow-up care.

Many of these adolescents and their families have had experience with therapies and therapists prior to hospitalization. They are frequently feeling frustrated and hopeless about the process of therapy. We attempt to use the leverage of the crisis situation and the hospitalization to point toward the need for something "different" to happen with the family during the hospitalization. The adolescent's symptoms frequently are manifestations of a family's stress. If we can broaden the focus during this initial session, the forces that are maintaining the symptom within the family will, it is hoped, appear and can then be the focus of our work. As identified in previous literature on the benefits of family therapy during hospitalization, "if the intervention can begin to restructure the family, far-reaching changes can be obtained within a relatively short period of time and can be enduring and supported by a useful aftercare program" (Mirkin et al., 1985).

We attempt to use our attending psychiatrist during this family session, particularly if he feels there is a need to provide medication to the adolescent. Since we do not want to reinforce what might be the parents' idea that the child is ill, the way the issue of medication is presented to the family is critical. We, in conjunction with the psychiatrist, present the medication as an adjunct to therapy, not as a replacement for individual or family work. As family therapists, we take a very active leadership role during these sessions. Particularly with families new to us, we attempt to form a tentative working hypothesis. At the same time, we try to reduce the family chaos and disorder that is usually present in families in crisis.

We continually reinforce the notion that not all the problems experienced by the adolescent and his or her family can be resolved during this crisis hospitalization. We assure the family that we will assist them in identifying what most needs to change in order for their child to safely return home. We also make ourselves readily available to the family by phone during this hospitalization. Frequently, if it becomes clear that there are marital issues that need to be addressed during the hospitalization, we will see the parents at our outpatient office. Separating the marital issues from the child's hospitalization tends to reinforce the restructuring of the hierarchy.

Suicidal behaviors are one of the most frequent presenting problems for which families request hospitalization. Adolescents' suicide attempts often occur as a plea for a change either in the behavior of family members or in the child's own life situation. It is imperative that we begin to uncover the often hidden reasons behind a family's request for hospitalization. A family's goal for hospitalization is significant in deciding what should occur during this brief stay.

If it is clear during this initial session that the family has exhausted its resources and the members feel their only solution is to extrude this child, we help them search for alternative living arrangements. We immediately involve the hospital social worker and work closely with the families to facilitate an expeditious referral to a safe living arrangement. Our focus continues to be on reunification, but at a future date. This hospitalization is framed as an opportunity for the family to be intimately involved in placement of their child outside of their home. In many cases, a brief stay at a shelter home or a temporary foster home will allow the family sufficient separation to regain equilibrium and begin working on family issues.

Discharge

Other authors agree that in a brief adolescent hospitalization, discharge planning must begin immediately upon admission. In addition, "goal setting, a clear explanation of what the patient can accomplish during the relatively short hospitalization (which directs both hospital unit resources, the family and the ADCT staff in the formulation of discharge plans), is a key to effective treatment planning" (Dalton, Bolding, Woods, & Daruna, 1987).

We discuss whether or not the child will be returning home at the end of the hospitalization and clarify what needs to be resolved before the family feels safe taking the adolescent home. If it is determined that the child will return home, a second family session is scheduled within two days. In many cases, this is the discharge session.

We attempt to involve as many resources as possible during the discharge session. Frequently, this session will be attended by the family, ADCT family therapist, hospital social worker, school personnel, and other therapists if the child was previously engaged with an outside agency. We will also ask our attending psychiatrist to be present to offer an explanation of the psychological testing, as well as to clarify any issue around medication. It is our goal to send parents home armed with as much information as possible. If the child is returning home, we will set up a date for our first postdischarge family session at the clinic. If out-of-home placement is being pursued, we will use this discharge session to allow the family to plan the goals of the placement, as well as formulate their reunification plan.

As has been well documented in previous literature, predicting a crisis and a possible relapse with the adolescent can be extremely useful (Mirkin et al., 1985). We encourage the family to plan specifically how they will deal with various difficult situations and variables as well as with a relapse, should it occur. The family is encouraged to contact ADCT should a crisis occur after the adolescent returns home. We have the ability to see families on a same-day basis and find that this is most effective in avoiding a rehospitalization. Families frequently need support immediately upon discharge if they are to continue using the newly learned, adaptive interactional patterns set in motion during our family therapy sessions in the hospital.

One of the primary goals of ADCT involvement on the inpatient unit is to enhance the motivation and opportunity for subsequent outpatient therapy. Throughout the adolescent's hospitalization, we stress the importance of continued family therapy. It has been our experience, as well as that of other such programs, that brief hospitalization in conjunction with aftercare services can be as effective as traditional, longer-term hospitalization in reducing levels of psychopathology and rates of rehospitalization and in improving social functioning (Endicott, Herz, & Gibbon, 1977; Goldstein & Horgan, 1988).

Pitfalls and Liabilities

Reducing the cost of mental health care without sacrificing quality often places the programs and staff in risk-taking positions as well as generating tension due to criticism from other professionals. Our staff, using this program, were able to reduce length of inpatient stays without shortcutting on quality of care. The staff of ADCT, the hospital, and the psychiatrists involved have been able to accept the added risk of venturing into new treatment waters. This was due, in large part, to their belief in this particular treatment modality. However, belief alone will not produce the type of success experienced in the program described above. There were several pitfalls that we had to successfully negotiate.

First, the outpatient staff of ADCT were deliberately recruited for this program design. It has been our experience that traditionally trained mental health professionals are often not equipped to handle high-risk cases of adolescent suicide without an overdependence on inpatient psychiatric units—typically until the insurance coverage is exhausted. ADCT staff are characterized by a combination of training, education, highly developed skills, and the "seasoning" that comes from a number of years of practice. Their background seems to be the most important ingredient in successfully implementing this model.

Second, administrative support is absolutely essential to the success of the model. Without it, the most highly skilled professional adolescent team would be handcuffed and left impotent. The ADCT staff was routinely challenged by demanding parents, traditional long-term inpatient treatment providers and, in some cases, collateral professionals such as county social workers and probation officers, school counselors, and employee assistance counselors. Faced with this second-guessing and pressure to abdicate their professional judgments, the ADCT staff required administrative support both privately, through internal discussions and financial commitments, and publicly, by demonstrated support in discussions and case review meetings with health plan representatives and other possible critics.

Third, as indicated earlier, without the right "fit," a hospital staff and/or attending psychiatrist could block, or at least diminish, the impact of this type of program. Haley (1980) advocates that mental health clinicians need to attempt to remain "in charge" of their cases, even when faced with inpatient treatment. Attending psychiatrists and hospital staff do not have the same sense of urgency to move adolescents (or adults) quickly toward discharge. Speeding up the evaluation and intensifying the family therapy sessions (if conducted at all) place more demands, pressure, and risk on these professionals and without any incentives to do so (Sherman, 1981). Slowing down the process for the purpose of "thoroughness," "comprehensiveness," and to look into the "family of origin issues" characterizes the more traditional 30- to 180-day LOS adolescent programs. Asking parents to take charge, be parents, stay involved, and assume responsibility is antithetical to the orientations of most traditional inpatient adolescent treatment programs. A compatible staff, and more importantly, a compatible psychiatrist, are the most important elements in successfully implementing this model of adolescent crisis treatment.

Future Directions

Can we continue to expect shorter and shorter LOSs and fewer admissions from managed mental health professionals? Yes and no. As others have indicated (Boaz, 1988), 5 to 10 inpatient days per 1,000 health plan enrollees is an ambitious, yet reachable target. Zero days per 1,000 may be unrealistic given the need to safeguard some psychiatric patients. Parents are not expected to change rapidly in their desire to have someone "change" their child rather than asking them to assume some responsibility for change.

Graduate programs in psychology and social work are not showing progress in recognizing the changing marketplace of mental health care delivery, despite the well documented and media-covered plight of our national health care costs. So what are the next developments? First, greater use of day hospital and day treatment facilities can be expected due to growing pressure to contain costs through preadmission certification and utilization review programs. LOSs could be cut dramatically if most programs were established for day-long treatment provision at the beginning rather than at the end of treatment. The innovative design of the "psychiatric inn" is an example of this type of programming (Gudeman, Shore, & Dickey, 1983). In addition, there is evidence to suggest that partial hospitalization may be as effective as traditional hospitalization for at least some patient populations (Kettlewell, Jones, & Jones, 1985; Lahey & Kupfer, 1979; Meyerson & Herman, 1983).

Second, led by the national establishment of diagnostic related groups for medical/surgical diagnoses and treatments, the psychiatric and psychological professional organizations are beginning to examine the viability of similar developments in mental health care. These developments will be coupled with existing sophistication in precertification and utilization review criteria to mandate fewer admissions and shorter LOSs. Support for these efforts from the major health insurance carriers would be logical given the compatible goals, yet many of these carriers are just beginning to awaken to the idea of "managed benefits." Third, given spiraling growth in the cost of national health care (Huntley, 1988), some form of programming at the national level may be required to bring cost control measures to more prominence.

While no one cost containment activity can limit all areas of health care inflation, a combination of the practices described above, along with a more sophisticated employer–buyer market may provide the necessary impetus to significantly reduce mental health care costs. The challenge before us is to achieve a reduction in costly inpatient services and still maintain (or improve) quality of care.

References

Abend, S. B., Kocholsky, H., & Greenberg, H. R. (1968). Reactions of adolescents to short hospitalization, *American Journal of Psychiatry, 124*, 149–155.

Abrams, G., Fullner, C., & Whitaker, C. (1971). The family enters the hospital, *American Journal of Psychiatry, 127*, 1363–1370.

Anderson, C. M., & Erstling, S. S. (1983). Common problems in application. In R. F. Luber & C. M. Anderson (Eds.), *Family intervention with psychiatric patients*. New York: Human Sciences Library.

Boaz, John T. (1988). *Delivery of mental health care: A guide for HMOs*. Chicago: Pluribus Press.

Dalton, R., Bolding, D., Woods, J., & Daruna, J. (1987). Short-term psychiatric hospitalization of children. *Hospital and Community Psychiatry, 38*(9), 973–976.

Endicott, J., Herz, M., & Gibbon, M. (1977). Brief versus standard hospitalization: The different costs. *American Psychiatric Association*, presented May 2–6.

Evans, H. A., Chagoya, L., & Rokoff, V. (1971). Decision-making as to the choice of family therapy in an adolescent in-patient setting, *Family Process, 10*, 97–110.

Goldstein, J., & Horgan, C. (1988). Inpatient and outpatient psychiatric services: Substitutes or complements? *Hospital and Community Psychiatry, 39*(6), 632–636.

Gudeman, J. E., Shore, M. F., & Dickey, B. (1983). Day hospitalization and an inn instead of inpatient care for psychiatric patients. *New England Journal of Medicine, 131*, 749–753.

Haley, J. (1980). *Leaving home*. New York: McGraw-Hill.

Hanrahan, G. (1986). Beginning work with families of hospitalized adolescents. *Family Process, 25*, 391–405.

Harbin, H. A. (1979). A family oriented psychiatric inpatient unit. *Family Process, 18*, 281–190.

Huntley, G. (1988, September 26). Higher and higher: 1988 health costs exceed estimates; no relief run in '89. *Business Insurance*, pp. 42–43.

Kettlewell, P. W., Jones, J. K., & Jones, R. H. (1985). Adolescent partial hospitalization: Some preliminary outcomes, *Journal of Clinical Child Psychology, 14*(2), 139–144.

Lahey, B. B., & Kupfer, D. L. (1979). Partial hospitalization programs for children and adolescents. In R. F. Luber (Ed.), *Partial hospitalization: A current perspective* (pp. 73–89). New York: Plenum Press.

Meyerson, A. T., & Herman, G. S. (1983). What's new in after-care? A review of recent literature. *Hospital and Community Psychiatry, 34*, 333–342.

Mirkin, M. P., Ricci, R. J., & Cohen, M. (1985). A family and community system approach to the brief psychiatric hospitalization of adolescents. In M. P. Mirkin, R. Ricci, & M. Cohen (Eds.), *Handbook of adolescents and family therapy*. New York: Gardner Press.

Sherman, C. F. (1981, November). *Delivery of psychological services for children in an HMO setting*. Paper presented at the 33rd annual meeting of the American Association of Psychiatric Services for Children, San Francisco.

10

Louis J. DeStefano and Karen H. Henault

The Treatment of Chronically Mentally and Emotionally Disabled Patients

The Setting

Community Health Care Plan (CHCP) is a staff model health maintenance organization in southwestern Connecticut, founded in 1971. It serves over 50,000 members in five different settings throughout the New Haven region. The mental health department employs more than 22 full-time equivalent staff including psychiatrists, doctoral psychologists, masters-level nurse specialists, social workers, and substance abuse counselors.

The treatment of chronically mentally and emotionally disabled patients is one of the most difficult problems facing the mental health community in this country today. With the proliferation of health maintenance organizations (HMOs) and other managed care systems, mental health providers are faced with the challenge of providing mental health services to a growing number of chronic patients while staying within the health insurance limits (Meier, 1981).

In this chapter, the authors outline a model for the treatment of chronically mentally and emotionally disabled patients that has evolved at Community Health Care Plan (CHCP) over the past 20 years.

Evolution of the CHCP Mental Health Service

At the outset, the mental health service was funded by a grant by the National Institute of Mental Health (NIMH) to study the feasibility of mental health care being provided by the collaboration of mental health and medical professionals.

Mental health professionals[1] were hired to provide both direct clinical care to the enrollees and consultation to primary care providers. The basic concept of the mental health service at CHCP was that primary care providers were encouraged

---

[1] The terms mental health professional/clinician are used in this paper to refer to members of the mental health staff who were clinical or counseling psychologists, Masters-prepared psychiatric nurse clinical specialists, and psychiatric social workers.

to carry the major responsibility for all health care, including mental and emotional problems.

The mental health service was built around the participation of the mental health clinician as an integral member of the primary care team. The mental health professionals were readily available for collaboration with the primary care providers who were either physicians, nurse practitioners, or physicians' assistants.

The primary care clinician had several options when presented with a patient in need of help with a mental or emotional problem: handle the problem alone; evaluate the patient and then consult with the mental health clinician on the team to determine the most effective treatment plan; or directly refer the patient to the mental health clinician.

The medical provider's choice depended on a number of factors: the treatment complexity of the problem, the amount of time available, knowledge of the patient, experience and familiarity with the problem, and the availability of mental health clinicians (Coleman & Patrick, 1975).

In support of the original program concept, an enrollee was not usually permitted to self-refer to a mental health clinician. Self-referrals were redirected to their primary care providers, except when the presenting problem was of an urgent nature. All routine referrals were screened by the primary care provider who had the opportunity to discuss the presenting problem with the enrollee and determine whether a mental health referral was necessary and appropriate.

Before 1975, when CHCP became a federally qualified HMO, its benefit package included unlimited visits to primary care clinicians for mental or emotional problems. Theoretically, outpatient services provided directly by the mental health service were limited to five visits, although this limit was never strictly enforced. An integral part of this model was the multidisciplinary primary care team, which met on a regular basis to discuss cases that both the primary care clinician and the mental health professionals shared. Sharing of responsibilities, mutual support, and consultations were obtained both informally and formally. The proximity of the mental health clinicians' offices to those of the rest of the team was an important aspect of this collaborative model.

After 1975, as a federally qualified HMO, CHCP provided its enrollees with a maximum of 20 mental health visits per year. There was a transformation of CHCP and the mental health service as the enrollment and staff size grew. When the NIMH grant ended, CHCP assumed fiscal responsibility for the provision of mental health care. Demands for service grew proportionately with the enrollment, and primary care providers had less time available to deal with the mental and emotional problems of their patients. Requirements for greater space for primary care services resulted in consolidation and relocation of mental health offices to a separate area. This relocation diminished the close collaboration of team members and increased the numbers of direct referrals to the mental health service. Although not as central, the primary care providers remained an integral part of the care and management of their patients.

Both inpatient and outpatient mental health benefits have increased steadily since CHCP's inception in conformance with state and federal regulations. Since 1988, CHCP enrollees have been entitled to up to 30 sessions of outpatient mental health care, 60 days of inpatient psychiatric hospitalization, and 45 days of inpatient substance abuse treatment per calendar year. Enrollees were never excluded from receiving mental health services on the basis of diagnosis or chronicity. Within the parameters of the benefit package, the mental health service must be cost-effective in order to provide for all of the mental health needs of the entire enrollment group. For example, 5.4% (approximately 2,500) of the enrollees of the New Haven region had mental health visits with one of the 16 full-time equivalent (FTE) mental health providers at CHCP in 1986 (Kisch & Austad, 1988).

The mental health service follows a short-term focused therapy approach to most mental health problems. On the average, enrollees referred to the mental health service in 1986 were seen for 6.6 sessions (Kisch & Austad, 1988). However, the short-term therapy approach had to be modified in order to meet the needs of the chronic patients due to the severity and enduring nature of their mental and emotional problems.

Definition of Chronic

The concept of chronic mental illness has been evolving over the years. Before deinstitutionalization, psychiatric hospitalization was the only criterion for chronicity. In recent years, three criteria (diagnosis, duration, and disability) have begun to define chronic mental illness.

In order to be considered "chronically mentally ill" individuals need to have a psychiatric condition or diagnosis of sufficient severity, be persistently ill over a long period of time, and be disabled in their social and occupational functioning. However, there is much confusion in the mental health literature about the definition of these terms: that is, which psychiatric conditions or diagnoses qualify as severe enough, how the persistence of the mental illness is defined, and what constitutes "disability" (Bachrach, 1988).

For the HMO, the salient factor about the chronic patient is the above-average use of mental health services. A small proportion of chronic patients do use a sizeable portion of all available mental health services. In a study conducted at Community Health Care Plan (CHCP) in New Haven, Connecticut, 292 of its 14,222 enrollees in 1974 were identified as chronically mentally ill. These patients, treated within the HMO context, used a significantly higher percentage of outpatient, inpatient, and pharmaceutical services than the average patient referred to the mental health service (Patrick, Coleman, Eagle, & Nelson, 1978). Furthermore, compared to their fee-for-service counterparts, HMO enrollees were much more likely to visit a mental health specialist (Manning, Wells, & Benjamin, 1987).

While the first author served as the coordinator of the intake system (1988), he found that 10% of the patients (who were seen 16 or more times per year) used up approximately 40% of the available mental health time. Obviously, in the closed-panel referral system of the HMO, meeting the needs of the chronic patient becomes a challenge.

Bennett and Wisneski (1979) have described the development of extended treatment services at Harvard Community Health Care Plan to provide long-term continuous care to the chronic patient. The provider group adapted treatment methods to patient needs, rather than to the benefits structure.

In addition to these chronically mentally ill patients, there are other patients with recurrent emotional problems (not of the severity of major mental illness) who make chronic use of the mental health services (Patrick et al., 1978). Although these patients do not suffer from major mental illnesses (the first criterion of Bachrach's definition), they do have a chronic emotional disability that requires continuing care. Therefore, for the purposes of this chapter, the authors define the chronic patient as one who suffers from mental or emotional disability of long duration that impairs adaptive functioning and requires continuing intervention by the mental health service.

The diagnostic groups that comprised most of the chronic population at CHCP included major mood and anxiety disorders refractory to treatment, chronic psychotic disorders, and persistent personality disorders.

Model of Treatment

HMO Psychotherapy

The evolution and development of a new style of psychological treatment labeled "HMO psychotherapy" has been described in greater detail elsewhere (Austad, DeStefano, & Kisch, 1988). In short, HMO psychotherapy is an integrative model of treatment borrowing heavily from short-term psychodynamic psychotherapy but also incorporating elements of behavioral, cognitive, existential, and Rogerian methods. The mental health staff are encouraged to be generalists and pragmatists who choose from a variety of treatments those that are the most effective and appropriate for each patient.

In addition to the eclectic integration of various therapies, the HMO mental health clinician selects in a flexible manner from an array of therapy modalities including individual, family, marital, and group psychotherapy.

Biological psychiatry in the form of pharmacotherapy is considered an integral component of the treatment plan whenever clinically indicated.

Referral

Generally, patients are referred by their primary care provider. This is consistent with the mental health service's philosophy of collaborative and integrated care. However, when in crisis, patients may bypass their primary care provider and self-refer. On occasion, a family member will initiate the referral when the patient's judgement and insight are so impaired as to preclude awareness of the need for professional intervention. Mental health staff rotate through the urgent visit service on weekdays and provide telephone consultation to medical providers on nights and weekends. Once assigned to a mental health clinician, barring any unusual circumstances, the patient continues to be followed by that clinician. When the need to resume treatment arises, the patient will, whenever possible, return to the same clinician. This system provides the chronic patient continuity of care and promotes efficient case management. Furthermore, patients are more likely to return to treatment, before their symptoms become very severe and disabling, since they are returning to a familiar therapist, and they are not delayed by having to renegotiate the referral system.

Rapid Assessment

An essential ingredient of all HMO therapy, including the treatment of the chronic patient, is the rapid formulation of an effective treatment plan (Austad et al., 1988). A complete initial evaluation including background history, mental status examination, diagnosis, formulation, and treatment plan is completed (in most cases) after the first session. If the patient is presenting in a crisis, such as an acute psychotic episode or with imminent suicidal or homicidal ideation or plans, crisis intervention becomes the focus of the initial mental health evaluation. Remaining parts of the evaluation such as extensive personal developmental histories are deferred until the patient is more stable.

The mental health professional develops a plan regarding the type of treatment, its duration, and the involvement of family members and significant others where indicated. Consultation and collaboration with the patient's primary care provider regarding medical conditions affecting the psychological state or regarding the prescription of medication begins immediately after the first session. If the primary care provider and the nonphysician mental health clinician have particular, unresolved questions regarding psychotropic medication, a consultation with a psychiatrist will be arranged.

Effective Parsimony

In developing the treatment plan, the HMO mental health professional uses those interventions that are the least disruptive to the patient's life and the least costly in terms of staff time and expenses. This model of HMO therapy has been labeled "effective parsimony" (Bonstedt & Baird, 1979). The goal is to return the patient to the previous level of functioning as quickly as possible and to help to prevent relapse. This principle allows for the development of creative, practical, and flexible treatment approaches.

In the HMO context, long-term psychoanalytically-oriented psychotherapy in its traditional format of ongoing weekly sessions, is considered to be neither the most appropriate nor the most cost-effective treatment for the chronic patient.

Collaboration with Primary Care Providers

As mentioned earlier, CHCP's mental health service was founded with the treatment philosophy that primary care providers (PCP's) could take major responsibility for all health problems of their patients, including mental and emotional problems. Although this original concept has evolved over time, primary care clinicians remain actively involved with the mental health treatment of many of their patients. When the PCP's remain actively involved, providing additional support and management of chronic patients, often these patients require fewer visits to the mental health clinician.

In order to foster the most effective care of chronic patients, CHCP's mental health professionals, who are mainly nonphysicians, collaborate closely with both primary care providers and psychiatrists regarding the prescription of psychotropic medications and the complications of any medical conditions. Primary care physicians continue to be primarily involved for the prescribing of all medications to their patients with mental and emotional problems. Inservice education programs, conducted by the psychiatrists, are given regularly to update the mental health and primary care providers on current trends in psychopharmacology and psychiatry to assist them in the care and management of their patients.

Pharmacotherapy

A discussion of treatment of the chronic patient would be remiss without a special focus on pharmacotherapy. While not all patients who are defined as chronic require medication for effective treatment, it has been noted that the single most important variable affecting the course and outcome in the treatment of major mental illness is pharmacotherapy (Sabin, 1978). Psychotherapy and pharmacotherapy interact synergistically: The proper use of medications can reduce the length of treatment; and the effective application of psychotherapy can lower the dose and the length of pharmacotherapy (Marder & May, 1986).

HMO mental health clinicians must have a sound basic knowledge of psychopharmacology in order to play an active role in the coordination of their patients' mental health treatment. Their extensive knowledge of pharmacotherapy allows them to instruct patients about psychotropic medications, their indications and side effects, and the importance of compliance.

For those patients who need to be maintained on antimanic, antidepressant or neuroleptic medications long-term, periodic monitoring by their primary care providers and a psychiatrist are coordinated by their mental health clinician. For example, current CHCP policy is that all patients on long-term (longer than six months) treatment with neuroleptic medications are evaluated by a psychiatrist once every six months. Patients on lithium carbonate and Tegretol (carbamazepine) for the treatment of mania have serum concentration levels monitored periodically, and have standard laboratory tests ordered at least every six months by their primary care providers. Routine laboratory tests may also be ordered once every six months for patients maintained on tricyclic antidepressant medications. Patients maintained on monoamine oxidase inhibitors (MAOI's) are monitored more closely by the psychiatrist and the primary care provider. Detailed instruction regarding the restrictive MAOI diet and the recognition of hypertensive reactions may be provided by the mental health clinician.

Patients on neuroleptic medications are routinely observed by the mental health professional for early signs of tardive dyskinesia, with prompt referral to the psychiatrist for formal testing with the Abnormal Involuntary Movement Scale (AIMS test). Other significant medication reactions, such as extrapyramidal symptoms or neurotoxicity are referred to the primary care providers with the consultation of a psychiatrist when indicated.

Timing of Sessions

Frequency and length of sessions will vary both with the severity of the problem and the clinician's knowledge of the patient. In a crisis situation, patients are often seen daily for brief sessions, for intensive therapy, and to monitor response to newly initiated medications. The focus is on rapid symptom reduction.

Suicidal thoughts and impulses are evaluated carefully by the clinician who decides whether a combination of medication and support from friends or family members will be sufficient to maintain the patient outside of the hospital. If these suicidal impulses are imminent and if social support is not forthcoming, an immediate admission to a psychiatric hospital is arranged.

In the case of the floridly psychotic patient, hallucinations are treated as symptoms of the acute phase of the illness. Neuroleptic medications are administered to reduce the hallucinations as effectively and as quickly as possible. Hallucinations are not interpreted in the traditional psychoanalytic sense, for they are not relevant to the short-term focused approach of HMO psychotherapy. However, mental health professionals may use their understanding of the patient's hallucinations in their formulation of the case and may, at their discretion, share this knowledge with the patient later, when the acute episode has resolved.

In the cases of personality-disordered patients who may use suicidal gestures to "act out" their emotional problems or unresolved aspects of the therapeutic relationship, the mental health professional develops an appropriate plan for managing these patients' "suicidality." This plan may include instructions to other mental health clinicians and medical providers as to how these patients' emergent contacts may be best handled.

Most cases do not present on an urgent basis. For the routine referrals for psychotherapy, sessions may be weekly and for the traditional "50-minute hour" at the beginning. However, as the patient's more acute symptoms become stabilized, the provider and the patient may agree to meet less frequently (e.g., once every two to three weeks) or for shorter sessions (e.g., one half hour) with the understanding that the provider is available in the case of an emergency. The frequency and length of sessions, therefore, are titrated according to clinical need.

As therapy progresses and the patient remains stable, sessions may be spaced even more widely, with the provision for more frequent sessions during periods of acute exacerbation. By remaining flexible, both the patient's and the HMO's needs can be satisfied. By seeing stable patients less frequently, according to clinical need, the mental health staff then have time available to service the more acutely disturbed patient when necessary. More importantly, chronic patients can feel secure in being followed by a concerned mental health clinician who is sensitive to their individual needs. A rigid adherence to the "50-minute" hour is not only unnecessary but may be too stimulating and anxiety-provoking for many patients. By maintaining this flexible approach, patients are empowered to be proactive in their treatment decisions.

Studies show that the duration of therapeutic contact over time seems to be more important than the frequency of visits. Furthermore there is evidence to suggest that weekly appointments are not necessary for all or even most patients (Sabin, 1978). For major mental illnesses, maximum therapeutic impact occurs over a long period of time. This model of spacing sessions can contribute to the management of the patient's mental and emotional problems while staying within the benefit package of the HMO.

Installment Therapy

For those patients who suffer from recurrent mental illnesses (with symptom-free periods) and for those patients who experience emotional adjustment problems at various stages of development, the HMO mental health clinician may choose to use "installment therapy."[2] This approach is characterized by brief, intermittent episodes of therapy without termination, but with interruptions when the patient is stable. The mental health needs of chronic patients, many of whom remain within the HMO system for years, are accommodated by the intermittent, long-term approach of installment therapy.

Cummings calls his similar model "brief intermittent psychotherapy throughout the life cycle," (Cummings, 1986). He emphasizes that the therapist does not terminate but rather interrupts treatment when the presenting problem is resolved.

A recent review of the literature on the long-term outcome in schizophrenia (Harding, Zubin, & Strauss, 1987) found that there was a more positive outcome in cases in which there was long-term intervention. Our model includes long-term follow-up of chronic patients on an intermittent basis. This is tailored to the individual patient's needs.

Involvement of Family and Significant Others

Because of eligibility requirements, most chronic patients in the HMO are either employed or the dependent of an employed person. Both the employer and family members often feel the impact of the patient's illness and it is important, when possible, to involve them in the treatment process.

The involvement of family members offers them the support and understanding necessary to deal with an ill family member. Those living with a chronic patient may help the patient to comply with medication regimens and to keep scheduled therapy appointments. Family members can also assist the mental health clinician by recognizing early signs of decompensation that may not be apparent to the patient. When a patient does have significant family involvement, it is important for the mental health professional to include family members early in the patient's treatment.

The mental health clinician can explain to the patient the need to include the family, discuss any concerns that its members may have, and reassure them that in most circumstances confidentiality will be maintained. Providing the family with education regarding the patient's illness, its course, prognosis, and appropriate treatment benefits both the patient and the family.

Employers of the chronic patient may also be included in his or her treatment. Certainly it is in the employer's interest that the patient maintain the highest level

---

[2] Attributed to a senior psychiatric social worker, Barbara Golden, who coined this term at a staff meeting circa 1986.

of functioning in order to remain a productive employee. Maintaining employment and adjusting to stressors in the work environment are important tasks for the chronic patient. If the patient's mental and emotional problems are identified promptly, the employer may be more likely to consider maintaining the patient in employment. The mental health clinician can move freely between providing direct care to the patient and indirect care (i.e., consultation) to the employer. The clinician can bring together the parties involved to plan mutually satisfactory approaches. These authors have found that a concerned supervisor can recognize early signs of decompensation and, with the patient's permission, can alert the mental health professional. The employer also needs to be consulted regarding permitting medical leave when the patient is experiencing a relapse. When the treatment is coordinated with the employer the patient receives not only support and understanding but also the potential for job security.

Group Therapy

Group therapy programs for chronic patients are one way of continuing to care for a large number of patients effectively. However, the HMO needs to be large enough to allow the formation of groups specific to diagnoses or problem areas. In a review of the literature, Sabin (1978) found that research gave some support to the conclusion that group therapy in the outpatient setting was associated with better outcome in the treatment of major mental illnesses, especially schizophrenia. Furthermore, these studies provided stronger support for the conclusion that group treatment was not inferior to individual treatment.

Several groups for chronic patients have existed over the years at CHCP. One such example was a psychotherapy group for depressed elderly women. The second author and her colleague estimated that by using group treatment, these patients needed approximately 10 to 30 fewer individual sessions annually (Austad & Henault, 1989). From this experience, the following recommendations could be made for similar group programs: Patients referred to groups should be thoroughly assessed and screened. The group should be regarded as the treatment of choice by the therapist and the patient should not be led to believe that group therapy is inferior to individual therapy. In order to maintain a successful group program, consistent communication among staff members about the availability of openings in the group and feedback about the appropriateness of referrals to the group is essential (Austad & Henault, 1989).

Hospitalization of the Chronic Patient

In addition to the demands put upon outpatient mental health professionals' time, chronic mentally disabled patients can be costly to the HMO in terms of inpatient hospitalization. At CHCP, every effort is made to keep hospitalization at a minimum. Rapid assessment, the use of psychotropic medications, and when necessary, more intensive crisis intervention on an outpatient basis are all important elements in minimizing the use of psychiatric hospitalization. Furthermore, when the patient is hospitalized, the CHCP mental health clinician plays an active role in coordinating treatment with the hospital treatment team and in arranging for immediate outpatient follow-up postdischarge.

The hospitals to which the HMO refers patients should have a philosophy of brief treatment, crisis intervention, and openness to collaborating with the outpatient mental health professional. The authors have found that ongoing consultation and liaison on the clinical and administrative levels are critical to achieving brief, cost-effective hospitalizations.

If hospitalization is to be kept brief, the hospital treatment team needs to focus on symptom reduction with the aim of rapid restabilization. The more enduring chronic symptoms can be the focus of outpatient treatment over time.

Currently, CHCP has an arrangement with a private psychiatric hospital to refer its patients in need of hospitalization. The hospital's admission and brief treatment unit has developed an inpatient treatment team specializing in HMO patients. The inpatient HMO team and the CHCP mental health staff, in becoming "telephone-familiar" with each other, have developed a collaborative relationship that has ensured briefer stays in the hospital and quick follow-up upon discharge. The Chief of the Mental Health Service has met with both the clinical and administrative staff of the hospital on many occasions to develop this arrangement, work on any ongoing problems, and conduct in-service education programs regarding the philosophy of HMO mental health care. Mutual trust, respect, and a degree of philosophical agreement enhance the collaborative effort and the quality of care.

Another mechanism to decrease hospital costs and provide the least restrictive treatment would be the establishment of a partial hospitalization program (PHP). The treatment philosophy of this program would need to be consistent with the HMO in being oriented toward using crisis intervention and brief treatment methods to achieve rapid restabilization. HMO's need either to be of sufficient size to support their own PHP, or to have access to an appropriate program in the community.

Case Studies

In addition to the above outline of the treatment of the chronically mentally and emotionally disabled patients within the HMO, we would like to share brief vignettes, taken from actual clinical practices, to illustrate how this form of treatment has been conducted at CHCP:

Case Illustration No. 1

The first author was referred this married woman in her sixties when she transferred from a private psychiatrist to CHCP after joining the plan. She had been employed, sporadically, in part-time office jobs and had three adult children, two of whom suffered chronic mental problems. Her husband, a retired professional in his mid-sixties, had suffered for many years from a severe personality disorder and in recent years had developed organic brain syndrome. The patient's presenting complaints were anxiety and depression in reaction to her husband's failing health. Further exploration revealed that she had had 30 years of psychotherapy including individual, marital, and group psychotherapy; nine psychiatric hospitalizations (apparently from major depression with psychotic features); and pharmacotherapy, including treatment with antidepressant, neuroleptic, anxiolytic, and sedative hypnotic medications in various combinations.

After having established a therapeutic alliance with the therapist, the patient felt comfortable with meeting once every three weeks on a regular basis, with the understanding that sessions would be scheduled more frequently during periods of greater distress. The therapist was also available by telephone between sessions, should a "crisis" arise. The patient was maintained on low-dose antidepressant and neuroleptic medications for the first three and one-half years of this treatment. In the fourth year of treatment, due to her complaints of anticholinergic side effects of the antidepressant (which had become less tolerable as she grew older), the consulting psychiatrist discontinued the antidepressant with no ill effects. She was then maintained only on low-dose neuroleptic medications.

This patient suffered from somatic delusions (mainly cancer phobia) during periods of decompensation. The therapist collaborated closely with her primary care provider in managing these episodes. This patient also attended a support group for elderly women for four years.

Her diagnosis was borderline personality disorder with prominent narcissistic features and periodic psychotic episodes. Despite nine prior hospitalizations, this patient has so far been maintained as an outpatient for five years.

The patient herself, a bright articulate woman, felt that the treatment she received at CHCP had been particularly beneficial and had helped to improve the quality of her life. She felt secure in the support network established for her in the HMO.

The above case illustrates how a chronically mentally disabled patient can be treated with infrequent individual psychotherapy sessions, a supportive group program, and pharmacotherapy in collaboration with her physician and the consulting psychiatrist. This patient required the involvement of both mental health and medical providers and received various modalities of treatment. However, her utilization of individual psychotherapy sessions was minimal (approximately 15 sessions per year). The fact that psychiatric hospitalization was never required speaks well to the benefit of providing a creative, integrated model of treatment.

Case Illustration No. 2

A 45-year-old woman, diagnosed as chronic schizophrenic, was referred to the second author after her husband had suddenly died from a severe cerebral vascular accident that had initially left him comatose. His physician had asked her to make the decision to remove her husband from life support systems. Shortly thereafter she was referred on an urgent basis by her physician. He presented her as grief-stricken and acutely psychotic, with the delusional belief that she was solely responsible for her husband's death.

After a brief psychiatric hospitalization (her eighth), she saw the second author individually for stabilization and maintenance over a 13-year period. She had many brief psychotic episodes but was never rehospitalized. Her psychotic episodes were characterized by delusional thinking, auditory hallucinations (in which she would hear her deceased husband calling to her), extreme agitation, and inability to sleep.

Many of these episodes were precipitated by stressful life events such as her stepson leaving for college, the death of a close relative, becoming involved in a new intimate relationship, or the anniversary date of her husband's death. During these acute episodes, the patient's sisters, whom the therapist had gotten to know well, would assist in the patient's care. They would bring the patient into the Health Center for treatment by both her therapist and her primary care provider. As the patient was unable to tolerate her medication orally, intramuscular phenothiazine was administered. The patient remained in the Health Center resting for approximately four to six hours after receiving the injection until she was calmer. At these times, her sisters would have her stay with one of them for a few days (she maintained her own apartment) supervising her medications until she was further stabilized. Throughout this time, the patient and the therapist maintained a therapeutic relationship. Sessions were on a monthly basis, and more frequently during a crisis, for a total of 12 to 16 sessions per year.

In the above case, the second author used both installment therapy and infrequent sessions to treat this chronically disabled patient with recurrent episodes of psychosis. Despite eight prior hospitalizations, she was not rehospitalized during her 13 years of treatment at CHCP. This therapy helped to maintain the patient's functioning over a long period of her life, with the least restrictive treatment. Collaboration with the medical providers was an essential element of her care. Often her psychotic episodes were stabilized entirely by the PCP. For example, the patient would present in crisis on a weekend (when her mental health clinician was unavailable). The medical providers would supervise the implementation of the treatment plan that had been previously established in collaboration with her therapist: medications would be administered, vital signs monitored, and general physical assessment performed. She felt secure in the knowledge that she was familiar to many of the health providers at the HMO and that an integrated, collaborative approach was made to her care.

Her family was given additional psychoeducational guidance and support to help them to remain supportive to the patient.

Case Illustration No. 3

The first author was referred this 49-year-old married woman of low average intelligence who was diagnosed with schizoaffective disorder. She had been treated for many years at a local mental health center and had required periodic hospitalizations. She had been unable to work successfully outside the home. After the birth of her son, who was age 20 at the time of her referral, she had experienced the first psychotic episode. These episodes were characterized by widely variable moods (depression to elation), auditory and visual hallucinations, and manic behavior (hypersexuality). Her medications were monitored and adjusted by her primary care provider and the consulting psychiatrist. She was maintained on a neuroleptic, an antidepressant, and an antimanic medication. The therapist saw her weekly for half-hour sessions for the first two years, and biweekly thereafter. Her physician saw her monthly; and the consulting psychiatrist evaluated her medication every six months. She was relatively free from psychotic symptoms and was not rehospitalized for three years. This patient was able to work part-time as a school monitor and has held this position for two years (at the time of her last contact with this chapter's first author).

The case demonstrates that the effective collaboration of the multidisciplinary treatment team can help to stabilize the chronically mentally disabled patient and prevent repeated hospitalizations. Also, the length and frequency of sessions were titrated to the clinical need. At first, the patient could tolerate only half-hour sessions but needed to be seen three times per week; gradually the sessions were lengthened and spaced more widely. Family sessions for psychoeducation were conducted with her husband and son. Furthermore, the therapist conferred with her employer to structure her work schedule to accommodate her mental condition.

Although this patient had a primary attachment to the therapist, she also felt very comforted by the care she received from other providers including her primary care physician and the consulting psychiatrist.

Case Illustration No. 4

A 39-year-old woman, diagnosed with schizophrenia (chronic, undifferentiated type) joined the HMO through her employer, a local food product factory. She lived at home with her parents. She had been working at a factory for four years, her longest continuous period of employment. The patient had been in treatment at the local mental health center for many years, and had required several brief hospitalizations. After joining the plan, she was referred to the second author by her primary care physician. The patient had been kept relatively stable on neuroleptic medications while in treatment at the local mental health center, and this medication regimen was maintained at the HMO.

Her first exacerbation occurred after four months of treatment. Her mother telephoned to inform her therapist that the patient had not been to work for three days, was spending most of her time in bed, and was not eating. The patient's father brought her to the Health Center to be evaluated. She was quite psychotic, with both auditory and visual hallucinations. She was also delusional, believing that she was President Kennedy's assassin and Hitler's mother, and was preoccupied with delusions of guilt and religiosity. She reported that she had stopped her medications about one week prior to this psychotic episode. Her medications were restarted and she was sent home with the understanding that her parents would supervise her medications. Her therapist notified her employer that a leave of absence was necessary. The patient reconstituted quickly and was able to return to work in approximately one week. Over time, a pattern was observed: Periods of decompensation would occur related to medication noncompliance, increased job stress, and difficulties at home. The patient and her family were seen more frequently during crisis. As she continued in treatment, the patient was able to identify the prodromal symptoms of another psychotic episode and would notify the therapist. Early intervention served to prevent or shorten these exacerbations of psychosis.

Also, the patient's supervisor became part of the patient's support system. He learned to recognize the initiation of bizarre behavior at work including difficulty staying at her job site and incoherent speech. The supervisor would bring the patient to the Health Center during these episodes. After being evaluated by her therapist, her medications were adjusted by her physician and she would then be monitored more closely until she recompensated. Her supervisor also became involved in her treatment, reminding her to take her medication when he recognized unusual behavior. The patient had consented to this level of involvement of her supervisor in her mental health care. The cooperation of her supervisor allowed the patient to remain employed.

This case indicates the importance of collaborating with the family and significant others, in this case, the employer. If they had not been involved to this extent, the patient would have become more dysfunctional, requiring repeated hospitalizations or residential treatment. The patient was helped to maintain her employment, which contributed greatly to her feeling of self-worth and well-being.

Conclusion

Mental health professionals in prepaid health care systems are faced with the dilemma of having to use limited resources to treat increasing numbers of chronically mentally and emotionally disabled patients. However, the mental health care of the chronic patient can be structured both creatively and flexibly in order to provide the most effective treatment to the largest number of enrollees while remaining within the benefits package.

The authors have presented one model of continuing care for chronic patients that has been developed over the past 20 years at CHCP. They have described the evolution of psychological treatment called "HMO psychotherapy." The hallmarks of this model applied to the chronic patient include easy access to the referral system and rapid assessment. Effective parsimony and judicious timing of sessions provide the least restrictive treatment for the chronic patient. One way to implement effective parsimony is through the use of "installment therapy," i.e., an intermittent series of psychotherapy sessions during times of increased mental or emotional problems. Patients are not routinely followed during periods of stability.

The psychoeducation of family members and employers encourages their support of the patient and enhances compliance with treatment. Pharmacotherapy is an essential component of the treatment of patients with major mental illness. Hospitalizations, when required, are kept brief with the emphasis on symptom stabilization followed by rapid and intensive outpatient intervention.

As the case examples illustrate, mental health providers have been able, with this model of treatment, to provide high quality care on a continuing basis to chronically mentally and emotionally disabled patients.

References

Austad, C. S., Kisch, J., & DeStefano, L. (1988). The health maintenance organization: II. Implications for psychotherapy. *Psychotherapy, 25*(3), 449–454.

Austad, C. S., & Henault, K. (1989). Group psychotherapy with elderly women. *HMO Practice, 3,* 70–71.

Bachrach, L. (1988). Defining chronic mental illness: A concept paper. *Hospital and Community Psychiatry, 39*(4), 383–388.

Bennett, M. J., & Wisneski, M. J. (1979). Continuous psychotherapy within an HMO. *American Journal of Psychiatry, 136*(10), 1283–1287.

Bonstedt, T., & Baird, S. H. (1979). Providing cost-effective psychotherapy in a health maintenance organization. *Hospital and Community Psychiatry, 30*(2), 129–132.

Brady, J., & Krizay, J. (1985). Utilization and coverage of mental health services in health maintenance organizations. *American Journal of Psychiatry, 142*(6), 744–746.

Coleman, J. V., & Patrick, D. L. (1975). *Integrating mental health services into primary care.* Unpublished manuscript.

Cummings, N. A. (1986). The dismantling of our health system: Strategies for the survival of psychological practice. *American Psychologist, 41*(4), 426–431.

Harding, C. M., Zubin, J., & Strauss, J. S. (1987). Chronicity in schizophrenia: Fact, partial fact, or artifact? *Hospital and Community Psychiatry, 38*(5), 477–486.

Kisch, J., & Austad, C. S. (1988). The health maintenance organization: I. Historical perspective and current status. *Psychotherapy, 25*(3), 441–448.

Manning, W. G., Jr., Wells, K. B., & Benjamin, B. (1987). Use of outpatient mental health services over time in a health maintenance organization and fee-for-service plans. *American Journal of Psychiatry, 144*(3), 283–287.

Marder, S. R., & May, P. R. (1986). Benefits and limitations of neuroleptics—and other forms of treatment—in schizophrenia. *American Journal of Psychiatry, 40*, 357–369.

Meier, G. (1981). HMO experiences with mental health services to the long-term emotionally disabled. *Inquiry, 18*, 125–138.

Patrick, D. L., Coleman, J. V., Eagle, J., & Nelson, E. (1978). Chronic emotional problems of patients and their families in an HMO. *Inquiry, 15*, 166–180.

Sabin, J. E. (1978). Research findings on chronic mental illness: A model for continuing care in the health maintenance organization. *Comprehensive Psychiatry, 19*(1), 83–95.

Herbert C. Schulberg and C. Paul Scott

Depression in Primary Care: Treating Depression with Interpersonal Psychotherapy

One of the most important tasks facing mental health clinicians in prepaid health care is the differential diagnosis of emotional disorders and the determination of how best to intervene with each person. The problems of diagnosis and treatment are particularly evident for depressive disorders in the primary care setting (in contrast to specialty care settings), as these disorders can be clinically confusing and are often significantly underrecognized by physicians (Schulberg & Burns, 1988). While many episodes of depression include a sad mood and other typical symptoms, depression may remain "masked" behind a complex array of somatic symptoms. Conversely, physical illnesses may present with primarily depressive symptoms.

It is essential for managed care to address these ambiguities in the assessment and treatment of depression. First, 6–9% of ambulatory medical care patients experience DSM-III depressive disorders (Schulberg, McClelland, & Burns, 1987). Another 10% display "masked" or atypical depressions not conforming to formal diagnostic nomenclature (Barrett, Barrett, Oxman, & Gerber, 1988). Second, the majority of patients seeking mental health care are treated in primary care settings (doctor's offices, clinics) rather than in specialty service settings (mental health centers, hospitals), and hence will be a significant component of any managed health care system (Wells, Manning, Duan, Newhouse, & Ware, 1987).[1] Proper diagnostic and treatment decisions must be made, since patients with a depressive disorder experience long-term distress, sometimes attempt suicide, and frequently overutilize medical services. While recommendations for the treatment of depression in specialty service outpatient settings are fairly clear (Klerman, 1990), there are many more problems in managing depression in primary care settings.

This chapter first examines the varieties of depressive disorders encountered in primary care settings and their relationship to physical illness. Clinicians working in health maintenance organizations (HMOs) and other primary care settings

---

[1] In fact, one of the advantages of managed health care is the potential involvement with a broader and more diverse patient base than usually reaches traditional specialty mental health care. See the chapter by Kisch, in this volume, for a more complete discussion of the relationship of primary care and mental health care.

may be unaware that there is a greater range of depressive disorders in primary care than in specialty mental health. We then briefly review prior research on patterns of physician recognition of depression, and the efficacy of treatments for depression in ambulatory medical practice. It is important for mental health clinicians working in primary care settings to recognize that primary care physicians may need help in recognizing and treating the depressive disorders they encounter. We then detail the principles of Interpersonal Psychotherapy (IPT) as developed by Klerman, Weissman, Rounsaville, and Chevron (1984) and their clinical application to adult and elderly patients who present in primary care settings with either clear or masked forms of depression (see Cummings' chapter in this volume regarding treatment of nondepressive somatization disorders). This psychotherapy has been extensively studied and found to be among the most effective methods of treatment for depressed outpatients in mental health settings (Elkin et al., 1989). It has great promise for working with depressed patients in primary care as well.

The Differential Diagnosis of Depression

In order to make proper treatment decisions for depressed patients, it is important to recognize depressive symptoms and to distinguish a "masked" depression that mimics a recognized medical disorder from depressive signs possibly indicative of an underlying medical disorder.

Somatic Concomitants of Depressive Disorder

Major depressive disorder (MDD) is a complex psychobiological syndrome involving mood disturbance, neurovegetative signs, and/or distorted cognitive schemata. From the physiological perspective, MDD involves multilevel impairment of brain neurotransmitters, hormonal systems, circadian rhythm, and rapid eye movement (REM) sleep (Katon, 1982). However, MDD can also be a severe reaction to overwhelmingly stressful life events and interpersonal losses. From a phenomenological perspective, the symptoms include a sad mood; loss of interest, motivation, and pleasure; increased guilt; impaired concentration; changes in appetite, weight, and sleep, and thoughts of death or suicide.

Some patients experience disturbing life events or losses but fail to report a depressed mood. When this happens, physicians may fail to consider the possibility of an underlying depression. Many patients will express their distress by somatic symptoms such as headache, nonspecific pain, gastrointestinal complaints, dizziness, fatigue, respiratory difficulties, and many others. Somatic manifestations of depression may serve to bind anxiety and relieve dysphoria in personally and culturally acceptable idioms (Katon, 1982) or may be a function of rigid defense mechanisms (Stoudemire, Kahn, Brown, Linfors, & Houpt, 1985). Patients who express their depression through somatic equivalents persist in this symptom expression from episode to episode even though the type of physical symptom may change across episodes. Early family patterns of illness behavior (for example, increased attention, or serious or frightening illness in childhood) may also predispose an individual to somatic rather than affective expression of depression. Physical symptoms can also generate the secondary gain of disability payments and dependency in a more acceptable form. Somatic symptoms, however, continue to affect the patient's social and vocational adjustment and the homeostasis of the family.

Sociocultural as well as psychodynamic factors can also influence and reinforce somatic expressions of depression. Some Western (Ludwig & Forrester, 1982) and non-Western (Katon, Kleinman, & Rosen, 1982) cultures lack proper terms for describing emotional states or pose strong sanctions against perceiving depression as an emotional state. When a patient's beliefs and practices about disease are not derived from modern science, physicians may fail to recognize depression expressed in the unique idiom of his or her culture of origin.

Given that many patients with an underlying depression seek help in the primary care sector for physical symptoms, do these persons present distinctive signs that can facilitate the diagnosis of depression? In depressed medical patients, the rates for physical pain range from 27% to 100% (Katon, 1982; Lesse, 1983). Other physical symptoms associated with depression in patients seeking medical care include musculoskeletal, neurologic, gastrointestinal, and cardiopulmonary types (Stoudemire, Kahn, Brown, Linfors, & Houpt, 1985). In a rigorous comparison of patients meeting Research Diagnostic Criteria for MDD with normal controls, the rate and level of somatic symptoms were found to increase with the patient's age and severity of illness (Casper, et al., 1985). In summary, no specific somatic symptoms, by themselves, are indicative of an underlying depression. In diagnosing depression when it presents as somatic symptomatology, the clinician needs to be attentive to the presence of concomitant depressive symptoms and to the patient's psychosocial context.

Depressive Concomitants of Medical Illness

What biological and psychological processes lead organic illnesses to resemble or generate depression? Katon (1982) concluded that it is unclear whether this form of somatopsychic illness results from pathological central nervous system monoamine changes stimulated by the medical disease, or whether it is a response to the stress of coping with such disease. A combination of both could be involved.

The possible medical conditions for which depressive symptoms are a frequent concomitant are extensive and pertain to most bodily systems (Cameron, 1987). Among the organic illnesses that most commonly cause depressive signs are hypothyroidism, hyperadrenalism, hypoglycemia, systemic infections, multiple sclerosis, temporal lobe and psychomotor epilepsies, essential hypertension, rheumatoid arthritis, pernicious anemia, diabetes mellitus, nutritional deficiencies, cardiovascular disease, and cancer (especially pancreatic and brain tumors). A wide range of neurological diseases and structural brain damage can also produce distinct affective symptoms (see the review by Tucker & Price, 1987). In addition to organic conditions that may potentiate a depression, various drugs ranging from birth control pills to antihypertensives produce depressive signs and symptoms (Zelnik, 1987).

These findings suggest that physicians and psychotherapists must be vigilant in distinguishing functional depression from medical illness with depressive symptomatology, regardless of its etiology and mechanisms. When the patient lacks a family history of depression, underlying medical illnesses should be considered.

Furthermore, women and older patients presenting with dysphoria or vegetative symptoms of depression (e.g., sleep changes, weight changes, appetite changes) should be evaluated for endocrine disorders. As a general principle, any physical symptomatology should be thoroughly evaluated before initiating psychosocial or psychobiological treatments. Further medical assessments also are warranted if the physical symptoms worsen or new ones appear during the course of treatment.

Recognizing and Treating the Depressed Patient in Primary Care

Several patterns of identification, diagnosis, and treatment of depression in the primary care setting have been described (Blacker & Clare, 1987; Katon, 1987; Schulberg, Block, & Coulehan, 1989; Schulberg & Burns, 1988). First, primary care practitioners underdiagnose this disorder. Rates of unrecognized depression range from 25% to 85%, depending on whether structured diagnostic instruments or a psychiatrist's formulation are used as the yardstick for diagnosing depression. Little is known about how primary care physicians elicit information, interpret cues, and formulate hypotheses about depression in medical populations. If physicians' awareness of depression is to be improved, researchers should examine the patient—physician interactions that facilitate or hinder diagnostic accuracy.

Second, even when accurately diagnosing depressive disorders, primary care physicians often do not treat them within state-of-the-art guidelines. In the previously cited reviews, physicians were found to provide depression-specific treatments to only 25% to 50% of patients diagnosed as depressed. When antidepressants were prescribed, physicians used relatively low dosages, rarely planed or effected dosage increases, and either discontinued the medication prematurely or did not discontinue it at all.

The third pattern emphasized is the growing uncertainty as to whether treatment guidelines developed with depressed patients in specialty mental health services can be transferred validly to depressed patients seeking treatment in primary care settings. This ambiguity may challenge the prevailing notion that proper treatment standards exist and that nonpsychiatric physicians fail to follow them. Indeed, there is evidence that the nature and severity of depressive symptomatology among primary care patients possibly differs from those of psychiatric patients. As was indicated previously, medical patients are thought to present more somatic complaints and fewer affective symptoms. Also, depressed persons seeking help from primary care physicians are often less clinically impaired than those turning directly to mental health professionals.

What knowledge exists about the efficacy of treatments for depressed patients in the primary care setting? Turning first to antidepressants, approximately 60% to 85% of ambulatory medical patients have been found to improve with active treatment, compared to 25% to 40% in the placebo condition (Schulberg et al., 1989). It is difficult to derive definitive conclusions from this body of work, however, since the investigators' methodologies vary on such design factors as subjects' inclusionary and exclusionary criteria; duration of treatment and time of endpoint assessment; and major outcome index. Blacker and Clare (1987) concluded that even the few antidepressant clinical trials conducted with primary care patients have significant limitations in their internal and external validity. Both a restricted range of severity and lack of clear depressive histories interfered with the validity of these studies. Finally, the presence of significant adverse side effects and noncompliance patterns further complicates the determination of an antidepressant's efficacy.

Consequently, even if antidepressants are superior to no treatment, their value is limited to patients who will accept them and not terminate treatment prematurely. At the least, it remains unclear which ambulatory medical patients benefit from drug treatment.

Assuming that only a segment of depressed primary care patients will benefit from antidepressants, effective alternative treatments are needed. Since stress and psychosocial difficulties are key concerns of this patient group, psychological treatments are well regarded and extensively used by primary care physicians (Daniels, Linn, Ward, & Leake, 1987; Fauman, 1983). Counseling procedures specifically pertinent to medical patients are described by Rodin (1984), Stuart and Lieberman (1986), and Castelnuovo-Tedesco (1986).

Psychological interventions alone with depressed patients in primary care, rather than specialty care, have not been studied empirically. Studies of brief psychotherapy conducted by Brodaty and Andrews (1983) and Klerman, et al. (1987) with ambulatory medical patients were not restricted to depressed subjects. Corney's (1984) "social work" with a depressed population included nonstandardized counseling and practical assistance. While research on psychotherapy alone is lacking, two primary care studies have analyzed this treatment's efficacy when combined with drugs. Blackburn, Bishop, Glen, Whalley, and Christie (1981) found no difference between the combined drug and cognitive therapy treatment versus cognitive therapy alone in the outcome of depressed medical patients. This contrasts with the conclusion that combined treatment produces an additive effect with depressed psychiatric patients (Conte, Plutchik, Wild, & Karasu, 1986; Weissman, 1979). Upon rectifying design flaws in Blackburn et al.'s work, Teasdale, Fennell, Hibbert, and Amies (1984) found that cognitive therapy combined with antidepressants significantly improved recovery upon posttreatment assessment; the increment over drugs alone was no longer evident, however, at three-month followup. Thus, the clinical efficacy of depression-specific psychological interventions validated with psychiatric patients remains to be established in primary care practice.

The timeliness of such outcome research is widely accepted. Indeed, in 1990 we initiated a clinical trial of psychotherapy's efficacy with this population (Schulberg et al., 1991). Pending findings from our research and that by others, the remainder of this chapter describes a psychotherapy intervention validated with depressed psychiatric patients that we deem generalizable to ambulatory medical patients experiencing a major depressive disorder. We will focus upon Interpersonal Psychotherapy (IPT), presenting its theoretical framework and procedures. IPT's applicability and feasibility in prepaid health care settings will be illustrated through clinical examples drawn from our work with depressed primary care patients.

Before undertaking IPT, however, the clinician must determine whether the depressed patient is best treated within the managed care facility or is better referred to a psychiatric facility. If the former, should the patient be treated by a generalist physician or by a mental health clinician when such a specialist is available? Schulberg et al. (1989) sought to answer this question through the use of decision analysis techniques that examine outcomes in the face of varied assumptions. However, insufficient empiric information was found in the literature to guide the choice of alternative treatment strategies. Even if incremental gains are expected when treatment is provided by a specialist rather than a generalist, wide variations in the availability of specialists and the sophistication of generalists make application of uniform guidelines tenuous in particular circumstances.

Given these realities, the choice of treatment setting and therapist typically results from a combination of clinician and patient variables. With regard to clinician factors, primary care physicians comfortable with affective disorders and trained in counseling procedures possibly could practice IPT, thereby maintaining responsibility for the depressed patient's psychiatric as well as medical care. The majority of generalist physicians, however, have no such aptitude or skill, and/or view psychotherapy as too time-consuming in an already overburdened work schedule. Such physicians should be encouraged to refer depressed patients to a mental health colleague within the managed health care center.

Patient influences on the choice of treating clinician include the patient's mental state and personality style. Depressed medical patients who are actively suicidal or psychotic, or both, or who have a history of bipolar illness are best treated by a mental health specialist. Sophisticated expertise with psychiatric illness also is required to treat patients with significant Axis II character pathology such as a borderline personality disorder. Finally, some patients are more likely to accept treatment from a medical provider rather than a mental health provider, because of stigma, defensiveness, or sociocultural concerns.

Interpersonal Psychotherapy (IPT)

Psychiatric treatment in prepaid health care facilities reflects the interplay of financial factors and the nature of the morbidity (Goldman, 1988). With regard to the former, prepaid primary care plans necessitate brief interventions since they typically limit psychiatric benefits. Altman and Goldstein (1988) found the modal duration of mental health treatment in a sample of HMOs to be between 10 and 20 sessions, a not unreasonable pattern given Bennett and Wisneski's (1979) finding that only two percent of an HMO population require long-term continuous psychotherapy.

Guidelines for sound mental health practice within the financial constraints of prepaid health care have been suggested by Bonstedt and Baird (1979) and Schneider-Braus (1987). (See Cummings, in this volume, for another perspective.) They emphasize the need for therapies causing the least disruption in a patient's life. Key elements of this approach are a goal-oriented contract negotiated by the patient and clinician, and a problem-solving orientation focusing upon present concerns. We suggest that this therapeutic orientation is quite applicable to depressive morbidity in primary care practice, since much of it is associated with difficult developmental transitions or stressful life events involving key interpersonal relationships. At these times, the patient's unresolved dependency needs thwart movement towards autonomy and individuation, and/or previously satisfactory adaptive capacities now prove inadequate.

If one accepts this formulation of the psychosocial stressors underlying many of the episodic depressions presenting in primary care practice, then there is need for a time-limited psychotherapy specifically geared to interpersonal issues. The psychotherapy must respect the patient's somatic presenting complaints while still dealing with the psychosocial context in which they arose or are experienced. The therapy should convey an optimism to the patient that particular relationship problems associated with the depression will be addressed and resolved, while others must await future consideration. Furthermore, termination must be addressed from treatment's onset since the therapeutic contract, for clinical and administrative reasons, is of a time-limited nature. Indeed, Siddall, Haffey, and Feinman (1988) conceive of most psychotherapy in an HMO setting as intermittent and brief rather than as discrete and terminable.

An intervention responsive to such requirements is the "Interpersonal Psychotherapy" (IPT) model developed by Klerman et al. (1984) specifically for the treatment of depression. IPT posits that depression, regardless of symptom pattern, severity, presumed biological vulnerability, or personality traits occurs in a psychosocial and interpersonal context. Understanding the interpersonal context associated with symptom onset and modifying its characteristics are important to the person's recovery and possibly for prevention of further episodes. This conception of the depressive disorder and strategies for its treatment derive from several sources. As outlined by Klerman et al. (1984), IPT's conceptual framework stems from the well-known and widely accepted theoretical contributions of such clinicians as Adolph Meyer and Harry Stack Sullivan who viewed psychiatric disorders as resulting from a person's inability to cope with environmental stressors. IPT also incorporates more recent empirical findings that demonstrate depression's association with disrupted affected bonds (attachment theory), the lack of an intimate confiding relationship, excessive stressful life events and social losses, and impaired social relationships.

IPT is a brief weekly psychological treatment, lasting approximately 16 sessions, that focuses on the quality of the depressed patient's current interpersonal functioning and seeks to remedy stressful interactions. IPT may be provided alone or in conjunction with antidepressants or other medications. Its efficacy in treating depressed psychiatric patients was determined through a series of New Haven studies (Klerman et al., 1984), and in the National Institute of Mental Health Treatment of Depression Collaborative Research Program (Elkin et al., 1989). A training manual that operationalizes this form of psychotherapy is useful in enhancing the consistency with which IPT is provided across patients and treatment settings (Rounsaville, O'Malley, Foley, & Weissman, 1988). IPT clinicians may be experienced psychiatrists, psychologists, social workers, or psychiatric nurses. There are no reports as yet of efforts to train primary care physicians in this form of counseling, although internal medicine nurse practitioners have been trained to provide a modified form of IPT (Klerman et al., 1987).

Managing the Depressive State

When the primary care physician determines that the patient's symptom pattern indicates a depressive disorder, several initial steps are initiated. The first, and often the most difficult with primary care patients, is educating the patient about the nature of depression and its contribution to his or her ill health. This education often takes the form of a detailed symptom review intended both to confirm the psychiatric diagnosis and to help the patient realize that vague, disparate, symptoms (particularly of the neurovegetative type) are part of a defined syndrome. This symptom review also stimulates the patient's thinking about the temporal relationship between stressful psychosocial experiences and preexisting or new physical ailments. The patient may better accept a psychiatric diagnosis if informed that six to nine percent of persons seen in primary care practice are similarly experiencing a depressive disorder. Using the IPT model, the physician can explain to the patient that depression responds to treatment, that improvement can be achieved in a 16-week time frame, and that the prognosis is good. This may reassure the patient who is feeling rather hopeless because previous physical and laboratory tests produced no definitive diagnosis.

The majority of primary care patients who present with a clearly diagnosable depression accept this formulation and agree to a mental health intervention, even if the depression is masked with somatic complaints. However, there is a subgroup of depressives unwilling to accept the psychosocial elements of their illness, which they insist is totally organic in nature. There generally is little clinical benefit to battling these patients and imposing the psychiatric diagnosis. They are better treated by the primary care physician with a combination of antidepressants and supportive counselling, perhaps with a mental health specialist serving as a consultant to the physician.

When the patient acknowledges the depression and initiates psychotherapy, a second aspect of managing the depression in the early phases of treatment is to counsel the patient in specific ways of controlling the vegetative and mood symptoms. These include the avoidance of stressful interactions, the temporary reduction of self-expectations, and the modification of daily commitments. The patient is granted the "sick role" and temporarily relieved from customary social obligations. However, while endorsing the sick role, the IPT therapist also emphasizes its brief duration and expresses optimism that the patient shortly will resume greater responsibility and autonomy. Depressed psychiatric patients typically appreciate and accept the legitimated curtailment of prior routines. However, it is possible that repeated sanctioning of behavioral limitations will be needed with depressed medical patients when they, or their families, or both still are struggling with the fact that irksome symptom patterns indicate an affective rather than physical disorder.

A still further aid to helping depressed patients manage disturbing symptomatology is to prescribe antidepressant medications for use in conjunction with IPT. This decision should be made in relation to the patient's role performance, severity of neurovegetative symptoms, medical contraindications, and prior drug response. We have found only five percent of depressed primary care patients to exhibit specific contraindications to tricyclic antidepressants (Coulehan, Schulberg, Block, Janosky, & Arena, 1990). Notably, many more are personally loathe to take such medications even when receptive to psychotherapy. In addition to a concern about uncomfortable side-effects, depressed primary care patients also are troubled by polypharmacy; they were found in the Coulehan et al. study already to be taking an average of three drugs for physical illness. At a deeper level, psychotropic medications may signify a loathsome psychiatric diagnosis to these patients; taking antidepressants may imply that they are "sicker" and possibly out of control.

Identifying Major Problem Areas

We stated previously that the time-limited nature of psychotherapy in prepaid health care programs necessitates a goal-oriented, problem-solving approach. IPT meets this criterion by selecting one or two key problem areas that therapist and patient contract to work on during the course of treatment. While the problem areas are potentially wide-ranging, IPT delimits them to four categories of interpersonal stressors found to be associated with depression. The psychotherapist's task is to permit patients to describe symptoms and problems in their own subjective terms but to reframe them in the context of recent or longstanding difficulties with key persons in their lives. Depressed medical patients may initially resist this reformulation, but we have found that most will accept a psychosocial perspective when perceiving it as a personal choice rather than as the therapist's demand. Therefore, even depressed medical patients harboring a concern that fatigue, loss of appetite, sleep discontinuity, and so forth truly indicate an undetected physical illness will simultaneously analyze current life circumstances and experiment with behaviors for resolving stressful relationships.

Interpersonal Problem Areas

IPT identifies four interpersonal problem areas as producing, or being associated with, depressive disorders. They are grief reactions, role transitions, interpersonal role disputes, and interpersonal deficits. These problem areas generally are distinct and readily identified through careful interviewing of the patient. However, they are not mutually exclusive and patients often will present difficulties in two or three areas. Furthermore, the targeted problem areas may shift as therapy progresses. With depressed psychiatric patients, difficulties in role transitions and interpersonal disputes predominate; indeed, they often occur simultaneously. It is our impression that depressed ambulatory medical patients more frequently experience unresolved grief that has been extensively somatized, or the combination of grief and role transition difficulties associated with chronic physical morbidity or loss of organs or limbs.

Occasionally, no distinct problem area is discernible from the patient's clinical history, or the patient and therapist fail to agree on the interpersonal problem area warranting therapeutic attention. In these circumstances, the therapist may: set very general goals with the hope of shortly becoming more focused; delay setting treatment goals until the patient's resistance diminishes; or accept the patient's initial perspective in anticipation of a subsequent change. When it is not possible to resolve the impasse and to establish a focused, mutually agreeable treatment contract, IPT should be terminated and an alternative intervention considered. We have found such an outcome to be rare. In the remainder of this section, we describe IPT's four problem areas. Each is illustrated with the case of a primary care patient whose depression exemplifies the relationship between the presenting complaints, the selected IPT problem areas, and suggested treatment approaches.

Grief Reaction

As Klerman et al. (1984) indicate, the experience of normal grief resembles a clinical depression, but the two conditions are not equivalent. Acute symptoms of grief reactions tend to resolve spontaneously within four to six months of the loss of a loved one as the bereaved person gradually distances himself or herself from emotions and experiences associated with that person. This process of symptom formation and resolution is normal, and depression-like bereavement is not considered a DSM-III disorder. When this process fails to occur within the expected sequence and duration, however, abnormal grief of the delayed or distorted type should be considered.

An abnormal grief reaction may be readily diagnosed when the patient's symptoms have a clear temporal relationship to the loss of a loved one. Often, though, the relationship is more subtle or indirect and requires careful probing by the therapist. With depressed primary care patients, the unresolved grief often presents as intense anxiety about serious personal illness or illness in a significant other. The patient may then display depressive symptoms but lack any awareness of their relationship to the past unresolved grief.

The IPT treatment of grief-related depression has two goals: facilitating the delayed mourning process, and helping the patient reestablish interests and relationships that can substitute for the lost loved one. Techniques for achieving these goals include: the elicitation of feelings and nonjudgmental exploration regarding events associated with the loved one's death; reconstruction of the relationship including hostile, angry affects; reassurance that total decompensation will not occur; and behavioral change in the direction of creating new relationships to fill the interpersonal void created by the loss.

Case illustration no. 1. A 48-year-old married man presented to the emergency room with acute onset sharp, left lateral rib cage pain, accompanied by numbness in both arms, rapid breathing, and diaphoresis. He was given nitroglycerin with equivocal results. An electrocardiogram (EKG) showed sinus tachycardia, and he was admitted to the coronary care unit to rule out an acute myocardial infarct (MI). The symptoms resolved quickly, and the patient had no enzyme elevations. However, he underwent a stress test and was considered for a coronary angiogram because of a positive family history, that is, his father had died of an MI when the patient was a teenager.

On initial questioning, the patient denied any recent life stress. He reported that he had been a "health nut" since his early 30s, at which time he had stopped smoking, begun a regular and rigorous exercise program, and followed a low-cholesterol diet. When asked if this was due to worries about his father's sudden early death, the patient denied this. He stated that, indeed, he had not thought much about his father "in years" and could not really remember events associated with his father's death. The patient mentioned in passing that he had assumed additional responsibilities at work. Upon further questioning, he revealed that his boss of 10 years had had a severe MI three months ago. The patient appeared sad but denied concern, stating that he had visited his boss in the hospital but since then had been "too busy" to talk with him.

In choosing a psychological treatment focus, the patient's striking denial of grief alerted the clinician to the well defended emotions of childhood loss. When attempts were made to elicit feelings and memories of his father's illness and death, the patient became controlled and distant. It was possible, however, to inquire further about the patient's relationship with his boss, who had been his mentor for many years. The patient had followed him up the corporate ladder; although he eventually achieved considerable independent responsibility, the patient still would "wander down the hall to run ideas past him" until the boss's recent illness. As he talked further about his boss and, in this attenuated way, worked through grief and guilt feelings, he obtained gradual symptomatic relief. Toward the end of therapy, frank exploration of feelings of loss about the therapist led to a reworking of these same issues in relation to his father's premature death.

Role Transitions

The multiple role that individuals play in society have long interested sociologists and social anthropologists. Psychologists and psychiatrists have focused particularly on the manner in which people cope with new roles and the impaired social functioning that results from the inability to manage a transition involving diminished status. When the new role (of an objectively negative or positive nature) is too difficult to manage, a clinical depression often results. Klerman et al. (1984) propose that depressions induced by role transitions stem from: (a) the loss of familiar social supports, (b) problematic management of the accompanying affect, (c) demands for a repertoire of new social skills, and (d) cognitive disturbances produced by diminished self-esteem.

Depressed primary care patients experience the same role-transitional problems as do depressed psychiatric patients, for example, coping with a job change, accepting a change in parental or marital status, retiring, and so forth. However, the medical group also commonly confronts severe role problems produced by the disabling effects of a chronic physical illness. Such illness can create major limitations in the person's social roles as parent, spouse, or coworker and require that he or she fundamentally reconceive the manner in which these roles are to be played. Depressive illness results when the person cannot accept the limitations produced by the physical morbidity, for example, dependency, loss of longstanding social relationships, the need to develop new social skills, altered social status and group identification, and so on.

The diagnosis of role-transition problems is based upon explicit, or perhaps implicit, indications that recent events have produced major changes in the patient's role constellation. The internal psychological meanings of these changes, rather than the change per se, are thought to trigger the depression. In clarifying the patient's reaction, it is useful to distinguish the feelings associated with the lost role (which may resemble a grief reaction) from difficulty in performing a new social role. For example, not all diabetic patients facing significant dietary restrictions, or insulin dependence, or both experience an affective disorder (Lustman, Amado,

& Wetzel, 1983). For those who do, it is valuable to understand the patient's cognitive beliefs about this illness, the subjective reactions to having a chronic condition, feelings such as dependency associated with needed medical procedures, and how the procedures affect the person's daily ability to function as student, spouse, wage earner, parent, and so on.

The goals of IPT in treating role-transition-related depression are to shift the patient's emphasis from the past loss to an appreciation of future opportunities for recovered self-esteem and rewarding social relationships. The therapeutic tasks include helping the patient objectively evaluate what has been lost, encouraging the appropriate expression of affect, establishing the social skills pertinent to the new role, and developing an appropriate social system. Patients must be actively supported as they disengage from old roles and experiment with new behaviors and affects.

Case illustration no. 2. A 51-year-old bridge worker was seen in the emergency room for acute shortness of breath, light-headedness, and diaphoresis. This was the most severe of several such recent episodes, the first having occurred when he felt dyspneic on climbing to a high beam. He has become anxious at that time and had asked to work on the bridge deck instead. Although this request was granted, the patient continued to experience a generalized feeling of unease as well as increasing irritability, sleeplessness, and despondency. He had smoked heavily for many years and had signs of mild emphysema on examination. The patient had toyed with the idea of suicide but felt that was the "coward's way out."

A clinical history revealed that the patient's father had also been a bridge worker, hard-driving, tough, and heavy-drinking. The father's readiness to brawl was legendary in the community. The patient had idolized him until early adolescence, at which time his own rebelliousness produced frequent conflict. One disagreement turned violent, and from that time the patient and his father had coexisted in a state of uneasy truce. As the patient's work situation and mood deteriorated, his relationship with his own teenage son became more bitter and antagonistic. When told by his doctor to stop smoking, the patient perversely increased this behavior and began to drive erratically.

Psychotherapy focused upon the role transitions occurring at work and at home, and their problematic echoes of the patient's never-resolved childhood identification and rivalry with his father. The patient spent several sessions denouncing his father and crying over their lost relationship. Subsequently, he was able to acknowledge that his father's way "to be a man" was not necessarily the only one. Having achieved this insight, the patient began to consider that a more sedentary job incorporating his many years of physical labor experience could allow further years of productive work. As he became cognitively and emotionally aware of his painful adolescent relationship with his own father, the patient became more receptive to his son's struggles for autonomy.

Interpersonal Role Disputes

Situations in which the patient and a "significant other" display widely discrepant expectations about their relationship have been characterized by Klerman et al.

(1984) as interpersonal disputes. Medical patients commonly report such disputes, but they become the focus of psychotherapeutic attention only when deemed significant in the depression's etiology or persistence. Typical maladaptive behaviors that maintain the dispute are the patient's poor communication patterns, truly irreconcilable differences, and/or the sense of helplessness and hopelessness intrinsic to the depression.

The nature of the interpersonal disputes upon which IPT focuses with depressed primary care patients may well resemble those presented by depressed psychiatric patients, e.g., physically abusive behavior by the spouse, altered but unsatisfactory roles upon the birth of a child, and so on. In the primary care setting, however, the therapist should carefully elucidate how physical illness has affected the patient's relationship with a significant other. Chronic illnesses like colitis or arthritis can profoundly disturb long-established marital roles and shift the prior equilibrium in conflicting directions.

IPT's treatment goals in the event of an interpersonal dispute are to: (a) help the patient identify the conflict, (b) guide the patient towards an awareness of choices and the formulation of alternative actions, and (c) encourage the patient to modify expectations of the significant other so that they are more realistic and achievable. A key task in developing the treatment plan is to determine the present stage of the dispute, that is, whether it is still being negotiated, is at an impasse, or is irretrievably disputed. The results of this assessment will guide the clinician's contract with the patient as therapy moves from exploring the characteristics of the dispute to a systematic review of the options available to the patient.

Case illustration no. 3. The patient was a 54-year-old married mother of three with a five-year history of severe rheumatoid arthritis. She had been an active and energetic young woman although she suffered a mild and transient postpartum depression with each child. The patient eagerly managed her home and children until the youngest entered kindergarten, at which time she again became transiently depressed. She improved spontaneously and was able to commit herself to volunteer work and the Parent–Teacher Association. Soon after the oldest daughter married and the youngest entered high school, the patient experienced the onset of severe joint pains, fatigue, and weight loss. These symptoms progressed rapidly, and a diagnosis of rheumatoid arthritis was made. The patient responded poorly to treatment. Short courses of steroids produced temporary relief, but her physicians were reluctant to keep her on maintenance doses. During one course of prednisone, the patient became depressed once again as the dose was lowered. Even weeks after the steroids were discontinued, the depression deepened. The patient slept poorly, lost appetite and weight, and withdrew from family and friends. She felt worthless and unable to care for her grandchild for fear she might "drop him."

Although all social relationships suffered, the patient was uncharacteristically irritable and short-tempered with her husband whom she accused of "not caring" about her pain. Upon questioning, it became apparent that, as the patient's dependency increased, her husband had turned away. He was working and traveling more as he secretly grieved the loss of a wife who had formerly taken such good care of him. The angrier she became, the more he withdrew until their time together was dominated by bickering and bitterness. Therapy centered on and clarified the patient's sense of losing her good health and roles as mother, grandmother, and volunteer. She recognized that she always had "mothered" her husband and experienced difficulty acknowledging her new dependency on him. In the middle phase of treatment, the patient's husband accompanied her to three sessions. They discussed the changes in their relationship and roles necessitated by the illness, and after sufficient ventilation of grief and anger were able to use their prior coping skills to renegotiate mutually acceptable tasks and responsibilities. As a new equilibrium was established in the marriage and as the patient accepted more of her physical limitations, she was again able to create a helping role. Not surprisingly, she chose at this time in her life to become active in a local arthritis self-help group.

Interpersonal Deficits

Exploration of the factors associated with a clinical depression may reveal that the patient has a history of social impoverishment marked by inadequate or unsustaining interpersonal relationships. Such persons may never have established intimate relationships as adults; indeed, disruption of important childhood relationships frequently is evident as well. Severe social isolation in a depressed patient potentially indicates a more severe level of pathology than is the case for the previously defined problem areas.

The diagnosis of depression accompanied by interpersonal deficits should seek to distinguish whether the patient is: (a) socially isolated because of longstanding or temporary deficiencies in interpersonal skills, (b) socially unfulfilled despite an adequate number and range of social relationships, or (c) socially withdrawn because of a persisting depression that has not been adequately treated. The third type is evident in primary care patients who have made poor adjustments to a chronic physical illness and whose relationships with others have become progressively withdrawn and limited. This pattern can also be seen in patients with AIDS or communicable diseases that lead them to avoid social contacts.

IPT's goal with depressed patients displaying interpersonal deficits is to reduce their social isolation. When there are no meaningful current relationships, the therapeutic focus may be on past ones, the relationship with the therapist, or behaviors needed to establish new social contacts. A review of past satisfactory relationships provides the patient with a model in which he or she participated actively, and alerts the patient to the possibility of once more engaging in meaningful social interactions.

Case illustration no. 4. This 37-year-old patient was raised in somewhat unusual circumstances. During childhood, his father maintained a second family in a neighboring town; the "secret" was probably known to all for years before his parents openly separated. The patient grew up with a feeling of shame and although he possessed a complement of superficial acquaintances, essentially he was isolated and alone. The oldest child in the family, he was academically able and competitive, and progressed in his job as an electrician to supervise a field crew before being promoted to a middle-level administrative position. In this new role, the patient felt conflicted between his supervisors and the frontline crews but was able to cope by working harder at noninterpersonal bureaucratic tasks. During a regional economic recession, fiscal pressures on the company became intense and the patient was no longer able to "keep the peace" in his work area through personal yeoman efforts. He became even more quïet and isolated at work and home; his wife noted increased temper outbursts that were particularly directed at his young son. The patient developed increasingly frequent headaches, which he ignored until one day he experienced a severe headache accompanied by transient numbness of the left arm and leg. When examined in the emergency room, the patient was severely hypertensive and required immediate treatment and hospitalization.

A masked depression was diagnosed. Psychotherapy focused on the relationship between the patient's social isolation and internalization of feelings and conflicts associated with the belief that "shameful" issues were not to be discussed with others. As the patient found that he could trust his therapist with these secrets and that disclosure brought relief from feelings of loneliness and tension, the patient accepted the need to learn new social skills. The depression lifted as he talked more openly with his wife and colleagues. The termination process permitted the patient to explore feelings about losing the therapist, an unusual opportunity for him to express sadness explicitly and directly.

Interpersonal Psychotherapy With Special Populations

The conceptual framework of IPT and its therapeutic interventions are pertinent to all depressed persons but variations of the model can enhance its efficacy with particular primary care populations. Perhaps the most refined IPT variations are those intended to meet the clinical needs of elderly persons. Sholomskas, Chevron, Prusoff, and Berry (1983) and Frank and Frank (1988) indicate from their experiences with this population that IPT's four problem areas are germane to formulating the nature of an elderly person's depressive episode. However, the specific objectives of the treatment contract and the manner in which they are achieved may require modifications with the elderly. Thus, when the elderly person's depression appears linked to an unresolvable interpersonal dispute, the usual therapeutic goal of helping the patient terminate the relationship may not be practical. Instead, treatment might focus on strategies for increasing tolerance of the stressful relationship, for example, by establishing alternative social outlets in which to invest one's energy. With regard to the therapist's interactions with an elderly depressed person, a full 50-minute session usually is unfeasible during the initial phase of treatment. The session's duration should match the patient's capacity for relatively focused attention. Additionally, a more active role typically is indicated for the therapist who also must tolerate the elderly patient's dependency needs to a greater degree than is customary.

Is IPT effective with patients displaying significant emotional distress but not necessarily at the diagnosable level? Indeed, should they be receiving this or any treatment? This issue is a key one in primary care practice, since 50% to 80% of patients scoring above the established cutpoint of a depression screening instrument fail to meet DSM-III criteria for a depressive disorder (Coulehan, Schulberg, & Block, 1989), or the disorder presents in an atypical or minor form (Barrett et al., 1988). Klerman et al. (1987) sought to address this issue by developing Interpersonal

Counseling (IPC) as a variation of IPT for use with HMO patients scoring high on the General Health Questionnaire. This psychosocial intervention of six half-hour counseling sessions was administered by nurse practitioners. The pilot study's finding that high-distress IPC-treated patients showed more rapid symptom reduction and improved social functioning than a comparison group suggests the value of continued efforts to modify IPT for use with the sizable number of primary care patients experiencing intense emotional distress of the subclinical type.

Conclusion

Depressive disorders are experienced by 6–9% of primary care patients, while another 10% display masked or atypical forms of this morbidity. Effective treatments are needed, therefore, within a framework that considers the clinical and organizational factors influencing prepaid care. A review of prior research indicates a dearth of studies demonstrating the efficacy of depression-specific psychological interventions with primary care patients. Pending such outcome research, we suggest applying a psychotherapy validated with depressed psychiatric patients to ambulatory medical patients experiencing an overt or masked major depressive disorder. The theoretical framework and therapeutic procedures of interpersonal psychotherapy (IPT) have been described and illustrated with case examples drawn from primary care practice. Variations of this intervention for use with the elderly and other populations should also be considered.

References

Altman, L., & Goldstein, J. (1988). Impact of HMO model type on mental health service delivery: Variation in treatment and approaches. *Administration in Mental Health, 15*, 246–261.

Barrett, J. E., Barrett, J. A., Oxman, T., & Gerber, P. (1988). The prevalence of psychiatric disorders in a primary care practice. *Archives of General Psychiatry, 45*, 1100–1106.

Bennett, M., & Wisneski, M. (1979). Continuous psychotherapy within an HMO. *American Journal of Psychiatry, 136*, 1283–1287.

Blackburn, I., Bishop, S., Glen, A., Whalley, L., & Christie, J. (1981). The efficacy of cognitive therapy in depression: A treatment trial using cognitive therapy and pharmacotherapy, each alone and in combination. *British Journal of Psychiatry, 139*, 181–189.

Blacker, C., & Clare, A. (1987). Depressive disorder in primary care. *British Journal of Psychiatry, 150*, 737–751.

Bonstedt, T., & Baird, S. (1979). Providing cost-effective psychotherapy in a health maintenance organization. *Hospital Community Psychiatry, 30*, 129–132.

Brodaty, H., & Andrews, G. (1983). Brief psychotherapy in family practice. *British Journal of Psychiatry, 143*, 11–19.

Cameron, O. (Ed.). (1987). *Presentations of Depression*. New York: Wiley.

Casper, R., Redmond, D., Katz, M., Schaffer, C., Davis, J., & Koslow, S. (1985). Somatic symptoms in primary affective disorder: Presence and relationship to the classification of depression. *Archives of General Psychiatry, 42*, 1098–1104.

Castelnuovo-Tedesco, P. (1986). *The twenty-minute hour: A guide to brief psychotherapy for the physician*. Washington, DC: American Psychiatric Press.

Conte, H., Plutchik, R., Wild, K., & Karasu, T. (1986). Combined psychotherapy and pharmacotherapy for depression. *Archives of General Psychiatry, 43*, 471–479.

Corney, R. (1984). The effectiveness of attached social workers in the management of depressed female patients in general practice Monograph Supplement 6. *Psychological Medicine*.

Coulehan, J., Schulberg, H., & Block, M. (1989). The efficiency of depression questionnaires for case finding in primary medical care. *Journal of General Internal Medicine, 4,* 541–547.

Coulehan, J., Schulberg, H., Block, M., Janosky, J., & Arena, V. (1990). Medical comorbidity of major depressive disorder in a primary medical practice. *Archives of Internal Medicine, 150,* 2363–2367.

Daniels, M., Linn, L., Ward, N., & Leake, B. (1987). A study of physician preferences in the management of depression in the general medical setting. *General Hospital Psychiatry, 8,* 229–235.

Elkin, I., Shea, M., Watkins, J., Imber, S., Sotsky, S., Collins, J., Glass, D., Pilkonis, P., Leber, W., Docherty, J., Fiester, S., & Parloff, M. (1989). NIMH Treatment of the Depression Collaborative Research Program: I. General effectiveness of treatments. *Archives of General Psychiatry, 46,* 971–982.

Fauman, M. (1983). Psychiatric components of medical and surgical practice: II. Referral and treatment of psychiatric disorders. *American Journal of Psychiatry, 140,* 760–763.

Frank, E., & Frank, N. (1988). *Manual for the adaptation of interpersonal psychotherapy to the acute treatment of depression in late life.* Unpublished manuscript, Western Psychiatric Institute and Clinic, Pittsburgh, PA.

Goldman, W. (1988). Mental health and substance abuse services in HMOs. *Administration in Mental Health, 15,* 189–200.

Katon, W. (1982). Depression: Somatic symptoms and medical disorders in primary care. *Comprehensive Psychiatry, 23,* 274–287.

Katon, W. (1987). The epidemiology of depression in medical care. *International Journal of Psychiatry in Medicine, 17,* 93–112.

Katon, W., Kleinman, A., & Rosen, G. (1982). Depression and somatization: A review. Part I. *American Journal of Medicine, 72,* 127–135.

Klerman, G. L. (1990). The psychiatric patient's right to effective treatment: Implications of Osheroff v. Chestnut Lodge. *American Journal of Psychiatry, 147,* 409–418.

Klerman, G., Budman, S., Berwick, D., Weissman, M., Damico-White, J., Demby, A., & Feldstein, M. (1987). Efficacy of a brief psychosocial intervention for symptoms of stress and distress among patient in primary care. *Medical Care, 25,* 1078–1088.

Klerman, G., Weissman, M., Rounsaville, B., & Chevron, E. (1984). *Interpersonal psychotherapy of depression.* New York: Basic Books.

Lesse, S. (1983). The masked depression syndrome: Results of a 17-year clinical study. *American Journal of Psychotherapy, 37,* 456–475.

Ludwig, A., & Forrester, R. (1982). Nerves, but not mentally. *Journal of Clinical Psychiatry, 43,* 187–190.

Lustman, P., Amado, H., & Wetzel, R. (1983). Depression in diabetics: A critical appraisal. *Comprehensive Psychiatry, 24,* 65–74.

Rodin, G. (1984). Expressive psychotherapy in the medically ill: Resistances and possibilities. *International Journal of Psychiatry in Medicine, 14,* 99–108.

Rounsaville, B., O'Malley, S., Foley, S., & Weissman, M. (1988). Role of manual-guided training in the conduct and efficacy of interpersonal psychotherapy for depression. *Journal of Consulting and Clinical Psychology, 56,* 681–688.

Schneider-Braus, K. (1987). A practical guide to HMO psychiatry. *Hospital and Community Psychiatry, 38,* 876–879.

Schulberg, H., Block, M., & Coulehan, J. (1989). Treating depression in primary care practice: An application of decision analysis. *General Hospital Psychiatry, 11,* 208–215.

Schulberg, H., & Burns, B. (1988). Mental disorders in primary care: Epidemiologic, diagnostic, and treatment research directions. *General Hospital Psychiatry, 10,* 79–87.

Schulberg, H., Coulehan, J., Block, M., Scott, C., Imber, I., & Perel, J. (1991). Strategies for evaluating treatments for major depression in primary care patients. *General Hospital Psychiatry, 13,* 9–18.

Schulberg, H., McClelland, M., & Burns, B. (1987). Depression and physical illness: The prevalence, causation, and diagnosis of comorbidity. *Clinical Psychology Review, 7,* 145–167.

Sholomskas, A., Chevron, E., Prusoff, B., & Berry, C. (1983). Short-term interpersonal therapy (IPT) with the depressed elderly: Case reports and discussion. *American Journal of Psychotherapy, 37,* 552–566.

Siddall, L., Haffey, N., & Feinman, J. (1988). Intermittent brief psychotherapy in an HMO setting. *American Journal of Psychotherapy, 42,* 96–106.

Stoudemire, A., Kahn, M., Brown, J., Linfors, E., & Houpt, J. (1985). Masked depression in a combined medical–psychiatric unit. *Psychosomatics, 26,* 221–228.

Stuart, M., & Lieberman, J. (1986). *The 15-minute hour: Applied psychotherapy for the primary care physician.* New York: Praeger.

Teasdale, J., Fennell, M., Hibbert, G., & Amies, P. (1984). Cognitive therapy for major depressive disorder in primary care. *British Journal of Psychiatry, 144,* 400–406.

Tucker, G., & Price, T. (1987). Depression and neurologic disease. In O. Cameron (Ed.), *Presentations of depression* (pp. 237–250). New York: Wiley.

Weissman, M. (1979). The psychological treatment of depression. *Archives of General Psychiatry, 36,* 1261–1269.

Wells, K. B., Manning, W. G., Duan, N., Newhouse, J. P., & Ware, J. E. (1987). Cost-sharing and the use of general medical physicians for outpatient mental health care. *Health Services Research, 22,* 1–17.

Zelnik, T. (1987). Depressive effects of drugs. In O. Cameron (Ed.), *Presentations of depression* (pp. 355–400). New York: Wiley.

12

Patricia J. Robinson

Providing Couples' Therapy in Prepaid Health Care

The Setting

Group Health Cooperative of Puget Sound is a health maintenance organization that was founded in 1947. It has a membership of approximately 360,000. There are seven mental health clinics that receive approximately 11,000 requests for new service per year. Most Group Health subscribers have a mental health benefit allowing 10 visits per year at no charge and another 10 or more with a copay requirement. Patients may self-refer or be referred by their primary care or specialty physician.

Consistent with data presented by Siddall, Haffey, and Feinman (1988), requests for marital or primary relationship therapy comprise up to 30% of requests for service. Approximately 35% of patients requesting services have been seen by the mental health service previously.

Marital stress and distress play a central role in the psychological and physical health of individuals and families. Adaptive coping and marital satisfaction are strongly related to general emotional adjustment (Ilfeld, 1980; Pearlin & Schooler, 1978). In addition, a good marriage is predictive of later life satisfaction (Mussen, Honzik, & Eichorn, 1982) and may be related to longevity and physical health (Kalish & Knutson, 1976). Conversely, marital conflict and marital separation can contribute to increased physical illness (Holmes & Masuda, 1974) and to depression (Coyne, Kahn, & Gotlib, 1976; Weissman & Paykel, 1974).

The prevalence of marital and family problems in managed mental health care is enormous. Shadle and Christianson (1988) report that 17% of health maintenance organization (HMO) clients use marital or family therapy, and problems in intimate relationships with a marital (or nonmarital) partner represent up to 30% of presenting problems in managed mental health settings (Siddall, Haffey, & Feinman, 1988). Clearly any comprehensive health care system needs to pay close attention to the treatment of marital and relationship dysfunction.

Appreciation is expressed to the Group Health Mental Health Department and the Group Health Medical Director for providing technical and financial support in the preparation of this chapter.

The Theory of Brief Treatment of Couples

One of the earliest models of brief therapy was developed at the Brief Therapy Center of the Mental Research Institute (MRI) in Palo Alto, California (Weakland, Fisch, Waltzawick, & Bodin, 1974). In this model, dysfunctional behavior in couples and families is seen as persisting to the extent that the problems are maintained by ineffective problem-solving behavior on the part of the patient or others in the interpersonal environment.

More recently, several clinicians have developed brief, behaviorally oriented therapy for couples seeking psychotherapy. In 1979 Jacobson and Margolin presented a behavioral marital therapy (BMT) approach to work with distressed couples. This model views marital distress as resulting from a low rate of positive exchange and the use of aversive consequences to control behavior, as well as from communication and problem-solving skill deficits. Another brief treatment approach for couples developed by Stuart (1981) grew out of a set of assumptions about relationships and behavior change, again based upon social learning theory. He advocates the use of cognitive change techniques to prompt new behavior and effect the repetition of desired behavior and the use of behavior change to facilitate new experience. Most recently Bornstein and Bornstein (1986) have integrated systems and behavioral communication approaches to marital therapy. Another model emphasizing the role of cognition in marital interactions has been developed by Beck (1988). In this approach, couples become more aware of their interpretations of their spouse's behavior and see much of their conflict as stemming from differences in perspectives. Group treatments using components of behavioral marital treatment have been developed for use with distressed (Contreras & Scheingold, 1984; O'Farrell & Cutter, 1984) and nondistressed couples (Markman, Floyd, Stanley, & Storaasli, 1988).

"Solution Oriented Brief Therapy" (DeShazer, et. al., 1986) is also used to successfully treat distressed couples. Interventions are aimed at expanding upon exceptions to the problems presented by the couple or individual representing the couple in treatment. When only one member of a couple is interested in change, this model identifies this person as the psychotherapy "customer" and treatment may proceed on an individual basis with this customer (Berg, 1988). This model shares common conceptual ground with both Systems Theory and with "Contextual Psychotherapy" (Hayes, 1987), which also reframes "resistance." In Solution-Oriented Brief Therapy, patients not interested in change are defined as "visitors" and like visitors they are complimented and treated kindly, but, of course, not expected to change. Likewise in Contextual Psychotherapy, patients are supported in finding ways to accept things "as they are" prior to pursuing change. Bergman (1985) provides yet another slant on systemic work with couples.

Current Research on Couples' Therapy

While data evaluating on the effectiveness of insight-oriented and strategic therapy with couples (Johnson & Greenberg, 1985; Weakland, Fisch, Waltzawick, & Bodin, 1974), have been slow in accumulating, and data on couples have not been leased out from data on all patients in available studies. DeShazer (1986) reports that 72% of a sample of 400 patients seen for Solution-Focused Brief Treatment indicated that either they had met their goals for therapy or that significant improvement had been made so that further therapy was not necessary.

Studies evaluating the effectiveness of behavioral marital therapy have proliferated in the past 12 years. Couples who participated in an eight-session treatment package demonstrated substantial improvement on both observational and self-report measures, as compared with a waiting list control group (Jacobson, 1977). Furthermore, 90% of the spouses reported marital adjustment scores within the normal range after therapy and maintained their level of satisfaction with positive changes at a one-year follow-up.

In the decade following this promising initial pilot study, numerous evaluative endeavors have produced important outcome and process information about behavioral marital therapy. The overall results are quite clear. Hahlweg and Markman (1988) report a meta-analysis of behavioral marital therapy in 17 outcome studies conducted in the United States and Europe involving 613 couples. They found that the average person who had received behavioral marital therapy was more improved than 83% of the people who had received either placebo or no treatment. Additionally, they concluded that the chance of improvement for couples in the treatment conditions was 72% as compared with a 28% chance for improvement in control groups. These results are stable cross-culturally and are maintained at 12-month follow-up. There is evidence that couples' therapy is an effective intervention in a group setting as well (Contreras & Scheingold, 1984; Wilson, Bornstein, & Wilson, 1988). However, when a "clinical significance" approach was employed in which scores on marital functioning measures from the Jacobson (1977) study were compared to scores of happily married couples, slightly more than one-third of the treated couples actually had changed their population status from "distressed" to "happily married" at the end of therapy. Sixty percent of these couples had maintained treatment gains at six-month follow-up (Jacobson et al., 1984).

Most recently, the therapeutic impact of specific components of a behavioral treatment of couples has been examined. This is particularly important in a managed mental health setting, where the efficiency and long-term effectiveness of the treatment program need to be evaluated carefully. Jacobson (1984) reported that behavioral marital therapy (BMP) comprised of both behavioral exchange (BE) and communication/problem-solving training (CPT) was no more effective than BE or CPT alone. A one-year follow-up of these couples, however, found that couples who had received the combined BMT treatment were the most likely to be happily married and least likely to be separated or divorced (Jacobson et al., 1984). Thus both components appear to be important for the long-term maintenance of positive outcome. Since as many as 35% of requests for mental health care come from repeat users of the mental health service, this information on the importance of both components seems to merit attention.

Jacobson suggests that expecting a brief, time-limited treatment program to provide a permanent solution to long-standing relationship problems may be naive. The use of planned, intermittent marital therapy "check-ups" may be more realistic (see Cummings in this volume for related views). This may be particularly true with couples with a highly affiliative wife and a highly independent husband (the "pursuer–distancer" relationship), who are less likely to benefit from behavioral marital therapy than other couples (Jacobson, Follette, & Pagel, 1986).

Finally, several studies (cf., Hahlweg & Markman, 1988; Markman et al., 1988) have examined the efficacy of cognitive–behavioral techniques with nondistressed couples in preventing marital distress. After participating in five three-hour couples' groups, these couples showed higher levels of both relationship satisfaction and sexual satisfaction and lower levels of problem intensity than control couples at a three-year, posttreatment follow-up. Interventions included communication and problem-solving skills, clarifying and sharing expectations, and sensual/sexual enhancement. While more data are needed, initial findings suggest that premarital interventions may be a cost-effective primary prevention program. Managed mental health offers an ideal setting for the delivery of psychoeducational prevention groups for couples.

Behavioral marital therapy, as delivered in research settings, does appear to gradually move couples toward a nondistressed status. The effectiveness of this approach to couples' treatment in managed mental health settings specifically is not available. Given the broad generalizability of the behavioral marital therapy outcome trials, such approaches are probably equally effective in managed health care settings. Research examining marital therapy in different economic contexts should pay close attention to definitions of successful treatments. Although change from the couple's degree of distress at intake is an important guide, a myriad of outcome measures could be used to develop quality assurance procedures (e.g., medical utilization rates, effective functioning in daily activities).

The Practice of Couples' Therapy: Basic Assumptions

Basic assumptions about the behavior of distressed and nondistressed couples guide the therapist's behavior in directing treatment. These premises may be phrased in the differing languages of different psychotherapy models. As noted by Coyne and Biglan (1984), there are many reasons to believe that pivotal concepts and interventions in therapy can be justified using seemingly different theoretical systems. In the HMO setting, however, identification of these assumptions and consistency in applying them within a specific therapeutic framework is particularly important. The assumptions must reflect the developmental, interpersonal–environmental model used in HMO mental health to ensure therapy effectiveness (see Austad & Berman, and Berman & Austad in this volume, for elaboration of these assumptions, also, Bennett, 1983, 1988).

The Meaning of Marital Distress

Marital distress is comprised of interpersonal domains where one or both partners experience a low level of satisfaction (e.g., in spending time alone as a couple). Operational definitions of unique problems (e.g., low frequency of occurrence and low rate of pleasure during time spent alone as a couple) include any and all transition factors occurring in the interpersonal context (e.g., birth of a child), the solutions used to solve a problem (e.g., avoiding spending time alone), the readiness of each partner to experiment with a new solution, and attributions about the "causes" of problematic behavior. Interventions based upon knowledge of all of these factors are the most likely to be useful to a couple.

Willingness to Learn

An underlying premise of cognitive behavior therapy with couples is that collaboration between spouses is closely related to their willingness to experiment with new behaviors. The therapist avoids power struggles over who will or will not "change" by openly presenting no change as an option throughout treatment, thereby reducing the potential for noncompliance (Patterson & Forgatch, 1985). This allows each member of the dyad to develop and implement potential solutions without any unnecessary degree of "risk." Solutions can be developed and implemented if they produce a beneficial effect for the couple and can be rejected otherwise. The therapist is active and directive in structuring treatment sessions in order to reduce the possibility of interactions that are potentially destructive to the already distressed relationship. Interventions aimed at increasing the couple's level of confidence in the marriage are critical early in treatment to engender the hopefulness needed for skill development later in treatment. The therapist acts as a consultant who assists the development and refinement of skills the couple can use in future difficulties in life.

Readiness to Learn

Communication, problem solving, and conflict resolution skills exist in a hierarchy, and the mastery of basic skills is prerequisite to learning more complex skills. The therapist starts at the skill level of the least skillful spouse and may refer one or both spouses for individual work prior to couples' therapy. Individual therapy may be necessary prior to conjoint work if one spouse is severely depressed, addicted, abusive, and/or clinging to beliefs that obstruct conjoint work. The therapist espouses a philosophy of learning and works actively to create an environment conducive to learning. Blaming and unproductive interactions are redirected, while experimenting is encouraged. The importance of applying skills between sessions is consistently stressed.

Application of a Cognitive–Behavioral Model

The cognitive–behavioral models for treating couples described by Jacobson and Margolin (1979) and by Stuart (1981) are readily implemented in the prepaid health care setting. They most clearly guide goal selection, assessment, and intervention strategies, and establish coherent time frames. With more difficult families (e.g., pursuer–distancers and treatment-resistant families), the techniques of Hayes (1987), Bergman (1985), or Weakland et al. (1974), Berg (1988), and DeShazer et al., (1986) may also be effective.

   The purpose of this section is to present basic guidelines for the therapist, including session objectives, relevant intervention techniques, homework assignments, and specific therapist behaviors. Treatment session outlines are presented for three phases of treatment, with each phase consisting of one to three sessions. This represents the typical time frame for work in managed health care. Case illustrations are provided to exemplify the application of this approach.

The Initial Phase of Treatment

Table 1 delineates the tasks to be addressed during the first phase of treatment. These tasks include collecting information, increasing positive exchange rates, planning treatment, and obtaining a commitment from each member of the dyad.

The therapist's goal in assessing the problem is to create an atmosphere of collaboration (Jacobson & Margolin, 1979). First, the problem is defined in specific terms that include contextual factors. This process allows the couple to discover new information that may increase their understanding of external factors influencing the problem and possible solutions. Further, this process allows each member

Table 1. Treating Couples in Prepaid Health Care: Initial Phase

Objectives	Techniques	Patient Assignments
Assessment of problem	Formal assessment Objectification Reframing	Relationship Belief Inventory Written statements of their part in problem
Assessment of satisfaction	Formal assessment Long- and short-term focusing	Marital Happiness Scale Dyadic Adjustment Scale
Assessment of communication skills	Observations	Communication practice sessions: Objectification, expressing appreciation
Increase in positive exchange	Refocusing attention Noting strengths Increasing rate of caring behaviors Defining collaboration	Sharing romantic or humorous memories "Caring Days" Recalling examples of collaboration
Planning and obtainment of commitment to treatment	"As if" participation Discussing model Pros and cons of participation Treatment contract	Listing questions or concerns Discussing beliefs about treatment Planning ways to deal with obstacles to completing Treatment

of the couple to both observe and practice the use of specific, clear descriptions of behavior. The therapist carefully reframes the problem in such a way that problem definitions involving blame and negative intentions are avoided. In so doing, the concepts of reciprocity, negotiation, and compromise are offered as viable alternatives. Reciprocity is particularly important as it characterizes positively reinforcing exchanges in ongoing, long-term relationships. Couples tend to reward and punish each other at equal rates over time. The reciprocity principle forms the basis for techniques aimed at increasing the amount of satisfaction experienced by partners in their relationship.

The level of satisfaction currently experienced by the couple in their relationship is an important focus of assessment and treatment. This type of information can be quickly obtained from the couple's responses to the Marital Happiness Scale (MHS) (Azrin, Naster, & Jones, 1987), which provides a rapid assessment of 11 areas of the marital relationship. Responses to the MHS can be examined quickly by the therapist and provide a structured assessment of the relationship, as well as an opportunity for the couple to think about their relationship in specific rather than global terms. The Dyadic Adjustment Scale (DAS; Spanier, 1976) is a self-report measure that provides more information than the MHS but requires more time to complete and to score. On occasion, a couple may be asked to complete the Relationship Belief Inventory (Eidelson & Epstein, 1982), which provides scores related to dysfunctional relationship beliefs.

Assessment of interactional skills is the third objective of the initial phase. The therapist can observe the couple's strengths and weaknesses as they discuss their problems. The couple may be asked to discuss problems that are not emotionally heated or conflictual, or simply to decide upon or plan an activity. Assessment of interaction or communication skills in a clinical setting is most commonly informal. In special cases, a structured assessment such as the Marital Interaction Coding System (Weiss, 1975) can be used to identify very complex interaction patterns, but in general it is too cumbersome and time-consuming for clinical work. An instrument that requires less time to complete, yet provides useful information, is the Verbal Problem Checklist (Thomas, Walter, & O'Flaherty, 1974). Regardless of the formality of the process, however, the assessment of interactions through enactment provides important data that individuals are often unable to provide through self-report.

The couple often benefits from an opportunity to reexperience positive aspects of their relationship. These are often forgotten in light of recent negative exchanges. Toward this end, the therapist uses positive control and positive exchange techniques (Jacobson & Margolin, 1979). Stuart's "Caring Days" procedure is one of the most workable behavioral exchange techniques. Several adaptations of Stuart's procedure are available (Bornstein & Bornstein, 1986), such as the "Catch Your Spouse Doing Something Nice" technique (O'Farrell & Cutter, 1984). The instructions for "Caring Days" techniques are simple, for example, "Make a list of specific things your partner could do to show he or she cares about you." Instructions retained on the list need to be behaviorally specific, positive (e.g., "Put your shoes away" versus "Don't leave your shoes out"), capable of being given on a daily basis, and not the subject of a recent conflict. The couple is asked to make a specific commitment to engage in six or more of the caring behaviors on their partner's list on a daily basis. Further, each member is asked to perform caring behaviors regardless of the performance of his or her partner. This neutralizes the tendency of distressed couples to use aversive counter-control strategies. Partners verify and record the occurrence of all caring behaviors. These written records help to increase the awareness of the efforts each partner is making.

In concluding the initial phase treatment tasks, the therapist offers a specific treatment plan and then fosters a discussion of the recommendations, leading to a verbal or written agreement with the couple. Explanation of the treatment model is very important. The therapist stresses that treatment might be difficult and will work only to the extent that the participants work at it. In some cases, the couple might be asked to list as a homework assignment obstacles to completing treatment. Success in treatment is defined as completing the treatment plan as agreed upon rather than any specific relationship outcome (i.e., reconciliation or divorce). "As if" behavior experiments are also described. These procedures demonstrate how a change of feelings about the marriage may follow from rather than precede change. The couple often sees this process in their initial "Caring Days" work, which helps bolster commitment to treatment even when marital distress escalates and motivation falters. The therapist and couple need to openly discuss beliefs about treatment at this point, and discuss its advantages (e.g., makes an honorable solution possible, reduces uncertainty) and disadvantages (e.g., feeling hurt, being disappointed, being inconvenienced). Treatment is conceptualized as an experiment with the general parameters (including length of time, format, goals, and possible activities) agreed upon by the therapist and couple.

The Middle Phase of Treatment

When the tasks of the initial phase are completed, treatment focuses upon more negative interactions and problematic situations for the couple (see Table 2). New techniques may be used for positive behavior exchange, such as the "Shared Recreation Activities" (SRAs) procedure suggested by O'Farrell and Cutter (1984). Each member of the couple is asked to make an individual list of possible SRAs. They then choose, plan, and implement several activities that appear on the lists of both partners. Further, the couple is asked to evaluate the amount of pleasure experienced in SRAs.

A major goal of the middle phase of treatment is increasing the couple's communication skills. The therapist uses written instructions, modeling, prompting, behavioral rehearsal, and feedback as intervention techniques. Jacobson and Margolin (1979) offer an excellent communications and problem-solving training manual for couples. Gottman, Notarius, Gonso, and Markman (1976) also provide couples with written information about interaction skills. Modeling is a highly useful teaching strategy and may be even more effective when employed by two therapists in a session (Jacobson & Margolin, 1979). Behavioral rehearsal is the process of having the couple practice modeling skills in the therapist's presence, when specific feedback can be given. The therapist needs to be sensitive, using humor and support to facilitate and shape the couple's increasing skillfulness. The therapist follows a repeating cycle of modeling, rehearsing, providing feedback, and reinforcing approximations to the desired behavior.

Table 2. Treating Couples in Prepaid Health Care: Middle Phase

Objectives	Techniques	Patient Assignments

Problem solving	Generating solutions
	Discussing pros and cons of
	  possible solutions
	Discovering obstacles
		Listing advantages and
		  disadvantages of present
		  solution

Increase of positive
  exchange
	Discussing and identifying
	  Shared Recreational
	  Activities (SRAs)
		Scheduling, doing, and
		  evaluating SRAs

Increasing communication
  skills: validating,
  listening, making specific
  positive requests
	Instructions, modeling,
	  behavioral rehearsal,
	  feedback
	Practice sessions
		Reading written
		  instructions

Introduction of role of self-
  talk and self-
  reinforcement
	Instructions, examples	Thought identification

The couple is given communication homework assignments. These assignments are given to help them learn to establish stimulus control over important communications. The couple is told to practice communication skills at a scheduled time and in a situation where they can talk privately in a face-to-face manner without interruptions. Additionally, the couple is asked to take turns in talking and to refrain from interrupting during practice sessions. The length and topic of at-home practice sessions varies according to the skills being practiced.

The Late Phase of Treatment

As can be seen in Table 3, focus continues on training in communication skills. The skill groups include expressing feelings directly and practicing all aspects of problem solving. Problem-solving skills include specifically defining the problem; accepting the problem (including each partner's feelings as accurate based upon his or her reality); setting a mutually acceptable, concrete, attainable goal; considering a broad range of solutions; compromising in reaching a solution; implementing the solution; collecting data and evaluating the solution, and revising and renegotiating a problem-solving plan. Couples may be asked to schedule regular problem-solving sessions to work on everyday problems. Bornstein and Bornstein (1986) suggest a notebook format in which couples record the date, problem discussed, and solution achieved. This format allows the therapist to monitor and assess the couple's efficacy at solving problems occurring in daily life, while allowing the couple to generalize skill development by applying them to a wide array of problems.

As the couple learns problem-solving skills, the therapist can introduce methods

Table 3. Treating Couples in Prepaid Health Care: Later Phase

Objectives	Techniques	Patient Assignments
Increasing communication skills: expressing feelings directly, negotiating, problem solving	Instructions, modeling, behavioral rehearsal, feedback	Holding a practice session Keeping a problem-solving notebook
Problem solving and revising	Discussing "good faith" and "quid pro quo" contracts	Writing, implementing, and evaluating contracts
Increasing abilities to monitor self-talk	Practicing in problem-solving and conflict deescalation situations	Listing thoughts Writing cognitive scripts
Relapse prevention planning	Discussing effective strategies Planning ways to maintain positive exchange rates Planning method to help maintain interaction skill usage Fading treatment	Making individual lists Choosing a monitoring method Deciding on cue to signal the need for a tune-up Planning a booster

of making agreements or contracts. In "quid pro quo" contracts, partners exchange behaviors directly and simultaneously, with each changing some aspect of his or her behavior in accordance with the other's wish. Control over reinforcement derives from the contingent nature of the exchange. In "good faith" or parallel contracts, couples form independent change agreements. The partner's independent behavior change is not made contingent upon the change in the other's behavior (Jacobson & Margolin, 1979). The couple is encouraged to choose "good faith" contracts in solving problems, as these provide opportunities for practice in making positive attributions regarding partner behaviors. At times, however, the "quid pro quo" contract is needed, for example when conflict and mistrust are extreme.

Both in-session problem-solving interactions and entries in the problem-solving notebook are used to generate information about the role of self-talk in influencing interaction behaviors. The couple may be asked to generate cognitive strategies for self-control and perseverance in problem-solving sessions. On occasion, couples may be asked to write out self-talk scripts or simple statements that serve to prompt their initiation of collaborative behavior in difficult situations. These scripts or directions to oneself may include self-reinforcing statements, and partners can always choose to reinforce each other for use of such tactics.

For example, Sam and Kristy developed a conflict deescalation plan that relied heavily upon self-talk tactics, as well as mutual reinforcement for compliance. Sam planned to ask himself, "How important will this be a year from now?" when he felt close to raising his voice. Kristy planned to tell Sam, "I am having trouble really listening to you at the moment and want to continue trying after a half-hour break" when she noticed herself thinking, "He'll never understand." Both planned to reinforce themselves for using these strategies and to engage in a mutually pleasurable activity (eating chocolates) when both succeeded in using the strategies and in choosing to verbally reinforce each other for so doing.

In preparation for ending treatment, couples are asked to generate self-talk possibilities that discourage continued use of newly learned behaviors. Couples usually produce thoughts such as, "Treatment didn't really help. . . . He'll/She'll never change. . . . There's no use in trying. . . ." In an effort to increase a couple's resiliency to these types of thoughts, thought acceptance strategies can be taught. Hayes (1987) offers several visually rich metaphors that couples can learn to use to help them creatively distance from "hot thoughts" enough to consider more plausible, cooling alternatives (e.g., "Treatment wasn't a panacea. . . . We still have to work hard. . . . These problems are difficult. . . . He/She has changed in some ways and he/she still has vulnerabilities. . . . How can I help myself and my partner right now?").

Relapse prevention is addressed in the last few sessions, which may be scheduled on a less frequent basis than earlier sessions. Relapse prevention planning identifies the most effective and practical techniques used by a couple in treatment and the application of these in some planned format. Couples may continue some aspect of "Caring Days" activities in a planned way or focus on cognitive strategies (e.g., keeping deescalation scripts nearby), and still others can engage in regularly scheduled communication practice or problem-solving sessions.

The following dialogue exemplifies use of the practical strategy of having couples tailor their own unique relapse prevention plan. Jeff and Joanna had increased their level of satisfaction regarding their activities as a couple and in regard to parenting. They had trained in listening, validating, making specific requests, identifying and solving problems, and use of contracts. Therapy had focused on issues related to Joanna's return to work, Jeff's frequent job-related traveling, household chores, and child care responsibilities.

Therapist: Let's spend a few minutes defining what you are doing differently that's making your relationship more workable and satisfying. Joanna, what comes to mind for you regarding changes you have made?

Joanna: I am protecting my sleep more because being rested is very important to all of our communications, especially problem-solving things about the kids and our careers.

Jeff: I am continuing to remind myself to listen to Joanna and to paraphrase what she says, especially about her job because this is important to her. I actually find learning about her work interesting. Oh, and I like helping her when she asks me to because she makes a big deal of it and gives me hugs and all.

Joanna: That's right. Jeff is wonderful in helping with the kids at night. I need to remember to ask him for help. He's taking care of the kids routinely several nights during the workweek now.

Therapist: How can you two use this information to keep your relationship going in the direction you're going? Have you come up with some ideas for keeping yourselves doing these things that increase your satisfaction with your relationship?

Jeff: We both plan to work on specific requests and to reinforce each other for such.

Joanna: Yes, and we are going to have weekly meetings on Sunday afternoons while the kids are asleep. We'll do a check on how we're doing with the kids and with making time for ourselves alone. And I want to use the problem-solving notebook for a while longer when we work on a conflict on Sundays. Jeff is less excited about this I think.

Jeff: Fine by me. I just want you to do the writing. Another thing we plan to do on Sundays is to offer to help each other if one of us is having a hard time. For example, Joanna might ask me how I was doing with my self-talk or if I had been particularly tired or whatever, in the event that she thought I hadn't been listening to her enough.

Joanna: Right. Remember to look for positive interpretations when one of us is not doing what the other one wants.

Therapist: Your plan sounds workable to me. You two are quite a pair. I think you'll probably continue on learning and helping each other out. Let's do talk for a moment, though, about what you might do in the event of a big problem that really challenges you, results in some pretty hot arguments, and so on.

Relapse prevention planning continues, with the therapist guiding the couple in their anticipation of specific problems and fluctuations in skills that they will likely encounter in the next year. The couple generates "plan b" interventions which may include scheduling a consultation in addition to the planned 6- to 12-month booster sessions or checkups that are recommended for most couples.

Conclusion

Considerable research on couples' treatment is now available to guide practitioners working with couples in relationship distress. However, the application of effective treatment programs for couples specifically within managed mental health has yet to receive empirical support. Studies currently underway at Group Health Cooperative will confirm the effectiveness of cognitive behavioral marital therapy in the prepaid setting. Several circumstances unique to prepaid health care may actually enhance practitioners' effectiveness with couples. The emphasis on prevention in many health maintenance organizations supports the development of primary prevention programs of an educational nature. Earlier intervention with less chronically distressed couples is probably cost-effective from both mental and physical cost perspectives.

Additionally, collaboration with other health care providers is encouraged in and facilitated by the managed care environment. Increasingly, care is being directed by decentralized primary care centers close to the patients' homes. At Group Health, more mental health services are being provided in the primary care centers, expediting treatment through more convenient facilities. In addition, this allows information sharing between the primary care physician and the mental health specialist, which potentially facilitates more skillful and confident referrals of distressed couples for either preventive or therapeutic intervention, as well as "checkups" when couples encounter new problems.

Collaboration with health care specialists is also quite feasible in this setting.

Group Health mental health staff are currently working with drug and alcohol treatment staff to develop educational group programs for recovering addicts or alcoholics and their spouses. We plan to evaluate the relationship between participation in this class and relapse, as well as several other health utilization behaviors of both alcoholics or addicts and their spouses.

Finally, opportunities for the development and evaluation of innovative programs are plentiful in managed mental health. Efforts are underway at Group Health to develop a Relationship Clinic that will allow practitioners specializing in work with couples to develop innovative individual and group interventions. This includes developing self-instructional workbooks and videotapes to supplement clinical work and to guide primary prevention efforts. Results suggest that this multimodal approach produces quality patient care, satisfied consumers, and increased professional satisfaction for therapy staff.

References

Azrin, N. H., Naster, B. M., & Jones, R. (1987). Reciprocity counseling: A rapid learning-based procedure for marital counseling. *Behavior Research and Therapy, 11*, 365–382.

Beck, T. (1988). *Love is never enough*. New York: Harper & Row.

Beck, T. (1988, October). Framed! *Health*, pp. 24–25.

Bennett, J. (1983). Focal psychotherapy—terminable and interminable. *American Journal of Psychotherapy, 35*, 365–375.

Bennett, J. (1988). The greening of the HMO: Implications for prepaid psychiatry. *American Journal of Psychiatry, 145*(12), 1544–1549.

Berg, I. K. (1988). Couple therapy with one person or two. In E. Nunally, F. Cox, & K. Chillman (Eds.). *Families in trouble*, (Vol. 3, pp. 28–54). Sage Publications.

Bergman, S. (1985). *Fishing for barracuda*. New York: Norton.

Bornstein, P. H., & Bornstein, M. T. (1986). *Marital therapy: A behavioral-communication approach*. New York: Pergamon Press.

Contreras, M., & Scheingold, L. (1984). Couples groups in family medicine training. *The Journal of Family Practice, 18*(2), 293–296.

Coyne, C., & Biglan, R. (1984). Paradoxical techniques in strategic family therapy: A behavioral analysis. *Journal of Behavior Therapy and Experimental Psychiatry, 15*(3), 221–227.

Coyne, J. C., Kahn, J., & Gotlib, I. H. (1986). Depression. In T. Jacob (Ed.), *Family interaction and psychopathology*. New York: Plenum.

DeShazer, S., Berg, I. K., Lipchik, E., Nannally, E., Molnar, A., Gingerich, W., & Weiner-Davis, M. (1986). Brief therapy: Focused solution development. *Family Process, Inc.* 207–221.

Eidelson, R. J., & Epstein, N. (1982). Cognition and relationship maladjustment: Development of a measure of dysfunctional relationship beliefs. *Journal of Consulting and Clinical Psychology, 50*, 715–720.

Gottman, J. M., Notarius, C., Gonso, J., & Markman, H. (1976). *A couple's guide to communication*. Champaign, IL: Research Press.

Hahlweg, K., & Markman, H. J. (1988). Effectiveness of behavioral marital therapy: Empirical status of behavioral techniques in preventing and alleviating marital distress. *Journal of Consulting and Clinical Psychology, 56*(3), 440–447.

Hayes, S. C. (1987). A contextual approach to therapeutic change. In N. S. Jacobson (Ed.), *Psychotherapists in clinical practice* (pp. 327–387). New York: Guilford.

Holmes, T., & Masuda, M. (1974). Life change and illness susceptibility. In B. S. Dohrenwend & B. P. Dohrenwend (Eds.), *Stressful life events: Their nature and effects*. New York: Wiley.

Ilfeld, F. W. (1980). Understanding marital stressors: The importance of coping styles. *Journal of Nervous and Mental Disease, 168*, 375–381.

Jacobson, N. S. (1977). Problem-solving and contingency contracting in the treatment of marital discord. *Journal of Consulting and Clinical Psychology, 45*, 92–100.

Jacobson, N. S. (1984). A component analysis of behavioral marital therapy: The relative effectiveness of behavior exchange and communication/problem-solving training. *Journal of Consulting and Clinical Psychology, 52*(2), 295–305.

Jacobson, N. S., Follette, V. M., Follette, W. C., Holtzworth-Munroe, A., Katt, J. L., & Schmaling, K. B. (1985). A component analysis of behavioral marital therapy: One-year followup. *Behavior Research Therapy, 23*(5), 549–555.

Jacobson, N. S., Follette, W. C., & Pagel, M. (1986). Predicting who will benefit from behavioral marital therapy. *Journal of Consulting and Clinical Psychology, 54*(4), 518–522.

Jacobson, N. S., Follette, W. C., Revensdorf, D. B., Baucom, D. H., Hahlweg, K., & Margolin, G. (1984). Variability in outcome and clinical significance of behavioral marital therapy: A re-analysis of outcome data. *Journal of Consulting and Clinical Psychology, 52*(4), 497–504.

Jacobson, N. S., & Margolin, G. (1979). *Marital therapy: Strategies based on social learning and behavior exchange principles.* New York: Brunner/Mazel.

Johnson, S. M., & Greenberg, L. S. (1985). Differential effects of experimental and problem-solving interventions in resolving marital conflict. *Journal of Consulting and Clinical Psychology, 53*(2), 175–184.

Kalish, R. A., & Knutson, F. W. (1976). Attachment versus disengagement: A life span conceptualization. *Human Development, 19,* 171–181.

Markman, H. J., Floyd, F. J., Stanley, S. M., & Storaasli, R. D. (1988). *Journal of Consulting and Clinical Psychology, 56*(2), 210–217.

Mussen, P., Honzik, M., & Eichorn, D. (1982). Early antecedents of life satisfaction at age 70. *Journal of Gerontology, 37,* 315–322.

O'Farrell, T. J., & Cutter, H. S. G. (1984). Behavioral marital therapy couples' groups for male alcoholics and their wives. *Journal of Substance Abuse Treatment, 1,* 191–204.

Patterson, G. R., & Forgatch, M. S. (1985). Therapist behavior as a determinant for client noncompliance: A paradox for the behavior modifier. *Journal of Consulting and Clinical Psychology, 53*(6), 846–851.

Pearlin, L. I., & Schooler, C. (1978). The structure of coping. *Journal of Health and Social Behavior, 19,* 2–21.

Shadle, M., & Christianson, J. B. (1988). *The organization of mental health care delivery in HMOs.* Excelsior, MI: Interstudy.

Siddall, L. B., Haffey, N. A., & Feinman, J. A. (1988). Intermittent brief psychotherapy in an HMO setting. *American Journal of Psychotherapy, 42*(1), 96–106.

Spanier, G. B. (1976). Measuring dyadic adjustment: New scales for assessing the quality of marriage and similar dyads. *Journal of Marriage and the Family, 38,* 15–28.

Stuart, R. B. (1981). *Helping couples change: A social learning approach to marital therapy.* New York: Guilford.

Thomas, E. J., Walter, C. L., & O'Flaherty, K. (1974). A verbal problem checklist for use in assessing family verbal behavior. *Behavior Therapy, 5,* 235–246.

Weakland, J. H., Fisch, R., Waltzawick, P., & Bodin, A. M. (1974). Brief therapy: Focused problem resolution. *Family Process, 13*(2), 141–168.

Weiss, R. L. (1975). *Marital interaction coding system-Revised.* Unpublished manuscript, University of Oregon, Eugene, OR.

Weissman, M. M., & Paykel, E. S. (1974). *The depressed woman: A study of social relationships.* Chicago: University of Chicago Press.

Wilson, G. L., Bornstein, P. H., & Wilson, L. J. (1988). Treatment of relationship dysfunction: An Empirical evaluation of group and conjoint behavioral marital therapy. *Journal of Consulting and Clinical Psychology, 56,* 929–931.

13

Kirk D. Strosahl

Cognitive and Behavioral Treatment of the Personality Disordered Patient

The Setting

The Group Health Cooperative of Puget Sound is one of the oldest staff model health maintenance organizations in the United States. Founded in 1947, it has a current enrollment of 360,000 in the greater Seattle, Washington area. There are a variety of mental health benefit packages, but most include 10 sessions at no charge and 10 sessions with a copay. The department of mental health employs psychiatrists, psychologists, nurse clinicians, social workers, and drug and alcohol counselors. There are seven mental health clinics, which handle over 11,000 new cases per year.

The multiproblem, distressed patient, usually diagnosed as suffering from an Axis II personality disorder, is the most theoretically and technically challenging patient treated in managed mental health care settings. Prevalence estimates of personality disorder in the outpatient mental health population vary widely and range up to 45%, with the most common diagnosis being antisocial and borderline personality (Reich, 1987; Robbins, Helzer, & Weissman, 1984; Salman, Byrne, & Doghramji, 1986). Multiproblem patients nevertheless account for a disproportionate amount of mental health utilization and a host of negative clinical outcomes. Although psychotherapy may produce transient symptom relief, these patients frequently drop in and out of therapy, present case management problems, engender staff conflicts, and engage in high-risk behaviors, such as repeated suicide attempts, violence, and drug or alcohol abuse (cf., Bloch, Bell, Hulbert, & Nasrollah, 1988; Dahl, 1986; Gabbard & Coyne, 1987; Gallop, 1988; Pfohl, Stangl, & Zimmerman, 1984; Stone, 1985; Widiger & Frances, 1985). In addition, health maintenance organization (HMO) practitioners have a high rate of "burnout" while working with multiproblem, distressed patients. It is ironic that multiproblem patients strip away the aura of healing power that is an essential ingredient of the mental health therapist's "comfortable" professional identity, at the same time revealing the many basic flaws in traditional models of insight-based behavioral change. Consequently, the label "per-

My appreciation is expressed to the Group Health Mental Health Department for technical and financial support in the preparation of this chapter. My appreciation also to Patricia Robinson for her helpful comments on an earlier version of this manuscript.

sonality disorder" has become synonymous with "trouble" and often functions to pejoratively label and punish unresponsive, resistent patients, who may or may not meet specific Axis II diagnostic criteria.

Behavioral psychology has always had an uneasy relationship with the concept of "personality disorder," no doubt due to longstanding skepticism about the utility of inferred, unobservable trait constructs such as "personality," which allegedly "cause" behavior (Strosahl & Linehan, 1986; Taylor, 1983). Consequently, social learning and behavioral principles have been less systematically applied to the description, assessment, and treatment of personality disorders. The principle contributions from psychology come from theorists who are clearly identified with either intrapsychic or trait orientations to personality (cf., Millon, 1981). More recently, cognitive theorists have engaged in some promising theoretical efforts to address the treatment of multiproblem patients (cf., Beck et al., 1990). However, empirical research evaluating treatments for personality disorders is absent from psychological journals, despite nearly three decades of prolific writing on the subject. Thus, a candid review of the "state of the art" would reveal a field top-heavy in theory with an insufficient empirical base to promote sound clinical interventions.

A major objective of this chapter is to present a behavioral approach to the assessment and treatment of personality disorders. This framework will allow the development of concrete, practical, and feasible guidelines regarding assessment and intervention with multiproblem patients within the constraints of the managed mental health setting. Topics will include selecting and screening patients, identifying goals, planning effective interventions, preventing relapse, and integrating intermittent follow-up care. Special clinical problems posed by multiproblem patients will be examined, including suicidal behavior, drug and alcohol abuse, compliance, resistance, and the patient/physician/therapist triangle. In order to accomplish these objectives, it is necessary to examine misconceptions about the nature of personality disorder, as well as problems and myths in the diagnosis and treatment of personality disorders.

Personality Disorders: Syndrome, Continuum, or Panchestron?

Many experts now agree that the current system for diagnosis of personality disorders is extraordinarily arbitrary and more related to theoretical schools and vested research interests than to a sound, empirically derived classification scheme (cf., Livesley, 1985). Proponents of the status quo defend DSM III's division of personality disorders into 11 types by pointing to research showing that experts independently agreed on what symptoms were specifically associated with a particular personality disorder. For example, showing that the symptoms of schizotypal personality could be distinguished from those of borderline personality was taken as evidence of the independent existence of these two syndromes (Spitzer, Endicott, & Gibbons, 1979). However, subsequent research has clearly demonstrated that Axis II does not meet the basic requirements of an effective taxonomic classification system. Reliability of diagnosis over the 11 disorders is unacceptably low. Symptom criteria overlap between disorders, are excessively inferential, and vary in number from disorder to disorder. Certain symptom criteria virtually never occur, and there is only modest agreement between *a priori* cardinal symptoms and empirically derived, prototypical features associated with each disorder (Frances, 1982; Livesley, 1985; Livesley & Jackson, 1986). Further, factor analytic and multidimensional scaling studies have, at best, partially replicated the symptom clusters that represent the Axis II disorders (Widiger, Trull, Hurt, Clarkin, & Frances, 1987).

Alternative classification systems have been proposed since the advent of DSM III. Without exception, these models follow a dimensional rather than categorical approach to classification. Millon's (Millon, 1981) three-dimensional representation of personality disorders includes: (a) self versus other orientation, (b) passivity–activity, and (c) pleasure–pain. A second alternative approach is the interpersonal circle, which consists of the dimensions of desire for affiliation and concern with power and control (Kiesler, 1986). Yet another approach involves the use of behaviorally anchored prototypes to define the cardinal traits of multiproblem disorders (Livesley, 1987).

A fundamental shortcoming of both categorical and dimensional models is that each assumes the existence of traits that "cause" behavior. Thus, obsessive personality is caused by an excess of an "obsessive trait" that, in turn, causes problems. Behavioral and social psychological researchers have attempted for the last decade to prove that traits exist but have consistently found that humans lack behavioral consistency across even slightly different situations (Strosahl & Linehan, 1986). It is now clear that *environmental guides interact* with *performance capacity* to determine actual performance. As amply demonstrated by the stable–unstable, borderline patient, one baffling characteristic of personality disorders is the occurrence of significant variations in behavioral competence often in remarkably similar situations. Although therapists are more than willing to ascribe trait-level explanations to such behavior, objective assessments of the same behaviors do not typically show trait-level consistency (Mischel & Peake, 1982).

Standard of Care Issues

Is there sufficient clinical evidence to conclude that long-term, intensive therapy should be the standard of care for personality disorders? There is no body of empirical literature to support this proposition. In fact, a growing literature suggests that beneficial effects can be obtained using time-limited, cognitive–behavioral, and psychopharmacological approaches. For example, personality-disordered patients may experience significant reductions in depression when exposed to cognitive therapy (Beck, Rush, Shaw, & Emery, 1979; Hollon & Beck, 1986). Linehan (1987) reports that self-injurious and suicidal behavior among borderline patients can be effectively controlled using cognitive–behavioral therapy. Psychopharmacology field trials suggest that neuroleptic and antiseizure medications are effective at reducing distressing cognitive and emotional symptoms experienced by borderline patients (Gunderson, 1986).

Conversely, this author was unable to locate a single study meeting contemporary scientific standards for single subject or group research that examined the efficacy of intensive psychotherapy with personality disorders. While research on the effects of long-term psychoanalytic psychotherapy by Kernberg and colleagues is underway, data are too premature to cast any light on this treatment (Berman, personal communication). At this point, the burden would seem to be on proponents of long-term therapy to demonstrate the clinical benefits and cost-effectiveness of this treatment approach.

A Cognitive–Behavioral Model of Multiproblem Behavior

The cognitive–behavioral approach emphasizes that contemporary cognitions, skill capacity, and environmental guides are the main influences upon behavior. Behavior is deemed functional or dysfunctional according to whether it satisfactorily addresses situational demands and produces a satisfactory emotional response or cognitive self-appraisal in the patient. The term "multiproblem" means that the patient repeatedly experiences performance problems in a variety of situations and, in turn, experiences negative external or internal outcomes.

A critical element of this model is that all behavior occurs in a larger "context," defined as "conditioned rules, beliefs, and experiences shared by the verbal community" (Hayes, 1987). Hayes identified characteristics common to the verbal community that encompass cognitions, affects, and behaviors. Most clients and therapists share assumptions about the relationship between thoughts, feelings, and behavior; what "causes" human behavior, what is required to change behavior; what is the meaning of negative mental events, and how they are to be addressed. In effect, these are the "mental ground rules" that guide all therapeutic transactions. The most influential of these shared assumptions are presented in Table 1, as are other important functional deficits often seen in this type of patient.

Contextual Factors

Verbal conditioning is an extraordinarily powerful determinant of success in therapy with multiproblem patients, as it directs the definition of problems, causes, and change options. In fact, it is the strategic use of rules suggested by this conditioning in therapy-wise, multiproblem patients, and their tacit acceptance by the therapist, that serve to limit or prevent behavior change.

One popular belief shared by patients and therapists alike is that one cannot experience disturbing thoughts or upsetting feelings if one is to live "normally." The multiproblem patient complains that functional behavior is impossible while disturbing thoughts or feelings are present and that the therapist must first help the patient "get rid of" these internal events. However, changing either thoughts or feelings is blocked by the presence of maladaptive behaviors! The circularity of these rules restricts the value of any skills presented by the therapist, as they cannot achieve the unachievable results required in this context.

A second context of multiproblem patients is the fallacy that understanding leads to change: "I need to understand how I developed this problem so I can change what causes me to act the way I do." The psychotherapist then seeks to develop "insight" into the dysfunctional behavior. However, reasons for behavior are not the same as causes of behavior (Hayes, 1987). Rather, behavior is multiply deter-

Table 1. Common Characteristics of Multiproblem Patients

I. *Contextual*

 Belief that understanding causes is necessary to change behavior
 Belief that negative mental events must be eliminated
 Belief in causal interdependence of thoughts, feelings, and behavior
 Belief that mental experiences are the same as "reality"
 Belief in necessity of harmony between thoughts and feelings
 Tendency to confuse description of events with causes of events

II. *Cognitive*

 Rigid, "black or white" thinking
 Perfectionistic, critical self-appraisal style
 Simplistic core schema
 Exaggerated negative self-schema
 Poor problem solving
 Catastrophic view of future
 Excessive focus on social humiliation/social rejection

III. *Emotional*

 Chronic negative affect
 Magnified affective response
 Lack of tolerance for negative affect
 Lack of affective regulation capacity

IV. *Behavioral*

 Deficient social/assertion capacity
 Poor conflict resolution skills
 Excessive use of negative reinforcement as self-control skill
 Low in pleasant and rewarding daily behaviors
 Poor behavior planning skills
 Deficient relaxation/tension reduction capacity
 Lack of self-change and behavior maintenance skills

mined, and most causes exist outside our limited awareness and processing ability. This leads to an eternal search for causes while functional behavior is put on hold.

A third context of the multiproblem patient is the intolerance of any suffering. For them, the goal of treatment is to *eliminate* uncomfortable thoughts or feelings. All too often, attempts to do so only serve to increase their intensity and provoke either an acute crisis or a therapeutic impasse.

Finally, multiproblem patients are conditioned to verbalize "hope" despite repeated failures in their efforts to change. Their reliance on "hope" makes them handle failure by intensifying efforts using the same problem-solving behaviors, in the belief that this tactic will overcome the few difficulties associated with a basically good solution. Multiproblem patients continue blatantly dysfunctional behavior despite overwhelming evidence that it will not work, or lapse into abject hopelessness about the actual results of their efforts.

Cognitive Factors

In addition to an overarching context, specific cognitive factors play an important role in the treatment of multiproblem patients. Beck and colleagues (Beck & Emery, 1985; Beck et al., 1979) have demonstrated that distorted cognitive processes are directly associated with affective disturbances such as anxiety and depression, which are extremely common in multiproblem patients. The most important cognitive characteristic of the multiproblem patient is the presence of rigid, impermeable, and simplistic core schema. Core schema, such as "I'm bad" or "I'm damaged goods" or "Because of my sins I don't deserve to be happy" are common among such patients. These beliefs may harken back to earlier traumatic events endured by the child or adolescent trapped in a destructive family system. The rule, "Never rely on a good thing," may in fact be very adaptive for a child who is the target of physical abuse by an unpredictable, alcoholic parent. Multiproblem patients, however, apply core rules in a generalized and obvious way long after they have ceased to be adaptive. These core schema are supported by complex information processing mechanisms that are generally impervious to insight interventions and change only in association with direct experience. Table 2 presents common core schema revealed in the process of treating the multiproblem patient.

An additional cognitive deficit in multiproblem patients is poor problem solving, defined as limited ability to operationalize problems, generate, implement, and evaluate solutions. The multiproblem patient shows a distinct preference for short-

Table 2.   Basic Beliefs of Multiproblem Patients

I. *Self*

I am flawed in a basic way
I cannot control or trust myself
I am irreparably damaged by past experiences
I am inadequate
I am ultimately going to die
I do not deserve happiness or success
I must suffer in silence
If I can't do it well, I won't do it at all
Where there's a will, there's a way
The more important it is, the less likely it is to happen

II. *Interpersonal*

I am unlovable
Other people can see right through me
Show a weakness and you'll be humiliated for it
Do unto others before they do unto you
I am a social misfit
Make a mistake and people will reject you for it
Other people do not have to bear the suffering I do and cannot understand my suffering
The expression of powerful feelings will lead to disastrous results.
People always let me down when I need them the most
People change their attitudes about me quickly and capriciously

---

term, "single shot solutions" to complex problems. This may explain why addictive behaviors and impulsive problem-solving acts are so prevalent in this population.

Affective Factors

The multiproblem patient experiences chronic difficulties with depression, anxiety, anger, and boredom (Bloch et al., 1988; Pfohl et al., 1984). The patient views to any type of negative emotional arousal as intolerable and requiring an immediate solution to eliminate these feelings. Multiproblem patients lack effective emotion regulation skills, most notably the ability to use "cognitive–affective scripts" to verbally mediate primary affective experiences such as loss/abandonment or social humiliation (Izard, 1979). This results in an accelerating cycle of emotional arousal that the patient is seemingly unable to verbalize or control.

Behavioral Skills

Multiproblem patients often exhibit performance deficits that lead to failures in certain situations. One such deficit is a lack of interpersonal effectiveness skills (Strosahl & Linehan, 1983). Multiproblem patients often fail to achieve specific assertion objectives, lack the social skills to manage relationships as a part of achieving objectives, or achieve objectives only at huge personal costs to self-esteem.

Multiproblem patients may exhibit poor self-control skills, using disproportionate amounts of negative reinforcement to change behavior. For example, a favorite strategy is to make a positive reward contingent upon completion of unrealistic "duties." Failure to complete required behaviors results in the elimination of positive reinforcement. There is a pervasive belief that self rewards should not be given for engaging in behaviors that previously were within the patient's range of performance. Behaviors that "should be" happening cannot be rewarded because personal weakness is responsible for their disappearance in the first place.

Another deficit is the inability to invoke relaxation and to diminish elevated physiological arousal. Multiproblem patients exist in a state of chronic overarousal and hypervigilance. They often react to relaxation therapy with heightened anxiety and physiological arousal. This constitutes part of a broad pattern of ineffective tension reduction skills.

A Cognitive–Behavioral Treatment Model

Most theories of personality disorder, such as that of the borderline personality, assume the patient is suffering from poorly integrated or distorted object relations (cf., Kernberg, 1984). Consequently, the preferred treatment is long-term, intensive psychoanalytic therapy (Kernberg, 1984; Kohut, 1977; Masterson, 1976). Prepaid health care systems are often criticized for failing to provide an acceptable standard of care (e.g., intensive psychotherapy) for multiproblem patients, but there is little empirical reason to believe that better outcomes are obtained with such patients in the fee-for-service sector.

The cognitive–behavioral model, in contrast, suggests a framework that allows effective treatment in a briefer period of time. There is less dependence on time-consuming and potentially ineffective individual therapy and greater use of intervention methods that tap the patient's own strengths and capacities. The remainder of this chapter will present practical guidelines for conducting cognitive–behavioral treatment with multiproblem patients within the managed mental health setting.

The hallmark of this treatment is that it is structured, time-limited, and psychoeducational in format. It is recommended that this treatment be implemented in a classroom model, using a student–teacher ratio of 10:1. The classroom is a powerful and flexible setting that, at strategic times, can guarantee a "safe haven" for the therapist. The teacher–student relationship has far different connotations than does the therapist–patient relationship. Often, interventions that would be rejected in therapy will be accepted in the classroom setting. The primary risk of one-to-one treatment is that the therapist will subtly reengage the traditional "context" of therapy with the patient. The use of a psychoeducational model allows teachers to discuss treatment as a "sampler" of potentially relevant skills. It is the student's responsibility to make skills relevant or helpful, thus removing dependence on the teacher as a potential problem. Treatment involves use of didactic lectures to introduce key concepts, supporting written materials, small and large group discussions, opportunities for experimental learning, and homework between sessions. Each session is guided by an outline of topics.

The general rule regarding patient selection is: "the more distressed and therapy-wise, the better." In general, most dysfunctional behaviors can be addressed within the framework of this model and are not considered detriments to participation. Behavioral problems such as suicidal or impulsive behavior do not automatically rule out participation in this treatment.

This treatment is contraindicated if one or more of three conditions is present in the patient: First, drug or alcohol addiction makes it unlikely that the individual will process sometimes confusing, contradictory, and challenging concepts presented in class. Such patients require drug or alcohol treatment and may reenter group treatment after a six-month abstinence. Second, the presence of a subtle thought disorder may interfere with the patient's ability to accurately process classroom information. Patients with signs of thought disorder such as self-referential thinking, loose associations, or semidelusional beliefs (the so-called schizotypal personality disorder) are much more effectively treated in individual supportive therapy, combined with appropriate medication. Finally, patients who experience debilitating social anxiety are initially better candidates for the one-to-one approach. Eventual participation in the classroom treatment may be a treatment goal. Table 3 lists the main intervention targets and associated strategies for each phase of the class.

Contextual Therapy

The basic goal of the contextual intervention is to immediately destabilize verbally conditioned rules, beliefs, and self-appraisal perspectives that preclude any real opportunity for change. Patients are taught "Comprehensive Distancing" (Hayes, 1987), or the act of detaching from distressing thoughts or feelings through a reformulation of the thought–feeling–behavior relationship. Self-observation and ac-

Table 3. Intervention Targets and Session Sequencing in the Cognitive–Behavioral Model

Phase	Goals	Strategies
		(in addition to didactic lecture and discussion)
I. Recontextualization (sessions 1–4)	• Challenge notion that thoughts and feelings cause dysfunctional behavior • Challenge contingent rules for change • Understand rule of mental events/affect tolerance • Challenge idea that reasons are causes • Develop awareness of basic rules of life • Undermine simplistic notions about commitment and willpower	• Eye contact exercise • Assign partner pairs (class only) and weekly check-in • Personal autobiography and creative rewrite • Employ creative hopelessness • "Rules of the Game" exercise
II. Cognitive therapy (sessions 5–8)	• Learn basic cognitive model • Change daily activity pattern to increase mastery and pleasure experiences • Learn to identify and challenge automatic thoughts • Learn to conduct personal experiments to test specific beliefs and assumptions • Learn to observe and detach from negative thoughts and aversive feelings	• Read *Feeling Good* (Burns, 1980) • Teach friendly observer technique • Teach monitoring and scheduling of activities • Teach use of daily record of dysfunctional thoughts • Teach use of triple column technique • Use personal experiments to test selected beliefs and assumptions
III. Behavioral skills training (sessions 9–11)	Teach one or more of the following: • Increase interpersonal effectiveness • Increase tension reduction capacity • Increase conflict resolution capacity	• Read *Control Your Depression* (Lewisohn et al., 1986) • Behavioral rehearsal with feedback • Modeling and role playing • Relaxation/awareness practice
IV. Relapse prevention/behavior change maintenance skills (sessions 12–14)	• Learn principles of self-directed behavior modification • Develop realistic expectations about relapse • Learn to integrate class skills into an intermediate life plan	• Teach self-monitoring, goal definition, and self-reinforcement skills • Behavior change plan 1. identify behaviors to be maintained 2. identify and troubleshoot potential obstacles 3. develop response plan in case of relapse or self-control failure

ceptance are emphasized instead of attempts to eliminate distress. Mental events and mentalistic explanations of behavior are continually reframed as one of many organ functions necessary for human survival. Just as the liver never ceases its filtering activity, the brain never stops generating thoughts. Thoughts are no more a substitute for "reality" than the action of the liver.

In comprehensive distancing, all internal events are viewed self-reflexively, that is, one can literally watch thoughts come and go without losing the separateness of "I," thoughts, and feelings. This has profound implications for the context of unpleasant mental events. Does suffering occur because of the events themselves or because of strategies for sampling and construing them? Does the tendency to regard thoughts as "reality" trap one in the literal meaning of thoughts? What would happen if distressing thoughts and uncomfortable feelings were allowed to occur without the futile attempts to control them or make them disappear?

Another important principle is that the environment is replete with guides to behavior, but these are missed because of a conditioned preoccupation with distressing mental events. Contextual therapy creates a readiness to use new skills when there have been discrepancies between knowledge and production of appropriate responses. There is a constant struggle between realism and verbally conditioned illusions. The major goal of treatment is to accept unpleasant feelings and thoughts while, at the same time, using environmental guides to behavior. The essence of the therapeutic message is: "Think what you think, feel what you feel, and do what you have to do" (Hayes, 1987).

The initial class session involves a description of the treatment and a discussion of the many obstacles that will be encountered. It is predictable at the outset that patients may find themselves engaging in the same self-immobilizing behaviors that have become so prominent in daily life. Commitment is simple in concept yet difficult in execution, especially when self-imposed obstacles are involved. A simple, five-minute eye contact exercise (i.e., keep eye contact without making a sound) will amply demonstrate how internal events can interfere with commitment. Inform patients that finishing treatment does not guarantee behavior change, making the willingness to commit doubly risky. The session ends with the assignment of "partners," who will have regular contact with one another outside of treatment to review progress on homework assignments, share experiences, and collaborate on developing intermediate-term goals. Clients are asked to sign a commitment ballot indicating their choice to participate in the treatment program. The decision not to go forward with the class is acknowledged as a legitimate commitment as well. In that case, suitable arrangements should be made for alternative treatment. Those choosing to go forward are asked to write a brief autobiography.

The second session is devoted to engendering "creative hopelessness." The teacher's agenda is to convince the class members that their situation is hopeless, given the requirements of the existing context. Predictably, this results in a backlash towards conditioned hopefulness. In this case, stories can be used to illustrate the concept that, before one can adopt new behaviors, old goals and their associated behaviors must first be stopped. Teachers are sometimes tempted to abandon comprehensive distancing at this point and to slip back into the traditional context of encouraging hopefulness, as part of their own verbal conditioning. The emotional level in the second class is usually quite intense: Some members feel angry and insulted, others feel a sense of relief, while others indicate confusion, fear, and uncertainty. Confusion is always emphasized as a positive developmental state, as it indicates destabilization.

Invariably one or more members of the class will argue that their problems are different and more severe than those of other class members. This produces confrontations between class members vying for special status because of the unspoken rule that there can only be *one* special person in the class. The session ends with the instruction to rewrite the autobiography from the first session from a creatively different perspective. Participants are to *focus* on and reinterpret the significance of the negative events in their autobiography that are usually seen as "causes" of current dysfunctional behavior. This will destabilize the notion that negative life events can only have a negative influence on development.

In the next two to four sessions, the relationship among thoughts, feelings, and behaviors, and the importance of understanding causes of behavior are debunked. Classroom exercises are used to show how difficult it is to locate causes. Surprisingly, patients feel relieved when they are freed of the requirement to having to understand the etiology of their problem.

These sessions also address the principle, "The less you want of a mental event, the more you get of it" (Hayes, 1987). Examples from class members are used to highlight how attempts to quell thoughts and feelings actually increase their frequency, intensity, and duration. Intriguing homework assignments go along with these sessions, one of which is the "rules of the game" exercise. The most powerful rules we carry are reflected in strongly held, internal sayings about life such as, "No pain, no gain," "If you have to do a job, do it right," and so on. Patients are told to identify and write down their favorite life sayings. This often reveals core schema to be targeted later in treatment.

Cognitive Therapy

The aim of the cognitive intervention is to teach skills for identifying, challenging, and correcting the distorted thoughts that play a prominent role in depression and anxiety (Beck et al., 1979; Beck & Emery, 1985). Cognitive therapy is the second intervention used in this treatment model. As basic beliefs and expectancies are destabilized in association with comprehensive distancing, the potential impact of cognitive restructuring is enhanced. To avoid the appearance of a conflict between contextual and cognitive principles, it is useful to point out that few people can consistently remain detached from "hot" thoughts or feelings and thus it is imperative to have techniques for managing one's responses when such perspective is lost.

Several useful principles, derived from cognitive therapy, can be applied to multiproblem patients. One basic principle is the value of detached and nonjudgmental observation of distressing thoughts and feelings (Beck & Emery, 1985). Learning techniques such as the "friendly observer" and the daily recording of dysfunctional thoughts teach patients that thoughts and feelings are not "reality," but our representations of it.

A second principle is that cognitions are arranged hierarchically. Multiproblem patients often find that trivial events trigger major cognitive, emotional, and behavioral reactions, which are then pointed to as proof of some basic character flaw. Explaining that cognitions are organized in terms of surface automatic thoughts, hidden assumptions, and basic rules about life is a sensible, less self-critical explanation.

A third principle is that beliefs are learned behaviors. Multiproblem patients frequently ask the question, "Where do these thoughts come from?" The cognitive model emphasizes that beliefs serve an adaptive function at some point but can outlive their usefulness. Most of the time, patients can see how a currently dysfunctional belief was adaptive at a prior time. This process defuses self-criticism in response to distressing cognitions.

A fourth cognitive intervention is behavioral activity monitoring and scheduling. As noted below, multiproblem patients arrange leisure and pleasure as contingent awards for perfectionistic performance. These patients identify certain behavioral goals that have come to symbolize the futility of attempts to change. Thus, use of activity planning can have a dual impact. The basic mix of daily activities can be rearranged to provide an effective blend of reinforcement and responsibility; behavioral goals seen as harbingers of progress can be achieved to establish positive therapeutic momentum.

A fifth aspect of cognitive therapy is the notion of "collaborative empiricism" in which the patient and therapist work together to help the patient establish methods of testing out ideas, beliefs, and assumptions. Multiproblem patients adapt readily to this problem-solving approach when there is a collaborative atmosphere. Often, it is helpful for the therapist to "think out loud," so patients can readily observe the personal scientist model in action.

Behavior Therapy

The selection of a specific behavior therapy is based upon a formal assessment of skill deficits and usually encompasses the last phase (four to six sessions) of treatment. Principle targets include tension reduction, interpersonal effectiveness, and behavior change maintenance skills.

When addressing relaxation and tension reduction skills, it is important to avoid suggesting that the ability to relax is a requirement for success in therapy. The consistent therapeutic rule is, "Any time something *has* to occur, the multiproblem patient will fail." Instructions in relaxation training highlight the importance of becoming aware of different or unusual sensations, including *increased* tension or vigilance, that occur during the awareness exercise. An open stance towards relaxation and awareness training allows each patient to feel success, despite the fact that "relaxation" may not have occurred. Second, the therapist can help patients identify naturally occurring tension reduction behaviors and integrate them into an arousal control plan.

Training in interpersonal effectiveness skills aims at improving social, assertion, and conflict resolution skills. An important step is to assess whether *capacity* is lacking for skillful behavior, or whether there is a cognitive basis for nonskillful behavior. This will suggest whether a cognitive or behavioral intervention is indicated. Situations used in training should be derived from the clients recent experience to enhance the generalization of learned skills.

Conflict resolution training is difficult to implement with multiproblem patients, who often exhibit an aversion to the expression of negative affect and have catastrophic beliefs about the consequences of interpersonal conflict. Often, conflict resolution training occurs in situ during class interactions. The therapist may restructure a problematic interaction between two class members in a way that mirrors the conflict resolution sequence. The teacher then role-plays conflict resolution behaviors, elicits discussion and feedback, then has the "conflicted" class members resolve their disagreement using the same skills.

Maintaining Behavior Change

A final goal of the treatment is to help each patient develop an intermediate term maintenance plan that incorporates newly learned skills. For all its practical appeal, relapse prevention planning is frequently a neglected part of work with the multiproblem patient. Relapse prevention emphasizes that unpleasant emotional, cognitive, or behavioral events are inevitable. It is the meaning attached to such events that is all-important. If one is prepared to accept setbacks, then there is a real opportunity to positively address these life demands without "adding insult to injury." Multiproblem patients often expect to be "cured" from emotional, cognitive, or behavioral problems, which makes relapse inevitable. The first problematic thought, feeling, or behavior is construed as evidence that treatment has failed. It should be emphasized that each patient can expect a lot of cognitive activity related to the idea of "cure."

Patients are encouraged to identify useful skills, develop ways to sustain their use, identify obstacles to their continued use, and identify early warning signs that skills have been dropped or their use reduced to an unacceptably low rate. Patients are encouraged to integrate realistic life objectives into this plan so that it functions proactively as well as preventing relapse.

Follow-Up Care

As with most HMO therapy, the concept of termination is not relevant to this treatment. The end of weekly meetings is labeled as a "field experiment," which will allow the patient to field-test the behavior change plan. In the classroom model, one- and six-month class reunions are held to assess the effects of the life change plan. The class reunion allows a preestablished check-in point with the mental health system, so that dysfunctional behavior is not required in order to gain access to the system.

Multiproblem patients may have achieved specific objectives but are certainly not "cured" of all difficulties. Should further therapy be used to correct these remaining difficulties? In general, life experience is a much better teacher than psychotherapy. Of approximately 60 multiproblem patients treated within this model at Group Health Cooperative, nearly 80% have achieved at least one or more of their stated therapeutic objectives. While this outcome is insignificant compared to traditional notions of cure, it is not meaningless to the patients themselves. For the first time in years, patients have positive experiences with attempts at change.

Follow-up interviews indicate that the majority of them do not reenter the system in a state of disarray and chaos, and often prefer to limit their use of mental health services.

Special Clinical Issues

Suicidal Behavior

A difficult aspect of work with multiproblem patients is the elevated risk of suicidal behavior (Frances, Fyer, & Clarkin, 1987). Linehan (1987) reports that the conditional probability of receiving a diagnosis of borderline personality disorder, given the presence of a repeated suicide attempt, is approximately 80%. The major principle of effective intervention is that suicidal behavior is a *learned* and *reinforced* problem-solving behavior that is designed to reduce or eliminate negative affect (Chiles et al., 1989; Strosahl & Chiles, 1984).

The cognitive–behavioral approach avoids reinforcing or punishing suicidal behavior while addressing the patient's sense of desperation (emotion) and hopelessness (cognition). The potential for suicidal behavior is not a focal point in therapy but is taken as a "given." Suicidal behavior often is related to a basic indignation about the quality of life one is experiencing and the perception that others do not have to bear this burden. The belief is, "Life is unfair." The therapist's response is understanding yet pragmatic and reality-based. The therapist recontextualizes suicidal behavior by pointing to how it might be seen as a way to get rid of negative feelings. The therapist emphasizes that he or she does not believe suicide is necessary, but that it is the patient's choice whether to terminate life. Discussions about suicidal behavior should be matter of fact, direct, with a strategic use of humor if possible. There is no place for shame, humiliation, coercion, or pejorative labeling. The therapist should adopt a collaborative stance on suicidal problem-solving behavior and explore other less aversive alternatives with the patient. The therapist is to avoid changing the scheduling, content, or work demands of the class because suicidal behavior is present. Thus, suicidal behavior is a legitimate, but costly, form of problem-solving behavior, which should not alter or change the reinforcement environment of the class in any significant way.

Compliance and the Patient–Therapist Relationship

Resistance as traditionally defined is a concept that has outlived its clinical usefulness. It is unlikely that patients have unconscious wishes to maintain a state of suffering. If this process occurs at all, it is generally conscious and understandable from a cognitive viewpoint. As Meichenbaum (1977) has suggested, resistance is the failure of the *therapist* to correctly understand the reality of the patient. When multiproblem patients do not perform, it is because the magnitude of the task is too large, the consequences of failure too great, or because of skepticism about the usefulness of the task in the first place.

The therapist should take full responsibility for the patient's performance failures. Asking the patient to perform a behavior is the *therapist's* responsibility, even if it might help the patient. The therapist is in a better position to accept failure and can adopt a "one down" strategy with the patient. This empowers the patient with responsibility for providing vital perceptual information to the therapist.

Multiproblem patients can be a source of burnout for therapists because they change in small increments or not at all. Therapists often develop negative feelings about them in relation to the lack of progress in therapy. In addition, their therapy-wise status makes them more than a match for the typical therapist. Issues also arise when the therapist and patient get into a power confrontation over dysfunctional behavior. Most therapists become very frustrated when someone is unable or unwilling to use clearly effective alternatives to self-defeating behavior, yet the multiproblem patient does exactly that! The most effective way to prevent burnout and relationship problems is to set realistic, specific, and attainable goals with the patient, and to not be averse to revising these goals downward if the situation demands it.

The Physician–Patient–Therapist Triangle

Neuroleptic and antiseizure medications may be useful in controlling cognitive and emotional symptoms reported by some multiproblem patients. Unfortunately, multiproblem patients attract unnecessary and potentially fatal medications like lightening rods. This may be due to the fact that such patients present with high levels of distress and physicians feel compelled to provide some sort of treatment.

The therapist, patient, and physician often triangulate over the issue of medication, particularly when no apparent benefits are being derived or when addictive drugs are involved. Often the expectancies of the physician, therapist, and patient are not clearly articulated, leading to fundamentally different ways of evaluating the success or failure of the medication treatment. Physicians often believe medications will improve global functioning and decrease office visits. The patient wants medication to "cure" distressing thoughts or feelings. The therapist wants to control specific symptoms that may be blocking progress in therapy. In any event, the way to prevent triangulation is to clearly define roles, communication rules, and limits of responsibility. The therapist and physician should provide each other with regular feedback about medical and psychological aspects of ongoing treatment. The patient needs to understand who is responsible for "medication type" versus "therapy type" questions. Most importantly, the therapist and physician need to interact as a "team" who must work together to achieve maximum benefits for the multiproblem patient.

Conclusion

There are many more questions than answers about the diagnosis and treatment of personality disorders. It is premature to conclude that existing conceptual models of multiproblem behavior are adequate or that any particular treatment approach has an established efficacy. While cognitive and behavioral approaches to multiproblem behavior are still in their infancy, they offer great promise for the managed mental health setting because of their parsimony, clarity, and practicality. Further theory development and associated empirical studies are needed to enhance general acceptance of cognitive behavioral approaches to this clinically challenging population.

References

Beck, A., & Emery, G. (1985). *Anxiety disorders and phobias: A cognitive perspective.* New York: Basic Books.

Beck, A., Rush, J., Shaw, B., & Emery, G. (1979). *Cognitive therapy of depression.* New York: Guilford Press.

Beck, A., Freeman, A., Pretzer, J., Fleming, B., Dans, D., Ottaviani, R., Beck, S., Simon, K., Padesky, C., Meyer, J., & Trexler, L. (1990). *Cognitive therapy of personality disorders.* New York: Guilford Press.

Bloch, D., Bell, S., Hulbert, J., & Nasrollah, H. (1988). The importance of Axis II in patients with major depression: A controlled study. *Journal of Affective Disorders, 14,* 115–122.

Burns, D. (1980). *Feeling good: The new mood therapy.* New York: NAL Penguin.

Chiles, J., Strosahl, K., Ping, Z., Michael, M., Hall, K., Jamelka, R., Senn, B., & Reto, C. (1989). Depression, hopelessness, and suicidal behavior in Chinese and American psychiatric patients. *American Journal of Psychiatry, 146,* 339–344.

Dahl, A. (1986). Prognosis of the borderline disorders. *Psychopathology, 18,* 3–10.

Frances, A. (1982). Categorical and dimensional systems of personality diagnosis: A comparison. *Comprehensive Psychiatry, 23,* 516–527.

Frances, A., Fyer, M., & Clarkin, J. (1987). Personality and suicide. In J. Mann & M. Stanley (Eds.), *Psychobiology of suicidal behavior (487,* pp. 281–315). New York: Annals of the New York Academy of Sciences.

Gabbard, G., & Coyne, L. (1987). Predictors of response of antisocial patients to hospital treatment. *Hospital and Community Psychiatry, 38,* 1181–1185.

Gallop, R. (1988). Escaping borderline stereotypes: Working through the maze of staff–patient interactions. *Psychosocial Nursing and Mental Health Service, 26,* 16–20.

Gunderson, J. (1986). Pharmacotherapy for patients with borderline disorder. *Archives of General Psychiatry, 43,* 698–700.

Hayes, S. (1987). A contextual approach to therapeutic change. In N. Jacobson (Ed.), *Psychotherapists in clinical practice* (pp. 327–387). New York: Guilford Press.

Hollon, S., & Beck, A. (1986). Cognitive and cognitive–behavioral therapies. In S. Garfield & A. Bergin (Eds.), *Handbook of psychotherapy and behavior change* (3rd ed., pp. 443–482). New York: Wiley.

Izard, C. (1979). Emotion expression and personality integration in infancy. In C. Izard (Ed.), *Emotions in personality and psychopathology* (pp. 447–466). New York: Plenum Press.

Kernberg, O. (1984). *Severe personality disorders: Psychotherapeutic strategies.* New Haven, CT: Yale University Press.

Kiesler, D. (1986). The 1982 interpersonal circle: An analysis of DSM III personality disorders. In T. Millon & G. Klerman (Eds.), *Contemporary issues in psychopathology.* New York: Guilford Press.

Kohut, H. (1977). *The restoration of the self.* Madison, CT: International Universities Press.

Lewisohn, P., Munoz, R., Youngren, M., & Zeiss, A. (1986). *Control your depression.* New York: Prentice Hall.

Linehan, M. (1987, November). Behavioral treatment of suicidal clients meeting criteria for Borderline Personality Disorder. In A. T. Beck (Chair), *Cognitive and behavioral approaches to suicide.* Symposium conducted at the meeting of the Association for the Advancement of Behavior Therapy, Boston, MA.

Livesley, W. (1985). The classification of personality disorder: II. The problem of diagnostic criteria. *Canadian Journal of Psychiatry, 30,* 359–362.

Livesley, W. (1987). A systematic approach to the delineation of personality disorders. *American Journal of Psychiatry, 144,* 772–777.

Livesley, W., & Jackson, D. (1986). The internal consistency and factor structure of behaviors judged to be associated with DSM III personality disorder. *American Journal of Psychiatry, 143,* 1473–1474.

Masterson, J. (1976). *Psychotherapy of the borderline adult: A developmental approach.* New York: Brunner/Mazel.

Meichenbaum, D. (1977). *Cognitive behavior modification: An integrative approach.* New York: Plenum Press.

Millon, T. (1981). *Disorders of personality: DSM III, Axis II.* New York: Wiley.

Mischel, W., & Peake, P. (1982). Beyond déjà vu in the search for cross-situational consistency. *Psychological Review, 89,* 730–755.

Pfohl, B., Stangl, D., & Zimmerman, M. (1984). The implications of DSM III personality disorders for patients with major depression. *Journal of Affective Disorders, 7,* 309–318.

Reich, J. (1987). Sex distribution of DSM III personality disorders in psychiatric outpatients. *American Journal of Psychiatry, 144,* 485–488.

Robbins, L., Helzer, J., & Weissman, M. (1984). Lifetime prevalence of specific psychiatric disorders at three sites. *Archives of General Psychiatry, 41,* 949–959.

Salman, A., Byrne, J., & Doghramji, K. (1986). The demographic profile of borderline personality disorder. *Journal of Clinical Psychiatry, 47,* 196–198.

Spitzer, R., Endicott, J., & Gibbons, M. (1979). Crossing the border into borderline personality and borderline schizophrenia. *Archives of General Psychiatry, 36,* 17–24.

Stone, M. (1985). Analytically oriented psychotherapy in schizotypal and borderline patients: At the border of treatability. *Yale Journal of Biological Medicine, 58,* 275–288.

Strosahl, K., & Chiles, S. (1984). Assessment and treatment of the suicidal patient. Paper presented at the 94th Annual Convention of the American Psychological Association, Toronto, Ontario, Canada.

Strosahl, K., & Linehan, M. (1983, August). *Assessment of interpersonal skills in suicidal psychiatric patients.* Paper presented at the 91st Annual Convention of the American Psychological Association, Anaheim, CA.

Strosahl, K., & Linehan, M. (1986). Basic issues in behavioral assessment. In A. Ciminero, K. Calhoun, & H. Adams (Eds.), *Handbook of behavioral assessment* (2nd ed.). New York: Wiley.

Taylor, C. (1983). DSM III and behavior assessment. *Behavioral Assessment, 5,* 5–14.

Widiger, T., & Frances, A. (1985). Axis II personality disorders: Diagnostic and treatment issues. *Hospital and Community Psychiatry, 36,* 619–627.

Widiger, T., Trull, T., Hurt, S., Clarkin, J., & Frances, A. (1987). A multi-dimensional scaling of the DSM III personality disorders. *Archives of General Psychiatry, 44,* 557–563.

14

Donald M. Gragg

Managed Health Care Systems: Chemical Dependency Treatment

The Setting

The Kaiser Permanente Medical Care Program is a group model HMO that comprises 12 regional programs throughout the United States. The southern California region provides medical care for over two million members through the combined efforts of the Kaiser Foundation Health Plan, the Kaiser Foundation Hospitals, and the Southern California Permanente Medical Group, a partnership of over 1,800 physicians who provide or supervise all the medical care.

The Chemical Dependency Recovery Program (CDRP) at Kaiser Permanente Medical Center in Los Angeles provides services to a local health plan membership of 350,000 with a staff of 1.4 (full-time equivalent) physicians and 12 counselors. Medical and psychiatric assessment, as well as hospital consultations, are provided by staff physicians. Closely supervised outpatient detoxification is conducted in the clinic, while more complicated cases are referred to other Kaiser Permanente facilities.

Assessment is provided in a 6-hour daily treatment program. An intensive, long-term outpatient program provides individualized therapy with from one to five group sessions per week during day or evening hours, in addition to individual and family therapy as needed. Codependent people (family members) are treated in a similar but separate track whether or not the addicted individual is in therapy. Adolescents are treated in a separate outpatient program.

Chemical dependency is a prominent problem in American society (Cahalan, 1987). Niven stated that "since 1950, alcohol consumption has continued on a steady upward path, from somewhat more than 2 gallons of absolute alcohol per capita to nearly 3 gallons in 1981. . . . That is about 591 12-oz. cans of beer or 115 fifths of table wine or 35 fifths of 80-proof whiskey, gin, or vodka" (1984, p. 1913). Alcohol has been shown to play a role in 10% of all deaths in the United States (National Institute on Alcohol Abuse and Alcoholism, 1983, p. vi). The official estimate of the fiscal costs to society for alcoholism and drug abuse exceeded $136 billion in 1980 (Harwood, 1984), and extrapolation suggests that this number may exceed $221.5 billion in 1990. Chemical dependency also increases health problems and health care utilization. For example, problem drinkers use 8 times more medical care, have 3.6 times more accidents on or off the job, and are absent 2.5 times more often than others (Lee, 1987).

Although estimates of the cost of treating addiction vary with type of medical coverage and with the manner in which costs are measured, there is little doubt that a mandate exists to find new ways to organize and deliver appropriate services (Sullivan, Flynn, & Lewin, 1987). A major challenge facing mental health providers today is to devise effective and affordable treatment services.

This chapter presents guidelines, and discussion of the programmatic features, that managed health care systems must deal with in accomplishing this task, drawing on my experience directing the chemical dependency program at Kaiser. This chapter is organized in four sections. Section one deals with program design and development by delineating major issues and significant details that any managed care system must consider in implementing a chemical dependency program. Section two outlines the general principles of addictions treatment. Section three discusses psychotherapeutic goals and issues, including the specific characteristics of patients and special populations. Section four deals with the distinctive influences of managed health care upon these treatment programs.

Program Design and Development

Philosophy of Program

Selecting an underlying treatment philosophy is an important first task for implementing any substance abuse program. A number of theoretical models offer tentative explanations for the causes of chemical dependency—including psychodynamic, sociocultural, neuroscience, and behavioral and disease models. A discussion of these theoretical perspectives is beyond the scope of this chapter and can be found in other sources (e.g., Bootzin & Accocello, 1988). This chapter will focus solely on addictions treatment programming based on the disease model.

Although no one method of treatment has shown consistently effective results, addressing addictions from a disease model perspective of diagnosis and treatment helps, in my experience, to provide a structure that seems to enhance clinical success. E. M. Jellinek and the Yale School for Alcohol Studies are credited with developing the disease concept of alcoholism during the 1940s. Actually, a much earlier version of this formulation was expounded by Benjamin Rush, a signer of the Declaration of Independence. Newly emerging evidence regarding genetic predisposition to alcoholism lends additional credence to the disease model (Goodwin, 1979).

The Alcoholics Anonymous movement has been the most influential force in the modern conception of, and in treatment approaches to, alcoholism and other addictions. Regardless of its roots, a powerful lobby of citizens and professionals support the disease model perspective of addictions (and the notion that the patient should not be considered responsible for acquiring the illness).[1]

---

[1] The term patient will be used in this chapter, but client could be substituted without alteration in meaning.

Considerable stigma and controversy still surround the disorders of chemical dependency. Dealing with addicted patients from the assumption that they are not responsible for having their disease reduces guilt and shame and facilitates the treatment process. The disease model of chemical dependency posits that patients lack culpability for acquiring the illness but are accountable for personal recovery, which is a critical concept and a difficult one to sustain consistently. Such a disease model differs from a pure medical model of disease, which does not hold the patient responsible for his or her own recovery. Addicted patients often try to place the responsibility for their recovery on treatment professionals, who are frequently all too willing to accept it. This tendency for the helping professional to inappropriately accept the responsibility for the patient's recovery is an element of co-dependency, which will be discussed later in this chapter.

The treatment of addictive patients within the context of managed care has unique advantages (and disadvantages). At Kaiser in Los Angeles, chemical dependency treatment implemented within a managed health care system follows some specific guidelines. Treatment of addictions is conducted in structured programs using predominantly group activities. The group mode of intervention is generally seen as more effective for addicted patients than for other mental health patients because the chemically dependent are considered a more homogeneous treatment group having more in common with one another. Educational programs, stress reduction methods, motivation enhancement, and denial reduction techniques are generally viewed as useful, and such programming can be carried out efficiently in structured group program settings. The 12-step programs, such as Alcoholics Anonymous and those patterned after it, are frequently used in the treatment of all addictive diseases, and such 12-step programs can be integrated into a comprehensive, structured therapeutic program delivered through a managed care system.

Input Variables

To develop appropriate chemical dependency treatment services in a prepaid health plan, a number of input variables must be considered in the design process. First, the characteristics of the enrollees of the managed care plan must be examined and understood. Second, the characteristics of the HMO must be considered in relation to its enrollees and their clinical needs. Third, treatment resources available within an organization and the surrounding community should be utilized and integrated appropriately. Fourth, decisions must be made concerning both the treatment services to be provided (including precise contract language regarding benefits) and whether the services will be provided in-house or by contracting with outside providers. Finally, federal, state, and local regulations must be known (and the policies and practices of the HMO must comply with them). Table 1 summarizes this group of input variables.

Characteristics of enrollees. It is extremely important, during the process of building an HMO substance abuse program, to become well-acquainted with the characteristics of the prepaid membership. It is incumbent upon the program originators to understand how the cultural, language, and drug use characteristics of enrollees can impact upon the potential treatment program.

Table 1. Input Variables in the Design Process

Characteristics and needs of the patient population
1. Common drugs of abuse
2. Cultural characteristics
3. Language
4. Geographic distribution and transportation systems

Characteristics of the HMO
1. Enrollment
2. Size and location of facilities
3. Existing treatment services or contracts

Existing community resources
1. Medical model addictions treatment programs
2. Social model addictions treatment programs
3. Programs for special populations (e.g., adolescents)
4. Self-help groups

Federal, state, and local regulations

Characteristics of the HMO. The feasibility of operating an in-house substance abuse program is determined by the size and composition of the health plan enrollment. A critical mass of substance abusers is necessary to operate a structured group treatment program. Factors such as the likelihood that patients can congregate in one place to attend sessions make a considerable difference in deciding upon what essential features must be built into a program. For example, a rural-based managed care program will require transportation facilities for its group members as an essential feature, but an urban-based program with easy access to public transportation may not.

Community and treatment resources. A survey of community resources yields information about possible contract providers and about current community standards of care to which the prepaid plan must be accountable. Since self-help group involvement is a desirable, if not an essential, element in each patient's recovery program, identifying and establishing good working relationships with the various 12-step and other self-help organizations is crucial to program development.

In-house programs versus contract providers. A number of factors must be considered in deciding whether to provide services by contract with existing providers or by developing an in-house program. Cost control, quality assurance, continuity of care in transitions between medical hospitalization, intensive addictions treatment, and long-term monitoring therapy may be better achieved with in-house programs. Contracting provides the advantage of offering a wider variety of options and may be less expensive when plan membership includes small numbers of patients.

Federal, state, and local regulations. If the prepaid health plan is a federally qualified HMO, it will be required to abide by the following federal regulations.

First, diagnosis and medical treatment for the abuse of or addiction to alcohol and drugs shall include detoxification for alcoholism or drug abuse on either an outpatient or inpatient basis, whichever is medically determined to be appropriate, in addition to the other required basic health services for the treatment of other medical conditions. Second, referral services may be either for medical or for nonmedical ancillary services. Medical services shall be a part of basic health services; prolonged rehabilitation services in a specialized inpatient or residential facility need not be a part of basic health services.

Treatment Components of a Chemical Dependency Program

There are a wide variety of treatment components that may be included in an addictions treatment program. These are listed in Table 2. While it is unlikely that any one managed health care plan will provide all of these services, each service should be considered in the planning process. Program planners will select the most appropriate and relevant components to suit their individualized needs. For example, program planners must decide how, and to what extent, their programs will provide consultation services related to addictions, emergency addictive services, detoxification, and rehabilitation. Decisions related to each of these services will be influenced by the size of the managed care system, the number of covered patients,

Table 2. Components of Addictions Treatment Programs

Hospital Consultations
  1. Assistance with detoxification and medical management
  2. Facilitate entry into long-term rehabilitation treatment

Night/weekend/emergency services
Inpatient (medical) detoxification
Outpatient (medical) detoxification
Social model detoxification
Hospital/residential rehabilitation (21–28 days)
Long-Term residential rehabilitation (3–12 months)
Outpatient rehabilitation, including day treatment programs
Family treatment

Special modalities
  1. Methadone detoxification and/or maintenance
  2. Aversion therapy
  3. Naltrexone therapy
  4. Disulfiram therapy

Special patient groups
  1. Adolescents
  2. Non-English speaking groups
  3. Cultural or other minorities (e.g., gay or lesbian groups)

Education of general medical staff regarding addictions

and whether the managed care system owns and operates its own inpatient and outpatient facilities.

It is important in any managed health care system to provide hospital consultation for substance abuse programs. This is financially important because it is well-known that addicted individuals are high users of medical services and clinically important because addicted individuals frequently deny their problems, thus hospital staff will play a key role in identifying individuals in need of intervention by the addictions treatment team.

All managed health care systems should also provide emergency services in the evening and on the weekend. Acute problems related to substances do not conveniently occur between 9 a.m. and 5 p.m. As with all components of an addictions treatment program, emergency services can be provided either in-house or under contract.

An essential component of any effective addictions treatment program is detoxification, which can be conducted on either an inpatient or an outpatient basis. This topic will be addressed in further detail below.

Finally, a managed health care system must determine the extent to which it is willing and able to engage in the long-term rehabilitation of addicted individuals. It is in the best financial interest of managed health care systems to coordinate the rehabilitation of individuals with addictive diseases so as to decrease their long-term inappropriate overutilization of health care services. Again, fundamental decisions must be made about inpatient rehabilitation versus outpatient rehabilitation, with specific attention directed toward treatment and support for nonaddicted family members and significant others.

Inpatient Versus Outpatient Treatment

Mainstream medicine has played an increasingly prominent role in the field of addictions, particularly alcoholism, during the past 20 years. This "medicalization" of the treatment of addictions has been accompanied by the development of many hospital-based treatment programs. Many people believe there is now a bias toward the inpatient treatment of addictions. The present overreliance on inpatient care resulted from several factors: the availability of hospital beds, insurance coverage for inpatient but not outpatient care, and an increased sense of clinical control.

Inpatient substance abuse programs have, in general, acquired good reputations, but their higher costs have encouraged employers and insurance companies to join HMOs in promoting outpatient alternatives. Highly structured, intensive outpatient or day hospital addiction treatment programs have been developed that provide excellent clinical care while the patient lives in his or her usual environment and continues to be productive in the workplace. Studies have shown no outcome differences in comparisons of the inpatient and outpatient care of patients whose addictions were *randomly* assigned to treatment methods (Annis, 1986; Miller & Hester, 1986).

In general, most managed health care systems will utilize outpatient intervention programs for addictive problems because of the lower costs involved in such care. However, such programs are also less disruptive to the patient, which frequently makes them preferable to the patient as well. Because all currently available research data suggests comparable outcomes for inpatient and outpatient programs for addictive programs, the choice of the least expensive alternative is also a professionally sound decision for the majority of patients with addictive disorders. However, clinical impressions suggest that patients with more advanced disease and with less social support need more intensive handling and may respond better to inpatient care.

Acute detoxification can frequently be conducted on an outpatient basis, particularly when it is carried out as part of a structured outpatient rehabilitation program with an experienced treatment team (Hayashida, et al., 1989). This should be the preferred (and most frequently utilized) detoxification approach for managed health care programs.

Indications for inpatient detoxification are (a) concurrent medical or psychiatric conditions that require hospitalization or, in conjunction with withdrawal symptoms, are expected to cause problems requiring hospitalization; (b) a history of complicated withdrawal (e.g., seizures or delirium) with a comparable quantity and duration of alcohol/drug use; (c) anticipated complicated withdrawal based on a history of alcohol/drug use, physical findings, and blood alcohol level determinations (a Breathalyzer is an invaluable aid); and (d) inadequate supervision and social support in the outpatient setting to assure abstention from alcohol/drug use or safe administration of necessary medications.

Alternative Program Designs

While a wide variety of program elements are possible and appropriate, three sample benefit packages and treatment programs are shown in Table 3.

A relatively small managed health care system, or a managed health care system covering a widely dispersed membership, may have a very small addictions

Table 3.   Sample Alternative Addiction Treatment Program Designs

Small or widely dispersed membership
1. Hospital consultations in-house
2. Detoxification, rehabilitation and family treatment by contract
3. Long-term residential rehabilitation and methadone treatment by referral (not covered benefits)

Alternative model for small membership
1. Hospital consultations and inpatient detoxification in-house
2. Outpatient detoxification and rehabilitation, and family treatment by contract
3. Short-term residential rehabilitation and methadone treatment by contract as supplemental (optional) benefits
4. Long-term residential rehabilitation, by referral (not a covered benefit)

Large membership
1. Hospital consultations, inpatient and outpatient detoxification, outpatient and short-term residential rehabilitation, and family treatment in-house
2. Long-term residential rehabilitation and methadone treatment by referral (not covered by benefits)

treatment staff and may choose to provide few services in-house. Such a system may provide hospital consultation in-house if the number of hospitalizations utilized by plan members is small enough. Most small managed care plans, or plans with widely dispersed membership, will want to provide emergency services, detoxification, rehabilitation, and family treatment by contract. Long-term residential rehabilitation and methadone treatment will generally not be covered benefits.

A relatively small managed health care system with at least one inpatient facility may wish to provide slightly more services in-house. In addition to hospital consultations, they may wish to provide their own inpatient detoxification services. Outpatient detoxification, rehabilitation, and family treatment may still be provided by contract. If there is sufficient need among the membership, short-term residential rehabilitation, as well as methadone treatment, might also be provided by contract, although in most smaller health plans this would need to be a supplemental or an optional benefit, probably involving an additional premium. Long-term residential rehabilitation is generally not a covered benefit, although referrals to such residential programs should be made when desired by the patient or when viewed as appropriate and needed.

Managed health care systems with larger memberships will generally provide a comprehensive set of in-house addictions treatment programs. In-house provision and management generally allow for greater control to managed health care providers, as well as better coordination of services on behalf of patients. Thus, larger systems often provide hospital consultation, emergency services, inpatient and outpatient detoxification, outpatient rehabilitation, and family treatment as in-house programs. Long-term residential treatment is generally not a covered benefit, although some plans may choose to provide short-term residential rehabilitation, depending on the needs of their covered population (with the same for methadone treatment).

Treatment Staff

For professionals with a wide variety of training and experience to perform well in the addictions field, they must be able to function as members of a team. An addictions treatment team should include both medical and nonmedical personnel. Two significant issues to be considered in staff selection are the use of recovering persons and the role of psychiatrists versus nonpsychiatrist physicians.

A large number of recovering chemically dependent persons have become providers who bring to the field a depth of insight to the addictive lifestyle and credibility with patients that is difficult to achieve with only professionally trained, nonrecovering staff. Such recovering individuals also facilitate good relationships with self-help groups and employee assistance programs. Recovering persons are usually expected to have a minimum of 2 to 3 years of continuous sobriety before they can appropriately assume professional responsibilities.

Nonrecovering staff can provide a sense of objectivity that may be difficult for recovering staff to demonstrate. Any nonrecovering staff members who are co-dependent (that is, have a family member or close friend who is chemically dependent) should have worked through their co-dependency status in Alanon or through another method prior to working professionally in an addictions treatment program.

In my experience, an ideal staff for an addictions treatment program consists of a mix of recovering and nonrecovering persons, with both groups having a high level of professional education and training in both the theory and practice of addictions therapy.

Earlier programs for the treatment of addictions have been viewed as marginally effective, in part because of overreliance on a psychoanalytic approach to the treatment of alcoholism. The leaders in the modern addictions field come from a range of medical and nonmedical specialties, including internists, family practitioners, pediatricians, psychiatrists, psychologists, nurses, and social workers. The modern medical treatment of addictions requires the skills of both the psychiatrist and the internist/family practitioner. This may be achieved by cross training such physicians.

Psychotherapy in Chemical Dependency Treatment

The principles and techniques of psychotherapy used with chemically dependent patients are of the same variety as those used in the treatment of other psychological and behavioral disorders. A detailed discussion of the psychotherapeutic treatment of addictive disorders is beyond the scope of this chapter.[2] However, some common elements in treating the addictive disorders have led to unique treatment approaches, which are sometimes organized into structured programs. The description that follows is intended to serve as an example, not as a single recommended program of therapy.

The Context of Therapy

The goals of chemical dependency treatment are the attainment of long-term sobriety and improved psychosocial functioning. Sobriety is used here to mean free of all mind-altering substances, with the exception of appropriately prescribed medications. Although some treatment programs attempt to aid patients in a return to controlled drinking, most authorities do not consider this to be an appropriate or acceptable treatment goal.

Treatment of addictive disorders should begin with an individualized assessment of the patient's problems and needs. An individual's desires regarding care may be inappropriate, such as the desire to learn to drink socially or to give up one drug while continuing to use others. Likewise, a patient may demand a type of therapy or setting which is not indicated. Carefully negotiating with the patient, while educating him or her about suitable goals and therapy, will help to retain commitment to the most effective overall program.

To some, using psychotherapy to treat chemical dependency implies that its purpose is to overcome some underlying psychopathology which is causing the addiction. In my experience, this approach is ineffective and potentially dangerous in that it supports the patient's denial of the true problem. It is imperative that treat-

---

[2] A variety of sources on the natural history of addiction, most typically alcoholism and recovery, exist in the literature. Two excellent sources for this information are Vaillant (1983) and Brown (1985).

ment be based on aiding the patient to cease the alcohol and/or drug use first. Only then should therapy be provided for residual disorders. Occasionally, patients may require treatment of a coexistent mental disorder concurrent with the initiation of addictions treatment. These cases are the exception rather than the rule. Care must be taken lest the therapist be misled into dealing with a consequence of the addiction as though it were the cause.

Motivation

Treatment failures with addictive disorders are often explained by a lack of patient motivation. After extensively reviewing the literature, Miller (1985) indicated five methods that can be effective in promoting patient motivation for recovery, a critical element of all phases of treatment: (a) the setting of specific and demanding but attainable goals, particularly when they are supplemented by feedback; (b) simple therapist initiations in maintaining contact, such as letters and telephone calls; (c) the encouragement of compliance via operant contingencies while consequences remain in effect, although the undermining of intrinsic motivation is a risk (this includes return to work slips, court letters, and urine drug screens); (d) the provision of (apparent) voluntary choices in the treatment planning; and (e) respondent procedures that decrease the attractiveness of the problem behavior. This includes the Alcoholics Anonymous principle of "keeping the last drink fresh" by repeatedly reviewing the adverse consequences of previous drinking as well as such formal techniques as the Johnson Institute intervention, described below.

Intervention

In an attempt to overcome resistance to treatment, family, friends, and professional helpers may plan a session in which the patient is confronted with descriptions of the impact of the addiction on the persons present. This is conducted in a nonjudgmental and caring way, but with a firm ultimatum that the patient must comply with treatment or experience certain prearranged consequences. I have found the audiovisual productions "The Enablers" and "The Intervention" are very useful tools in planning interventions.[3]

The Induction of Sobriety

Initially, therapy focuses on promoting acceptance of the illness and willingness to receive help. The processes of motivation, education, and support shift the balance toward the state of acceptance or surrender in which treatment is possible. Conversely, the process of denial shifts the balance in the other direction. The concept of surrendering as a therapeutic process refers to overwhelming the denial mechanism to achieve a peaceful, positive state of acceptance of the illness and a willingness to cooperate in therapy (Tiebout, 1949).

---

[3] These audiovisual productions are available from the Johnson Institute, 7151 Metro Boulevard, Minneapolis, MN 55435–3425.

The goals for this initial stage of therapy are detoxification, abstinence, acceptance of the disease model of chemical dependency, and development of the ability to experience and express feelings. Treatment consists of education regarding the illness; supportive psychotherapy focusing on establishing a sense of self-worth; aids to abstinence, such as disulfiram, aversion therapy, and naltrexone; and health assessment and medical treatment, if needed.

Relapse Prevention

It is recognized that addictions are chronic diseases. Relapses are, therefore, to be expected and should be dealt with as positively as possible. Patients should not be blamed or punished, but the circumstances leading up to the relapse should be analyzed and used as tools in treatment to prevent future recurrences. A growing body of knowledge about therapies focusing on relapse prevention can aid the clinician in applying this principle to individual treatment plans and therapies (Annis & Davis, 1988; Brownell, Marlatt, Lichtenstein, & Wilson, 1986; Gorski & Miller, 1984; Marlatt & Gordon, 1985).

Ongoing Therapy

After the patient has achieved a period of abstinence, the focus of therapy can be broadened to include emphasis on other life problems and mental health issues. Intervention may take the form of individual or group sessions within the treatment program, separate mental health programs, self-help groups such as Alcoholics Anonymous, or any combination of the above. Decisions about the specifics of treatment must be based on the individual needs of each patient.

Most patients do not require extensive psychotherapy after the establishment of sobriety, but they do need a long-term recovery program. Regular participation in 12-step approaches such as Alcoholics Anonymous, Narcotics Anonymous, Cocaine Anonymous or Alanon, in my opinion, should be a part of recovery.

Characteristics of the Patient

As stated earlier, the disease model perspective forms a helpful framework from which to view the addicted patient. This promotes a greater degree of compassion in providers who work with addicted patients as well as in family, friends, and employers.

The belief that the individual is blameless for acquiring the illness but accountable for personal recovery is a helpful tool for working with the chemically addicted. Dealing with these patients from the assumption that they are not responsible for having the disease reduces guilt and shame and facilitates the treatment process. Other methods of confronting defenses and providing encouragement are discussed below.

Defenses

Those with addictive diseases usually deny the presence and severity of their illnesses. As the defense mechanism of denial is broken down through therapy, a low level of self-esteem may ensue due to the stigma and guilt associated with the condition. Group therapy is extremely useful for addressing these aspects of treatment. Patients identify the disease of addiction much more readily in others than in themselves. In groups, they are commonly able to relate to the other person's condition and, therefore, to identify their own addiction. The caring, support, and acceptance provided by a group is also valuable in combating low self-esteem.

Disease Course

Since chemical dependency is a chronic, relapsing illness, long-term therapy is appropriate. The typical patient attempts to discontinue formal therapy prematurely, so a major portion of treatment efforts may be directed toward maintaining the patient in a recovery program indefinitely. Because relapse is a major source of complications and health care costs, this long-term psychotherapy is a cost-saving measure. Thus, the most widely accepted current model of addictions treatment is long-term group therapy in structured programs, where patients usually receive similar management regardless of their specific drug of abuse as well as any warranted individualized therapy.

Special Populations

Whether the drug is nicotine, alcohol, or heroin, chemical dependency or addiction is characterized by impaired control of drug use and continued use despite adverse consequences. The complete diagnostic criteria for psychoactive substance dependence and related diagnoses are contained in the *Diagnostic and Statistical Manual of Mental Disorders* (American Psychiatric Association, 1988). Clinical management is influenced by which particular drug or drugs are involved, by the setting and circumstances of drug use, and by the social and cultural characteristics of the user. Subpopulations with unique treatment needs also exist. For example, adolescents have such distinctive needs that they must be treated separately from members of other groups. Other special populations, such as women, the elderly, and ethnic minorities, can be treated in a common program provided that special consideration is given to their individual needs. Most programs have shown that mixing alcoholics with street drug abusers works effectively. In fact, the majority of substance abusing patients today use both alcohol and other drugs. Abusers of prescription medications who obtain their drugs through legitimate channels frequently have difficulty identifying with the street addict and may require separate therapy.

Dual Diagnosis

It has been estimated that up to 30% of chemically dependent patients also have an additional mental disorder. In some instances, the other disorder antedates the addiction and may have played a role in its development. In these cases the addiction is considered secondary to the other mental disorder and may be called a *secondary* addiction. In other cases, the addiction antedates the other illness and is thus a *primary* addiction. Secondary addictions are usually considered to be more difficult to treat than primary addictions.

From 10–15% of chemically addicted patients have diagnosable affective disorders (major depression or bipolar illness), another 10% have antisocial personality disorder, and 7–10% have anxiety disorders (generalized anxiety disorder and panic disorder). Psychotherapy or pharmacotherapy of these conditions should be undertaken only when the substance abuse is also being appropriately treated. If treatment of the second condition is provided by a separate program, it is imperative that there be close coordination and cooperation between the therapists involved.[4]

The Family

A large but frequently overlooked component of the addiction dilemma is the role of the family. In the earliest description of alcohol problems in the Judeo-Christian tradition (Genesis, 9:20–27), the father's drinking is noted to create serious domestic conflicts. It is recognized today that the family may become as sick as the addicted person as its members develop dysfunctional responses to deal with the abnormal behavior of the patient. Treating the family along with, or independently of, the substance abuser is standard practice. Intervening in the family interaction may improve the treatment success of the patient and may reduce the utilization of health care by nonaddicted family members.

For what reason is the family treated? The concept of co-dependence characterizes the pathological degree of helping, or dependency, which is common in family members and others close to chemically dependent persons (Beattie, 1987; Cermak, 1986). These co-dependents act in a manner conducive to the persistence of addiction. They become enmeshed in the addictive process and may themselves become ill with a variety of psychosomatic complaints secondary to the anxiety, guilt, and anger emerging from the self-perpetuating cycle of dependency and co-dependency.

A recent arrival on the alcoholism treatment scene is the recognition of the nature and extent of the residual problems experienced by many adult children of alcoholics. Although many aspects of this syndrome are similar to the difficulties experienced by children in any form of dysfunctional family, enough characteristic features exist to make separate identification and management worthwhile. The literature on the subject continues to expand (Cermak, 1985), and there are now Adult Children of Alcoholics (ACOA) self-help groups throughout the country.

Influence of the Prepaid Practice Setting

A wide variety of addictions treatment programs exist in most communities. Individuals select the program that personally appeals to them, that offers the best

---

[4] Prevalence data for dual diagnoses vary widely from study to study because of variations with sex, drug of abuse, and other population variables. The numbers cited are estimates for a typical HMO population based on data from various studies.

chance of success, or that is most affordable. Patients may also be referred to specific programs after a professional assessment has indicated that a particular approach is warranted.

A major advantage to managed health care addictions treatment is that services are prepaid and, therefore, are available to all who need them. In the HMO setting, all beneficiaries have equal entitlement to treatment. However, the HMO has a limited ability to offer the specific treatment programs on demand that a patient may feel meet his or her unique needs. This means that the natural matching process of patient to program that generally occurs in the fee-for-service sector may not occur. As a result, patients may feel that they are deprived of the idealized program that they would have chosen if unimpeded freedom of choice had guided their decisions. Since expectations of success or failure may play a significant role in actual clinical success or failure, when patients believe they are receiving inferior or inappropriate therapy, the probability of success can be reduced.

Minimizing the above problem might be accomplished by providing a flexible in-house program or by contracting with a variety of treatment facilities, thus permitting good patient-program component matches as well as allowing significant patient input into decision making. Convincing patients that their program can work for them is essential to therapeutic success and can be fostered by patients observing the achievements of others in a group treatment setting.

Another problem encountered in HMO addictions therapy is that the prepayment feature may undermine the efforts of patients who are best motivated by financial incentives. There is some truth in the adage, "You get what you pay for." Patients tend to value more highly the treatment in which they are financially invested. For this reason, some programs find it advantageous to charge a co-payment, although for some patients this may represent a barrier to needed attention.

The HMO Image and Chemical Dependency Treatment

Health care providers are committed to rendering quality services whether they are practicing in the prepaid, "not for profit," or "for profit" sectors. Sometimes suspicions exist that the "for profit" provider is attempting to make a profit by delivering services that may not be absolutely essential and that the prepaid provider is attempting to reduce costs by withholding services that might be beneficial. When the precise effectiveness of different therapies is not proven, accusations of overuse or underuse abound, as is the present case in the field of substance abuse. Due to limited addictions treatment coverage in many HMO benefit packages and to the use of less expensive therapeutic approaches by HMOs, the prepaid practice sector has received much adverse publicity. It is incumbent upon the providers in this field to ensure that appropriate, adequate treatment is delivered.

Costs Versus Savings

In today's health care marketplace, costs are a constant issue. Any attempt to develop new or expanded health services raises the question, How are we going to pay? Many studies show that treating alcoholism, and to some degree other addictions, decreases health care costs by reducing the need for the care of complications resulting from untreated addictions (Luckey, 1987; Hunter, Plotnick, Adams, & Rowe, 1982). Although these studies are helpful for persuading administrators of the necessity of treatment needs, cost savings are not easily defined and are not immediately available for program planning and development.

Program Evaluation

The provision of quality care requires continuing evaluation of treatment and outcome. Sophisticated outcome evaluation is a complex and difficult process that requires special expertise and resources. However, simpler forms of ongoing evaluation can be conducted in all programs.

Reviewing the program design and operation against established policy and practice is one such technique. Edwards (1980) described key elements in a best buy approach:

1. Different patients require different types of help, and alcoholic populations are not homogeneous. To run a program by a rulebook is not sensible.

2. Assessment of patients matters very much and is a clinical responsibility that must be scrupulously met. The time presently allocated to treatments of unnecessary intensity should be reallocated to more thorough initial assessment.

3. Underlying and accompanying conditions must be identified and treated. Staff must therefore have within the team a high level of general medical and psychiatric competence.

4. The moment of help seeking has to be sympathetically understood in terms of its meaning for patient and family. Everything possible must be done to confirm the potential of this moment.

5. Goals have to be agreed on rather than imposed, and this implies due attention to the process of decision making. The goals should be explicit and should be worked out practically and in detail, both for the long-term and the short-term. Short-term goals should be attainable and immediately rewarding. Once a decision has been made by the patient, an invitation to firm the commitment may aid the keeping of the commitment.

6. The therapist matters. He or she should be positively encouraging, should be willing to show warmth, and should convey a message of hope and possibility.

7. Self-determination and self-responsibility should be emphasized, not only in the spoken message but also in the program content as it is delineated by the patient once goals and methods have been identified. The therapist must not teach or reinforce helplessness.

8. Methods for working toward agreed goals should include review and discussion of the patient's coping repertoire and encouragement of substitute activities. Relapse precipitants should be identified and strategies for future avoidance should be made.

9. Self-monitoring should be encouraged, by note-keeping or diary-keeping.

This information should be reported back to the therapist and used in further planning.

10. The spouse should be involved in the initial assessment, in goal setting, and in the whole follow-through.

11. Treatment (including detoxification) should be conducted on an outpatient basis to the maximum extent possible, except when inpatient care is necessary for the treatment of underlying or accompanying conditions, or where disease is extreme and few social supports exist, or where indicated as a life-saving intervention.

12. The intensity of treatment should be kept to a sensible minimum, with emphasis on facilitating and monitoring the patient's own exploitation of his or her natural resources.

13. The social dimension of treatment, that is, the patient's dealing with external realities, is of importance, and goals and methods in this area will require clarification. This is a prime area for the rewarding exercise of self-determination.

14. Alcoholics Anonymous referral should be routinely made and discussed when an abstinence goal has been chosen. It is freely available but not to be forced.

15. The cost of treatment should be monitored with constant willingness to revise deployment of resources so as to maximize benefits.

The staff of an addictions treatment program within a managed health care system can annually conduct a critical "self-study" of themselves as individuals and of their overall intervention program by comparing their actual functioning with their stated beliefs and operating principles. This can be done in different ways at different times. For example, five successful cases and five unsuccessful cases can be re-reviewed and discussed to compare and contrast how well each person and the overall team achieved their stated intervention ideals in each case.

Summary

A significant portion of the membership of any managed health care system will have addictive disorders requiring intervention and treatment. Thus, it is essential that all managed health care systems have some type of addictions treatment program. The program may primarily comprise a series of service contracts headed by a single addictions services clinical coordinator in-house, or it may comprise a comprehensive series of inpatient and outpatient intervention and rehabilitation programs provided on an in-house basis, or it may offer a service structure at a point any place between these two extremes. However, regardless of the specific structural elements of the program, it is essential that all managed health care systems provide treatment for addictive disorders.

Psychotherapy is a valuable component within addictions treatment programs. Initial psychotherapeutic interventions are most typically conducted on an individual basis, but the preferred long-term psychotherapeutic approach is generally group therapy. Group therapy of individuals with addictive disorders is typically long-term because of the chronicity of the problem and the high potential for relapse. Twelve-step approaches are frequently critical to long-term maintenance of sobriety. Psychotherapeutic intervention and education with family members are also essential.

The majority of addictions program services within a managed health care system can and should be provided on an outpatient basis. Research has found no differences in the clinical effectiveness of inpatient and outpatient treatment programs, but a clear difference is obvious cost. The provision of less expensive but clinically effective outpatient care permits a managed health care system to provide cost-effective long-term care group therapy to individuals with addictive disorders.

References

American Psychiatric Association. (1988). *Diagnostic and statistical manual of mental disorders* (3rd ed., rev.). Washington, DC: Author.

Annis, H. M. (1986). Is inpatient rehabilitation of the alcoholic cost-effective? Con position. *Advances in Alcohol and Substance Abuse, 5*, 175–190.

Annis, H. M., & Davis, C. S. (1988). Relapse prevention. In R. K. Hester & W. R. Miller (Eds.), *Handbook of alcoholism treatment approaches*. New York: Pergamon.

Beattie, M. (1987). *Co-dependent no more*. Center City, MN: Hazelden.

Bootzin, R., & Accocello, J. R. (1988). *Abnormal Psychology: Current Perspectives* (pp. 281–310). New York: McGraw Hill.

Brown, S. (1985). *Treating the alcoholic: A developmental model of recovery*. New York: Wiley.

Brownell, K. D., Marlatt, G. A., Lichtenstein, E., & Wilson, G. T. (1986). Understanding and preventing relapse. *American Psychologist, 41*, 765–782.

Cahalan, D. (1987). *Understanding America's drinking problem: How to combat the hazards of alcohol*. San Francisco: Jossey-Bass.

Cermak, T. L. (1985). *A primer on adult children of alcoholics*. Pompano Beach, FL: Health Communications.

Cermak, T. L. (1986). *Diagnosing and treating co-dependence*. Minneapolis, MN: Johnson Institute.

Edwards, G. (1980). Alcoholism treatment: Between guesswork and certainty. In G. Edwards & M. Grant (Eds.), *Alcoholism treatment in transition*. Baltimore, MD: University Park Press.

Goodwin, D. W. (1979). Alcoholism and heredity: A review and hypothesis. *Archives of General Psychiatry, 36*, 57–61.

Gorski, T. T., & Miller, M. (1984). *The phases and warning signs of relapse*. Independence, MO: Herald House—Independence Press.

Harwood, H. J. (1984). *Economic costs to society of alcohol and drug abuse and mental illness: 1980*. Research Triangle Park, NC: Research Triangle Institute.

Hayashida, M., et al. (1989, February 9). Comparative effectiveness and costs of inpatient and outpatient detoxification of patients with mild-to-moderate alcohol withdrawal syndrome. *New England Journal of Medicine, 320*, 358–365.

Hunter, H., Plotnick, D., Adams, K., & Rowe, J. (1982). Treating alcoholics in group practice HMOs: Implications for management, marketing and medical care. *The Group Health Journal*, Summer, 21–31.

Lee, F. C. (1987). Purchasers address escalating psychiatric and substance abuse utilization. *Employee Benefits Journal*, March, 9–13.

Luckey, J. W. (1987). Justifying alcohol treatment on the basis of cost savings: The "offset" literature. *Alcohol Health and Research World*, Fall, 8–15.

Marlatt, G. A., & Gordon, J. R. (1985). *Relapse prevention*. New York: Guilford Press.

Miller, W. R. (1985). Motivation for treatment: A review with special emphasis on alcoholism. *Psychological Bulletin, 98*, 104–107.

Miller, W. R., & Hester, R. K. (1986). Inpatient alcoholism treatment: Who benefits? *American Psychologist, 41*, 794–805.

National Institute on Alcohol Abuse and Alcoholism. (1983). *Fifth special report to the U.S. Congress on alcohol and health*. DHHS Publication No. (ADM) 84–1291, printed 1984. Rockville, MD: Author.

Niven, R. G. (1984). Alcoholism—A problem in perspective. *Journal of the American Medical Association, 252*, 1912–1914.

Sullivan, S., Flynn, T. J., & Lewin, M. (1987). The quest to manage mental health costs. *Business and Health*, February, 24–28.

Tiebout, H. M. (1949). The act of surrender in the therapeutic process. *Quarterly Journal of Studies on Alcohol, 10*, 48–58.

Vaillant, G. E. (1983). *The natural history of alcoholism*. Cambridge, MA: Harvard University Press.

15

Hyman L. Kempler

The Treatment of Chronic Pain

The Setting

Harvard Community Health Plan (HCHP) is a prepaid group practice with more than 400,000 members in the greater Boston area. Its guiding principles are the provision of "excellent prepaid, integrated health care at a reasonable cost. Member satisfaction is the primary measure of success . . . we innovate and pursue new initiatives." These values have led to an emphasis on the development of consumer involvement and patient services such as an extensive mental health program that is integrated within the primary care system (Dorsey & Bennett, 1979; Budman, Feldman, & Bennett, 1979).

One of the innovations that HCHP has fostered is the patient's increased responsibility for his or her own health. In mental health this has meant promoting briefer therapies and interventions that elicit patient strength rather than psychopathology. The patient is expected to be more active, assume more control and not focus exclusively on the caregiver for his or her well-being. The use of eclectic therapies, perspectives, and skills inherent in different disciplines, and interdisciplinary collaboration have been favored. In a closed-panel prepaid system like HCHP, providers commit to the treatment of a population of patients. They practice with an awareness that if a provider makes one service inaccessible, for example, mental health, it is likely that the patient will seek entry to another, for example, internal medicine. Finally, consumer involvement includes participation in decisions that affect care options and cost.

Treating Chronic Pain: Problems and Issues

The "chronic pain patient" demonstrates persistent pain behavior, such as complaining, frequent visits to the doctor, drug taking, and physical incapacity for a period of six months or longer. This type of pain behavior is deemed medically incongruent in that the intensity of pain seems out of proportion to the known or observable tissue damage. Chronic pain is a compelling sensation that motivates many patients to seek remedies offering relief or, preferably, cure. But often medical

I am grateful to Michael J. Bennett, Lesley Fishelman, Susan Imus, and Arnold Miller for their helpful comments on an earlier version of this paper.

care provides only temporary relief while cure remains elusive. While searching for a cure, the chronic pain patient might be overlooked in a typical fee-for-service structure. However, in the health maintenance organization (HMO) setting, where medical care is monitored and coordinated, the chronic pain patient is likely to become very visible.

In the last two decades, pain clinics have been created to deal with such patients. Staffed by interdisciplinary teams that may consist of physicians, psychologists, nurses, physical therapists, or others, these clinics are in ambulatory or inpatient settings. The magnitude of the problem is illustrated by the steady increase in the number of clinics from 35 in 1976 to 1,500 in 1988 (Aronoff, 1988). However, only 125 of these are currently accredited, free-standing or hospital-based programs.

Cost factors are a significant consideration in the treatment of chronic pain patients. These patients use significantly more medical services at HCHP than other members, averaging 10.1 compared to 1.9 visits during a six-month period (Fitzpatrick & Kempler, 1990). Neurological and orthopedic assessment and frequent office visits are costly. While pain clinics are a valuable treatment resource, pain control treatment is also expensive, as illustrated by one Boston facility's charge of $18,000 for one month of inpatient treatment! Cost issues are particularly relevant in settings such as HMO s, where cost controls are vital to the well-being of the organization. Providing quality treatment for the chronic pain patient at reasonable cost is a challenge in these settings.

The particular treatment for chronic pain patients outlined below is more easily understood in light of the setting of HCHP, a prepaid group practice with more than 400,000 members. It is committed to continual improvement of quality and service and to strong consumer involvement along with cost consciousness. Staff satisfaction is also an important value.

Each member typically has a primary care physician who manages his or her overall care including specialty referrals and treatment. Patients with pain as their primary symptom can pose difficult management and treatment issues for health care providers (Fitzpatrick & Kempler, 1990). Because these patients don't get well easily, they often frustrate the treatment efforts of those trying to care for them. Indeed, they may complain to administrators about unsatisfactory treatment and request approval for HCHP paid extramural treatment.

Chronic pain patients are also not a homogeneous group. When tested with the MMPI (Minnesota Multiphasic Personality Inventory), they reveal at least three distinct personality groups: (a) a relatively healthy group; (b) a moderately distressed group with abnormal scale elevations on hysteria, depression, and hypochondriasis; and (c) a significantly disturbed group with additional scale elevations including schizophrenia (Armentrout, Moore, Parker, Hewett, & Feltz, 1982).

The HCHP Pain Management Program

The Pain Management Program (PMP) began in May, 1988 and is affiliated with the Department of Neurology at HCHP. Although it is staffed primarily by mental health clinicians, association with the mental health department was deliberately avoided in order to minimize patient anxiety about the program. Experience prior to the advent of PMP had indicated that chronic pain patients seemed to benefit little from psychological treatment. Patients misunderstood or did not acknowledge the mind–body relationship and thus psychological mechanisms and experience were not seen as having physical consequences, such as, endorphin production. As a result, psychological interventions were rejected and their suggestion by a provider was often regarded as insulting because of a perceived challenge to the patient's mental status. We sought to avoid these complications by incorporating two operational principles: (a) acceptance of the patients' pain complaints without judgment about etiology, and (b) elicitation of the patients' motivation by offering choices to participate in various aspects of the program.

Referrals

HCHP providers (usually internists or specialists who have exhausted other treatment options within HCHP) make referrals to the program. Patients who have complained of pain for at least six months are eligible. Before they are accepted, appropriate evaluations, (e.g., orthopedic, neurologic) must have been made, and an adequate trial of expected treatment, (e.g., physical therapy, medication, TENS unit (transcutaneous electrical nerve stimulator) must have been attempted. Algorithms for the treatment of the most common pain problems, that is, back pain and headaches, have been developed to ensure that a complete work up and trial of treatment have taken place. In cases where such standards are not met, the patient is sent for further evaluation, and treatment, or both. The evaluative approach makes the PMP available to as many providers and patients as possible. This orientation is consistent with PMP's commitment to assist other medical providers in the care of these patients and HCHP's mandate to provide relevant health services to its subscribers.

Evaluation

Following the referral, the patient contacts, or is contacted by, the program for a three-step evaluation.

Step 1: Interview. In Step 1, after reviewing the medical records, a clinician interviews the patient to determine his or her appropriateness for the program. In the interview, which lasts up to one hour, the clinician obtains a brief history of the patient's current pain problem, physical health, medication use, and relevant family background. The clinician describes the program while assessing the patient's interest and motivation. The clinician also ascertains that the patient's participation is voluntary and that the patient is not severely disturbed, for example, psychotic or suicidal. The patient's intellectual level and English language comprehension is also approximated from the patient's behavior and background.

Step 2: Evaluation battery. In Step 2, the interviewer asks potential patients to complete a packet of written materials. The items in the battery, selected after a review of the literature on pain evaluation, were chosen for their relevance to treatment goals such as pain coping skills and increased pain control. Their simplicity, brevity, allowance for patient judgments, prediction of treatment outcome, and repeatability at the end of PMP and a six-month follow-up were also considered.

Information from the battery is shared with the patient or the referring provider on request. The evaluative battery consists of the following:

1. Pain rating. This is a measure of subjective pain experience. The patient indicates the worst pain experienced in the past month and the "severity of your pain on the average over the past four weeks" on a 10-centimeter visual analogue scale whose end-points are marked "no pain" and "pain as bad as it could be."

2. COOP Scales. Used in ambulatory medical practice, this rating scale checks on the patient's view of his or her status in the past month (Nelson et al., 1987). The patient appraises eight areas of functioning on a five-point ordinal scale. Each point scale is illustrated by a drawing that depicts a level of functioning. The areas are physical condition, emotional condition, social activities, pain, overall condition, change in condition, quality of life, and social support. If possible, a second rating by a significant other is also obtained.

3. SCL-90-R is a 90-item self-report inventory of problems involving physical and emotional distress (DeRogatis, 1977). It is also a measure of psychological well-being. Item are rated on a five-point scale and responses are scored in terms of nine dimensions common to medical and psychiatric patients namely: somatization, obsessiveness, interpersonal sensitivity, depression, anxiety, hostility, phobic anxiety, paranoid ideation, and psychoticism. A measure of general psychological distress is also obtained (GSI). The scale has had considerable use with chronic pain patients (Shutty, DeGood, & Schwartz, 1986).

4. Coping Strategies Questionnaire (CSQ). Developed to assess cognitive and behavioral methods of coping with pain, this 42-item instrument asks patients to rate their frequency of use of the following: diverting attention, praying/hoping, coping self-statements, reinterpreting pain sensations, increased behavioral activities, ignoring sensations, catastrophizing, and pain behaviors (Rosenstiel & Keefe, 1983). In addition, the patient rates his or her global ability to control and decrease pain. The scale predicts, to some degree, behavioral and emotional adjustment in some chronic pain patients (Keefe et al., 1987).

5. Millon Behavioral Health Inventory (MBHI). This is a 150-item true–false self-report inventory with a prognostic index for pain treatment (Millon, Green, & Meagher, 1979). It also purportedly measures attitudes relevant to coping with illness, with particular attention to the role of psychosomatic and psychogenic factors such as chronic tension and social alienation, and personality styles such as "cooperative," "inhibited," and "forceful." The inventory is machine-scorable, and generates a clinical report.

In addition to the information obtained directly from the patient, two other indices of patient behavior are gathered: (a) number of contacts (from the medical record), and (b) use of pain medication. These are to be used for program evaluation.

Step 3: Appointment. A follow-up appointment is scheduled with the patient after the testing packet is completed. In the interim, the staff reviews intake and testing material and reaches a decision on whether to accept the patient. During the follow-up visit the patient is told of the staff's decision, which is generally to accept. For example, in the second treatment cycle of the PMP, of 31 patients who were evaluated, only one was rejected. This patient displayed evidence of major psychiatric illness. Patients can also decide not to enter the pain management program at this point, but few decline.

This phase of the process is concluded with the patient's choice of either the modified or intensive treatment program, following the interviewer's explanation of them. Before leaving, the patient signs a contract specifying the program chosen and a commitment to attend. A goal intention form that lists achievements expected, such as less pain, improved social activities, better sleep, and increased physical activity is also completed.

Guiding Program Selection

PMP staff help the patient select the program in which he or she wishes to participate. The interviewer may make suggestions based on patient motivation, condition, psychological time resources, group composition, and system issues. However, the patient's choice is accepted most of the time. Since participation in the program is voluntary, this approach is assumed to enhance motivation and thus the chance for a positive outcome.

At times staff strongly recommend or insist on a particular track. The more chronic, intractable, and dysfunctional the patient, the more likely it is that the patient would be directed toward the intensive program. For example, a patient addicted to narcotic medication and making frequent medical visits for pain relief would be urged to take the intensive track. But on other occasions, a resistive patient might be encouraged to start with a modified track because he or she is too frightened to make a stronger commitment. This treatment might suffice, at least for a while. If the patient subsequently desired further treatment, additional help can be arranged. Patients who could regress by participation in the program—for example, those who are severely psychologically impaired—also are often counseled into a modified component. In one instance, a patient with a borderline personality disorder and a depressive disorder who had recently been discharged from a psychiatric hospital was referred because of chronic migraine headaches. She was offered the modified track although she requested the intensive track. The rationale for the staff's decision—that the latter program was potentially too stimulating and could upset her and the other patients—was explained to her and she agreed.

Patients' progress through the program is monitored by the program coordinator, who performs many of the evaluations, does expressive arts and movements therapy, and is available to patients daily. (Patients in the intensive program can request up to four sessions of individual consultation and others can request follow-up visits.) Two other staff members work with patients. A psychiatrist, who is the Director, evaluates referrals and sees patients for medication and treatment issues. A psychologist (the author) evaluates patients and consults with them on psychological evaluations and treatment concerns. Clinical issues are reviewed regularly in weekly staff meetings and informal contacts.

Program Options and Treatment Groups

The PMP is a program developed and conducted by an interdisciplinary team of mental health professionals, such as psychiatrist, psychologist, and expressive arts and movement therapists and includes concepts and techniques from cognitive–behavioral, psychodynamic, hypnotherapeutic, psychopharmacologic, and psychoimmunologic treatment models. The program favors approaches that empower patients to be active in their own recovery and enable them to achieve mastery over obstacles to health through focused self-examination and relevant actions. This makes it possible to capitalize upon and elicit each patient's unique strength rather than noting conflicts and psychological liabilities.

Because group treatment has been shown to be both effective and economical, the program was devised around a series of groups or modules designed to accomplish the following therapeutic aims:

1. Challenging beliefs: Maladaptive notions about pain and ways in which they are maintained by the patient and the environment are identified, reexamined, and modified. For example, the notion that pain is invariable or that pain intensity and suffering are identical is explored and challenged. Turk and Holzman (1986) note that reconceptualization and enhancement of coping skills are common to all chronic pain treatment methods.
2. Consciousness raising: Awareness of the individual psychological patterns that have created and maintained the pain "illness," is enhanced, and ways in which these patterns may be managed or overcome are examined. Attention to a more autonomous and fulfilling life despite the presence of pain is stressed.
3. Coping methods: Ways of coping with pain such as relaxation, meditation, and self-hypnosis are taught. These are intended to increase the patient's self-efficacy in the control and reduction of pain.
4. Education: Information about life-style changes that emphasize health, such as exercise, body mechanics, and discipline are provided.
5. Therapeutic Milieu. Participation is encouraged within a community of fellow patients and therapists that promotes discussion and learning about chronic pain. Patients also experience personal validation, occasions for constructive conflict and confrontation about resistance, and exposure to new behavior and beliefs.

The groups that were developed include: Ways to Wellness, Expressive Arts Therapy, and Hypnosis. These groups are combined into treatment alternatives or tracks labeled *modified* or *intensive*. These two tracks were chosen because they were consistent with treatment objectives, were likely to appeal to patients, fit the skills of the staff, and met budgetary allowances.

The modified track consists of Ways to Wellness, a seven-week two-hour evening group. A patient can supplement this with a Hypnosis Group, or an Expression Group, or both. The intensive track consists of the Ways to Wellness group and the Hypnosis group, which meets for one and a half hours weekly for five weeks during the daytime. In addition, two group meetings, a one-hour Expressive Arts Group prior to Ways to Wellness and a one-hour multimodal group before the Hypnosis Group are provided. The latter session broadens and reinforces learnings from the other groups using verbal and nonverbal techniques.

Each track has its strengths. The modified track, unless supplemented, is basically a two-hour, seven-week group meeting and offers a powerful therapeutic opportunity. Patients with some motivation and autonomy, who are concerned about taking time away from work find this approach useful. It interferes minimally with a patient's everyday routine, since it convenes in the evening. The intensive track, providing five and a half hours weekly of both day and evening meetings, with some held in small groups, allows for more individual attention and more in-depth therapy. Patients who are significantly impaired by their pain and are highly motivated for help, or whose condition appears intractable, or who seem to require a more comprehensive approach participate in this track.

Other groups—Dynamic Relaxation and Pool Therapy—were developed and offered on an "as-needed basis" (depending upon patients' interest). The latter is recommended for patients with impaired mobility or restricted movement. A nominal fee is charged for the group because of costs incurred to the program for the use of facilities outside of HCHP. The "Booster Group," a weekly support group for former PMP participants, is also provided. All aspects of the program except for pool therapy are covered as part of the patient's benefit package. A description of the groups follows.

Ways to wellness. This module is the main treatment vehicle offered to all patients and is conducted in seven weekly two-hour sessions. Originally developed by HCHP staff for patients whose physical illness was intensified by psychosocial factors (Hellman, Budd, Borysenko, McCelland, & Benson, 1988), it was adapted for chronic pain patients (L. N. Fishelman, personal communication, May 13, 1988). Its goals are to increase self-awareness about the integration of one's mind and body in illness and behavior and to foster the assumption of greater responsibility for improving one's health.

A combination of didactic material, discussion, homework assignments, and group experiences are offered in seven weekly 2-hour sessions. For example, one session begins with a meditative task that helps patients to focus their attention on the free associations that follow their pain complaints. The patient's capacity for self-observation is enhanced and stimulated further through additional practice and homework including journal writing, visualization, and meditation. Reports of these activities are shared in the group and sometimes between meetings among the patients. Rituals like the disidentification exercise—a recitation that reinforces the notion that the person is more than his body or his symptom—are performed in the group and assigned for homework. In these ways, emphasis is placed on changing schemas that relate to the pain condition through self-examination and action. A central therapeutic message is that the pain experience is to be distinguished from the suffering that accompanies it. The latter is the result of a "personal story" which, if discovered and understood, can lead at least to symptom relief and control and ultimately to increased life enhancement and autonomy.

The personal story unfolds through the discovery of the patient's "subpersonality." This subpersonality embodies a character trait, such as "critic," "people pleaser," or "worrier," that dominates the ego (Assagioli, 1965). The distortion of the self that is represented by the chronic pain syndrome is facilitated by a particular subpersonality. For example, some patients with migraine headaches are "eager pleasers." That is, conflict and anger are absent from their family relationships and overresponsibility is ever present.

Following the identification of the subpersonality, the patient is helped to learn its origins and the particular psychological rewards that maintain it. These may involve primary relationships in childhood or adolescence that emerged in response to traumatic events. In the concluding meeting, a forgiveness ritual is introduced in which the patient writes a letter forgiving others or themselves for such traumatic experiences as hurt, abuse, overprotection, or death. Emotionally powerful letters are read and discussed in the group to amplify their significance.

Hypnosis. The hypnotic module of PMP involves five weekly group sessions, each lasting 1.5 hours. Hypnosis can improve coping and self-efficacy in the control of chronic pain, both on an individual basis (Barber & Adrian, 1982; Hilgard & Hilgard, 1983; Sachs, Feurstein, & Vitale, 1977) and on a group basis (Toomey & Sanders, 1983). The goals of the module are: (a) to improve patients' capacity to reduce and alter pain sensations and/or suffering through hypnotic trance, and (b) to help patients learn about the psychological factors influencing their pain and modify them through hypnotic suggestions.

A brief lecture on the history of hypnosis and its application in various medical and healing contexts begins the module. Potential patient resistance to hypnosis is also discussed, followed by a trance experience in which a suggestion for arm levitation is embedded. Indirect suggestions about disassociation of pain, time distortion, and posthypnotic suggestion for pain relief are also included. Patients are asked to repeat the experience daily at home for one week by listening to a tape that contains some of the lecture and the hypnotic discourse. The initial sessions also may include a demonstration with a patient volunteer of hypnotic phenomena, such as glove anesthesia, or a trance during which pain reduction is suggested. Afterwards the effects of the trance on the patient's pain, other perceptions, and well-being are discussed.

Subsequent sessions are devoted to ratifying trance experiences, practicing different inductions, introducing pain control approaches such as displacement, altering sensations (e.g., hot to cold, pain to numbness), and practicing self-hypnosis. Special tapes have been produced to facilitate the learning of sensation alteration and self-hypnosis.

Sessions often include group trances in which indirect suggestions for pain relief are included and the dynamic issues relevant to certain problems such as lower back pain are discussed indirectly. For example, reference is made to how some people have learned to cope with "back-breaking burdens." Following trance, patients sometimes discuss issues that were stimulated by the trance.

Finally, the sessions also contain opportunities for individual patients to do hypnotherapeutic work. Some patients with posttraumatic stress disorders have been able to abreact painful affects and have responded to suggestions for letting go of some of their pain. Other patients, for example, one with postsurgical pain and another with multiple-sclerosis-related pain, have also participated in brief hypnotherapeutic experiences. The positive response of these patients helps their more resistant colleagues to confirm the value of hypnosis.

   Expressive arts therapy. The group is conducted in six weekly one-hour sessions. This module involves the patient in an exploration of his or her inner resources and their external representation through expressive media such as art, music, dance, and story telling (Robbins, 1980). It is particularly appropriate for two extreme segments of pain patients; those who have difficulty verbalizing and those who are verbose but avoid expressing themselves affectively. The purpose of the group is to discover meanings and affects and their relationships with parts of the self (that is, subpersonalities) that have been submerged or exaggerated as a result of pain. As patients recover repressed memories and learn to create metaphors of their experience, awareness and increased self-expression follow. Pain symptoms often diminish or are experienced with less anxiety.
   In the meetings, patients' images and movement metaphors of pain, feelings of self-worth, and body mapping are developed. Giving form through the creative process helps the patients to bring their feelings under symbolic control. The concretization of inner experience is used to support a belief in patients' responsibility for pain relief. Patients are encouraged to learn, in effect, that "I made the pain. I control it. I can change it." Some participants in this module have produced dramatic pictorial and kinesthetic representations of their pain experience and ensuing reductions in pain symptoms.

   Dynamic relaxation. This therapeutic group is offered in five weekly sessions, each lasting one hour and fifteen minutes. The group combines Tai Chi, a Chinese Martial Art form used for its meditational values; Barteneiff fundamentals of movement, a series of body exercises to enhance body awareness and communication; relaxation; visualization; and other dance–movement therapy approaches such as Chacian Whitehouse, approaches named after their originator.

   Pool therapy. This group is offered in five weekly one-hour sessions. It conducts a form of movement therapy in an aquatic setting. While voluntary, it is especially recommended for patients with impaired mobility associated with back and leg pain.

   Other educational offerings. Presentations on nutrition, time management, body posturing, fitness flexibility, and cardiovascular conditioning also have been given. These are offered by staff from other departments at HCHP or *pro bono* by professionals from the community. PMP patients are invited to attend on a voluntary basis. The PMP staff constantly emphasizes the integration of these concepts and techniques into daily life. In addition, the staff makes available a list of community referrals for massage therapy, acupuncture, and Alexander technique (a form of body manipulation aimed especially at the spine and head to improve physical and psychological balance), which patients are free to pursue at their own expense.

Program Evaluation

PMP staff have been concerned both about the program's usefulness to primary care providers and its clinical effectiveness. We will consider each issue below.

In the first year and a half of its existence, 266 (57%) of the 464 patients referred, were evaluated. Two hundred and twenty three began treatment and 172 completed it (108 modified; 64 intensive). The treatment cost was estimated at $1,000 per patient. No patient requests for referral to extramural pain management programs have been authorized since the inception of the program. These data suggest that the program is able to serve a large number of patients who might otherwise be referred outside of HCHP or might not receive any treatment. In addition, it has been possible to avoid exceedingly costly inpatient programs. Primary care physicians clearly refer to the program frequently.

However, the data indicate that more than 40% of the referrals are not activated by patients and about 30% of those evaluated do not begin treatment. Phone contact with a small random sample of the former group revealed various reasons for noncompliance including rejection of the holistic orientation of the program and pursuit of more strictly physical treatment such as steroid injections; use of other community resources; and situational and family complications.

The data also indicate a 23% rate of drop-out from treatment. While comparable to other ambulatory programs (Kerns and Haythornthwaite, 1988; Moore and Chaney, 1985), we hope to reduce this figure by responding more effectively to patient resistance through program modification.

There are various ways to assess PMP's clinical effectiveness. Statistical analysis of pre- and postprogram testing profiles are underway, and medical utilization data are being amassed. Comparison of patients from the first two treatment cycles (N = 25) suggests that subjective ("worst") pain ratings decrease significantly at the conclusion of the program. Treated patients (N = 33) visit their physicians less in the six months after treatment than in the preceding six months. Differences in utilization between modified and intensive track patients and between noncompliant with referral, drop-outs, and treated groups are being investigated.

The staff believes that effective treatment results in lower subjective distress (e.g., less pain and suffering), and decreased medical utilization. It may also lead to greater control of pain, improved individual functioning (e.g., return to work, better sleep, more physical activity) and enhanced self-regard. These goals are also seen to be in keeping with what patients want from the program, since patient satisfaction ratings of the program are generally very positive. Our impression is that patients achieve these goals to varying degrees. We will illustrate the workings of the program through a review of the treatment of three patients.

Case Illustrations

Case illustration no. 1: Mary. Mary is a 24-year-old woman who was working in a local computer company as a technician when she was accidentally caught in a revolving door. Her arms and hips were squeezed, and she developed unremitting pain in her neck, arm, hip, and leg. She was unable to work and filed a compensation claim. Neurological and orthopedic evaluations were normal. Various treatments including physical therapy, ultrasound, and traction were only partially successful. The patient's pain complaints persisted. A trial on elavil to reduce pain and improve her sleep failed. After six months, Mary's depression worsened. She was referred to the pain program with a diagnosis of post-traumatic stress disorder and chronic pain syndrome.

Mary's initial evaluation indicated that her subjective pain ratings were relatively low but her functioning capacity was perceived as severely compromised. Her husband viewed Mary as slightly less dysfunctional than Mary herself. Her most prominent pain coping strategy was catastrophizing. Thus the staff's initial impression of Mary was of a fragile, scared, and overwhelmed woman whose high level of tension contributed to her pain. She accepted the recommendation to join the intensive program. Although shy, Mary bonded quickly with two other female patients who had started the intensive track with her. In the "Ways to Wellness" group, Mary identified a perfectionistic subpersonality that often made her tense and led to feelings of failure. These patterns were magnified by her accident. While a return to work was one of her main goals, she presumed that she had to be perfectly healthy before returning. These ideas were challenged in the group.

In the Hypnosis group she succeeded in working through some of her anger and the fear of doors and elevators that she had developed since the accident. She became less anxious about returning to work and more confident that she could master her fears. In Expressive group therapy Mary became more aware of the way in which her anxiety was expressed physically.

The staff was gratified by Mary's progress. At the end of the program she returned to work part-time. Her improvement was also reflected in reduced subjective pain ratings, reduced catastrophizing (as measured by CSQ), and the substitution of more adaptive pain coping strategies and improved general functioning.

Case illustration no. 2: Jim. Jim is a 39-year-old man with two children who was referred for pain management by his orthopedist. Persistent severe pain in his lower back and right leg prevented him from continuing with his technical but physically strenuous position at the telephone company. Two laminectomies performed in the previous two years had not terminated the pain associated with diseased lumbar discs. The residual pain was presumably caused by a disc fragment, for which the patient did not want to risk further surgery. While some pain relief was achieved through epidural steroid injections, Jim accepted referral to the pain program in order to obtain additional assistance.

When seen for evaluation, Jim's pain ratings revealed moderate pain intensity. He viewed himself as quite impaired socially and vocationally (having been on workers' compensation for three years) but his wife regarded him as somewhat more impaired emotionally than he did. However, he indicated a considerable fund of coping skills on the CSQ. In view of these and some of his other responses, the staff was uncertain about the extent to which Jim would participate in the intensive program.

In treatment Jim initially manifested a confident, pessimistic, challenging, but honest attitude. For example, in the first hypnotic session he minimized the hypnotic process and declined to attempt trance. However, he later acknowledged that he had been afraid and apologized to the therapist for his critical behavior. In a subsequent meeting he volunteered to work and was able to achieve freedom from pain while in trance. In addition, he voiced feelings of "sadness, weakness, and emptiness" when the pain disappeared. Moved to tears, he left the room only to return and reveal to the group that he had been a star soccer player in his native South American country. The loss of strength and mobility as a result of his back problems was humbling to this once proud athlete. Jim identified subpersonality elements centering on an unemotional, controlled, uncaring, rigid, invulnerable persona. The tension in the muscles of his back and the persistent preoccupation with his back pain was another representation of his inflexible character. The group process was partially helpful to Jim in that it provided the setting for him to acknowledge the concerned and caring parts of himself that he denied but which others perceived and liked. He was able to relax more effectively and examine a range of options for more purposeful living.

Jim's work in Dynamic Relaxation resulted in some pain-free days through his learning moving meditations. Awareness of body posturing along with the relaxation and inner comfort achieved enabled him to reduce tension in his body. Although his posttreatment evaluation revealed modest perceived improvement in pain reduction and control, and little change in overall functioning and pain coping strategies, there was some evidence for decreased psychological stress. This change coincided with the staff's perception of a significant positive shift in Jim characterized by increased optimism and self-esteem and less focus on the persistent pain resulting from the nerve irritation in his back. A note from his internist at the end of the program confirmed that Jim was more optimistic about his health and had agreed to return to at least part-time work. Jim continues to participate in the PMP Booster group.

Case illustration no. 3: Susan. Susan is a middle-aged woman with a history of migraine headaches beginning in childhood. Although medications and the surgical correction of a nasal defect provided some relief, the headaches frequently occurred on almost a daily basis, seriously interfering with her work and social life. Psychotherapy had been of some help, but no clear pattern of stress or interpersonal difficulty was found to correlate with the headaches. Her therapist referred her for pain management in the hope that the headaches might be reduced. Susan's evaluation indicated minimal to moderate subjective distress. However, coping strategies appeared lacking. Because she was working, Susan opted to participate in the modified track and Expressive therapy. In the Ways to Wellness group her overresponsible subpersonality was identified, and its relevance to her long-standing guilt about her psychiatrically disturbed father and sister was elaborated. Her well-intentioned emotional but frustrating tie to these family members had become a constant burden of unhappiness that was expressed in her headache. Her forgiveness letter involved a symbolic letting-go of responsibility for the dysfunctional members of her family. Through the media of writing, and block and clay sculpture, Susan reinforced the awareness gained in Ways to Wellness. An enhanced appreciation of what could be called "survivor guilt" and its manifestation in headaches finally gave Susan some freedom to abandon her burden.

At the completion of the program, the staff was impressed by her increased self-awareness, her positive attitude, and the decrease in her headaches. Posttreatment evaluation showed a marked increase in positive coping strategies. When asked to volunteer to make a video about the program three months later, Susan reported infrequent headaches and a reduction in her use of antidepressant pain medication. She continued to practice the relaxation and body awareness techniques learned in PMP and was planning a return to school to broaden her career.

Conclusion

The following discussion outlines clinical impressions of working with chronic pain patients and aspects of treating these patients in a prepaid setting. Chronic pain patients are often angry and resistive to treatment. These reactions may be demonstrated indirectly, such as through nonattendance at a session or noncompliance with a homework assignment or directly, for example, by devaluation of the program or by refusing to start treatment. In addition, patients are often quite discouraged and depressed and these feelings may be projected onto the therapist. Thus the therapist may, in turn, become discouraged with the treatment and the patient's response. If the source of these feelings is not identified and understood, treatment may be negatively affected. The structure of PMP helps to protect staff from too much negativity toward patients in several ways. First, the team approach helps the therapist be more realistic about the patient's motivation, strength, and progress. Second, other patients facilitate treatment by noting resistance in their colleagues and confronting it. This can help the therapist regain perspective about the therapeutic process.

We have outlined an intervention program for a particular population, which emanated from the unique culture of HCHP, a prepaid group practice with a tradition of well-financed mental health services. A distinct advantage to treating chronic pain patients in such a prepaid group setting appears to be the opportunity for patients to receive coordinated and planned care. Another may be that the care is provided economically. On the other hand, despite its service commitment, HCHP's treatment options are limited. Some chronic pain patients may require program elements that are more highly individualized, more intensive, and more varied (such as biofeedback, physical rehabilitation, and family involvement) than one program can offer. Perhaps further experience will enable us to indicate more specifically the kind of patients most likely to respond to our program.

References

Armentrout, D. P., Moore, J. E., Parker, J. C., Hewett, J. E., & Feltz, C. (1982). Pain patient MMPI subgroups: The psychological dimensions of pain. *Journal of Behavioral Medicine, 5*, 201–211.

Aronoff, G. M. (1988, November). *Pharmacotherapy of chronic pain patients*. Paper presented in symposium, Complications of Pain Therapy, conducted at the joint meeting of the American and Canadian Pain Societies, Toronto, Ontario, Canada.

Assagioli, R. (1965). *Psychosynthesis*. New York: Hobbs, Dorman.

Barber, J., & Adrian, C. (Eds.). (1982). *Psychological approaches to the management of pain*. New York: Brunner/Mazel.

Budman, S. H., Feldman, J., & Bennett, M. J. (1979). Adult mental health services in a health maintenance organization. *American Journal of Psychiatry, 136*, 392–395.

DeRogatis, L. R. (1977). *SCL-90: Administration, scoring and procedures manual*. Baltimore: Johns Hopkins Press.

Dorsey, J. L., & Bennett, M. J. (1979, October). Mental health services in the Harvard Community Health Plan. *Proceedings of the Medical Directors Conference*. (Medical Directors Division), 4, p. 2. Group Health Association of America: Group Health Foundation. Dallas, TX.

Fitzpatrick, R., & Kempler, H. L. (1990). Integrating care for chronic pain patients. *HMO Practice, 4*, 87–93.

Hellman, C. J. C., Budd, M., Borysenko, J., McClelland, D. C., & Benson, H. (1988). A study of the effectiveness of two group behavioral medicine interventions for patients with psychosomatic complaints. Unpublished paper, Harvard Community Health Plan, Cambridge, MA.

Hilgard, E. R., & Hilgard, J. R. (1983). *Hypnosis in the relief of pain* (Rev. ed.). Los Altos, CA: William Kaufman.

Keefe, F. J., Caldwell, D. S., Queen, K. T., Gil, K. M., Martinez, S., Crisson, J. E., Ogden, W., & Nunley, J. (1987). Pain coping strategies in osteoarthritic patients. *Journal of Consulting and Clinical Psychology, 55*, 208–212.

Kerns, R. D., & Haythornthwaite, J. A. (1988). Depression among chronic pain patients: Cognitive–behavioral analysis and effect on rehabilitation outcome. *Journal of Consulting and Clinical Psychology, 56*, 870–876.

Millon, T., Green, G., & Meagher, R. (1979). The MBHI: A new inventory for the psychodiagnostician in medical settings. *Professional Psychology, 10*, 529–539.

Moore, J. E., & Chaney, E. F. (1985). Outpatient group treatment of chronic pain: Effects of spouse involvement. *Journal of Consulting and Clinical Psychology, 53*, 326–334.

Nelson, E., Landgraf, J. M., Hays, R. D., Kirk, J. W., Wasson, J. H. Keller, A., & Zubkoff, M. (1987, October). Dartmouth COOP proposal to develop and demonstrate a system to assess functional health status in physicians' offices. (Final report to the Henry J. Kaiser Family Foundation, Grant No. 85-3180). Pub: Dartmouth Medical School, Hanover, NH.

Robbins, A. (1980). *Expressive therapy: A creative arts approach to depth-oriented treatment*. New York: Human Services Press.

Rosenstiel, A. K., & Keefe, F. J. (1983). The use of coping strategies in chronic low back pain patients: Relationship to patient characteristics and current adjustment. *Pain, 17*, 33–44.

Sachs, L. B., Feurstein, M., & Vitale, J. H. (1977). Hypnotic self-regulation of chronic pain. *American Journal of Clinical Hypnosis, 20*, 106–113.

Shutty, M. S., DeGood, D. E., & Schwartz, D. P. (1986). Psychological dimensions of distress in chronic pain patients: A factor analytic study of SCL-90 responses. *Journal of Consulting and Clinical Psychology, 54*, 836–842.

Toomey, T. C., & Sanders, S. (1983). Group hypnotherapy as an active control strategy in chronic pain. *American Journal of Clinical Hypnosis, 26*, 20–25.

Turk, D. C., & Holzman, A. D. (1986). Commonalities among psychological approaches in the treatment of chronic pain: Specifying the meta-constructs. In A. D. Holzman & D. C. Turk (Eds.), *Pain management: A handbook of psychological treatment approaches* (pp. 257–267). New York: Pergamon Press.

Nicholas A. Cummings

The Somatizing Patient

The Setting

American Biodyne is a mental health maintenance organization (MHMO) that was founded in 1985. It is a privately held Delaware corporation that provides unlimited mental health/chemical dependency outpatient and hospitalization services to enrollees of Blue Cross/Blue Shield, Humana, Lincoln National, and several other health plans in 10 states. It currently serves contracts representing 2.5 million covered lives.

In the mid-1950s, the Kaiser Permanente Health plan, the forerunner of the modern health maintenance organization, was startled to find that 60% of all visits to a physician by its two and a half million enrollees in California were by patients who had no physical illness (Follette & Cummings, 1968). At the time, this surprising figure was thought to reflect a propensity of the HMO: When access to medical services is no longer blocked by limitations, copayments, and deductibles, patients tend to overutilize medical facilities. In those early days, the relationship between stress and physical symptoms that is now known as "the somatization syndrome" was not clearly understood. Yet to label these patients "hypochondriacal," as physicians were likely to do in that era, would have suggested that hypochondria was so widespread as to be nearly universal. The term "No Significant Abnormality" was adopted and was entered as "NSA" in the medical chart by the physician. This term was not satisfactory because of its inaccuracy: These patients did, indeed, have a significant abnormality—the somatization of stress. The term that was adopted years later and which remains in use, is the "worried well."

The Kaiser Permanente staff believed for many years that the somatization syndrome was peculiar to HMO patients. But in 1976, in his testimony on behalf of the American Medical Association to the U.S. Senate Subcommittee on Health, John Kelly stated that in the United States between 60% and 70% of all patients visiting a physician have no physical disease but are somatizing stress. Why had this figure emerged so early in capitated medicine while it remained obscure and hidden for so many years in fee-for-service medicine?

The answer was obvious. In fee-for-service medicine, the physician must enter an acceptable or suspected diagnosis on the reimbursement form before the third party payor will reimburse for service. The physician who is capitated, as was the case with the Kaiser Permanente HMO, has no need to enter an approximate diagnosis when a definite one does not exist inasmuch as that physician is paid by *prospective* reimbursement to render all subsequent medical care to a group of patient enrollees.

The History of Somatization

Historically the impact of psychological or emotional problems on physical health was acknowledged intuitively. Not only was the nature of this impact poorly understood, but also it lacked empirical validity. Early experiments in what was termed "psychosomatic medicine" focused on discovering personality types that correlated with certain physical complaints such as peptic ulcers, migraine headaches, colitis, and so forth (Weiss & English, 1948). These experiments, conducted between 1930 and 1950, failed to find any significant relationship between personality type and physical illness, and interest in psychosomatic medicine waned.

During the same period, other researchers, notably psychologists who were convinced of a relationship between emotional distress and physical symptoms, continued to research the impact of psychotherapy on people's lives. Identified with this research are such experimenters as Bergin, Luborsky and Strupp (Bergin & Lambert, 1978). The major difficulty with this psychotherapy outcome research, as it came to be called, was the nature of the outcome criteria. A host of soft outcome variables, such as changes in psychological test scores, patient reports of "happiness," and measures of being "well adjusted" or "maladjusted," simply did not discriminate the patient's status before and after psychotherapy. One of the notable contributions of the Cummings and Follette studies (1967, 1968, 1976) and the Cummings studies (1979, 1983, 1985) was the discovery of a hard measure of psychotherapy outcome: a reduction in somatization as indicated by a tabulation of medical utilization before and after psychotherapy (Budman, Demby, & Feldstein, 1984).

The translation of stress into physical symptoms with consequent overutilization of medical services was observed in England years before in patients with no physical disease (Balint, 1957). Great Britain, with its national health care system, began grappling with the problem of the somatizer after the conclusion of World War II. The problem was also discovered in West Germany before it surfaced in the United States (Jones & Vischi, 1979), and there is some early evidence that somatization of stress, with consequent overutilization of medical facilities, exists in Japan (M. Sayama, personal communication, 1984).

How Does Somatization Take Place? A Case Illustration

Modern medicine, because of the way it is dispensed, inadvertently encourages somatization. The physician, trained to find disease, becomes frustrated if he or she can not find it in the presence of seemingly physical symptoms. Doing the job well requires that the disease reflected in the symptoms be identified, so evaluations (including laboratory tests, X-rays, and CAT-scans) are intensified. Eventually, the physician gives up, sometimes telling the patient that these symptoms are imaginary. The patient, convinced that he or she has a physical disease, then seeks out another physician with whom the entire process is repeated. We have seen patients who serially exhausted over a dozen physicians in this manner. An example may be helpful in understanding the process:

Bill was in his mid-fifties when the owner of the company where he worked, who was his closest friend, retired. Bill, an accountant, held the title of controller in this firm. The owner's son, fresh from graduate school with his new M.B.A. degree, assumed management of the company. One of his first projects was to computerize the accounting department. Bill, like many people his age, had a fear of computers and was convinced that he could never master them. He worried that he would be on the job market in his mid-fifties, unemployed, and in despair. He began to suffer from a general malaise that included loss of appetite, loss of interest in his surroundings, and inability to sleep. He consulted his physician who found no physical disease, gave him reassurance, and admonished him that since he was not as young as he used to be, he ought to cut back his work schedule. (Bill was a conscientious man who tended to work long hours.) He was also told to come back in a month if he did not feel better, which Bill did as his malaise steadily increased.

The fact is that Bill was depressed due to his fears of being unemployed and too old to find a new job. He gave his physician a clue when he said at the end of his examination, "You know, Doc, I have this new young boss and he is really on my back." The physician, pressed for time and faced with a waiting room bulging with patients, did not hear this. In a subsequent visit, in which all of the tests again yielded negative results, Bill repeated his remark. "You know, Doc, this young boss is *really* on my back. He's making me nervous." This time Bill said the magic word "nervous" and received a prescription for Valium. Again, he was told to return in a month or two if he did not feel better.

This sequence was repeated a couple more times during which Bill began to complain of low back pain. (Neither he nor the physician recalled at that moment his having said "My boss is on my back.") This time the physician referred Bill to an orthopedist. Over time Bill's backache grew so severe that the specialist signed him out on sick leave. Now Bill did not have to confront the distasteful job situation. By the time the orthopedic surgeon had given up on Bill and referred him to the author for psychotherapy, Bill had an emotional investment in remaining sick and avoiding the job. His was not an easy case, but after six sessions he enrolled in a community college computer class, lost his backache, and returned to work. His medical utilization, which had soared in the past several months, dropped dramatically.

Somatization and the Physician

Highly skilled physicians consistently fail to recognize patients with somatization disorders, in spite of repeated opportunities to diagnose the behavior. Twenty to 30 physician visits per year might be typical for a somatizing patient, and over 100 physician visits is not a rare occurrence, as reported by a five-year study that tracked a population of over 100,000 persons (Cummings, Dorken, Henke, & Pallak, 1989). The medical utilization histories of these patients demonstrate exhaustive physician work ups with numerous procedures and even operations. It is not unusual for such patients to become drug-dependent since the frustrated physician may rely heavily on overmedication. Iatrogenic exacerbation of their symptoms frequently results from physicians' repeated attempts to find their physical cause. When an enlightened physician orders yet another laboratory test to reassure the patient that there is no disease, the net effect is to operantly condition the patient to continue the somatizing behavior and even escalate the symptoms (Quill, 1985).

Originally, physicians regarded somatization as a form of hysteria. Later, it was redefined as Briquet's Syndrome, a diagnosis that required the presence of no fewer than 25 of 60 symptoms drawn from at least 9 of 10 symptom groups lacking in organic explanation. Further, this multisystemic group of symptoms had to appear before the patient reached the age of 35 (Quill, 1985). This stringent definition of somatization syndrome seemed to reflect physicians' resistance to accepting the widespread existence of somatization in the general population. The third edition of the Diagnostic and Statistical Manual of Mental Disorders (DSM III) reduced the number of symptoms required to make the diagnosis to 12 for men and 14 for women. Then, as if to reverse its acceptance of these less stringent criteria, DSM III lowered to 30 years the age before which the syndrome of persistent, vague, multisystemic symptoms had to appear (Quill, 1985). Given such continued resistance to the somatization paradigm, it is no wonder that skilled physicians continue to underdiagnose the disorder.

A Pragmatic Definition of Somatization

Somatization is the translation of stress or emotional distress into seemingly physical symptoms where no organic etiology for these symptoms exists. The most frequent symptoms are neurodermatitis, heart palpitations, backaches, chronic headaches, abdominal pains that can change quadrants, chronic malaise, hyperventilation, low blood sugar, unusual allergies, bruchism, hyperemesis, and frequent urination or the inability to urinate freely (Quill, 1985). The somatizer can replicate any symptoms in the medical lexicon, often presenting a baffling array of them. Somatization can occur at any age following a stressful event and at any developmental stage in the life cycle, such as entering school, puberty, adolescence, graduation, adulthood, marriage, parenthood, divorce, bereavement, middle age, old age, and retirement. It can take the form of a single symptom or a group of symptoms that become the focus of the person's life and mask the precipitating stressors. The patient is increasingly convinced, despite all medical findings to the contrary, that the basis for the symptom or symptoms is organic illness and embarks on a never-ending quest for the right physician or the medical procedure that will discover the organic etiology. In the meantime, the psychological stressors go untreated while medical utilization and symptomatology escalate. It is not uncommon for somatizing patients to be hospitalized for an extensive number of medical tests after outpatient procedures have failed to detect organic etiology. If enough of them are administered, one or two inevitably will show marginal findings, as they would with any normal person. This only spurs the frustrated physician to look harder for the elusive, nonexistent organic cause.

Curiously, in spite of the pain and suffering shown by the somatizer, no primary anxiety or depression is present. It is as if the anxiety and depression associated with the stressors have been bound in the somatic symptomatology. Overt anxiety or depression is usually secondary to the somatized condition: "How would you feel if you were sick all the time?"

The author's 30 years of research on somatization have demonstrated that, for most somatizers, the behavior was rewarded in the early days of childhood: "Daddy, I didn't take out the garbage last night because my head was hurting too much from doing my homework." Parents often gave an overabundance of affection and attention when the child was ill, while remaining relatively aloof when the child was physically well. As the offspring of nurses, some somatizers learned in childhood that illness would bring attention from a dedicated caregiver.

The Medical Offset Phenomenon

The pioneering research at Kaiser Permanente that demonstrated a reduction in medical utilization among somatizers following psychological intervention has been replicated over 30 times with similar results (Jones & Vischi, 1979).

Initially Kaiser Permanente experimented with a number of attempts to provide long-term therapy for all subscribers manifesting emotional distress. These efforts were prompted by the belief that short-term therapy was not as effective as long-term, and by the discovery that providing easily available comprehensive health services as part of a prepaid plan fostered the somatization of emotional problems and the consequent overuse of medical facilities by patients with no physical illness. The result of providing long-term therapy was a long waiting list, a high dropout rate, and only partially successful attempts to reduce the ever-growing waiting list by providing crisis intervention. After several years on such an unsatisfactory course, a series of evaluative studies began that spanned two and a half decades. During this period, an efficient, treatment system emerged that was both therapeutically and financially effective.

In the first of a series of investigations into the relationship between psychological services and medical utilization in a prepaid health care setting, Follette and Cummings (1967) compared the number and type of medical services sought before and after psychotherapeutic intervention in a large group of randomly selected patients. Outpatient and inpatient medical utilization for the year immediately prior to the initial interview in the Department of Psychotherapy, as well as for the five years following it, were studied for three groups of psychotherapy patients. These three groups consisted of patients who had been seen for (a) one therapy session only; (b) brief therapy, with a mean of 6.4 interviews; and (c) long-term therapy with a mean of 33.9 interviews. A "control" group of matched patients demonstrated similar criteria of distress but had not, in the six years under study, been seen in psychotherapy. The findings indicate the following:

1. Persons in emotional distress use both inpatient (hospitalization) and outpatient medical facilities significantly more than average health plan patients.

2. Emotionally distressed individuals who received psychotherapy used medical

services significantly less than a "control" group of matched emotionally distressed health plan members who were not accorded psychotherapy.

3. These declines remained constant during the five years following termination of psychotherapy.

4. The most significant declines occurred in the second year after the initial interview, especially those patients who received only one session of brief therapy (two to eight sessions) did not require additional psychotherapy in order to maintain the lower utilization for five years.

5. Patients seen for two years or more in continuous psychotherapy demonstrated no overall decline in total outpatient utilization inasmuch as psychotherapy visits tended to supplant medical visits. However, there was a significant decline in inpatient utilization in this long-term therapy group from an initial rate several times that of the health plan average, to a level comparable to that of the general adult health plan population.

In a subsequent study, Cummings and Follette (1968) found that intensive efforts to increase the number of referrals to psychotherapy by using computerized psychological screening to perform early detection of somatization and alert physicians to its presence did not have that effect. The authors concluded that in a prepaid health plan setting already maximally employing educative techniques to both patients and physicians and already providing a range of prepaid psychological services, the number of subscribers seeking psychotherapy reached an optimal level and remained constant thereafter.

To summarize nearly two decades of prepaid health plan experience, Cummings and Follette (1976) demonstrated that there is no basis for the fear that increased demand for psychotherapy will financially endanger the system. It is not the number of referrals that drives costs upward, but the manner in which psychotherapy services are delivered. The finding that one session only, with no repeat psychological visits, can reduce medical utilization by 60% over the following five years was surprising and totally unexpected. Equally surprising was the 75% reduction in medical utilization over a five-year period in those patients receiving two to eight psychotherapy visits (brief therapy).

In an eighth-year telephone follow-up, Cummings and Follette (1976) sought to answer whether the previously described results could be attributed to therapeutic, deleterious, or extraneous factors. It was hypothesized that if a patient had achieved better understanding of the problem through the psychotherapy sessions, he or she would recall the actual problem rather than the presenting symptom. It was also hypothesized that the presenting symptom would have disappeared and that the patient would be coping more effectively with other problems. The results suggested that the reduction in medical utilization was the consequence of resolving the emotional distress reflected in the symptoms and in the visits to the doctor. The modal patient in the eight-year follow-up can be described as follows: He or she denied ever having consulted a physician about the symptoms for which the referral was originally made. Rather, the underlying problem discussed with the psychotherapist was recalled as the reason for the psychotherapy visit. Although the problem was resolved, this resolution was attributed to the patient's own efforts and no credit was given to the psychotherapist. This affirms the contention that the reduction in medical utilization reflected the diminution in emotional distress that was originally expressed in symptoms presented to the physician.

In their earlier work, Cummings and Follette (1968) addressed the question of cost-effectiveness by demonstrating that savings in medical services offset the cost of providing psychotherapy. However, they insisted that the services provided must also be therapeutic in that they reduce the patient's emotional distress. Therapeutic success was predicted in a model that involved the analysis of transference and resistance, uncovered unconscious conflicts, and had all of the characteristics of long-term therapy except length. In fact, over a five-year period, 84.6% of the psychotherapy patients chose to come for 15 sessions or fewer (with a mean of 8.6). Follow-up showed that, far from being "dropouts," these patients had achieved a satisfactory state of well-being that continued to the eighth year after termination of therapy. Of the remainder, 10.1% were found to be "interminable," in that once they began psychotherapy, they seemingly continued with no indication of termination.

In another study, Cummings (1979a) addressed the problem of the interminable patient for whom treatment was neither cost-effective nor therapeutically effective. The concept that some persons may be so emotionally crippled that they may have to be maintained for many years or for life was unacceptable: If five percent of the patients entering psychotherapy were in that category, within a few years a program would be hampered by a monolithic case load. (This has in fact happened in many public clinics where psychotherapy is offered at nominal or no cost.) The hypothesis of the study was that these patients required more intensive intervention, and the frequency of psychotherapy visits was doubled for one experimental group, tripled for another and held constant for the control group. Surprisingly, the cost–therapeutic effectiveness ratios deteriorated in direct proportion to the increased intensity of treatment: that is, medical utilization increased and the patients manifested greater emotional distress. It was only by reversing the process and seeing these patients at spaced intervals of once every two or three months that the desired cost–therapeutic effect was obtained. These results are surprising in that they seem to disprove traditionally held notions in psychotherapy, but they demonstrate the need for ongoing research, program evaluation, and innovation if psychotherapy is to be made available to everyone.

The Cost-Therapeutic Effectiveness Ratio (Cummings, 1979) and the 38 Criteria of Distress (Follette & Cummings, 1967) have proven to be useful evaluation tools at Kaiser Permanente, American Biodyne, and other large-scale health systems, enabling them to innovate cost–therapeutically effective programs for somatization, alcoholism, drug addiction, the "interminable" patient, chronic psychosis, problems of the elderly, severe character disorders, and other conditions considered by many to be too costly, and therefore, uninsurable.

Methods, Tools, and Interventions for the Treatment of Somatizers

"Outreaching" the Somatizer

In testimony before the United States Senate (Cummings, 1985a), it was reported that patients who are experiencing emotional stress generally find "an unsympathetic or uncomprehending ear" when they attempt to discuss their distress with their physician. They quickly begin to translate their problems into the form of X-rays, laboratory tests, prescriptions, and return visits to the primary care specialist. Outreach programs are needed to bring these patients into a psychological service where the causes of their stress can be addressed.

Physician education. The best way to outreach the somatizer is by educating the physician. This task is not as easy as the statement implies. Physicians are trained to find physical disease and are not trained or rewarded for thinking psychologically. Rarely does a physician look for the signs of somatization syndrome. Rather, the typical approach is to eliminate the presence of disease, using exhaustive medical tests. This process only reinforces the patient's belief that he or she has a physical illness while it frustrates the physician who eventually loses interest in the patient. The patient responds with feelings of hurt and betrayal that are reflected in increased demands on the physician for attention.

Adjusting the system of compensation. The form of compensation often influences practice as it relates to the somatizer. In one large health system where physicians were capitated in the style of the HMO, they identified and referred 83% of their somatizers for psychological intervention, while fee-for-service physicians referred fewer than 6% (Cummings, 1988; Cummings & Dörken, 1986). In the latter group, there were too many physicians in the community competing for the same patients. Unfortunately, somatizers can represent a substantial portion of a physician's income. This may be true especially of dermatology, where 50% to 60% of patients may suffer from neurodermatitis, a clearly somatized condition. This does not mean that physicians are dishonest or cynical. Rather, it reflects unconscious motivation; the capitated physician has no reward for holding on to the somatizer, while the fee-for-service physician has an unrecognized reward for keeping him or her in the medical system.

Because physicians vary in their ability to identify and refer these patients for psychological intervention, it is often necessary to outreach the patient. Integral to effective treatment is a program that can triage the patient out of the medical system into a psychological system. All patients who have made 20 or more physician visits in one year should be contacted. Of these, somewhat fewer than half generally have a chronic physical illness that requires regular, sustained medical intervention, and more than half will be somatizers. Although some somatizers make fewer than 20 physician visits in one year, this number is the cut-off point at which it is efficient to target outreach. The upper range can exceed 300 such visits in one year, with 32 as the mean and 28 as the mode. Where psychologists have contracted to provide services for an existing health plan, the client organization is usually more than willing to provide a computer print-out of patients who have made more than 50 visits in a 12-month period.

Contact by telephone. Psychiatric nurses are ideal professionals to conduct telephone outreach because they have extensive knowledge of physical illness, are familiar with somatization syndrome, and possess psychotherapeutic skills. Medical social workers have similar knowledge and skills and are an acceptable substitute for psychiatric nurses. Psychologists can also perform telephone outreach if using this level of professional is cost-effective.

The outreach worker is responsible for calling a predetermined number of high medical utilizers. At the time of the phone contact, the patient's belief in the somatic nature of his or her complaints should not be challenged. The patient's interest can usually be aroused by the statement, "Someone who has had as much illness as you certainly must be upset about it." This usually elicits an immediate reaction, ranging from an exposition of symptoms to the complaint that physicians don't seem to understand or to be sympathetic to the patient's plight. After hearing the patient out sufficiently to permit the development of some initial trust, the patient is invited to explore how the counselor (a less threatening term than mental health provider) might be of help. It is suggested that together they can perhaps investigate alternatives to treatments that have not worked, or that the patient can be put in touch with a more sympathetic physician, should the difficulty be better appraised. An initial appointment for psychotherapy is made.

Contact by mail. Periodic mailing is another method used in an attempt to bring somatizing patients into psychotherapy. Brochures or newsletters can remind these high medical utilizers of the services available to them. In addition, the regular newsletter of a health plan can feature articles about a specific somatic complaint in each issue. The condition can be described and discussed with accompanying recommendations for change, along with the suggestion that an appointment with a counselor may be appropriate.

Community education programs. Outreach personnel are also encouraged to take part in presentations to the community and to local industries in an attempt to further identify high utilizers and encourage their participation in psychotherapy. This allows the prospective patient or potential referer (employer, friend, or coworker) to view the members of the psychological service in vivo and achieve a degree of comfort they otherwise might not have.

Triage. Once the patient comes to the office, it is vital that the therapist not challenge the somatization but marshall his or her interviewing skills to detect the underlying problem. Once the problem or set of problems are determined, the therapist treats these without ever directly relating them to the physical symptoms. In fact, most patients conclude therapy with a relief of somatic symptoms and no conscious knowledge of the relationship between psychological factors and previous physical complaints.

It is important to note that our model of triaging somatizers out of the medical system and into a psychological system was not developed as a cost containment measure. Rather, it was developed primarily to bring therapeutic effectiveness and relief of pain, anxiety, and depression to the patient in psychological distress. It became an integral part of a therapeutically effective, comprehensive mental health treatment system, and only then was it discovered to be cost-effective as well.

In cases of any concurrent actual physical illness, the therapist accepts the illness as a given. At that point, the therapist concentrates on the patient's reaction to the condition (depression, rage, despair) and also to any neurotic conflicts that may be impeding recovery. These issues are then addressed in the course of psy-chotherapy.

Preventive Health Care

Garfield et al. (1976) enunciated a method of triage in which the "worried well" are referred to a health education bypass that is essentially educative, psychological, and behavioral in nature. This relieves the physician of having to identify the somatizer by a process of elimination following weeks, months, and even years of expensive medical diagnosis procedures.

As a result of extensive cumulative research and through the use of the cost–therapeutic effectiveness ratio, a series of focused brief therapy protocols targeted to 68 specific psychological stress conditions have emerged. Along with an outreach system, these protocols enable practitioners to be of real assistance to individuals during stressful points in their lives (Cummings, 1985a). The model that has evolved is called Brief Intermittent Therapy Throughout the Life Cycle. These psychological interventions are not only efficient, in that an average of only 6.4 sessions is required but also effective in that problem-solving is highly focused. The interventions are applied only at times of stress, rather than protracted over months and probably years as is done in the traditional model of psychotherapy.

Such stressful periods may coincide not only with developmental milestones, but also with marriage, divorce, births, deaths, bankruptcy, surgery, job changes, geographical relocations, retirement, and so forth. Wide individual variations in handling stressors exist, but the typical maladaptive response in somatization is a dramatic increase in medical utilization. Using a reduction in medical utilization as a measure of resolution of stress, a wide range of preventive health studies have been undertaken. The following examples provide a sample of their findings.

High pediatric utilization. High medical utilization by children often reflects the unhappiness or marital conflict of the parents. An example is the somatization of stress in children whose parents are threatening each other with divorce. The child often learns that his or her "illness" temporarily brings the parents together over concern for the child's health, resulting in an escalation of pediatric utilization as talk of divorce escalates. Psychological intervention with the parents reduced pediatric utilization by 63% the following year. This contrasted with the control group of high pediatric utilizers whose utilization increased slightly but not significantly.

Bereavement. Following the death of a spouse, medical utilization often in-creases dramatically. In some cases, the symptoms may replicate those of the de-ceased's terminal illness. Psychologically, this is a way of keeping the deceased "alive" (introjection) or assuaging guilt for negative behavior toward the deceased while still alive. This reaction can represent total somatization, or the promulgation of an actual disease such as cancer, heart disease, or stroke. It has been noted that there is a 20% rise in such actual physical illness following the death of a long-standing spouse. Bereavement counseling reduces medical utilization to expected levels in cases of somatization. An experiment is underway to determine if bereavement counseling can reduce the number of subsequent actual physical illnesses compared with those of a control group.

Surgery. Presurgical counseling by a psychologist can reduce hospitalization by an average of 1.3 days. Similar results have been demonstrated in a number of other studies (Olbrisch, 1979). Typically, this counseling takes place on an outpatient basis before the surgery, but in cases where the need for treatment is sudden, can be conducted in the hospital on the eve of the surgical procedure. Although it is an effective intervention in a number of procedures ranging from appendectomy to henioraphy, it is particularly effective in cases where the procedure has intense psychological meaning to the patient (e.g., hysterectomy) or in cases where the postoperative recovery is long, and accompanying depression is typical (e.g., open heart surgery).

Asthmatic children. Children who have severe asthmatic attacks often are reflecting their parents marital conflicts. In a typical case, the child might be awakened on a Friday night by the sound of his or her parents quarreling. The parents are tense about having to spend the whole weekend together. Unconsciously, the child has learned that a severe asthmatic attack necessitating an emergency room visit will terminate the quarrel and temporarily bring the parents together. Marital counseling was found to eliminate such emergency room visits, which nonetheless continued for the control group.

Alcoholism. Alcoholics are high utilizers of medical services, but their illness is seldom diagnosed by their primary care physicians, in spite of such severe side effects as cirrhosis, acute pancreatitis, bone fractures, and accidental burns. The medical utilization rates of alcoholics who followed a successful substance abuse program and remained sober during the subsequent year dropped by 77%, and there was a significant reduction in school problems among their children.

Step-parenting. In a search to identify psychosocial stressors, it was noted that a group of high pediatric utilizers had in common the recent acquisition of a step-parent. Group step-parenting counseling with both the natural and step-parents reduced this overutilization by 61% in the year after counseling. The control group maintained its level of pediatric overutilization. The critical factor in the counseling was the subsequent relaxation of the step-parent, who had been trying to achieve the approval and acceptance of the step-child.

Heart attacks. Parents who suffer myocardial infarction (MI) and who demonstrate signs of depression on a psychological questionnaire return to work weeks later than those patients who do not show those depressive signs (Friedman, Ury, Klatsky, & Siegelaub, 1974). MI patients receiving psychological intervention returned to work significantly sooner than those not receiving such intervention. The sooner the counseling occurred following the MI, the more positive was the outcome.

Retirement. Even though most people look forward to retirement, it is a stressful time of abrupt change. Often the marital equilibrium is upset by a husband who is now constantly at home, yet is reluctant to change his life-style by beginning to perform new behaviors such as sharing the household chores. Medical utilization, which often shows a sharp increase immediately following retirement, can be maintained at customary levels with preretirement counseling. It is important to prepare not only the retiree but also the spouse for the disequilibrium the new life-style will bring.

Problems and Disadvantages of Outreach Programs

Two caveats are important when using the method of outreaching and triaging the somatizer. The first pertains to resistance that will be engendered on the part of the somatizer if the therapist directly challenges the patient's belief that a physical disease exists. The patient will bolt, only to continue to pursue physical verification through still another physician. Future attempts to reach this patient will be decidedly more difficult. The therapist must win the patient's confidence and address his or her stress without ever challenging the belief that the symptoms represent a physical disease. Most somatizers, once the cause of the stress is ascertained and ameliorated, will abandon the symptomatology and reduce medical utilization. Often, they will leave psychological treatment without ever having made the connection. To insist on linking the symptom with the stress may result in such a loss of self-esteem that gains may be undone.

The second caveat involves the use of overly zealous outreach programs that may result in actual physical disease being overlooked. Cummings (1985b) reports a computerized outreach program that had to be discontinued because it significantly increased the number of medical diagnoses missed by participating physicians. It was almost as if the physicians had so espoused the concept of somatization that they dispensed with the kinds of physical examination and medical tests that would have elicited an existing disease.

Conclusion

The most frequent manifestation of stress is somatization. Appropriate medical intervention that treats the stress will result in a dramatic reduction of medical utilization: the so-called medical offset phenomenon. Reduction in medical utilization is a reliable and useful measure of stress resolution. Stress points and stress factors occur throughout the life cycle and are, to some degree, predictable. A combination of triage by the primary care physician and aggressive outreach programs will alleviate the symptoms of stress by directing the worried-well into problem-solving brief therapy. This results in a preventive health care system that directly promotes the mental health of individuals and their families.

Advice to HMO Practitioners

The medical offset literature has demonstrated that somatization can significantly tax medical resources in any health care system. Through outreach, HMO psychotherapists are in an excellent position to triage the somatizer out of the medical system and into a psychological system where the patient will receive relief from suffering and the HMO will save substantially more than the cost of providing the psychological interventions. Even though the physician compensation structure in an HMO is conducive to appropriate referral, there is still a need to educate the physician on how to make the referral without insulting the patient's belief in the medical nature of the symptom. It is equally important for the psychotherapist not to challenge the belief system while still addressing the causes of stress.

An appropriate outreach and treatment program for the somatizing patient must involve the physician, HMO management, and even the community. Although the savings in medical costs are an incentive for the HMO, the therapist's reward is the satisfaction that comes from the provision of appropriate treatment and the consequent recovery of a patient whose pain was escalating in response to inappropriate medical treatment.

References

Balint, M. (1957). *The doctor, his patient, and the illness.* New York: International Universities Press.

Bergin, A. E., & Lambert, M. J. (1978). The evaluation of therapeutic outcome. In Garfield, S., & Bergin, A. E. (Eds.), *Handbook of psychotherapy and behavior change* (pp. 330–343). New York: Wiley.

Budman, S. H., Demby, A. B., & Feldstein, M. L. (1984). A controlled study of the effects of mental health treatment on medical utilization. *Medical Care, 6,* 31–41.

Cummings, N. A. (1975). The health model as entree to the human services model in psychotherapy. *The Clinical Psychologist, 29*(1), 19–21.

Cummings, N. A. (1979). The anatomy of psychotherapy under national health insurance. *American Psychologist, 34,* 711–718.

Cummings, N. A. (1979a). Prolonged or "ideal" versus short-term or "realistic" psychotherapy. *Professional Psychology, 8,* 491–505.

Cummings, N. A. (1985a, June 25). Testimony to the United States Senate, *Congressional Record: Senate,* S8656–S8659.

Cummings, N. A. (1985b). Assessing the computer's impact: Professional concerns. *Computers in Human Behavior, 1,* 293–300.

Cummings, N. A. (1986). The dismantling of our health system: Strategies for the survival of psychological practice. *American Psychologist, 41,* 426–431.

Cummings, N. A. (1988). Emergence of the mental health complex: Adaptive and maladaptive responses. *Professional Psychology: Research and Practice, 19,* 308–315.

Cummings, N. A., & Dorken, H. (1986). Corporations, networks and service plans: Economically sound models for practice. In H. Dorken & Associates (Eds.), *Professional psychology in transition.* San Francisco: Jossey-Bass.

Cummings, N. A., Dorken, H. Henke, C., & Pallak, M. (1989). *The impact of psychological services on medical utilization in a Medicaid population.* Report on the Hawaii Medicaide Study. Baltimore: Health Care Financing Administration.

Cummings, N. A., & Fernandez, L. E. (1985, March). Exciting future possibilities for psychologists in the marketplace. *Independent Practitioner,* pp. 38–42.

Cummings, N. A., & Follette, W. T. (1968). Psychiatric services and medical utilization in a prepaid health care setting: Part II. *Medical Care, 6,* 31–41.

Cummings, N. A., & Follette, W. T. (1976). Brief psychotherapy and medical utilization: An eight year follow up. In H. Dorken & Associates (Eds.), *The professional psychologist today.* San Francisco: Jossey-Bass.

Cummings, N. A., & VandenBos, G. (1978). The general practice of psychology. *Professional Psychology, 10,* 430–440.

Duhl, L. J., & Cummings, N. A. (1987). *The future of mental health services.* New York: Springer.

Follette, W. T., & Cummings, N. A. (1967). Psychiatric services and medical utilization in a prepaid health care setting. *Medical Care, 5*, 25–35.

Friedman, G. D., Ury, H. K., Klatsky, A. L., & Siegelaub, A. B. (1974). A psychological questionnaire predictive of myocardial infarction. *Psychosomatic Medicine, 36*, 73–87.

Garfield, S. R. (1976). Evolving a new model for health-care delivery. *Orthopaedic Review, 5*, 31–37.

Garfield, S. R., Collen, M. F., Feldman, R., Soghikian, K., Richardt, R. H., & Duncan, J. H. (1976). Evaluation of an ambulatory medical care system. *New England Journal of Medicine, 294*, 311–327.

Jones, K. R., & Vischi, T. R. (1979). Impact on alcohol, drug abuse, and mental health care utilization. *Medical Care, 17*(12), 43–131.

Kiesler, C. A., Cummings, N. A., & VandenBos, G. R. (1979). *Psychology and national health insurance: A sourcebook.* Washington, DC: American Psychological Association.

Quill, T. E. (1985). Somatization disorder: One of medicine's blind spots. *Journal of the American Medical Association, 254*, 3075–3079.

Weiss, J. R., & English, O. S. (1948). *Psychosomatic medicine.* New York: Plenum Press.

Part IV _____

Summary and Future Directions

17

Patrick H. DeLeon and Gary R. VandenBos

Psychotherapy in Managed Health Care: Integrating Federal Policy with Clinical Practice

President Nixon's 1971 Health Message to the Congress was, for all practical purposes, what brought the concept of managed mental health care into modern health policy. The President's expressed goal under his National Health Strategy was to "build a true 'health system'—and not a 'sickness' system alone. We should work to maintain health and not merely to restore it" (Nixon, 1971).

This idea of a health care system emphasizing health maintenance, disease prevention, and wellness was adopted, along with the concept of the "health maintenance organization" (HMO), by the Nixon administration (and all subsequent Republican administrations). These concepts were subsequently expressed in the Health Maintenance Organization Act (HMO Act) of 1973 (PL 93–222). The HMO Act provided federal funding to partially underwrite the development of new HMOs, with the intent of providing $325 million over the first five years of the initial ten-year plan (HMO law, 1974). The Act also created a certification process, known as "federal qualification," for HMOs meeting certain financial and organizational standards. The new law superseded some aspects of state law and required that many employees in the United States be offered the option of joining an HMO, as an alternative to their employer's existing health plan, if they so desired. To qualify for federal loans or subsidies, HMOs were required by law to provide a comprehensive set of basic services, including outpatient mental health care and crisis intervention services.

Amendments to the HMO law in 1976 and 1978 resulted in further expansion of HMOs. The 1976 amendments liberalized HMO requirements and created widespread industry acceptance of federal qualification. The 1978 amendments were aimed at further legislative refinement to help the HMO program to become even more competitive in the marketplace.

This chapter is based in part on the article "Managed Mental Health Care: A History of the Federal Policy Initiative" by Patrick H. DeLeon, Gary R. VandenBos, and Elizabeth Q. Bulatao, which appeared in the February 1991 issue of *Professional Psychology*. This chapter represents a significant condensation in some sections as well as a major expansion in other areas, specifically in terms of the implication for clinical practice within HMOs. The authors acknowledge the contribution of Elizabeth Q. Bulatao to content in selected portions of the present manuscript.

The Status of Mental Health Within Federal HMO Legislation

It was a very positive sign of recognition and acceptance for the mental health field to have outpatient psychological care and crisis intervention services included in the 1973 HMO Act. In retrospect, it is even somewhat surprising. In the early 1970s there were numerous questions about the effectiveness of psychotherapy, and most mental health providers were not recognized in the majority of reimbursement plans, either public or private. Medicare only covered psychiatrists and had an artificially low annual limit. Psychologists and social workers were not eligible providers under CHAMPUS. The majority of private insurance plans did not include the coverage of outpatient psychotherapy among their basic benefits. But in the last 40 years there has been an explosive growth in the field of psychology in the United States, coupled with a growing recognition of the applied role that professional psychologists play in medicine, mental health, education, industry, law, and other areas. The strides that have been made toward full recognition and equality for psychologists as service providers are the result of the maturing of the profession and of years of aggressive collective action taken by psychologists at the local, state, and national levels. Thus, it was quite gratifying to the mental health field to be acknowledged in the initial HMO legislation.

Worry about the possibility of overutilization, inappropriate utilization, and runaway costs were major concerns related to the inclusion of a mental health component (both outpatient psychotherapy and inpatient psychiatric hospitalization) in comprehensive managed health care plans in the early 1970s. However, in an evaluation of Kaiser Permanente's experience with psychotherapy and medical utilization, Cummings and VandenBos (1981) showed that the inclusion of psychotherapy within a comprehensive health care plan did not bankrupt the health care financing system. Early in Kaiser Permanente's experience of providing capitated health care, the value was discovered of providing psychotherapy to prevent overutilization of medical facilities by individuals who were somatizing psychological conflict and stress (Follette & Cummings, 1967). This is now referred to as the "medical offset effect" of the provision of psychotherapy (Jones & Vischi, 1979; Mumford, Schlesinger, Glass, Patrick, & Cuerdon, 1984; VandenBos & DeLeon, 1988). It should be noted that almost all of this research was conducted in HMO settings.

The Kaiser experience showed that the cost of providing quality mental health coverage is not uncontrollable: average mental health costs within Kaiser increased only 3.5% per year between 1959 and 1979, while nationwide general medical costs increased between 12% and 20% per year (Kiesler, Cummings, & VandenBos, 1979, p. 206). To achieve its cost-effective managed health care system, Kaiser used multiple entry points for gaining access to psychotherapy. This avoided the high cost, inefficiency, lack of responsiveness, and bias inherent in a single entry point system controlled by one profession with one orientation. Kaiser found that when a patient believes he or she should seek psychological treatment, both quality-of-care and cost-efficiency are best served by allowing him or her to directly seek and obtain outpatient psychotherapy. Despite providing "service on demand" psychotherapy, the Kaiser plan demonstrated that mental health utilization rates were predictable and that mental health is insurable; utilization rates at Kaiser rose to a predictable level and remained stable thereafter.

Unfortunately, the majority of HMOs do not provide patients with unrestricted access or multiple entry points to psychotherapy and other mental health care services (Shadle & Christianson, 1988). In fact, HMO "gatekeeper" mechanisms involving primary care physicians generally have been viewed as barriers to the appropriate utilization of psychological services in HMOs. This is true from a clinical perspective, in terms of the need to educate physicians about where and how to make referrals (Cummings & Follette, 1968). "Gatekeeping" mechanisms have also been criticized for their failure to provide adequate access to care and quality of care. (Buie, 1987, 1989a, 1989b; Welch, 1986a, 1986b).

Despite the Kaiser experience and the initial inclusion of psychological care in the 1973 federal HMO legislation, psychotherapy and other mental health services have never had a solid legislative mandate regarding the inclusion and provision of psychological care in HMOs. Just three years after the initial HMO legislation was passed, the legislative position of psychological services was somewhat weakened. In enacting the Health Maintenance Organization Amendments of 1976 (PL 94–460) the congressional committees with jurisdiction over the program noted the following (Senate Report No. 94–884):

> Since the Act's inception, progress in implementation has been slow . . . [the bill] is intended to correct the identified deficiencies in the original law, improve the administration of the program, and make HMOs meeting the law's requirements more competitive with traditional insurance programs and health delivery systems. . . . It is clear that some of the requirements of the original Act are excessively strict and have the effect of placing developing HMOs at a competitive disadvantage with other parts of the health care system. This has been demonstrated by a survey by the General Accounting Office (GAO) as a part of its mandated responsibilities under the original Act. (pp. 4–6)

Particularly noteworthy for mental health professionals was the GAO finding that the over 500 organizations surveyed had highlighted the high cost of providing the required basic and supplemental mental health services as a major problem. The 1976 amendments provided greater administrative flexibility for the HMO program, making it more practical for interested groups to become "federally qualified." Authority was granted, for example, allowing HMOs to contract for professional services with individual health professionals or groups of health professionals that did not qualify as medical groups or IPAs, provided that the amount contracted for did not exceed a specified value. Similarly, HMOs were now authorized to use the clinical expertise of "other health care personnel" (which would include nurse practitioners and clinical psychologists for the first time since the program's inception). Modifications were also made to the provisions governing reimbursement under Medicare and Medicaid; these essentially provided that only "federally qualified HMOs" were eligible for financial support.

Further amendments to the HMO Act have appeared periodically from 1975 until the present. The majority of them have not held major unique implications for mental health services within HMOs. For example, the Health Maintenance Organization Act Amendments of 1978 (PL 95–559) were enacted during a period of slow but steady expansion by HMOs, even though there was some evidence of increasing acceptance by the business and labor communities. The resulting congressional view was that further legislative refinement was necessary for the program to become even more competitive in the marketplace. In proposing to reauthorize the program for an additional five years, the Senate committee with jurisdiction noted that: "While HMOs are not the final answer to the health care cost problem, they do give providers strong incentives to reduce unnecessary expenditures; and they create much-needed competition for the health care dollar. HMOs have now proven their cost-saving abilities" (Senate Report No. 95–837, pp. 3 & 8). Although the mental health field had actively lobbied for expanded and explicitly articulated HMO mental health services, the 1978 HMO amendments fundamentally ignored mental health issues. The initiative of the coalition of mental health providers seeking greater coverage ran counter to the Congress's desire to provide HMOs with greater administrative and programmatic flexibility. As a result, psychological services in HMOs were ignored.

Subsequent HMO amendments in the early and middle 1980s were also primarily geared towards administrative and structural matters. Procedures and monitoring mechanisms were put in place to curb financial abuses. A few technical matters related to the mental health field did, however, occur during this period. As a provision of the Deficit Reduction Act of 1984 (PL 98–369), psychologists were recognized as providers under medicare when risk-sharing HMOs were authorized to provide the services of clinical psychologists. The Mental Health Organizational Amendments of 1986 (PL 99–660) explicitly listed psychologists as among the authorized HMO professions, whereas prior to this modification their services had only been recognized under the broad heading of "other health care providers." This 1986 amendment represented the first official recognition of psychologists in any medicare-related legislation. A year later, the Omnibus Budget Reconciliation Act of 1987 (PL 100–203) amended the Social Security Act to include coverage of clinical social worker services provided by HMOs to their enrollees.

The U.S. Congress and the federal administration remain convinced that actively encouraging prepaid and managed health care efforts are in the nation's best interest. The Health Maintenance Organization Amendments of 1988 (PL 100–517) continued the trend of providing administrative flexibility. With the 1988 amendments, it was no longer necessary to require firms with 25 employees or more to specifically provide an HMO health benefit; however, the historical financial non-discrimination provisions were not repealed. The 1988 Amendments also included language that would override state laws and regulations deemed to prohibit HMOs from meeting the federal HMO requirements.

The Bush Administration's continued support of HMOs was evident at Secretary Sullivan's 1991 Senate Appropriations Committee hearings when he stated that "Our legislative agenda includes several initiatives which will encourage the provision of health services in managed care settings. We believe managed care is the best means of assuring quality service and appropriate care for Medicare and Medicaid beneficiaries" (see Adler, 1990).

Thus, the expansion of health care delivery by HMOs has been the explicit national health policy for the United States for over 18 years. Each surgeon-general of the United States has explicitly endorsed HMOs and managed care. This national policy has had an impact, as noted by the fact that one out of every seven Americans now receive their health care via managed health care systems. All indications are that the federal HMO initiative will continue for the foreseeable future. Therefore, it is critical for the mental health field to work actively on future legislation to modify the federal HMO law, and to continue to develop and refine innovative clinical interventions targeted at specific psychological and behavioral problems. These interventions should be structured in such a manner as to make their incorporation into HMO services simple and effective.

The Growth of HMOs and Managed Care Systems

Prior to the 1973 HMO Act, the Department of Health, Education and Welfare (now the Department of Health and Human Services) had been encouraging the development of prepaid health plans. However, the passage of the 1973 legislation allowed the federal government to foster and stimulate HMO growth. The HMO movement has grown and matured since 1973.

Managed care systems such as HMOs are now an established part of the U.S. health care system. In 1970 there were 33 HMOs covering three million persons (1.5% of the U.S. population), and in 1980 there were 236 HMOs serving 9.1 million members, or about 4% of the U.S. population (National Industry Council for HMO Development, n.d.). The growth of HMOs continued in the early 1980s, but slowed later in the decade. Thus, the number of HMOs reached an all-time high of 707 plans in 1987, but the number of plans decreased in 1988, 1989, and 1990. By the end of 1989, there were 623 operating HMOs, down 5.5% from 1988. This number is expected to decrease to 612 by the end of 1990, with further decreases projected through 1994, when there will be 568 plans in operation. The decrease in the number of operating HMOs is explained by industry sources as reflecting continued consolidation in the industry as HMOs are shut down, become insolvent, or are acquired by other HMOs. However, total enrollments were up 3.9% to 35.03 million in 1989 (or 14% of the U.S. population), compared with 1988 when 659 HMOs served some 33.7 million members. Enrollments are expected to reach an estimated 36.9 million in 1990 and 53.2 million by the end of 1994 (Marion Laboratories, Inc., 1989; Marion Merrel Dow Inc., 1990). Thus, the percentage of the U.S. population actually covered by HMO systems tripled during the 1970s, and more than tripled again during the 1980s.

The "classic" model of an HMO was a prepaid group practice (or prepaid staff practice) system. In the early and middle 1970s, there were criticisms of such models by both consumers and providers, which led to the development of loosely contracted individual practice association (IPA) models of managed health care. In the late 1970s and early 1980s, the majority of the new HMOs used the IPA model, which was often strongly physician-dominated.

In 1986 a major national survey of HMOs was conducted with funding from the National Institute of Mental Health (Shadle & Christianson, 1988). One part of the study examined the growth and changes within individual HMOs and within the managed care industry.

Three major trends were noted by Shadle and Christianson (1988) in the managed health care industry. First, the mix of organizational structures of HMOs has changed. Among HMOs three years or younger, 75% are IPA models. In 1989, IPAs made up about 62% of all HMOs, as compared to about 37% in 1981. Second, the HMO industry has undergone a change in the mix of for-profit versus not-for-profit firms. Sixty-two percent of all HMOs in 1987 were for-profit, with three-fourths of the plans under three years of age being for-profit. Virtually all new HMOs established in 1988 and 1989 were for-profit (Marion Merrel Dow Inc., 1990). While data on the profit status of HMOs is not consistently available over time, it is evident that the role of the for-profit HMOs has steadily grown. While not-for-profit HMOs still enroll 60% of all HMO members, enrollment in for-profit HMOs grew by 19% in 1986 versus a 3% growth rate for not-for-profit plans. Third, there has been a continuing shift in the HMO industry away from small, independent HMOs towards multistate networks of HMOs linked by common ownership and management. In 1986, about 50% of all HMOs were linked to national firms, and these multistate health care firms enrolled 60% of all HMO members. By 1989, it was reported that 47 multistate HMO chains owned and operated 411 or 66% of HMO plans, enrolling 73.8% of all HMO members in the United States (Marion Merrel Dow Inc., 1990).

Mental Health Care in HMOs

Mental health care (which primarily means psychotherapy, but also includes behavioral interventions and psychopharmacology) is a relatively new service with HMOs, having emerged in the late 1960s and early 1970s. Despite their commitment to comprehensive care, the prototype HMOs of the 1940s and 1950s did not include outpatient treatment for mental illness. One exception was the St. Louis Labor Institute HMO. The Health Insurance Plan of Greater New York provided only mental health diagnosis and consultation, while Kaiser Permanente provided mental health services on a reduced-fee fee-for-service basis in this pre-1960 era.

In the 1960s, partially in response to the influence of large contractor groups (e.g., the Federal Employees Health Benefits Program, and union and employee groups), HMOs started including outpatient mental health care on an optional (rider) basis. New HMO plans that emerged in the late 1960s, such as the Harvard Community Health Plan, included substantial mental health care as a basic benefit (Bennett, 1988).

With the passage of the 1973 HMO Act, prepaid health plans that wished to be federally qualified had to meet the requirements for emergency and outpatient crisis intervention services of providing up to 20 mental health care visits per year. Alcohol and substance abuse services were also required (HMO law, 1974). The initial legislation was somewhat imprecise concerning the nature and extent of mandated mental health coverage, and administrative interpretation of this legislation has allowed considerable latitude in services provided (Cheifetz & Salloway, 1984).

The survey of HMO mental health programs noted earlier (Shadle & Christianson, 1988) gave a useful overview of the nature of mental health services currently provided in managed care systems, based on a 60.5% response rate by all U.S. HMOs as of December 31, 1985. Almost 70% of responding HMOs reported that they delivered all or most of their mental health services internally, with about

47% reporting that they delivered all of their mental health services internally. Conversely, 17.6% of HMOs reported using external providers for all or almost all of their mental health care. Both staff model HMOs (69.2%) and group model HMOs (48.3%) were more likely to offer all mental health services internally. Likewise, large HMOs were more likely than smaller HMOs to directly provide mental health care.

Slightly over half of responding HMOs reported having a specific mental health director or coordinator, of whom 42% were psychiatrists, while 28% were psychologists. Older HMOs and larger HMOs were more likely to have a mental health director, and IPAs were by far the least likely to have such a specialty coordinator.

In the vast majority of HMOs, the primary care physician is viewed as the gatekeeper to mental health specialists or specialty units (contrary to what the Kaiser Permanente experience would advise). About 75% of HMOs indicated that the "approval" of the patient's primary care physician was required before any ADM service could be obtained, although the relative frequency of this requirement varied among types of HMO structures. In general, HMOs that were older, larger, and/or not-for-profit were slightly less likely to control mental health access via "physician approval" than newer, smaller, and for-profit HMOs. IPA model HMOs were much more likely (88%) to require physician referral than staff model HMOs (58%).

However, the use of HMO gatekeepers does not necessarily mean that self-referral for psychological services is forbidden. Slightly more than half of responding HMOs reported that self-referral for mental health care was permissible, and it was reported that half of all mental health utilization was self-initiated.

Among HMOs using external providers, over 75% reported using the services of private practitioners for outpatient therapy services. Sixty percent reported that they also had outpatient subcontracts with community mental health centers, and about 45% reported contracts with hospital-based outpatient clinics. For inpatient residential services, over 85% of HMOs reported contracts with community/general hospitals, and about 70% with private psychiatric hospitals.

Seventy-one percent of all outpatient mental health service provided was in the form of individual psychotherapy. Group therapy, couples' therapy, and family therapy made up most of the rest of the utilization. For HMO enrollees using outpatient mental health care, 63% were treated in fewer than 10 sessions; 26% were seen for between 11 and 20 sessions; and 11% had more than 20 sessions. The average length of treatment, by our estimate, was between 9.56 and 11.62 sessions. In terms of inpatient care, 80% of HMO enrollees receiving such care were hospitalized for less than two weeks.

The Shadle and Christianson survey did not address issues of quality of care or possible barriers to care. Most early advocates of HMOs argued for health care services by HMOs for two distinct and separate reasons: (a) they viewed it as providing more care and more appropriate care to the largest number of patients; and (b) the "managed" aspects of HMOs allowed the health care system to control and eliminate truly unneeded health care, whether instigated by the patient or the provider. Thus, among HMO advocates, there was an attempt at a creative merger of the two potentially conflicting goals of access to care and cost containment. Many of the current complaints about HMO services (and speculation about the inappropriate use of HMOs as cost containment mechanisms) have centered upon whether the early ideals of the HMO movement are still being adhered to or whether cost containment goals are leading to inappropriate barriers to psychological services, access to a limited array of psychological services, and unrealistically brief "treatment" in HMOs (Buie, 1989b, 1990; DeLeon, Uyeda, & Welch, 1985; GAO, 1988).

Improved Services or Cost-Containment?

In the early years of the HMO movement, much of the interest seemed to center on the delivery of accessible, high-quality health care to a fairly large population at an affordable cost. In the view of some, there has been far less attention to HMOs as vehicles for improving the quality of, and access to, health care since 1980. The rapid development and proliferation of HMO delivery systems have generated considerable debate and criticism from health care professionals and the public (Buie, 1989a; 1989b). In recent years, some have seen HMOs as concentrating unduly on containing costs, providing investment opportunities, and restructuring the medical care system (Luft, 1987; Shulman, 1988; Welch, 1986a; 1986b). For example, in Florida, numerous complaints prompted the U.S. General Accounting Office to conduct an investigation of the new Medicare HMOs (Welch, 1986a). GAO found these HMOs to be underregulated by the federal government and that the regulations that did exist were not being enforced—to the detriment of their medicare patients (GAO, 1988).

The primary areas of concern to psychologists within managed care settings can be categorized into three central issues: access, quality, and consumer/provider awareness.

First, the profession of psychology has generally advocated improving patients' access to all forms of health care. Delivery of mental health care and other services to consumers in HMOs and other managed care systems may be restricted because of the physician "gatekeeping" process. Despite the fact that the Kaiser Permanente experience suggests that patients should have immediate, direct, and easy access to psychological care (for both cost-efficiency reasons and quality of care reasons), many HMOs continue to use insensitive mechanisms to attempt to control access to psychotherapy (and, hence, cost). The use of such "gatekeeper referral" controls becomes more questionable when the gatekeeper has a financial incentive to block access to needed care (Welch, 1986b). The Omnibus Budget Reconciliation Act of 1986 (OBRA) restricted the use of some such cost containment mechanisms that provided financial incentives to providers to limit access to care (and possibly to lower the quality of care).

Managed care entities often place unrealistic limits on the amount of psychotherapy provided to clients. In some cases HMOs refuse to provide any psychotherapy to a patient requesting it, if in their opinion they can not guarantee that the problem can be successfully addressed in short-term psychotherapy. HMOs and other managed care operations are not typically structured to provide continuation of mental health treatment.

Second, the quality (and appropriateness) of so-called "mental health services" provided through managed care systems are often considered inadequate (Buie, 1989b). The minimal amount of psychotherapy provided in managed care systems and the use of physician "gatekeepers" who are typically untrained in the mental health area are often cited as evidence of the lack of concern about quality and appropriateness of care.

Further, there is continuing.debate on the definition, value, and effectiveness of the "short-term (not to exceed 20 visits), outpatient evaluation and crisis intervention mental health services" stipulated in the 1973 HMO Law. Because the law is not precise concerning the nature or extent of mandated mental health services, administrative interpretation of this legislation encourages considerable latitude in services provided. All HMO service providers, including psychologists, are limited in their participation by problems of definition; it is still not clear precisely what outpatient mental health care services HMOs must provide. Individual HMOs may exercise considerable latitude in the eligibility criteria they develop for outpatient mental health services and in the range of such services provided. Thus, the extent and costs of mental health services provided are actually dictated less by law and regulation than by how HMOs interpret and implement them (Cheifetz & Salloway, 1984). The relationship between time limits and effective psychotherapy is still a matter of debate. While more and more literature is written and research is conducted regarding time and brief psychotherapy, some psychologists have argued that most HMOs provide a few hours of "crisis intervention" that is labeled "psychotherapy" (Buie, 1989b).

Third, in the area of consumer awareness, consumers are often provided incomplete information about the operation of the managed care plan and the financial arrangements it offers. Welch (1986a) considers this "misleading advertising." Managed care entities tend to emphasize only the favorable comparisons between their services and those of traditional health insurance (i.e., that office visits and routine physicals are free, and that there are no deductibles or coinsurance features). Other (negative) features that directly affect access to care and quality of care, such as long delays in the scheduling of nonemergency services or excessively time-consuming procedures for applying for psychological care, are not readily apparent to consumers until they want or need such care. In addition, consumers often lack full information about the cost control mechanisms operating within the managed care setting, such as artificial barriers to psychotherapy. Plans generally do not inform consumers of their use of physician incentive plans that link a provider's decision to refer a patient to a specialist to how much income that physician will receive. The GAO (1988) study of federally qualified HMOs concluded that the practice of HMOs using salary withholds, bonuses, and other incentive arrangements as a way to keep down the costs of patient care could be jeopardizing the quality of care delivered by the plans. These financial arrangements are common throughout the managed care industry. Likewise, health care providers themselves often are not adequately informed about the managed care system before entering into a legal binding relationship with the HMO.

The Impact of Federal HMO Legislation on Clinical Practice

Clinical practice in HMOs has been shaped by HMO legislation as well as by market factors, innovations in the field, and other factors. Moreover, the clinical experiences of mental health practitioners working in HMO settings have had a broad impact on the rest of the mental health field (and in fact all of health care). This has come about because HMO mental health professionals are exposed to an array of other health care professionals with whom they would not otherwise have contact, an array of clinical problems not normally seen in mental health settings, and a broad array of patient populations.

When psychological services were initially included in the federal HMO legislation, the routinely available mental health services could be lumped into a few small categories: crisis intervention, psychotherapy, inpatient psychiatric hospitalization, and inpatient detoxification programs (and, maybe, psychological testing). In reality, the majority of services provided were either some type of short-term inpatient custodial care or outpatient psychotherapy that was either psycho-dynamic or eclectic in orientation. Because of the intentionally planned time/resource constraints in HMOs, as well as the broader array of patient problems confronted by the behavioral specialists in HMOs, mental health providers in HMOs have been among the leaders in developing planned, short-term psychotherapy approaches to a wide range of psychological and behavioral issues. They have also been among the leaders in the development of certain areas of behavioral medicine and health psychology. Many of these innovations are noted in the earlier chapters of this book.

While some people have complained that mental health professionals working in HMOs have "abandoned" either psychotherapy approaches or some traditional mental health patient populations, one can also view HMO mental health providers as contributing to the expansion of the armamentarium of the mental health field, both in terms of specifically designed programs to address specific problems as well as in the nature and types of problems addressed.

Socialization into Expanded Roles

HMOs are integrated health care systems. Their basic goal is to provide compre-hensive health care. This means that all components of health service—preventive, diagnostic, therapeutic, consultative, rehabilitative, inpatient and outpatient, phys-ical, and mental—should be conveniently and continuously available to patients (Schofield, 1976). To achieve this goal, an effective HMO system requires a smoothly functioning team or teams of varied health care professionals, support staff, and business experts who can work together with mutual respect (Belar, 1989). Within HMOs, there is much greater sense of a team approach to clinical work (Budman, 1985). Mental health team members are expected to interact and communicate with the internal medicine providers with whom they work most closely. This approach facilitates entry of patients into the mental health department, as well as discussion of the patient's case, and the joint development of a treatment program for the patient.

The sharing of expertise enables team members to quickly learn and understand the specialties of their coworkers. Psychologists quickly learn the physiological concerns of their physician and nurse colleagues—how they think and how they work, while physicians and nurses gain insights into the psychological components of medical problems. Likewise, there is value in psychologists and other nonphy-sician mental health providers seeing primary care nurses and other allied health

personnel functioning almost as autonomous health professionals (but still struggling with problems of physician control).

Access to New Classes of Patients

The mandating of psychological services as a result of HMO legislation brought
opportunities for psychologists and other nonphysician mental health providers to
assume new and diverse functions. To a lesser extent, this was also true of psychiatrists. Because the basic goal of the HMO is to provide comprehensive health care,
all mental health practitioners in HMOs must assume broader roles as health
professionals who can contribute meaningfully to the evaluation and management
of health problems (Schofield, 1976; Wiggins, 1976). They are able to and often do
assume multiple roles in HMOs. They work as administrators, organizational consultants, patient ombudsmen, clinical consultants, teachers, supervisors, researchers, and clinicians (Belar, 1989; Sank & Shapiro, 1979).

While mental health practitioners affiliated with HMOs continue to provide
services to "psychiatric" (or mentally ill) patients, they have also been drawn into
early intervention and prevention services, particularly with children and adolescents. These experiences have provided both expanded opportunities for psychologists, for example, to think about clinical intervention with children experiencing
psychological and behavioral problems, and exposure to an array of pediatric problems that most psychologists in routine mental health practice are less likely to
see. The HMO situation has also exposed mental health providers to patients not
typically seen as mentally ill, who are experiencing physical difficulties or leading
lifestyles known to be detrimental to the maintenance of good physical health (e.g.,
heavy smokers, obese patients, and alcoholics).

The Changing Nature of Training

The rapid growth of HMOs requires that graduate education and training programs
for nonphysician mental health professionals must respond to these health care
market changes. Among psychologists, for example, relatively few understand the
nuances of an integrated delivery system, and the majority have little or no practical
experience working within the various "managed care" models. One reason for this
is because the majority of our training institutions have developed isolated, rather
than integrated, practice models. As a result, psychology students do not routinely
interact with their colleagues in the various medical specialties. Because of this
isolation in the training process, psychological services may seem alien to those
more established medical specialties that serve as the core of current managed care
systems (DeLeon, 1989).

Another element that should be addressed in the training of nonmedical health
care professionals is the tendency to ignore cost factors when conceptualizing "what
would be the best clinical regimen for the patient." Clinical psychologists, for example, must learn to maximize the cost-effectiveness of their services by using
"psychological extenders" or "psychological assistants" for the routine aspects of
clinical care (such as the administration of certain phases of the testing protocol),

as is done in medicine and dentistry. It is neither cost-effective nor beneficial for HMO clients in general when psychologists act as if they had to personally attend to every aspect of psychological service for each client seen. Such a process unnecessarily ties up a clinician's time, which could be used more effectively to assist more patients.

Belar (1989) emphasizes the need for the socialization of psychology students for broadened and cooperative roles in HMOs. Ways this could be achieved during the graduate training program include emphasizing the value of successful teamwork and providing training in applied research. In preparing trainees for the team approach, graduate programs must carefully examine the attitudinal set that they model for trainees. Professional isolation is not tolerated by HMO managements, and adequate training in teamwork should be designed to reduce the frustrations and ego blows the trainee is likely to experience in HMO settings. In the area of research involvement, graduate psychology programs must provide applied research training as there is little support for basic research in HMOs. However, HMOs, as corporate health care units, are very data-oriented, and the empirical orientation of well-trained behavioral researcher/clinicians would be most appropriate.

Conclusion

Modern managed mental health care is now almost 20 years old, and it has gone from serving less than 1% of the population to providing care for at least 14% of the population in 1990. Psychotherapy and other mental health services have been a component of managed care throughout this period. However, the details of access to care, the specifics of the services delivered, and quality of care, as well as consumer awareness, service limitations, and restrictions vary considerably among various HMOs and other managed care entities.

It is essential that all mental health professionals work to ensure that high quality and appropriate psychological services are available within managed care systems to those individuals who choose to have their health care needs met through such organizations. This will necessitate the socialization of mental health professionals into new and different roles for work with new and different classes of patients and will require significant changes in the educational training of future mental health professionals.

References

Adler, T. (1990, April). HMO fever: Bush budget spotlights managed health care. *APA Monitor, 21*, pp. 17–18.

Belar, C. D. (1989). Opportunities for psychologists in health maintenance organizations: Implications for graduate education and training. *Professional Psychology: Research and Practice, 20*, 390–394.

Bennett, M. J. (1988). The greening of the HMO: Implications for prepaid psychiatry. *American Journal of Psychiatry, 145*, 1544–1549.

Budman, S. H. (1985). Psychotherapeutic services in the HMO: Zen and the art of mental health maintenance. *Professional Psychology: Research and Practice, 16*, 798–809.

Buie, J. (1987, September). Evidence of HMO flaws mounting. *APA Monitor, 18*, p. 45.

Buie, J. (1989a, June). Given lemons, they make lemonade. *APA Monitor, 20*, p. 20.

Buie, J. (1989b, November). Managed care debate covers pros and cons. *APA Monitor, 20*, p. 21.

Buie, J. (1990, March). HMO's quality of care challenged by lawsuits. *APA Monitor, 21*, p. 13.

Cheifetz, D. I., & Salloway, J. C. (1984). Mental health services in health maintenance organizations: Implications for psychology. *Professional Psychology: Research and Practice, 15*, 152–164.

Cummings, N. A., & Follette, W. T. (1968). Psychiatric services and medical utilization in a prepaid health plan setting: Part II. *Medical Care, 6*, 31–41.

Cummings, N. A., & VandenBos, G. R. (1981). The twenty years of Kaiser Permanente experience with psychotherapy and medical utilization: Implications for national health policy and national health insurance. *Health Policy Quarterly, 1*, 159–175.

DeLeon, P. H. (1989). New roles for old psychologists. *The Clinical Psychologist, 42*, 8–11.

DeLeon, P. H., Uyeda, M. K., & Welch, B. L. (1985). Psychology and HMOs: New partnership or new adversary? *American Psychologist, 40*, 1122–1124.

Flinn, D. E., McMahon, T. C., & Collins, M. F. (1987). Health maintenance organizations and their implications for psychiatry. *Hospital and Community Psychiatry, 38*, 255–263.

Follette, W. T., & Cummings, N. A. (1967). Psychiatric services and medical utilization in a prepaid health plan setting. Part I. *Medical Care, 5*, 25–35.

General Accounting Office. (1988). *Medicare physician incentive payments by prepaid health plans could lower quality of care.* (GAO/HRD–89–29). Washington, DC: U.S. Government Printing Office.

HMO law includes mental health services as basic benefit. (1974). *Hospital and Community Psychiatry, 25*, 257–261.

Jones, K. R., & Vischi, T. R. (1979). Impact of alcohol, drug abuse, and mental health treatment on medical care utilization. *Medical Care, 17*(12), 1–82.

Kiesler, C. A., Cummings, N. A., & VandenBos, G. R. (Eds.). (1979). *Psychology and national health insurance: A sourcebook.* Washington, DC: American Psychological Association.

Luft, H. S. (1987). *Health maintenance organizations: Dimensions of performance.* New Brunswick (U.S.A.) and Oxford (U.K.): Transaction Books.

Marion Laboratories Inc. (1989, October). *Marion managed care digest update*, Kansas City, MO: Author.

Marion Merrel Dow, Inc. (1990). *Marion managed care digest—HMO edition*, Kansas City, MO: Author.

Mumford, E., Schlesinger, H. J., Glass, G. V., Patrick, C., & Cuerdon, T. (1984). A new look at evidence about reduced cost of medical utilization following mental health treatment. *American Journal of Psychiatry, 141*, 1145–1158.

National Industry Council for HMO Development. (n.d.). The health maintenance organization industry ten year report, 1973–1983, "A history of achievement, a future with promise." Washington, DC: Author.

Nixon, R. (1971). Special message to the Congress proposing a National Health Strategy. In *Public papers of the presidents of the United States* (pp. 170–186). Washington, DC: U.S. Government Printing Office.

Sank, L. I., & Shapiro, J. R. (1979). Case examples of the broadened role of psychology in health maintenance organizations. *Professional Psychology, 10*, 402–408.

Schofield, W. (1976). The psychologist as a health professional. *Professional Psychology, 7*, 5–8.

Shadle, M., & Christianson, J. B. (1988). Organization of mental health care delivery in HMOs. *Administration in Mental Health, 15*, 201–225.

Shulman, M. E. (1988). Cost containment in clinical psychology: Critique of Biodyne and the HMO. *Professional Psychology: Research and Practice, 19*, 298–307.

VandenBos, G. R., & DeLeon, P. H. (1988). The use of psychotherapy to improve physical health. *Psychotherapy, 25*, 335–343.

Welch, B. (1986a, October). Professional point. *APA Monitor, 17*, p. 35.

Welch, B. (1986b, December). Professional point. *APA Monitor, 17*, p. 30.

Wiggins, J. G. (1976). The psychologist as a health professional in the health maintenance organization. *Professional Psychology, 7*, 9–13.

18 _____

William H. Berman and Carol Shaw Austad

Managed Mental Health Care: Current Status and Future Directions

The purpose of this book has been to describe optimal mental health care as it is practiced by clinicians in managed health care systems. Many of these practitioners have experienced a significant discrepancy between their graduate training in the mental health field and the realities of clinical practice in managed health care systems. In these settings, the demand for effective and timely services with rapid engagement, intervention, and disengagement is essential. Although some experience frustration, disillusionment, and burnout (Austad, Henault, Steefel, & DeStefano, in press), others have begun to revise their formulation of their work and changed their method of practice to accommodate both the constraints of managed care and their increasing awareness of alternative methods of treatment.

The contributors to this volume have adjusted their practice in different ways. Some have developed new conceptualizations of mental health care, drawing on alternative theoretical models of health and psychopathology. Others have adapted existing treatment models such as cognitive–behavioral (Jacobson & Margolin, 1979), interpersonal (Klerman, Weissman, Rounsaville & Chevron, 1984) or dynamic brief therapies (e.g., Budman & Gurman, 1988; Davanloo, 1980; Sifneos, 1979; Strupp & Binder, 1984), so that they are more consistent with the demands of managed health care. These new models reflect a view of the individual that emphasizes healthy development, normal personality, and humanistic and interpersonal values.

Current Status: Innovations in Theory, Assessment, and Treatment

In Chapter 1 we described some of the basic assumptions of HMO (health maintenance organization) psychotherapy. In many instances these reflect a change from the traditional assumptions of mental health care in the United States. Although these changes are not necessarily unique to HMO mental health, they are essential to good practice in HMOs.

Managed mental health care systems have accepted the idea that multiple interventions may be necessary throughout a person's life. The role of the primary care based, psychological "family doctor" is to provide a framework that allows for a continued relationship between the patient and therapist. This model emphasizes brief contacts at points of particular distress over an extended time span. The panel

264

of patients is broad, and they are seen as the need arises. Based on an ongoing therapeutic alliance, primary care based treatment facilitates the long-term availability of mental health services, while using less intensive, "intermittent" therapeutic input. Cummings articulates this approach to psychotherapy, which uses therapists whose role is similar to that of Patterson and Berman's "primary mental health practitioners." The subfield of health psychology implicitly relies on a primary care model. Application of the primary care approach has been described in several chapters of this book, including those on the use of psychopharmacology, the treatment of life crises, adolescent psychopathology, and somatization disorders. It was perhaps most clearly demonstrated in the chapter on treatment of the chronic patient. An ongoing involvement with this population was found to facilitate patient adaptation and decrease the need for rehospitalization.

HMO psychotherapy also emphasizes an interpersonal philosophy that assumes that developmental transitions or disruptions may trigger significant emotional difficulties for many patients. In general, people will find options for growth and development, even though they experience periods of turmoil and distress. Most patients treated in this context will be able to recover with relatively brief, focused interventions. The chapters in the theory section describe approaches to individual and group psychotherapy that use and this philosophy of treatment. Similar approaches to intervention with somatizing patients, depressed patients, and marital and family crises are consistent with life-span developmental research (Levinson, 1978; Vaillant, 1977). Even hospitalized adolescents and people with personality disorders are viewed as having the potential to significantly improve their lives using intermittent, developmental interventions rather than the long-term treatment so frequently recommended for them.

A relationship between patient and therapist that emphasizes a pragmatic therapeutic alliance is consistent with these philosophies. The contract that should exist between all therapists and patients in an HMO was described thus by Cummings: "I will never abandon you as long as you need me. In return for that, I want you to join me in a partnership to make me obsolete as soon as possible (p. 40)." The intermittent model of treatment strongly emphasizes the importance of both patient and therapist working toward a common set of realistic goals. The patient and therapist develop a strong bond that is maintained over an extended period of time, even if contact is infrequent. In addition, both patient and therapist also consider the needs of the membership as a whole, rather than focusing exclusively on the dyad (Bennett, 1988b). A strong, positive treatment alliance, without constant involvement, is important in all of the approaches described in this volume, and particularly emphasized in family crisis intervention and substance abuse treatment.

Responsibility for treatment is an important component of the therapeutic alliance. All brief psychotherapy requires the therapist to take responsibility for the content and direction of the therapy. Training HMO psychotherapists to be active and directive is an important aspect of HMO work. However, the patient and his or her family have the ultimate responsibility for treatment. The patient is responsible for acting in accordance with the therapeutic contract, for completing homework if assigned, and for using and implementing the therapy outside of therapeutic contacts. It is particularly important in treating personality disorders, chemical dependency, and chronic pain that the patient is responsible for his or her own behavior.

Mental health care in general is moving toward more structured, planned interventions based on a synthesis of diagnostic and psychosocial factors (Beutler & Clarkin, 1990; Frances, Clarkin & Perry, 1984). Several chapters in this book have implicitly, if not explicitly embraced this approach. The model of group psychotherapy described by Folkers and Steefel strongly emphasizes a programmatic approach in which particular problems or disorders are targeted for a preestablished, comprehensive treatment. Behavioral medicine also emphasizes programmatic interventions that are targeted to specific problems, some of which are not encompassed by traditional diagnoses. Programmatic interventions for psychotic disorders, families in crisis, emotionally and behaviorally disturbed adolescents, substance abuse, and chronic pain account for individual needs while also providing a consistent intervention that can be evaluated and modified.

Unlike the traditional solo mental health practitioner, the HMO psychotherapist works within an open system involving primary care, specialty medicine, and mental health. The primary care practitioner provides the therapist with important information about patients and their families. Primary care providers and specialty providers can be involved so as to increase the system's efficiency and provide continuity of care after an acute episode is over. Staff collaboration is particularly important in treating chronic pain with medical, pharmacologic, and psychological interventions. Both nonmedical and medical mental health expertise are required to make these interventions parsimonious yet comprehensive. This same expertise is required to treat other psychological disorders, as well as depression, psychosis, chemical dependency, and somatization disorder. Behavioral medicine plays an increasingly important role in health maintenance as the growth of HMOs continues with legislative and corporate support. Within such a system, "professional preciousness" has little place; mental health disciplines must work in an integrative fashion to provide effective treatment in the most efficient manner.

Future Directions

Quality of Care in Prepaid Mental Health Services

One of the essential questions about mental health services in managed care is whether quality care can ever be provided, or whether a conflict of interest is inherent and unavoidable. Inevitably, prepaid health care, particularly in the increasingly common "for-profit" organization, produces a strong economic incentive for practitioners to restrict access to and involvement in mental health services. It has been stated that any system in which the provider stands to gain by a reduction in service will invariably provide substandard care (Backus, 1987; Eisenberg, 1986).[1]

---

[1] The minor premise of this argument often is that optimal mental health services are inherently long-term, labor intensive, and with outcome that is definable only on a case-by-case basis. Although this belief is not central to the conflict-of-interest critique, it frequently arises in debates about mental health care. It has been well noted that there is no current evidence—beyond anecdotal reports and uncontrolled, single-cell, pre–post research designs—that long-term dynamic psychotherapy is an effective intervention for significant Axis I disorders (Klerman, 1990).

Thus, the potential for conflict of interest certainly exists in managed mental health. Barriers to utilization and underreferral for mental health services have been documented (Buie, 1987, 1988; Karon, 1989). However, traditional payment systems also have the potential for conflict of interest, as exemplified by abuses of medicare and medicaid financing. When the provider of any service is reimbursed only for those services that he or she provides, the provider is likely to encourage the highest utilization of services possible (Muszynski, 1985). Since mental health services are provided in an expertise-based, noncompetitive market, consumers tend not to search for the balance between the lowest cost and the best service; rather, they make choices based on personal referrals or convenience. This eliminates a significant cost-limiting regulatory mechanism.

The chapters of this book support the belief that effective, high-quality mental health services can be provided in a system that has limited resources and controlled costs. However, not all managed mental health systems are of equal quality. Quality assurance mechanisms are needed to examine the adequacy of each managed care system individually. The solution to quality of care conflicts in managed health is a two-tier approach. First, intentional barriers to treatment and obstacles to needed care that result in abuse of the reimbursement systems must be addressed by legislative action. Particular attention should be paid to the use of adverse selection criteria and cost-shifting of high utilizers to indemnity or state programs. DeLeon and VandenBos have addressed many of these issues in their chapter in this volume.

Second, the managed mental health field must develop and establish quality of care standards. In general health care, quality is determined on the basis of three factors: structure, process, and outcome (Cohen, 1988; Donabedian, 1968). In mental health, however, it has traditionally been defined by structure and process variables, such as frequency of contact, rather than by outcome or the relationship of process and outcome (Rodriguez, 1988a). Definition of the relevant factors for treatment traditionally has been based on psychodynamic models with little demonstrated reliability and validity (Klerman, 1990). In addition, the fields of mental health were unable to agree among themselves what defines appropriate treatment or positive outcome. Cohen (1988) has argued that there are significant methodological problems with an outcome-based definition of quality in mental health. This argument is most clearly stated in a recent American Psychiatric Association Office of Quality Assurance statement (1988, p. 19):

> Quality of care is a determination that the treatment given . . . meets the explicit and implicit standards of care accepted by the profession. . . . In most areas of medicine, quality can be evaluated by looking at quantitative measures of outcome. *However, in psychiatry, the lack of such outcome measures, except of the most general kind, means that the review of quality is based on the process of care and the ongoing response of the patient; that is, measures of process and progress, rather than outcome* (italics ours).

When an empirical, outcome-based approach to quality assurance is used, the efficacy of the HMO therapy model can be accurately evaluated.

The second tier of quality care provision combines structure, process, and *outcome variables* in mental health service delivery. Outcome-based evaluation of mental health services is essential both to evaluate whether individuals suffer as a result of the particular economic system of treatment, and to critique and refine the services that are provided (Rodriguez, 1988b). It is important to examine the following components of mental health services within any mental health service in prepaid care.

Process Variables

Are appropriate numbers of patients being treated? Research has consistently demonstrated that more patients are seen in prepaid mental health services than in indemnity or fee-for-service policies, both on a yearly basis (Diehr, Williams, Martin, & Price, 1984; Kisch & Austad, 1988; Levin & Glasser, 1979; Taube, Goldman, Burns, & Kessler, 1988; Williams, Diehr, Drucker, & Richardson, 1979), and over a period of years (Manning, Wells, & Benjamin, 1987). An estimated 25% or more of managed mental health patients return for further treatment because of new difficulties, feeling they benefited from the prior contact (Kessler, 1984; Siddall, Haffey, & Feinman, 1988).

Variations in the use of mental health services and barriers to treatment in prepaid mental health care (e.g., Brady & Krizay, 1985; Buie, 1987; Glasser, Duggan, & Hoffman, 1975) should be examined. Blocking early access to mental health care may increase the severity of problems and increase overall costs in the long run (Durenberger, 1988, 1989). Case flow into managed mental health services should occur at or above the rate for traditional services, thus providing a measure of the availability of services and ensuring that gatekeeper functions are not being abused.

Are patients treated for an appropriate length of time? A significant body of literature demonstrates that most people are in psychotherapy for only a short-term course of treatment (Budman & Gurman, 1988; Garfield, 1978). Statistics from 600 community mental health centers from 1970 to 1978 show that patients receive an average of five sessions of therapy (Phillips, 1985). Only 50% of those receiving treatment returned after the initial visit, and 70% had terminated by the sixth session. Other studies have demonstrated that the median number of sessions is between four and five (Horgan, 1985; Taube, Kessler, & Feuerberg, 1984). Even in a long-term treatment setting, the median length of treatment is 12 sessions (Howard, Davidson, O'Mahoney, Orlinsky, & Brown, 1989). While there is an increased benefit from additional sessions for some patients, there are significantly diminishing returns, with the largest benefit occurring in the first eight sessions. Patients with personality disorders take the longest to benefit and need the most extensive intervention, according to this research (Howard, Kopta, Krause, & Orlinsky, 1986).

Research on the number of sessions for which patients are seen in HMOs is quite consistent with these data (Hoeper & Nycz, 1981), and suggests that the major difference between HMO treatment and traditional reimbursement procedures is "short-term by design" versus "short-term by default" (Budman & Gurman, 1988). In addition, the mean length of treatment in traditional insurance plans is elevated by the inclusion of high-functioning, high-utilizers (Taube, Goldman, Burns, & Kessler, 1988), a population that prepaid health plans overtly try to reduce (Kisch & Austad, 1988). Documentation of comparable duration of psychotherapy, except

for patients targeted for reduced utilization, is a second important oversight variable, unless of course equivalent outcome can be demonstrated in fewer sessions.

Conversely, extended duration of treatment is an appropriate marker for individual case evaluation. A prolonged intervention may indicate potentially inappropriate treatment. Although there are no assurances of complete recovery for
chronic pain patients, the procedures described by Kempler (see chapter 15, this
volume) suggest that treatment review is indicated if the patient still requires
frequent narcotic injections after 15 weeks of a pain management program. Similarly, if a patient has shown no change in depressive symptoms after several weeks
of intervention, a case review should be initiated to determine whether appropriate
treatment is being given. On a system-wide basis, a cutoff related to the mean
length of treatment could be used as a case review point. For example, if the mean
length of treatment is 6.5 sessions ± 3 sessions, a case review of any patient
receiving more than 10 sessions could be used to ensure that patients were receiving
the best possible care.

Outcome Variables

For assessment of quality of care, outcome refers either to the alleviation of signs
and symptoms, and return to the prior level of functioning, or to achieving jointly
defined goals in the least restrictive context and at the least cost to the individual
and society. Some of these variables are available or determinable at the present
time. Others have not yet been established, but could be with available data. Some
of the outcome criteria have not been evaluated, in part because the bias has been
strongly in opposition to these kinds of questions.

*Have symptoms been alleviated? Has the patient returned to his or her prior level
of functioning?* The goal for active treatment is to return the patient to the level
of functioning demonstrated prior to the onset of difficulties, with the symptoms
that brought the patient into treatment no longer prominent.

The Office of Quality Assurance of the American Psychiatric Association (1988)
finds that in any treatment setting,

> active treatment is . . . the process of restoring the patient with an acute illness
> or acute exacerbation of a chronic illness to the level of health and functioning
> present before the acute episode. . . . [and is] aimed at symptom reduction and
> stabilization of behavior. (p. 4)

Change in overt symptoms is the optimal outcome measure for establishing
quality of care. While therapeutic change is difficult to quantify for patients who
qualify for long-term psychoanalytic psychotherapy, this is not the case for most
patients treated by the approaches described in this book. If treatment is effective,
then depressed patients should be free of depressed mood and neurovegetative symptoms. Scores on a reliable measure of depression will show a decrease. Similar
outcome measures can be used for anxiety disorders and phobias. Patients with
substance abuse disorders should be abstinent of any psychoactive substance except
prescription medications. Psychotic patients and their families should report no

major disturbances in the behavior or thinking of the patient. Chronic pain patients should report less subjective pain, decreased dysphoria, and increased coping ability compared to when they presented for treatment. Somatizing patients should be less involved in medical utilization, and more able to function in family, social, and work life.

Assessment of prior level of functioning is more difficult, since acute or first-episode patients are unlikely to have any documentation of their level of functioning. However, discussion with the patient and the patient's family can give clues. In general, patients who worked prior to treatment should return to gainful employment. The person should be able to maintain a level of social contact similar to that experienced prior to the episode. And nuclear family relationships should have a clear and stable resolution, such that the relationship is not a prominent cause of personal distress and disruption.

Other variables that relate to outcome can be included in any evaluation of an individual case or a mental health service. For many Axis I psychiatric disorders, the relapse rate can be used as a standard of evaluation. Patients who have higher-than-average relapse can be identified and targeted for additional intervention around such factors as treatment compliance, high expressed emotion (Vaughn & Leff, 1985), or relapse prevention (Marlatt & Gordon, 1985). Obviously, morbidity and mortality rates can be evaluated to ensure that patients at high risk for suicide or accidental death are being adequately treated. Finally, the nonresponder rate of patients in a given health plan can be compared to the community-wide rate. Individuals who are not responding can be identified and evaluated for mitigating factors and treatment alternatives.

Have jointly defined goals been achieved? A majority of cases (Siddall et al., 1988) in managed health care do not meet the criteria for Axis I disorders. For these patients, standards for quality care can be determined by jointly defined goals of treatment, rather than by theoretical assumptions or individual experiences (Barrett, 1981). Few patients come to treatment requesting personality restructuring. When a patient initiates treatment for a particular symptom, the treatment needs to address that symptom. Most often, patients want help with negative feelings, problematic interpersonal relationships, or personal failure. In all brief therapies, a period of contracting around a particular focus is essential for good outcome (Budman & Gurman, 1988; Cummings, this volume; Strupp & Binder, 1984). The particular contract for any therapy can be used to evaluate outcome and often is beneficial per se, even in the long-term treatment of severe borderline states (Clarkin, personal communication, December, 1989). Barrett (1981) has used a goal-oriented rather than a process-oriented approach in a community mental health center, with significant improvement in their assessment of quality of care. Others have used a combination of process and outcome measures to examine quality of care in an empirically sound manner (Feldman, Wilner, & Winickoff, 1982; Hankin & Locke, 1982).

Has treatment occurred at the least cost to the individual and society? Psychosocial and pharmacologic interventions are expensive, time-consuming, and stressful activities that interfere to some degree with one's daily life. In a time of cost-consciousness and limited resources (Berman et al., 1988), one important component of outcome is the cost of the intervention to the individual and to society. Both intensive outpatient intervention (Langsley, Pullman, Machotka, & Flomenhaft, 1968) and brief hospitalization (e.g., Endicott, Herz, & Gibbon, 1978) have been shown to be equally effective and less costly to the individual, family, and society than standard inpatient treatment. A recent study by Hayashida et al. (1989) found that outpatient detoxification for mild-to-moderate alcohol withdrawal syndrome was briefer, equally safe and effective, and significantly less expensive than inpatient detoxification. However, these data are not often reflected in clinical practice. Decreasing the negative impact of treatment must be a component of quality care evaluation. Unfortunately, norms are difficult to establish, as prevailing community standards are often not generalizable. Norms can be established for variables such as workdays missed and patient expenditures, and should be used in establishing quality standards. Questions related to individual and social cost include: How many work days were missed? How long were patients in the hospital? What was the cost of psychotherapy, medication, and laboratory work? How long was the person in acute distress before treatment began?

Was the least restrictive environment used? The concept of the "least restrictive alternative" has been a central component of patients' rights for 15 years (Ennis & Emery, 1978). This can be applied to mental health care for the general population just as it was to the involuntary and incompetent patient when it was developed. It can refer to the right of patients to have access to partial hospitalization, brief therapy, or group therapy rather than more traditional approaches to intervention. Could the patient have been treated at home, or in a day hospital, for example? Could less frequent contact have been as effective?

It is not always the case that more treatment is better. Therapists are at times guilty of overestimating their own impact and underestimating the impact of life changes, maturation, and informal social supports on an individual's mental health. In extreme cases, psychotherapy can continue for months or years despite a significant negative reaction and increased dysfunction (Grunebaum, 1986). The least restrictive environment can be interpreted to mean that patients have a right to make changes in their lives and increase their self-esteem by acting on their own after a brief psychotherapy contact.

Directions for Research

Research is essential to develop creative solutions to mental health problems. However, conducting research in managed health care is difficult because it takes place in an economically competitive setting where the emphasis is on service delivery (Bennett, 1988a). Often administrators in managed care settings are reluctant to support research, as they perceive that it will interfere with and prolong interventions as well as increase costs. Moreover, any additional work for the clinicians, who are already producing at a high capacity, is viewed with disdain.

However, research can be closely tied to the services that are provided for the membership. All mental health services are subject to utilization review and quality control; research can become an integral part of maintaining quality of care, for example as has been done on occasion at Harvard Community Health Plan (Feldman et al., 1982). A recent study by Siddall, Haffey, & Feinman (1988) is another good example of research integrated into the provision of care.

Fundamental questions regarding quality of care require the development of research projects. Further comparison of prepaid and indemnity plans with respect to structural (e.g., types of therapists, types and amounts of medication), process (e.g., number of patients seen) and outcome (e.g., change in symptoms, least cost to the individual, least restrictive alternative) variables can address questions of quality care in managed mental health. These studies can occur on either a macro level, using multiple sites and broad outcome variables, or on a micro level, emphasizing specific populations or interventions, and clinically rich data. The most ambitious of the former type, the Rand Health Insurance Experiment (Brook et al., 1984; Wells, Manning, Benjamin, 1986), provided important data regarding the impact of insurance benefits on utilization of health services. A current project by RAND, the Medical Outcome Study (Wells, personal communication, February 1989) involves the study of medical outcome in different health insurance programs, including the treatment of depression. Identification and treatment of underserved populations, such as children and those suffering from chronic disorders need much more extensive study. Greater understanding of the "high utilizer" is also essential to developing effective interventions with this population. Finally, the role of psychiatric comorbidity in medical disorders has not been investigated in the context where it could be most useful: the primary care setting of managed health care. It is possible that this is as important to overall medical care as the medical offset effect is to mental health care.

While large-scale, extensive studies are essential, small-scale, intensive studies are usually more feasible, and provide equally important data. Chart review, observational, and intervention studies that are rich in clinical information are crucial to ensuring quality care and developing more effective interventions. The mental health programs such as those described in this book would benefit from outcome and process research. Contrasting intervention techniques can be effectively introduced in prepaid health care in a way that does not hinder patient care, and costs little for the insurer. Strosahl's approach to the personality disordered patient could be compared to the approach already used by HMO psychotherapists. Patients could be randomly assigned to the two treatments, and outcome measures taken as a part of the evaluation of treatment. Alternatively, individual and group versions of the treatment could be compared, with little added burden to either clinicians or patients. An example of this kind of study is the use of interpersonal counseling in a primary care setting (Klerman et al., 1987), in which a targeted, programmatic intervention was applied to patients in primary care experiencing psychosocial difficulties.

Training and Staff Development

It is a common complaint of both psychotherapy researchers and clinicians that the advances in psychotherapy research the rarely reflected in practitioner behavior (Strupp, 1989). Although briefer and more focal treatments, emphasis on the individual's adaptive capacities, and changing formulations of some psychiatric disorders are common in academic psychology and psychiatry, there is little evidence of their integration into treatment settings. Managed mental health practice has a unique potential to foster integration of these perspectives into clinical practice because of the need for brief, targeted, efficient approaches to psychological problems. Most clinicians working in these settings perceive the treatment as more difficult and more demanding than the work for which they were trained (Austad et al., in press). As noted in several other chapters, the typical psychotherapist is poorly trained for the prepaid setting. Hoyt (see Chapter 7) has delineated many of the characteristics of a good brief therapist, including a preference for parsimony, an emphasis on strengths, and a focus on solutions. Moreover, he has noted the importance of a sound theoretical orientation and effective diagnostic skills.

Training of prepaid mental health providers must take place on two levels: the early training of psychiatric residents, psychology trainees, master's-level nurses, and social workers, either during graduate programs or as postdoctoral training; and concurrent staff training and development. Managed mental health clinicians need training in areas beyond those provided by most graduate programs. Theories of human behavior emphasizing life cycle development and plasticity rather than rigidity of development are important (e.g., Levinson, 1978; Vaillant, 1977). Models of brief psychotherapy, as well as models of behavioral, family, or psychodynamic psychotherapy are central to fostering versatility in treatment. Clinicians must be familiar with alternatives to traditional psychodynamic psychotherapy including group, family, hypnotherapy, and behavioral interventions. Nonmedical practitioners need training in pharmacotherapeutics to work collaboratively with physicians and psychiatrists in the treatment of severe disorders.

Students seeking training in this modality should have a basis in more traditional mental health care. A second-year internship or postdoctoral year for psychologists in managed mental health would provide significant skills for intervention in this setting. Similarly, the PGY-IV year would be an appropriate time for psychiatric residents to receive training in managed mental health services. The experience of outpatient chronic care, collaborative psychopharmacology, and consultation-liaison programs available in managed care settings would facilitate their ability to function as independent health care providers. Finally, second year placements for social workers and master's-level nurses would provide a reasonable basis of knowledge, particularly if supervision were continued after completion of the degree. Training for all of these groups would place an emphasis on integrated assessment during intervention, and specific interventions based not only on DSM-III diagnosis, but also on the current context of the problem and the patient's social network. Models of treatment decisions such as Differential Therapeutics (Frances et al., 1984) could be used to facilitate training in these settings.

In-service training is also essential in prepaid health care. Clinicians often feel overwhelmed by the volume of care they need to provide. They can easily feel less respected than mental health professionals in other settings and experience their work as more routinized and uncreative, leading to lowered enthusiasm and burnout (Fielding, 1984). An understanding of the process of mental health in managed systems, as described in several chapters in this book, will foster motivation to continue working in this modality. The development of new clinical skills, the sharpening of preexisting skills, and the supportive examination of difficult or problematic cases is essential for an effective treatment milieu. As an example, Community Health Care Plan has organized a weekly mental health case conference, in which each clinician presents cases with a particular question to discuss. All staff attend, providing alternative clinical perspectives and personal support for the clinician. At times, effectively treated cases are presented, fostering motivation and interest in managed treatment models. In addition, once or twice a year, experts are brought in to develop alternative strategies for intervention, often drawing on current research in brief interventions. Finally, financial support is provided to encourage therapists to attend professional meetings on theoretical issues and treatment interventions.

Program Development

We have repeatedly emphasized that optimal managed mental health care provides the opportunity for the development of the most effective treatment strategies for the most people, at the least cost to the individual and to society. The development of new forms or structures for intervention that meet these goals is essential to progress in managed mental health care. Mental health clinicians can use their own expertise and experience within the managed care setting to design interventions consistent with their theoretical beliefs and therapeutic practice. All of the chapters in the second section of this book illustrate innovative treatment programs or preexisting psychotherapies adapted to the particulars of managed health care.

Inpatient treatment is an important area in which significant change is necessary to ensure the most effective care. The most serious, life-threatening disorders often come to attention first because of a crisis requiring an inpatient admission. Inpatient treatment is the most disruptive to an individual's life, affecting family, work, and financial situation. In addition, it is the most expensive form of treatment. Chapter 9 on inpatient adolescent treatment describes an important model for basic inpatient treatment. Although the criteria for admission to an inpatient unit are similar for all inpatient settings, the authors' approach is unique in its emphasis on family involvement and decision-making. One of the main goals of brief hospitalization is development of an alliance that will facilitate outpatient therapy. Symptomatic treatment is actively addressed, but the family is often the most important target of psychosocial interventions.

Adult inpatient treatment programs could benefit from similar interventions. Adult programs can use creative treatment strategies that reduce costs and decrease the degree of disruption in the least restrictive setting for the patient. Day or partial hospital programs have demonstrated a high degree of efficacy for patients who are not imminent risks, but who cannot yet function in their normal daily setting. Night hospital programs have also been used for patients who are able to function in their jobs, but have particular difficulties in their home environment, such as intense marital conflict aggravating a depression, or a lack of family and social support. Finally, extremely brief inpatient units in which the patient is maintained only for one to three days and then moved to a less restrictive environment (Gudeman & Shore, 1985) can be of significant benefit to the large majority of patients in managed care, who have social supports and jobs awaiting them.

Treatment of Chronic Patients

Statistics on use and duration of mental health services indicate that less than 0.5% of the membership of managed health care cannot be treated within mental health benefits mandated by the Federal HMO Act. In practice, many HMOs provide services for a broad range of patients, including those with psychotic and personality disorders. The treatment of the chronically and catastrophically mentally ill, however, is *de facto* shifted to public facilities, in that few HMOs have social service programs or cover long-term treatment for any type of illness or disorder (Schlesinger, 1986). The rationale for separating out what Goldman and Taube (1988) referred to as the high-impaired high-utilizers is usually a cost-based argument, although there is increasing evidence that it is extremely difficult to provide adequate services to the severely ill in capitated programs. As a result, public mental health programs may continue to provide the most effective services for these high-risk patients.

There is a small population of patients who do not meet the operational definition for chronic care, yet require long-term psychotherapy in order to function. Patients who experience repeated exacerbations of symptoms despite pharmacologic compliance or significantly increased medical utilization when mental health care is stopped are examples of this need. Treatment must be available for these patients in any comprehensive mental health delivery system. Psychotherapists with specific and specialized skills in various approaches to long-term intensive treatment are needed as more patients are covered by managed mental health. Family mental program, clinicians could refer appropriate patients to long-term psychotherapy based on severity of psychopathology, psychosocial and familial factors, and the specialty skills of the long-term psychotherapist.

Many staff model HMOs have well articulated approaches to the treatment of psychotic patients. Chapter 13 identified the central aspects of this approach. Unfortunately, few of the (Individual Practice Association/Preferred Provider Organization) models of managed care are equipped to intervene with the inpatient, except from a retroactive cost-denial or concurrent review system. Many of these IPAs could benefit from a program that would facilitate the transition of such patients out of the hospital and back to their daily lives.

Conclusion

Health maintenance organizations were begun in the 1920s to provide medical care to workers who were not receiving effective care in the current health care market (Eisenstein, 1981; Nelson, 1987), and to meet the increasing health needs of all Americans (Bennett, 1988b; Roemer, 1985). Cost-containment and profitability have largely replaced social consciousness as the driving motivation behind the growth of managed health care. Nevertheless, as the health needs of Americans grow, the fee-for-service and indemnity models have not provided adequate medical or mental health care. Recent research into depression, as just one example, indicates that less than 30% of those people needing treatment are actually receiving mental health care (Goodwin, 1989).

The managed health care movement offers a unique opportunity to provide high-quality mental health services to a large proportion of Americans. It also provides an opportunity to critically examine many of the basic assumptions about mental health services and to begin to integrate research on the utilization and practice of mental health care into the daily activities of clinicians. This book demonstrates the efforts made by practitioners in HMOs toward the development and integration of creative, effective mental health care as it is practiced in the prepaid sector. It further demonstrates that assessment, goals, and interventions can be clearly delineated and provided in the context of a brief but potentially recurrent therapeutic relationship. The practitioners who have contributed to this book show their commitment to both their patients and the philosophy of prepaid mental health. Continued growth of the theory and practice of psychotherapy in managed mental health will be determined by the motivation of all practitioners (and their commitment) to those Americans who need mental health services.

References

American Psychiatric Association, (Office of Quality Assurance). (1988). *Concepts and definitions in psychiatric quality assurance and utilization review.* Washington, DC: American Psychiatric Association.

Austad, C. S., Henault, K., Steefel, N., & DeStefano, L. J. (in press). Psychotherapists in independent practice and managed health care settings: A comparison. *Psychotherapy in Private Practice.*

Backus, V. P. (1987). HMOs: Not always the best medicine. *Hospital and Community Psychiatry, 38*(3), 229.

Barrett, T. (1981). Simplifying quality review systems through the use of organizational goals. *Quality Review Bulletin, 7,* 4–9.

Bennett, M. J. (1988a). Quality assurance activities for mental health services in health maintenance organizations. In G. A. Striker & A. R. Rodriguez (Eds.), *Handbook of quality assurance in mental health* (pp. 421–438). New York: Plenum Press.

Bennett, M. J. (1988b). The greening of the HMO: Implications for prepaid psychiatry. *American Journal of Psychiatry, 145*(12), 1544–1549.

Berman, W. H., Kisch, J., DeLeon, P. H., Cummings, N. A., Binder, J. L., & Hefele, T. J. (1988). The future of psychotherapy in the age of diminishing resources. *Psychotherapy in Private Practice, 5*(4), 105–118.

Beutler, L., & Clarkin, J. F. (1990). *Systematic treatment selection.* New York: Brunner/Mazel.

Brady, J., & Krizay, J. (1985). Utilization and coverage of mental health services in health maintenance organizations. *American Journal of Psychiatry, 142,* 744–746.

Brook, R. H., Ware, J. E., Rogers, W. H., Keeler, E. B., Davies, A. R., Sheibeirne, C. A., Goldberg, G. A., Lohr, K. N., Camp, P., & Newhouse, J. P. (1984). *The effect of coinsurance on the health of adults: Results from the Rand Health Insurance Experiment.* Santa Monica, CA: The Rand Corp.

Budman, S. H., & Gurman, A. S. (1988). *Theory and practice of brief therapy.* New York: Guilford Press.

Buie, J. (1987, September). Evidence of HMO flaws mounting. *APA Monitor,* p. 22.

Buie, J. (1988, March). New data show HMO dream unfulfilled. *APA Monitor,* p. 32.

Cohen, L. H. (1988). Research on mental health quality assurance. In G. A. Striker & A. R. Rodriguez (Eds.), *Handbook of quality assurance in mental health* (pp. 65–79). New York: Plenum Press.

Davanloo, H. (1980). *Short-term dynamic psychotherapy.* New York: Jason Aronson.

Diehr, P., Williams, S. J., Martin, D. P., & Price, K. (1984). Ambulatory mental health services utilization in three provider plans. *Medical Care, 22,* 1–13.

Donabedian, A. (1968). The evaluation of medical care programs. *Bulletin of the New York Academy of Medicine, 44,* 117–124.

Durenburger, D. (1988). Rectifying an archaic payment policy. *American Journal of Psychiatry, 145,* 81–82.

Durenburger, D. (1989). Providing mental health care services to Americans. *American Psychologist,* *44*, 1293–1297.

Eisenberg, L. (1986). Health care: For patients or for profits. *American Journal of Psychiatry, 143*(8), 1015–1019.

Eisenstein, J. P. (1981). *Health Maintenance Organizations: From social health reform to marketplace conservatism.* Unpublished master's thesis, Yale University, New Haven, CT.

Endicott, J., Herz, M. I., & Gibbon, M. (1978). Brief versus standard hospitalization: The differential costs. *American Journal of Psychiatry, 135*, 707–712.

Ennis, B. J., & Emery, R. D. (1978). *The rights of mental patients.* New York: Avon Books.

Feldman, J., Wilner, S., & Winickoff, R. (1982). A study of lithium carbonate use in a health maintenance organization. *Quality Review Bulletin, 8*, 8–14.

Fielding, S. L. (1984). Organizational impact on medicine: The HMO concept. *Social Science and Medicine, 18*(8), 615–620.

Frances, A., Clarkin, J., & Perry, S. (1984). *Differential therapeutics in psychiatry: The art and science of treatment selection.* New York: Brunner/Mazel.

Garfield, S. L. (1978). Research on client variables in psychotherapy. In S. L. Garfield & A. E. Bergin (Eds.), *Handbook of psychotherapy and behavior change* (3rd ed., pp. 213–256). New York: Wiley.

Glasser, M. A., Duggan, T. J., & Hoffman, W. S. (1975). Obstacles to utilization of prepaid mental health care. *American Journal of Psychiatry, 132*, 710–715.

Goodwin, R. (1989, May). Current status of the treatment of depression. Paper presented at meeting of the American Psychiatric Association, San Francisco, CA.

Grunebaum, H. (1986). Harmful psychotherapy experience. *American Journal of Psychotherapy, 40*, 165–176.

Gudeman, J. E., & Shore, M. F. (1985). Public care for the chronically mentally ill: A new model. In S. S. Sharfstein & A. Beigel (Eds.), *The new economics and psychiatric care.* Washington, DC: American Psychiatric Press.

Hankin, J. R., & Locke, B. Z. (1982). The persistence of depressive symptomatology among prepaid group practice enrollees: An exploratory study. *American Journal of Public Health, 72*(9), 1000–1007.

Hayashida, M., Alterman, A. I., McLellan, T., O'Brien, (1989). Comparative effectiveness and costs of inpatient and outpatient detoxification of patients with mild to moderate alcohol withdrawal syndrome. *New England Journal of Medicine, 320*(6), 358–365.

Hoeper, E. W., & Nycz, G. R. (1981). Utilization and cost of mental health care when integrated in a health care system. *Journal of Psychiatric Treatment and Evaluation, 3*, 217–226.

Horgan, C. M. (1985). Specialty and general ambulatory mental health services. *Archive of General Psychiatry, 42*, 565–572.

Howard, K. I., Davidson, C. V., O'Mahoney, M. T., Orlinsky, D. E., & Brown, K. P. (1989). Patterns of psychotherapy utilization. *American Journal of Psychiatry, 146*, 775–778.

Howard, K. I., Kopta, S. M., Krause, M. S., & Orlinsky, D. E. (1986). The dose–effect relationship in psychotherapy. *American Psychologist, 41*, 159–164.

Jacobson, N. S., & Margolin, G. (1979). *Marital therapy: Strategies based on social learning and behavior exchange principles.* New York: Brunner/Mazel.

Jones, K. R., & Vischi, T. R. (1979). Impact of alcohol, drug abuse and mental health treatment on medical care utilization. *Medical Care, 17*(12, Suppl.), 1–82.

Karon, B. P. (1989, August). *Problems of psychotherapy under managed health care.* Paper presented to the Annual Convention of the American Psychological Association, New Orleans, LA.

Kessler, L. G. (1984). Treated incidence of mental disorders in a prepaid group practice. *American Journal of Public Health. 74*(2), 152–154.

Kisch, J., & Austad, C. S. (1988). The health maintenance organization: 2. Historical perspective and current status. *Psychotherapy, 25*(3), 441–448.

Klerman, G. L. (1990). The psychiatric patient's right to effective treatment: Implications of Osheroff v. Chestnut Lodge. *American Journal of Psychiatry, 147*, 409–418.

Klerman, G. L., Budman, S., Berwick, D., Weissman, M. M., Damico-White, J., Demby, A., & Feldstein, M. (1987). Efficacy of a brief psychosocial intervention for symptoms of stress and distress among patients in primary care. *Medical Care, 25*(11), 1078–1088.

Klerman, G. L., Weissman, M. M., Rounsaville, B. J., & Chevron, E. (1984). *Interpersonal psychotherapy of depression.* New York: Basic Books.

Langsley, D. G., Pullman, F. S., Machotka, P., & Flomenhaft, K. (1968). Family crisis therapy: Results and implications. *Family Process*, 7(2), 145–158.

Levin, B. L., & Glasser, J. H. (1979). A survey of mental health service coverage within health maintenance organizations. *American Journal of Public Health*, 69(11), 1120–1125.

Levinson, D. (1978). *The seasons of a man's life*. New York: Random House.

Manning, W. G., Wells, K. B., & Benjamin, B. (1987). Use of outpatient mental health services over time in a health maintenance organization and fee-for-service plans. *American Journal of Psychiatry*, 144(3), 283–287.

Marlatt, G. A., & Gordon, J. R. (1985). *Relapse prevention: Maintenance strategies in the treatment of addictive behaviors*. New York: Guilford Press.

Muszynski, I. L. (1985). Prospective pricing: The common denominator in a changing health care market and its implications for psychiatric care. In S. S. Sharfstein & A. Beigel (Eds.), *The new economics and psychiatric care*. Washington, DC: American Psychiatric Press.

Nelson, J. (1987). The history and spirit of the HMO movement. *HMO Practice*, 1(2), 75–85.

Phillips, E. L. (1985). *Psychotherapy Revised: New Frontiers in Research and Practice*. Hillsdale, NJ: Erlbaum.

Rodriguez, A. R. (1988a). An introduction to quality assurance in mental health. In G. A. Striker & A. R. Rodriguez (Eds.), *Handbook of quality assurance in mental health* (pp. 3–36). New York: Plenum Press.

Rodriguez, A. R. (1988b). The effects of contemporary economic conditions on availability and quality of mental health services. In G. A. Striker & A. R. Rodriguez (Eds.), *Handbook of quality assurance in mental health* (pp. 137–168). New York: Plenum Press.

Roemer, M. I. (1985). I. S. Falk, the Committee on the Costs of Health Care, and the drive for national health insurance. *American Journal of Public Health*, 75(8), 841–848.

Schlesinger, M. (1986). On the limits of expanding health care reform: Chronic care in prepaid settings. *The Milbank Quarterly*, 64(2), 189–215.

Siddal, L. B., Haffey, N. A., & Feinman, J. A. (1988). Intermittent brief psychotherapy in an HMO setting. *American Journal of Psychotherapy*, 42(1), 96–106.

Sifneos, P. (1979). *Short-term dynamic psychotherapy*. New York: Plenum Press.

Strupp, H. H. (1989). Psychotherapy: Can the practitioner learn from the researcher? *American Psychologist*, 44, 717–724.

Strupp, H. H., & Binder, J. L. (1984). *Psychotherapy in a new key*. New York: Basic Books.

Taube, C. A., Goldman, H. H., Burns, B. J., & Kessler, L. G. (1988). High users of outpatient mental health services: 1. Definition and characteristics. *American Journal of Psychiatry*, 145(1), 19–24.

Taube, C. A., Kessler, L., & Feuerberg, M. (1984). Utilization and expenditures for ambulatory mental health care during 1980. In *National Medical Care Utilization and Expenditure Survey: Data Report 5*. Washington, DC: Department of Health and Human Services.

Vaillant, G. E. (1977). *Adaptation to Life*. Boston: Little, Brown.

Vaughn, C., & Leff, J. (1985). *Expressed emotion in families: Its significance for mental illness*. New York: Guilford Press.

Wells, K. B., Manning, W. G., Benjamin, B. (1986). Use of outpatient mental health services in HMO and fee-for-service plans: Results from randomized controlled trial. *Health Services Research*, 21, 453–474.

Williams, S. J., Diehr, D., Drucker, W. L., & Richardson, W. C. (1979). Mental health services: Utilization by low-income enrollees in a prepaid group practice plan and in an independent practice plan. *Medical Care*, 17(2), 139–151.

Index